www.bma.org

D0322119

*the*
# COMPLETE
# FACILITATOR'S
*handbook*

# *the*
# COMPLETE
# FACILITATOR'S
# *handbook*

## John Heron

KOGAN
PAGE

First published in 1999
Reprinted 2000, 2002, 2004, 2005, 2006, 2008 (twice), 2009, 2010

120 Pentonville Road
London N1 9JN
United Kingdom
www.koganpage.com

525 South 4th Street, #241
Philadelphia PA 19147
USA

4737/23 Ansari Road
Daryaganj
New Delhi 110002
India

© John Heron, 1999

**British Library Cataloguing in Publication Data**

A CIP record for this book is available from the British Library.

ISBN 978 0 7494 2798 6 (pbk); ISBN 978 0 7494 2972 0 (hbk)

# *Contents*

# *Preface*

## *A Little History*

The first edition of this book was called *Dimensions of Facilitator Style*. It was published conjointly by the Human Potential Research Project, University of Surrey, and the British Postgraduate Medical Federation, University of London, in 1977. It presented a model of facilitation which had been gradually evolved, over a seven year period, for the training of facilitators from many settings, through professional development programmes at the University of Surrey.

From 1977 this model was, for a further decade, used by myself and my colleagues for facilitator training, both in the two university settings mentioned above, and in courses run by the Institute for the Development of Human Potential, founded in London in 1977. This intensive work called for further evolution of the conceptual structure of the model, making explicit what had hitherto been implicit in its formulation. So *Dimensions of Facilitator Style* was fully revised and became *The Facilitators' Handbook*, published by Kogan Page in 1989.

In 1992, I had discussions with Kogan Page about a further book on facilitation skills which would develop in depth themes only touched on in the Handbook. This work was published in 1993 as *Group Facilitation: Theories and Models for Practice*.

Then, in 1997, Kogan Page proposed a new and revised edition of *The Facilitators' Handbook* to coincide with bringing it out for the first time in paperback. After eight years of continuous use of the *Handbook* by myself and others in diverse settings, the model of facilitation it puts forward has proved its relevance at the workface of facilitator training, both for beginners and for experienced practitioners. However it was clear, once again, that, as a result of this extended application in the field, further developments of its latent potential were called for. I agreed to revise the *Handbook* and suggested that at the same time I integrate it in one volume with a revision of *Group Facilitation*. Hence the present work, which we decided to call *The Complete Facilitator's Handbook*.

Please note this new title does not refer to the complete handbook of the facilitator. It refers to the handbook of the complete, that is, accomplished, facilitator.

## Guidance for the Reader

Here are a few pointers to help you find you way round the book:

- The core model of the book is provided by the six dimensions, interacting with the three modes, of facilitation, together with the account of group dynamics, and the issues involved in creating a facilitator style.
- An overview of all the dimensions and modes is given in Chapter 1, the group dynamic theory is found in Chapter 4, and the creation of a facilitator style is discussed in Chapter 18.
- How each one of the six dimensions interacts with the three modes, in terms of a whole range of facilitator interventions, is covered in a separate chapter. The six chapters are 5, 6, 10, 11, 13 and 15.
- The chapter or chapters *between* any of the key chapters I have just mentioned develop issues or items contained in the immediately preceding key chapter.
- The Contents pages list all the sub-sections within each chapter, and so provide a useful and detailed summary of what is in the book.

And here are three suggestions about the use of the book:

- It can be used as a reference manual for facilitators on the job, and as a resource manual for trainers of beginners and of in-service facilitators.
- It has to be applied selectively and imaginatively, flexibly and adaptively. The meticulous analyses of items and issues need to be refracted through existential realities.
- It is best regarded as a set of perspectives and practices which are in principle open to revision and enrichment through further experience and reflection.

# *Acknowledgements*

In presenting this book, I wish to express my gratitude to three groups of people. I thank the large number of those who, in several parts of the world over the past twenty eight years, have participated in my trainers' and training the trainers' workshops. Their intelligent and caring commitment to their work has contributed an immeasurable amount to my thinking about facilitation. I am grateful to my many colleagues at the universities, institutes and centres where I worked, either as a staff member, or a visiting facilitator, for raising my consciousness about vital issues and distinctions. And I acknowledge a special debt of gratitude to other authors in the field, whose influence over the years I have assimilated into my thinking.

John Heron
San Cipriano
October, 1998

# 1 Dimensions and Modes of Facilitation

This opening chapter defines basic terms, outlines the modern revolution in learning, and introduces the six dimensions and three modes of facilitation, which comprise the core model presented in this book.

## Background

This work is a new compilation: it fully revises, integrates, and extends with additional material, four earlier books, *Dimensions of Facilitator Style* (University of Surrey, 1977), *The Facilitators' Handbook* (Kogan Page, 1989), *A Handbook for Leaders* (University of Surrey, 1990b) and *Group Facilitation: Theories and Models for Practice* (Kogan Page, 1993). It also takes note of ideas expressed in *Feeling and Personhood* (Sage, 1992), and *Co-operative Inquiry* (Sage, 1996a). It presents a current account of my perspective on the theory and practice of facilitation.

## The Facilitator and the Experiential Group

What I mean by a facilitator in this book is a person who has the role of empowering participants to learn in an experiential group. The facilitator will normally be formally appointed to this role by whatever organization is sponsoring the group. And the group members will voluntarily accept the facilitator in this role.

By an experiential group I mean one in which learning takes place through an active and aware involvement of the whole person – as a spiritually, energetically and physically endowed being encompassing feeling and emotion, intuition and imaging, reflection and discrimination, intention and action (Heron, 1992). This potentially covers a wide spectrum: traditional therapy groups, sensitivity training groups, encounter groups, personal development groups in a particular mode (such as psychodrama, co-counselling, bio-energetics, primal, Gestalt, transpersonal, etc), interpersonal-skills training groups for personal or professional development, management training groups, social action training groups. The spectrum also extends into all contexts where learning is rooted in self-direction and whole personhood.

A strong, but by no means exclusive, focus throughout the text is on personal development and interactive skills groups, of the various kinds just mentioned. This is because the widest range of searching issues for the facilitator come up in these arenas. However, I must stress that the model applies equally to groups which, learning through experience, action and practice, are dealing with more external and technical skills, such as nursing and medical skills, or with other specialist skills; and with the theoretical knowledge that underpins such skills. Furthermore, and most fundamentally, it applies to all groups in higher, adult and continuing education of any kind where facilitators are committed to empower the autonomy and holism of the learner; and the book deals with important issues which arise in these contexts.

## The Modern Revolution in Learning

There has been a radical change in the theory and practice of higher education over recent decades (Boud, 1988; Heron, 1993; Knowles, 1980). This is most evident in the fields of tertiary, adult and continuing professional education. The basic and very simple premise of this change is that student learning is necessarily self-directed: it rests on the autonomous exercise of intelligence, choice and interest. From this many other points unfold, which I express here in terms of my own thinking about the basic issues involved:

1. **Facilitation of learning.**   Teaching is no longer seen as imparting and doing things to the student, but is redefined as facilitation of self-directed learning. How people learn, and how to bring about this process, become the focus of concern, rather than the old-style pre-occupation with how to teach things to people; and with this goes a significant shift in the onus of responsibility. In the old model, the teacher is principally responsible for student learning. In the new model, the primary responsibility rests with the self-directing learner; and only secondarily with the facilitator.

2. **Manifold learning.**   Learning itself I see as having four interdependent forms, which in many different ways complement and
support each other.

- **Practical learning.**   This is learning how to do something. It
  involves the acquisition of a skill and it is expressed in the
  competent practice of that skill. This is the will, including the
  physical, level of learning.
- **Conceptual learning.**   This is learning about some subject
  matter, learning that something is the case; and is expressed in
  statements and propositions. This is the intellectual, verbal-
  conceptual level of learning.
- **Imaginal learning.**   This is learning configurations of form
  and process. It involves an intuitive grasp of a whole, as shape
  or sequence. It is expressed in the symbolism of line, shape,
  colour, proportion, succession, sound, rhythm, movement.
  And, toward the interface with conceptual learning, is the
  metaphorical, evocative and narrative use of language, as in
  the work of the poet, novelist and dramatist. This the imaginative, intuitive level of learning.
- **Experiential learning.**   This kind of learning is by encounter,
  by direct acquaintance, by entering into some state of being. It
  is manifest through the process of being there, face-to-face,
  with the person, at the event, in the experience. This is the
  feeling, resonance level of learning.

These four forms of learning are distinct; they cannot be reduced
to each other. At the same time, however, they inform, support
and enhance each other. They constitute an up-hierarchy, with the
ones higher in this list being grounded in those that are lower, as
shown in Figure 1.1.

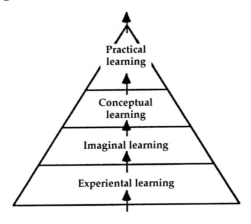

**Figure 1.1**   *Manifold learning*

We encounter the world (experiential learning); identify patterns of form and process in it (imaginal learning); these become the basis for the development of language and knowledge (conceptual learning) which is applied in a wide range of skills (practical learning). Henceforth, I use 'experiential learning' to refer to the whole hierarchy. This hierarchy states what kind of learning rests epistemologically on what other kind. The four forms can also be construed as a cycle in which the practical skills at the apex lead over into enriched experiential learning, thence into imaginal and conceptual learning, and so on.

3. **Holism in course design.**    The learner is a whole person, and the whole person needs to be involved in learning. Learning is extended from its traditional restriction to the theoretical and applied intellect, into the domains of body awareness, emotions and attitudes, interpersonal relations, social and political processes, psychic and spiritual awareness. This means three things.
   - **Confluent education.** The holistic, multi-stranded curriculum which attends – with differing degress of emphasis (depending on the primary learning objectives) – to body, intention, action, intellect, imagination, intuition, emotion, empathy, psychic and spiritual dimensions of the person.
   - **Task-process integration.** The interweaving of a concern for human process at all levels with a commitment to the external tasks of learning about the world and how to apply knowledge to it.
   - **Experiential learning cycle.** This cycle both grounds thought in practice and encounter; and generates thought out of practice and encounter. So there are two complementary processes within the cycle. In the first, a concept is taken into an appropriate experience, then revised in the light of so grounding it. In the second, a certain kind of experience is distilled into a conceptual model, then further developed and refined in the light of that model. Both processes enrich each other.

4. **Participation with staff.**    The concept of learning as self-directed only appeared in the old approach as students working on their own on prescribed tasks. The new approach applies it to participating with staff in three main areas of educational decision-making (Heron, 1988). To educate persons means to facilitate their self-direction:
   - In learning what the content of a discipline is.

- In learning how to learn that content.
- In learning whether they have learnt it.

Hence the importance of the following two kinds of participation.

- **The learning contract.** The student, at the appropriate stage, is invited to co-operate with staff in decisions about learning objectives, timetabling, pacing, teaching and learning methods, and the use of human and physical resources. Such collaborative course design may involve both one-to-one contracts and one-to-group contracts between facilitator and learners.
- **Collaborative assessment.** The student takes part with the facilitator in determining criteria for assessment; each assesses the student's work in the light of these criteria, and together they negotiate the final grade. I have written about this in some detail elsewhere (Heron, 1988).

5. **Co-operation with peers.** Persons can only be self-directing and become whole in reciprocal relations with other self-directing persons who are becoming whole. The autonomy and holism of the learner entails a context of co-operation with other learners. Hence the importance of group-based learning, of student interdependence with regard to both experience and reflection, of peer problem-solving and decision-making, of peer feedback on practice, of self- and peer assessment. The autonomous and whole person learning group is an essential context for the new educational approach.

These five points taken together constitute the educational rationale for this book, and its account of facilitator options. It is committed to the view that the facilitator is a midwife eliciting the emergence of self-directed and peer, holistic learning.

## The Parameters of Experiential Learning

The participants are learning from experience. There are the objectives of learning: the knowledge, skills, changes of attitude, affect and character structure, and deeper transformations of being to be acquired by the learners.

These, in turn, determine the programme of learning, that is, the curriculum, the course or workshop design which distributes different topics and sorts of activity over a timetable.

This design includes the methods of learning: the different ways in which the participants acquire their knowledge and skills, and realize their other learning objectives. And these methods involve the use of various human and physical resources. The design also includes space for the assessment of learning; and for evaluating the learning objectives and the programme as a whole, including topics, timetable, methods, resources, assesment and facilitation.

There are the dimensions of facilitation: different basic issues in relation to which the facilitator can influence the learning process.

Then come the modes of facilitation: the different ways in which the facilitator can handle decision-making within each dimension.

Here I summarize the dimensions and the modes.

## *The Six Dimensions of Facilitation*

1. **The planning dimension.**   This is the goal-oriented, ends and means, aspect of facilitation. It is to do with the aims of the group, and what programme it should undertake to fulfil them. The facilitative question here is: how shall the group acquire its objectives and its programme? Full details in Chapter 5.
2. **The meaning dimension.**   This is the cognitive aspect of facilitation. It is to do with participants' understanding of what is going on, with their making sense of experience, and with their reasons for doing things and reacting to things. The facilitative question is: how shall meaning be given to and found in the experiences and actions of group members? Full details in Chapter 6.
3. **The confronting dimension.**   This is the challenge aspect of facilitation. It is to do with raising consciousness about the group's resistances to and avoidances of things it needs to face and deal with. The facilitative question is: how shall the group's consciousness be raised about these matters? Full details in Chapter 10.
4. **The feeling dimension.**   This is the sensitive aspect of facilitation. It is to do with the management of feeling and emotion within the group. The facilitative question is: how shall the life of feeling and emotion within the group be handled? Full details in Chapter 11. The vital distinction between feeling and emotion is discussed in Chapter 3.
5. **The structuring dimension.**   This is the formal aspect of facilitation. It is to do with methods of learning, with what sort of form is given to learning within the group, with how is it to be shaped. The facilitative question is: how can the group's learning be structured? Full details in Chapter 13.
6. **The valuing dimension.**   This is the integrity aspect of facilitation. It is to do with creating a supportive climate which honours

and celebrates the personhood of group members; a climate in which they can be genuine, empowered, disclosing their reality as it is, keeping in touch with their true needs and interests. The facilitative question is: how can such a climate of personal value, integrity and respect be created? Full details in Chapter 15.

Now these six dimensions interweave and overlap, being mutually supportive of each other. Nevertheless, I hold that each one has in practice an independent identity which will claim the facilitator's attention. They need to be distinguished from each other in thought and action to achieve effective facilitation. Yet they also need to be interrelated continuously in their application: they are to be distinguished only in order to be woven into an integrated mastery of the learning process. The challenge is to keep an eye on each dimension, and organize them all, over time, into a well-balanced whole.

What characterizes them, and the specific interventions that fall under each of them, is that they are pitched at the level of human intention. They are about the facilitator's purposes, about what he or she is seeking to achieve, with regard to various kinds of learning in the group. The full form of the facilitative question is: given that my purpose is to elicit and empower learning through an effect on this or that dimension, how can I go about it? Each intervention intends to achieve a certain result in a certain way.

## The Facilitative Question

The facilitative how question, defined under each dimension above, has a two-part answer. One part deals with who will decide about the issue raised by the question. Will it be the facilitator alone, the facilitator and the participants together, or the participants alone? And this takes us into the three political modes of facilitation, given below. The other part deals with what intervention is to be used in dealing with the issue. This, combined with the modes, is covered in the substantial inventory of facilitative interventions given in the chapters on each of the six dimensions.

## The Three Modes of Facilitation: the Politics of Learning

Each of the above six dimensions can be handled in three different ways. It is one of these three ways which will provide the answer as to who should make decisions on each dimension. From now on, in the description of modes and interventions, I shall refer to the facilitator in the second person, as 'you'.

1.  **The hierarchical mode.** Here you, the facilitator, direct the learning process, exercise your power over it, and do things for the group. You lead from the front by thinking and acting on behalf of the group. You decide on the objectives and the programme, interpret and give meaning, challenge resistances, manage group feeling and emotion, provide structures for learning and honour the claims of authentic behaviour in the group. You take full responsibility, in charge of all major decisions on all dimensions of the learning process.

2.  **The co-operative mode.** Here you share your power over the learning process and manage the different dimensions *with* the group. You enable and guide the group to become more self-directing in the various forms of learning by conferring with them and prompting them. You work with group members to decide on the programme, to give meaning to experiences, to confront resistances, and so on. In this process, you share your own view which, though influential, is not final but one among many. Outcomes are always negotiated. You collaborate with the members of the group in devising the learning process: your facilitation is co-operative.

3.  **The autonomous mode.** Here you respect the total autonomy of the group: you do not do things for them, or with them, but give them freedom to find their own way, exercising their own judgment without any intervention on your part. Without any reminders, guidance or assistance, they evolve their programme, give meaning to what is going on, find ways of confronting their avoidances, and so on. The bedrock of learning is unprompted, self-directed practice, and here you delegate it to the learner and give space for it. This does not mean the abdication of responsibility. It is the subtle art of creating conditions within which people can exercise full self-determination in their learning.

These three modes deal with the politics of learning, with the exercise of power in the management of the different dimensions of experience. They are about who controls and influences such management. Who makes the decisions about what people learn and how they learn it: the facilitator alone, the facilitator and group members together, or the group members alone? The three modes comprise a higher order, political dimension which runs through all the basic six.

As an effective facilitator, you are someone who can use all these three modes on each of the six dimensions as and when appropriate;

|  | Planning | Meaning | Confronting | Feeling | Structuring | Valuing |
|---|---|---|---|---|---|---|
| Hierarchy |  |  |  |  |  |  |
| Co-operation |  |  |  |  |  |  |
| Autonomy |  |  |  |  |  |  |

**Figure 1.2**  *Dimensions and modes*

and are flexible in moving from mode to mode and dimension to dimension in the light of the changing situation in the group. This is no doubt a counsel of perfection, but it broadens the facilitative imagination to entertain the total 18-part grid of options in the back of the mind, as in Figure 1.2.

Too much hierarchical control, and participants become passive and dependent or hostile and resistant. They wane in self-direction, which is the core of all learning. Too much co-operative guidance may degenerate into a subtle kind of nurturing oppression, and may deny the group the benefits of totally autonomous learning. Too much autonomy for participants and laissez-faire on your part, and they may wallow in ignorance, misconception and chaos.

The modes can include each other. You can be basically hierarchical, but with elements of co-operation and autonomy. Thus, within hierarchically given exercises, members will always be autonomous, self-directing in active practice when taking their turn. This is the heart of learning particular skills and awarenesses. Alternatively, the group as a whole may be in an autonomous phase, and call you in to do a piece of hierarchical work, etc.

## The Use of the Modes: Stages and Presumptions

Each experiential group, depending on its learning objectives, will require a different balance of the three modes. And any given group may need this balance to change at different stages in its development, each stage depending on certain presumptions. The three stages below are not a formula for any learning group. It all depends on the objectives and the prior experience of group members.

Some groups, especially those attending in-service training courses for skilled people, may start at stage 2 or stage 3. But the three stages given here are classic ones for training absolute beginners, as they are for parenting. It is important to remember they can overlap, the earlier ones running on, in reduced form, beside the later ones.

1. **Hierarchy early on.**   At the outset a clear hierarchical framework may be needed within which early development of co-operation and autonomy can occur. The presumption here is that participants are insecure and dependent in the area of learning, with lack of knowledge and skill, and have little ability therefore to orientate themselves. They will benefit from your command of events. There is also the presumption that your use of the hierarchical mode, making decisions for the learners, is based on their consent. Within the hierarchical framework, there will of course be autonomous practice and co-operative exchanges with you.
2. **Co-operation mid-term.**   In the middle phase, more open collaboration with group members may be appropriate in managing the learning process. You negotiate the curriculum with them and co-operatively guide their learning activities, with various forms of staff–student contracting and agreement. The presumption here is that they have acquired some confidence in the area of learning, with a foundation of knowledge and skill. In this way, they are able to orientate themselves and participate with you in decisions about how the learning should proceed.
3. **Autonomy later on.**   In the later phase, much more delegation and scope for the group to be autonomous and self-directed may be needed, with peer learning contracts and self- and peer assessment. The presumption here is that group members have considerable confidence in the area of learning and have acquired evident competence in a sizeable body of knowledge and skill. They benefit from full self-determination in their learning.

## *Participation in Educational Decision-making: the Classic Dilemma*

People in our society carry around a lot of unprocessed distress caused by having been the victims of oppressive educational methods from the earliest years – both at home and at school – where their needs and rights as embryonic persons have not been fully honoured or realized. One result of this oppression is that they lack certain basic human skills: skills in handling their own emotions, skills in interacting with other persons, skills in self-direction and collective decision-making. There has been a gross deficiency in the range and depth of their education and training.

This leads to the classic dilemma of all educational reform. Students have the need and the right to be released from oppressive forms of education and should be encouraged to participate in educational decision-making. But they are conditioned and disempowered by these forms, and may not have the motivation, or the personal, interpersonal and self-directing skills required, to break out of them. So they may be neither satisfied nor effective when encouraged to co-operate with you and to be participative.

The resolution of this dilemma lies in mastery of the three modes and the three classic stages outlined in the preceding section. Only give away an appropriate amount of power at a time, otherwise neither you nor the students will be able to cope. And realize the huge array of options you have in combining the three modes in different ways, with varying degrees of emphasis, in relation to so many diverse facets of the educational process (for more on this see Chapter 5). There is no need to hasten inappropriately forward by gross leaps, when you can proceeed slowly by innumerable subtle steps.

## The Many Forms of Autonomy

The autonomous mode I have defined above as you, the facilitator, giving space for unprompted self-directed learning activity in the group. But this occurrence of autonomy can take place in three ways. It can be conferred by you on the group, put forward directively, in the hierarchical mode. Or it can be evolved by negotiation between you and the group, in the co-operative mode. Or it can be self-generated by the group – participants reverse the roles, and become the hierarchs who divest you of your presumption to control and negotiate. This third way is a learning revolution which, if it occurs, is a critical – and potentially fruitful – turning point in the history of a group.

There is also the obvious distinction between individual autonomy and group autonomy. They can be at odds: what I choose may conflict with the consensus choice among my self-directing peers, who thus become my controlling hierarchs, directing my action. Therefore group autonomy does not necessarily guarantee the autonomy of every one of its members.

Finally, you can delegate leadership, or delegate without leadership. The former means that you direct, or negotiate with, someone to be the acting group leader while you step out of the role. This is done either as a special exercise for skills-building in training group facil-itators, or as part of general group process and group dynamic learning. If you delegate without leadership, this means that you give space for a self-directed peer group.

## Task and Process in Experiential Learning

The distinction between task and process is most obvious when the task is to bring about change in the environment. If a group is busy making a pyramid out of the furniture in the room, this is its task. The social phenomena that go on during this task, constitute the group's process: they can be described in relative independence of the task – how leadership and other roles are allocated, how decisions are made, how commmunication networks and contribution rates become established, what psychodynamic interactions between people and intrapsychic states within each person are evident, and so on.

The distinction still holds in personal development work or inter-active skills training. The task is to re-enact some bit of your past in a psychodrama, or to practise some skill in a certain situation within a role play. The process is to do with the intrapsychic and interpersonal phenomena that go on as warp to the woof of the task. Here it is still possible to describe process issues independently of task issues, but although the two are distinct they lend themselves readily to being interdefinable.

The distinction is collapsed when the task of the group is to explore its own emerging process – as in a traditional sensitivity training group. Then there are two levels of process: there is the process, not being explored or attended to, that is involved in exploring the process that is being attended to. Hence any pure process group is located within a recondite regress. Foreground process 1 has a back-ground process 2, which, when it is brought into the foreground, will have a background process 3, etc.

If we now bring in the concept of learning, then there are three areas for it: learning about the task; learning about the group process; and learning about the learning process itself. The last of these means understanding what is involved in getting to understand the task or the process: upper-level learning about ground-floor learning.

Of the four sorts of learning mentioned earlier, let us take the two most commonly considered: conceptual learning (about something) which can be expressed in statements; and practical learning (how to do something) which can only be expressed in terms of some practical skill. For example, to learn about group process is to understand it and to be able to make informed statements about it; to learn how to do, i.e. participate in, group process is evident in the learner's intrapersonal and interpersonal skills.

If we put all these notions together, we get the table in Figure 1.3: the four empty boxes on the left are first-order or ground-floor learning; the eight empty boxes on the right are second-order, upper-level learning.

| | Task | Process | Learning about: Task | Learning how to: Task | Learning about: Process | Learning how to: Process |
|---|---|---|---|---|---|---|
| Learning about: | | | | | | |
| Learning how to: | | | | | | |

**Figure 1.3**  *Sorts and levels of learning*

So if we take the bottom row, there is learning how to do the task, learning how to handle process, learning how to learn about the task, learning how to learn how to do the task, learning how to learn about process, and learning how to learn how to handle process.

## The Concept of Facilitator Style

Facilitator style, in my view, transcends rules and principles of practice, although it takes them into account and is guided by them. There are good and bad methods of facilitating any given group, but there is no one right and proper method. There are innumerable valid approaches, each bearing the signature of different, idiosyncratic facilitators.

By facilitator style, I mean the unique way a person leads a certain group, and more generally, the distinctive way that person leads any group. We can analyse the style in terms of the dimensions, modes and particular interventions given in this book, and how these are put together. We can also see it as a function of the facilitator's values and norms, psychological make-up, degree of skill and development, of the objectives and composition of the group, and of a wider cultural context. But in the last analysis it is you, the imponderable person, that determines your style.

So there is a crucial gap between everything in this book, and the generation of your style: it can only be filled by the unique, distinctive process of your creative and selective imagination, and of your way of being present in and to the world.

## One-to-one, One-to-some and One-to-all Interventions

This account of facilitation was originally developed out of my *Six Category Intervention Analysis*, first published in 1975, and now in a revised and enlarged fourth edition entitled *Helping the Client: A Creative, Practical Guide* (Heron, 1990a). The six category model is used for training one-to-one practitioners, whereas this facilitator style model is entirely for training those who lead groups.

Nevertheless, the two models usefully go together: the group facilitator will frequently have one-to-one interactions with a group member, and will then use many of the six category interventions, especially the very specific catalytic and cathartic ones, some of which I have included in this book. In what follows, I shall assume your familiarity with the six category system, and at some points will refer you to it. Lack of such familiarity, however, will not limit your understanding.

In the text, I have included, across the dimensions and modes, a mixture of interventions. There are those that relate to all of the group, those that relate to some of the group; and there are a few that relate only to one of the group, where such interventions seem fairly central to what goes on in experiential groups. I must ask the reader to get used to switching between one-to-all, one-to-some, and one-to-one interventions, and their many combinations, since this is the reality of the facilitator's role.

For details of the full range of one-to-one interventions which a group facilitator will frequently use, see my *Helping the Client* (Heron, 1990a). However, note that some basic one-to-one interventions can also be used for some or all of a group and these are included here in their one-to-some or one-to-all forms.

## Education and Training

The present model is for use in developing facilitators, both beginners and those with experience. The latter particularly will find it helpful in extending their skill. In a workshop setting, the model has at least three uses.

- **Education.**  To raise consciousness about the range and subtlety of options available to all facilitators and about the implications of different facilitator profiles across the dimensions and modes.
- **Assessment.**  To provide a tool for self-assessment and peer assessment, so that facilitators get more insight into their strengths and weaknesses.
- **Training.**  To provide the basis for a set of exercises that build up skill both within particular dimensions and modes, and within a selected profile across the dimensions and modes.

I assume throughout this book an educational model for experiential learning groups of all kinds, including psychotherapy groups and personal development groups. Whatever the sort of group, its members are acquiring new understanding of themselves and others, and new skills in managing their own process and in relating to others. To extend education into personal development and the management of emotions, social skills, decision-making, and the combinations of these, makes it truly education for living.

## The 18 Basic Options

I conclude this chapter with an overview of the dimensions and modes combined into the 18 basic options for the group facilitator. This gives a summary outline of the content of Chapters 5, 6, 10, 11, 13, and 15. For convenience, I have numbered each option as in Figure 1.4.

Don't be misled by the simplified statement of each option. The different modes within each dimension are not mutually exclusive: they can all be used on the same course, at different times, and with respect to different aspects of the given dimension.

|  | Planning | Meaning | Confronting | Feeling | Structuring | Valuing |
|---|---|---|---|---|---|---|
| Hierarchy | 1 | 4 | 7 | 10 | 13 | 16 |
| Co-operation | 2 | 5 | 8 | 11 | 14 | 17 |
| Autonomy | 3 | 6 | 9 | 12 | 15 | 18 |

**Figure 1.4**  *Dimensions and modes*

1. **The planning dimension: hierarchical mode.**   You here plan for the group. You choose what the group will learn, deciding unilaterally on the content of the course programme and making decisions for the learners.

2. **The planning dimension: co-operative mode.**   You plan the programme with the group. You are committed to negotiate, to take into account and seek agreement with the views of group members in constructing the timetable, which integrates their ideas and yours.

3. **The planning dimension: autonomous mode.**   You delegate the planning of the programme to the group. You are getting out of the way, affirming the group's need to work out its own course design.

4. **The meaning dimension: hierarchical mode.**   You make sense of what is going on for the group. You give meaning to events and illuminate them; you are the source of understanding what is going on.

5. **The meaning dimension: co-operative mode.**   You invite group members to participate with you in the generation of understanding. You prompt them to give their own meaning to what is happening in the group, then add your view, as one idea among others, and collaborate in making sense.

6. **The meaning dimension: autonomous mode.**   You choose to delegate interpretation, feedback, reflection and review to the group. Making sense of what is going on is autonomous, entirely self-generated within the group.

7. **The confronting dimension: hierarchical mode.**   You interrupt the rigid behaviour, and point to what is being avoided. You do this directly to people and for people – in such a way that those concerned may take up the issue and thereby show some awareness of their avoidance.

8. **The confronting dimension: co-operative mode.**   You work with the group and its members to raise consciousness about avoided issues and defensive behaviour. You prompt, invite and ask people, consult them, compare and share views with them. Consciousness-raising is collaborative.

9. **The confronting dimension: autonomous mode.**   You now hand over all consciousness-raising about defensive, avoidance behaviour to the group. You create a climate and learning structures which enable group members to practise self- and peer confrontation.

10. **The feeling dimension: hierarchical mode.**   You take full charge of the affective dynamic of the group for the group,

directing its process and deciding how it will be handled. You think for group members, judging what methods of managing feeling and emotion will suit them and their purposes best.

11. **The feeling dimension: co-operative mode.** You work with the group, eliciting, prompting, and encouraging views, discussing with members different ways of handling feeling and emotion. You practise collaborative management of the affective dynamic of the group.

12. **The feeling dimension: autonomous mode.** You give the group space for – and delegate to it – the process of managing its own affective dynamic, its life of feeling and emotion.

13. **The structuring dimension: hierarchical mode.** You structure learning activities for the group. You design the learning exercises and directively supervise their use by the group.

14. **The structuring dimension: co-operative mode.** You structure learning methods with group members, co-operating with them in devising how the learning shall proceed. They collaborate with you in designing the structured exercises, and in supervising the running of them.

15. **The structuring dimension: autonomous mode.** You delegate to group members control over their own learning process. They are entirely self- and peer directed in the design of structured exercises, and in supervising the running of them.

16. **The valuing dimension: hierarchical mode.** You take strong initiatives to care for group members. You manifest directly to them, in word and deed, your commitment to their fundamental worth as persons.

17. **The valuing dimension: co-operative mode.** You create a community of value and mutual respect with group members. You are inclusive and interactive, collaborating with them as all emerge as self-creating persons.

18. **The valuing dimension: autonomous mode.** You choose to delegate the affirmation of self-worth to group members. You give them space to celebrate the value of personal identity and emergence in their own way.

## Criteria of Validity

This whole system of dimensions and modes is pitched at the level of human intention. It maps the range of purposes out of which facilitators can create their style. As such, and as with any account of human intention and purpose, it presupposes some very general values and norms. Therefore its validity is, in part, to do with its moral justification. What are the ethical values and principles that underlie it, and are these sound?

Its validity is also, in part, phenomenological, to do with personal experience in the midst of action. The system articulates processes and options relevant in the current human world. It gives voice to a radical empiricism, an experiential awareness of the basic phenomenal categories that make sense of events and actions in the facilitation of group learning. It is open to any experientially sensitive group participant or facilitator to engage in this kind of action inquiry, or first person research (Reason and Torbert, 1999).

Then there are obvious logical criteria involved in its validity. Is the system comprehensive and inclusive of all the main parameters? Is it internally coherent, are the main elements consistent with each other? And, whatever the degrees of interdependence and overlap, are the main elements relatively independent of each other?

Each reader can apply these three sorts of criteria – the ethical, the phenomenological, and the logical – in their own personal action, experience, and reflection. For their systematic use in collaborative relations with other people, the research paradigm of co-operative inquiry (Reason, 1988; Heron, 1996a; Heron and Reason, 1997) offers a powerful way forward, and I give an overview of this in Chapter 7.

# *2 Authority, Autonomy and Holism*

In the light of the dimensions and modes presented in the previous chapter, this chapter redefines the nature of facilitator authority, considers its relation to autonomous and whole person learning, and looks in detail at two of the three main forms of it.

## Three Kinds of Facilitator Authority

The facilitator has three kinds of authority – tutelary, political and charismatic. These are three threads interwoven through the tapestry of dimensions and modes introduced in the previous chapter. I discuss them here in the context of higher, continuing and adult education.

### Tutelary Authority

The facilitator is:

- Competent in some body of knowledge and skill.
- Competent in the appropriate teaching and, above all, learning methods for students to acquire that knowledge and skill.
- Competent to communicate effectively with learners through the written and spoken word and other presentations.
- An attentive guardian of learners needs and interests, rights and duties.

Tutelary authority manifests, particularly but not exclusively, through the meaning and structuring dimensions. A more traditional, and limited, phrase for it is cognitive authority.

### Political Authority

Facilitators take decisions that affect the whole programme of learning. Political authority involves the exercise of educational decision-making with respect to the objectives, programme, methods, resources, and assessment of learning. It manifests through the use of the three decision modes of hierarchy, co-operation and autonomy, especially, but not exclusively, on the planning dimension.

### Charismatic Authority

Facilitators influence learners and the learning process by virtue of their presence, style and manner, and through the way this personal presence manifests within their exercise of tutelary and political authority. Charismatic facilitators empower people directly by the impact of their way of being and behaving. It manifests on all the dimensions and especially through the feeling, confronting and valuing dimensions.

## Authority and Authoritarianism

We need here to distinguish a benign, luminous and truly educative authority from a punitive, indoctrinating and intimidating authority. Genuine authority proceeds from those who are flourishing from their own inner resources and can thereby enable other people to flower in the same way. It manifests as the facilitative ability to empower. So charismatic authority as I defined this in the preceding section is really central to it, interacting with tutelary and political authority.

Oppressive authority is rigid authoritarianism and proceeds from people who are denying some of their basic inner resources and can only use a model of restrictive control in trying to educate others. It manifests at the best as a benign and blinkered compulsion to do too much in a limiting way for students, at the worst as a manipulative urge to dominate and intimidate them. It has been the bane of education at all levels. Traditional teaching, still strongly with us, is beset by authoritarianism. It runs the different kinds of authority into each other, as I suggest in the next section.

Facilitative authory is distress-free, and presupposes a good measure of emotional competence, which includes, among several other important skills, the ability not to transfer old hurt-laden agendas into current situations (Heron, 1992; Postle, 1991). Oppressive authority, by contrast, is driven by repressed emotional distress from the past, unawarely displaced into the teaching role. What is blindly at work is the unprocessed fear and anger from the authoritarian teacher's own early life when he or she was subject to oppressive regimes at home and school.

## Traditional Confusion of Three Kinds of Authority

Old-style teaching confuses the three kinds of authority in the crudest possible way. It assumes that because teachers have cognitive authority – as repositories of knowledge – they should therefore exercise total political authority in a *directive* way, making all educational decisions *for* their students. And then it assumes that because they have to direct everything that students do, they should exercise their charismatic authority as controlling power, that is, as disciplinarians and judges, meting out punishments to the disobedient, and judging the learners' conformity by acts of unilateral assessment.

Thus the traditional teacher decides what students shall learn, when and how they shall learn it and whether they have learnt it; and presides over this regime with a forbidding authoritarian charisma. Student autonomy is relegated to in-the-head following of many long lectures, to answering questions or asking them, to discussion in tutor-led seminars, and to doing homework on prescribed reading, writing or practical tasks.

## Need for Authority

The challenge of all teaching is to integrate a genuine authority in the facilitator with the autonomy of the learner. But why have any kind of educational authority, however benign? The obvious answer is so that knowledge and skills, accumulated within the culture of a discipline, can be passed on. Otherwise everyone has to learn everything from experiential scratch – which would be the *reductio ad absurdum* of experiential learning theory. Herein lies the tension, between the passing-on on the one hand, and the self-generated nature of personal learning on the other.

## Learning as Autonomous and Holistic

Learning by its nature is autonomous. It is constituted by understanding and skill, retention and practice, interest and commitment. There is an obvious connection between learning and the first four of these, for they are what we mean by it. To learn is to come to understand something or to acquire a skill, either of which is retained by practice or rehearsal. And these are all necessarily self-generated: no-one else can do your understanding or retention or practice for you. But there is also a very close connection between learning and interest and commitment. We learn what interests us, that is, what is useful or intrinsically worthwhile or both; and because it interests us we are committed to stay the course until we have learnt it. Both interest and commitment are also necessarily self-generated: they are negated or distorted by any attempt to impose them.

But while the immediate process of learning is self-generated, does it follow that a whole programme of learning is necessarily self-directed? Up to a point it clearly does: interest and commitment of any authentic sort call for some degree of self-directed planning in how to fulfil learning goals (Boud, 1988). They cannot be sustained in a programme that is entirely directed by others, without degenerating into compulsive prudence – conforming to the system in order to survive as effectively as possible. There are two other arguments in favour of self-direction in educational decision-making about the procedures of learning.

The first is to do with the end product of the educational process, namely educated professionals. What society rightly expects in such persons is that they can monitor and intelligently manage their competence while they are working (Schön, 1983), they can learn from work experience by reflecting on it, they can assess their work in retrospect when it is done, and they can keep their work up to date by being a self-directed life-long learner. All these interdependent skills of being self-monitoring, self-reflective, self-assessing and self-directing need to be acquired, in increasing measure, throughout the undergraduate learning process – by participating in setting learning objectives and planning learning programmes, through the use of the experiential learning cycle, and by participation in assessment (Heron, 1988). If they are not, then we cast inadequately prepared professionals into the public arena.

The second argument is to do with rights. The doctrine of natural rights was first clearly formulated by Locke in the 17th century, and has been on the march ever since. Now it is invoked in terms of human rights, which point to those moral principles that apply to people simply by virtue of their humanity and that transcend prevailing law, fiat or convention. One basic right is the right of people to participate in decisions being made about them. This has been applied historically in the political sphere and has been used and is still being used world-wide to press the case for demo-cratic forms of government, in which people participate in political decision-making through their elected representatives.

However it is also a right calling for more widespread application, and it is this generalized extension which is still problematic and contentious for many people in our society who take for granted the political application. Growing children have a right to participate increasingly in parental decisions about their lives and welfare. Workers have a right to participate in managerial decisions that affect their work. Subjects in research experiments have a right to partici-pate in researcher decisions that generate knowledge that purports to be about them. So too in the educational sphere, students in higher education – who are considered old enough to die for their country – have a right to participate in staff decisions that claim to educate them.

As well as being autonomous, learning is also necessarily holistic, that is, it involves the whole person, a being that is physical, percep-tual, affective, cognitive (intellectual, imaginative, intuitive), conative (exercising the will), social and political, psychic and spiritual. It may involve the whole person negatively by the denial of some of these aspects and their exclusion from learning. In this case we get alien-ation, such as intellectual learning alienated from affective and imag-inal learning, with the result that the repression of what is excluded distorts the learning of what is included. Alternatively the involve-ment of the whole person is positive and all these dimensions are intentionally included in the learning process. But again, the unfolding and integration of multiple sides of the learner is a matter of self-development. A person blooms out of their own formative potential, in accordance with their own choices. The idea of someone who, after appropriate initiation, continues to live out an externally imposed, other-directed, programme of whole person development is a contradiction in terms. So autonomy and holism are interdependent.

An important supporting argument about holistic learning draws from general systems theory (von Bertalanffy, 1972; Laszlo, 1972), which, applied to psychology and learning, looks at people in terms of relation and integration. On this view the person is a system whose nature arises from the interactions of its parts. To educate such a person is to take account of the simultaneous and mutually interdependent interaction between his or her multiple aspects. Systems theory also asserts the primacy of self-organization in any dynamic system, and thus also underlines the arguments for autonomy in learning.

## Paradox of Facilitator Authority

The facilitator has to pass on some body of knowledge and skill – the content of learning – by a process of learning that affirms both the autonomy and wholeness of the learner. We thus get the paradox of facilitator authority exercised to generate free and rounded learning. This paradox is exacerbated in this era because it is a watershed time between two educational cultures. An authoritarian educational system, using oppressive forms of teacher authority, is still wide-spread; hence learners who emerge from it are conditioned to learn in ways that are relatively short on autonomy and holism. In a special sense they need leading into freedom and integration, when they enter another more liberated educational culture where these values are affirmed.

## Authority as a Means of Initiation

The concept of *initiation* is, I think, the best one to illuminate this paradox. The facilitator's authority – tutelary, political, charismatic – is used to empower people through *rituals of entry* into their inner resources, their wellsprings of freedom and wholeness, the heritage of their personhood. This does call for a careful rethinking of what these three kinds of authority mean, especially the political kind. What happens to the facilitator's authority – tutelary, political and charismatic – in the model of teaching as initiation that empowers people with their autonomous and whole personhood? I will discuss each of these in turn, focusing most fully upon political authority. This is a very different concept of initiation to that originally evoked by R S Peters who used it to argue for the traditional model of unilateral staff control of the educational process (Peters, 1966).

## Tutelary Authority as Initiation

Tutelary authority replaces the old idea of cognitive authority and is a much more sophisticated notion. I defined it in the opening section as applied particularly within the meaning and structuring dimensions of learning. It involves mastery of some body of knowledge and skill and of appropriate teaching and learning methods for students to acquire it, effective communication to learners through the written and spoken word and other presentations, and guardianship of learners needs and interests, rights and duties. By comparison with the old tradition, what is acquired and the ways of acquiring it become much more comprehensive and varied. I will refer to these, respectively, as subjects and procedures.

In relation to the subject, facilitators are not only intellectually competent in it, but also bring emotional, interpersonal, practical, political, spiritual and other competences to bear upon their attitude to and presentation of it. They have a holistic grasp of the subject and can reveal it in a way that shows its interconnections with all the aspects of the person and with other interdependent subjects.

In relation to procedures, facilitators have a much more expanded repertoire than many traditional teachers in higher education, who have a limited range of methods and have received little or no training in the area. Being knowledgeable about diverse learning methods and skilled in their facilitation is essential for honouring autonomy and holism in learners.

## Tutelary Procedures

1. **Open learning.**   There is a great emphasis on the provision of open learning materials: systems and packages of information and exercises – words and graphics – which are presented in a way that takes account of the self-pacing, self-monitoring learner.
2. **Active learning.**   Much importance is given to the design and facilitation of holistic, participative methods – games, simulations, role plays, and a whole range of structured activities – which will involve learners in self-directing action and reflection, in affective and interpersonal transactions, in perceptual and imaginal processes, in subtle and spiritual attunement. The facilitator uses the experiential learning cycle in various formats: this grounds learning in personal experience, and releases learning as reflection on that experience.
3. **Real learning.**   Projects, field-work, placements and inquiry outside the classroom, case studies, problem-oriented learning, all these become vital aspects of the learning process, so that it is dynamically related to what is going on in the real world.
4. **Peer learning.**   The autonomy of the learner needs the supportive, interactive context of other autonomous learners, hence the importance of the peer learning group for student co-operation in teaching and learning, in experience and reflection, in practice and feedback, in problem-solving and decision-making, in interpersonal process, and in self and peer assessment.

5. **Multi-stranded curriculum.** The curriculum is holistic and multi-stranded. This means several different and related things:
   - The main subject on the curriculum is balanced by complementary minor subjects.
   - Each subject is presented by the facilitator in a way that brings out its interconnections with the whole person and with other interdependent subjects.
   - The active learning methods used within a subject involve various aspects of the whole person, and may empower learning by evoking deep inner resources.
   - The active learning methods used within a subject also bring out its implications for different aspects of human life, and its interdependence with other subjects.
   - Other activities in the classroom are not to do with the formal subject, but to do with the self and others in ways that involve various aspects of the whole person.
6. **Contract learning.**   The student is supported and helped to plan their own programme of learning and to participate in assessment of learning, by the use of collaborative contracts (see Chapter 5) and collaborative assessment (see Chapter 6) with the facilitator. This item overlaps with the facilitator's exercise of political authority, which I discuss below.
7. **Resource consultancy.** The amount of stand-up teaching becomes greatly reduced compared with the old approach. The facilitator becomes much more a resource and consultant, available to be called in when needed by the self-directing, active learner – to clarify, guide, discuss and support.
8. **Guardianship.** The facilitator cares for and watches over students as a guardian of their needs and interests, alerts them to unexplored possibilities, to new issues of excitement, interest and concern; and reminds them of issues discussed, of commitments made and contracts agreed. These eight items are illustrated in Figure 2.1.

The main tension in this list is focused between items 5 and 6, holistic teaching and contract learning. This especially applies where students have come from a very non-autonomous and non-holistic educational background, as is often the case with those who move from secondary to tertiary education. If these students start early on in a course to use learning contracts and thus to plan their own learning to a significant degree, then they are likely to do so in terms of the old familiar non-holistic learning methods they have brought with them. If, however, facilitators are going to initiate students into

**Figure 2.1**   *Tutelary procedures*

holistic methods, then the facilitators will have to plan a lot of the learning until students have internalized these methods and can manage them autonomously (Boud and Miller, 1996; Heron, 1996b).

This tension between autonomy and holism in learning is, I believe, a major issue in the educational revolution that is afoot. In my view, it has not been sufficiently spotlighted in earlier studies in experiential learning (Weil and McGill, 1989; Mulligan and Griffin, 1992). Many teachers are moving forward to use learning contracts and enhance student autonomy without considering whether the resultant learning process is holistic.

## *Political Authority as Initiation: the Three Decision-modes*

I defined political authority at the outset as the facilitator's exercise of educational decision-making with with respect to the objectives, programme, methods, resources, and assessment of learning. It manifests through the use of the three decision-modes of hierarchy, co-operation and autonomy, especially, but not exclusively, on the planning dimension.

A crucial shift is taking place in the use of this kind of authority in education, and so the concept of it needs to undergo a complete redefinition. I believe that the full implications of this have not as yet been fully articulated and grasped. In a nutshell, the shift is from deciding in terms of just one decision-mode to *deciding which decision-mode to use*. The result is a vast increase in facilitator flexibility and enabling power. By a decision-mode I mean one of three basic ways of making educational decisions in relation to learners. You can make decisions for them, you can make decisions with them, or you can give them space to make decisions on their own, by themselves. In Chapter 1, I call these hierarchy, co-operation and autonomy. I will also call them, respectively, direction, negotiation and delegation.

What the decisions are being taken about, centrally, are the basic elements of the learning process: learning objectives, the programme (which interrelates topics with their pacing and progression over time), the teaching and learning methods, the human and physical resources to be used, the criteria and methods of assessment. There is also higher-order evaluation of how all these elements of the learning process have been put together.

If we combine topics with pacing and progression in the one item of the course programme, or timetable, and leave out overall course evaluation, then we have five immediate areas for educational decision-making: the objectives of learning, the programme of learning, the methods of learning, the resources (human and physical) for learning, and the assessment of learning. The three decision-modes and these five elements of the learning process are shown in Figure 2.2.

|  | Objectives | Programme | Methods | Resources | Assessment |
|---|---|---|---|---|---|
| Direction: Facilitator alone |  |  |  |  |  |
| Negotiation: Facilitator/Learners |  |  |  |  |  |
| Delegation: Learners alone |  |  |  |  |  |

**Figure 2.2**   *Decision-modes for planning learning*

The three modes were defined in general terms in Chapter 1. I will now go over them again in relation to the elements of the learning process.

1. **Direction (hierarchy).** Direction, in the traditional full-blown form that is still used throughout most institutions of higher education, means that you exercise educational power unilaterally. You decide everything in the five areas *for* your students. You decide, without in any way consulting students, what they will learn, when they will learn it, how they will learn it and with what resources, and by unilateral assessment you decide whether they have learnt it. Students' performance with respect to objectives, the programme, methods, resources and assessment is entirely subordinate to your commands. Their self-direction can only be exercised in a minimal way within the complete framework of learning which you prescribe.

2. **Negotiation (co-operation).** Full-blown negotiation means that you exercise educational power bilaterally: you decide everything *with* your students. Your decision-mode is co-operative. You take into account student self-direction as well as your own views, consult them about everything and seek to reach agreement in setting up mutually acceptable contracts about objectives, the programme, methods, resources and assessment. Assessment will be collaborative, involving a negotiation between students' self-assessments and your assessments of their work.

   Of course, not everything is negotiable. You will believe in certain educational values, principles and practices which are non-negotiable, and which provide the base from which your negotiation proceeds. I develop this important point a little further on.

3. **Delegation (autonomy).** Delegation means that you give space for the unilateral exercise of educational power by students themselves. In full-blown delegation, you have declared your own redundancy, and students are entirely self-determining with respect to their objectives, programme, methods, resources and assessment. Everything, including assessment, is self and peer determined in autonomous student groups.

Each of these decision-modes in its full-blown form as defined above is unacceptable as the exclusive basis for running any course in higher education. What is called for on an empowering course is that direction, negotiation and delegation are used in differing serial and concurrent ways as the course unfolds.

The old-style political authority of the teacher lacks any sophistication. It blindly applies the decision-mode of direction across the board of all educational decisions. The new facilitative political authority is more subtle and challenging: it means exercising liberating power by choosing the appropriate decision-mode – whether direction, negotiation or delegation – for these learners, at this stage of their learning, in respect of this or that aspect of the educational process. It means that you can influence the degree and the pacing of empowerment.

The three decision-modes apply to all the six distinct dimensions of the learning process – planning, meaning, confronting, feeling, structuring and valuing. However, it is in their application to the planning dimension where political authority is most fully exercised.

## *The Four Decision-mode Levels*

Political authority is evident in the mastery of these decision-modes at four different levels of planning. There is the main level, already mentioned, of planning the learning process in all its six aspects: learning objectives, the programme, the teaching and learning methods, the human and physical resources to be used, the criteria and methods of assessment, evaluation of the whole process. This main level is level 2 in the fourfold scheme, as we shall see.

As I have said, you can plan all this by yourself; or you can negotiate a plan with the learners; or the learners can put one together on their own; or all three methods can be used with different parts of the plan. Below this, there is the ground-floor level 1 of the immediate learning activity, what is going on in the classroom here and now. Here too, you can manage it for the learners; or you can manage it co-operatively with the learners; or the learners can manage it on their own; or all three may be used for different activities.

It is important to note that these two levels are quite distinct in the sense that different decision-modes can be used on them, and a lot of educational wisdom is involved in using these differences. Thus you can *directively* plan and structure a whole series of learning activities which, once they are up and running, are *autonomously* managed by the learners. This is a relevant combination for initiating people into deeply holistic forms of learning.

There is also a third level, the level of deciding – by direction, negotiation, delegation, or a mixture – whether to use direction, negotiation, delegation, or a mixture, when planning. In other words, on level 3 you choose all by yourself a decision-mode for planning, or you negotiate with students in choosing a decision-mode for planning, or students all by themselves choose a decision-mode for planning, or all three of these are used for different areas of planning. Many facilitators are probably not aware of level 3. They are unawarely unilateral at this level without realizing there is a choice to be made between direction, negotiation and delegation.

Suppose you are going to negotiate with students at level 3. Then this means that before the course starts you take them aside and say: 'I want to invite you to take a conjoint decision with me as to whether I plan the course, you and I plan it co-operatively, or you plan it all by yourselves'. Such a consultation might result in a meta-plan in which you plan some parts of the course on your own, other parts are planned co-operatively, and yet further parts are planned by the students on their own.

There is a also fourth level for decision-mode use, *but it is necessarily and exclusively reserved for the directive mode*. This level is the final resting place of the facilitator's political authority. It is the level at which you decide which decision-mode to use at level 3, that is, which decision-mode to use in choosing a decision-mode for planning. It is at level 4 that you decide unilaterally, all on your own, whether at level 3 you will choose a decision-mode for planning by yourself, negotiate the choice with your students, or delegate to them the choice of a decision-mode for planning.

If at level 4 you choose negotiation at level 3, then you have unilaterally decided (at level 4) that you are going to ask your learners to negotiate with you (at level 3) in deciding whether you do the planning, or you do it co-operatively with them, or they do it. As I say, this level 4 decision needs to be directive: you make it on your own.

It could be argued that you could negotiate or delegate at level 4, but then the decision to do either of those will have been taken directively at level 5. In other words there is an infinite regress of deferred decision-making, unless the series is closed by unilateral direction at some level, and level 4 is the highest possible level for rational closure. It is neurotic or mad to go beyond it. The four levels are shown in Figure 2.3. This figure provides a convenient anatomy of the exercise of facilitator power on any kind of educational course. The three decision-modes of direction, negotiation and delegation given in the figure refer to the options open to the facilitator at the different levels.

Level 4 is a sophisticated level and many facilitators won't use it intentionally at all. Without noticing what they are doing, they will in effect decide directively at level 4 to decide directively at level 3 to use this, that or the other decision-mode in planning at level 2. If they

| Level 4: Choosing a decision-mode to use in choosing a decision-mode in planning | Direction | | |
|---|---|---|---|
| Level 3: Decision-mode to use in choosing a decision-mode for planning | Direction | Negotiation | Delegation |
| Level 2: Decision-mode used in planning learning activities | Direction | Negotiation | Delegation |
| Level 1: Decision-mode used in learning activity | Direction | Negotiation | Delegation |

**Figure 2.3**    *Decision-mode levels*

are very, very unaware they will decide everything directively even at level 2, the level of planning, *without realizing they have other choices at that level.*

The simplest possible account of this figure is as follows. I decide at level 4 whether I, we or you decide at level 3 whether I, we or you plan at level 2 the programme of learning activities which will be managed by me, us or you at level 1. I will go over these levels again in Chapter 5.

## Empowerment through Mastery of Decision-mode Levels

I notice that facilitators tend to wilt rather when I go on about levels 3 and 4. Now it does require something like an extended state of consciousness to keep effectively alert at those levels. But I take the stringent view that until we have mastered those levels and know that we are using them and how we are using them – which usually means being directive at 3 as well as 4 and so unilaterally choosing decision-modes for level 2 – then we have not really taken charge of our power to empower our learners.

In other words, facilitators are, at crucial points in the most student-centred programmes, exercising a subtle kind of unilateral directive authority. They cannot abdicate from it at level 4, and will usually use it at level 3. Unless they are exercising it intentionally, and really know what they are up to, there is the ever present issue of unaware overcontrol or undercontrol of the empowering process.

## Unilateral Direction on Principle at Level 3

Many progressive facilitators are, even if they have not made this fully conscious to themselves, entirely directive at level 3 *on principle.*

For example, they may believe strongly in a significant measure of student autonomy, such as student participation in programming their own learning and in assessing their own learning, both in conjunction with staff. They are committed to learning contracts and collaborative assessment as a matter of principle. And this principle is non-negotiable. This means they are not open to their learners negotiating them back into unilateral educational decisions. So if at level 2 there is to be negotiated programming, this use of negotiation at level 2 is itself non-negotiable at level 3.

Again, progressive facilitators may be committed to holism on principle, to educating many aspects of the person, so that both course content and learning methods are multi-dimensional. So they are non-negotiably directive at level 3 about being directive at level 2 with respect to holistic elements in programme design and in learning methods. Incidentally, facilitators who are committed at level 3 to both autonomy and holism face the challenge, at level 2, of using *negotiation* to affirm the autonomy, and *direction* to establish the holism. This is the creative tension between autonomy and holism to which I have already referred.

This business of being directive at level 3 on principle is entirely right and proper, so long as it is fully conscious and intentional. Authentic educators stand for certain inalienable and non-negotiable values to which they are deeply committed. If they do not stand for anything on principle and can be negotiated into *any* position, then they are not really educated and have no real authority of any kind, tutelary, political or charismatic. It is, ultimately and paradoxically, our non-negotiable values that empower people – or disempower them, depending on the values.

## The Importance of Advertising Non-negotiable Values

What all this means is that facilitators' non-negotiable educational values – whether about autonomy or holism or both – which make them directive at level 3, should be consciously held, and above all clearly identified and made explicit in the course prospectus, and again at interview, so that the prospective learner can make a free and informed choice to join this particular community of value.

What the facilitators need to say loud and clear is: 'This is the kind of educational community we run, and we are committed in principle to students being autonomous and holistic in these various ways which we have specified. If this appeals to you, come and join us and explore this way of learning with us. If it is not what you want, we respect that, and invite you to look elsewhere for what you do want.'

This kind of pre-course clarity and openness is vital in principle, and especially in practice in a watershed culture where old and new models of education exist side by side and learners are moving between them. It is clearly immoral and not at all empowering to spring the new educational values on students in their first weeks after enrolment, when everything they have so far read or heard about the institution has led them to expect that it would deliver the old authoritarian values of unilateral direction of all learning by staff. If this surprise event happens to them, they have a valid moral case that the institution's implied contract to deliver traditional teaching has been broken. Many teachers who are enthusiastic to try new things make this mistake, and then fail to realize that they are not just meeting with some kind of psychological resistance to new methods, but even more so with a genuine moral grievance. Until students feel that their *moral* grievance is fully heard and honoured, there is not much chance that they will be able to work through their *psychological* resistance.

It may be best for progressive facilitators to be entirely directive at level 3 precisely because we live in this watershed culture between the old and the new educational values. If your learners are heavily conditioned by the old values, to negotiate with them or delegate to them at level 3 may simply mean that they unawarely press the claims of these old values. So it is better to decide directively at this level, make it clear in all the course publicity what your values are, and invite learners to join you if these values appeal to them, and to recommend that they do not join you if these values do not appeal. You need to offer an unequivocal contract to potential students about your mode of practice.

## A Full-blown Level 3 Course

However, there may come an era when the values of autonomy and holism are the norm in the educational culture. Then we have the prospect of a full-blown level 3 course in which students are included in negotiation at this level. So the course is advertised as one where the learners will be asked on arrival to co-operate with the staff in deciding whether the five main elements of the learning process will be planned by the staff, by staff and learners, or by the learners, or in different respects by each of these groups. Such a course does indeed sound empowering and full of potential learning.

Even now in professional development courses it can be realistic and grounded. I have used it on a course to train experienced GPs to become trainers of young hospital doctors entering general practice for the first time. To get a relevant course going I needed to agree, with the trainers coming to the course, on who should plan what: I certain things, they and I other things, they certain things.

## Charismatic Authority as Initiation

The third aspect of authority, charismatic authority, I defined at the outset as the facilitators' influence on learners and the learning process by virtue of their presence, style and manner, that is, through their personal delivery of tutelary and political authority. Charismatic facilitators empower people directly by the presence of their own inner empowerment. Such presence manifests on all the dimensions and especially through the feeling, confronting and valuing dimensions.

It means eliciting the emergence of the autonomy and wholeness of learners through a behavioural manner, a timing and tone of voice, as well as choice of language and ideas, that proceed from the autonomy and wholeness of the facilitator. It is this expressive presence that generates self-confidence and self-esteem in learners, and enhances their motivation toward independence and integration of being. I address this theme more fully in Chapter 12.

# 3 Whole Person Learning

In the previous chapter I introduced the notion of holistic learning and proposed that learning necessarily involves the whole person. In the present chapter I explore the implications of this theme in depth.

## Distinctions Within the Field

What is holistic, or whole person, learning? The answer depends on what you think a whole person is and how you believe such a being functions. So we are into personality theory: the structure and dynamics of the person. Before getting into all this, let me separate out some of the different sorts of things that holistic learning can include.

The first basic distinction is between holistic learning in the world – in living and in working – and holistic learning in the classroom or group room.

The second main distinction is between learning some ordinary subject or skill by being involved as a whole person, and learning how to become a whole person. The first of these is about educational development – using holistic methods to enhance the learning and teaching of different disciplines. The second is about personal development. Of course they are not mutually exclusive. If you learn accountancy by a holistic method, you may also gain a little personal development thereby. And if you attend a workshop for your personal development, you will expect to find holistic methods being used. Nevertheless, the difference is clear.

Within each of these two quite different sorts of holistic learning, some further important practical distinctions can be made. Let's look at learning a specific subject or skill by being involved as a holistic learner. This can mean that the holistic methods are *inside* the learning: their use is related to mastering the content of the lesson. So you play a game in Spanish as part of the business of learning

Spanish. Or it could mean that holistic activities are *alongside* the learning. They are not directly to do with the content of the lesson but are interspersed throughout it to minister to various aspects of the whole person and to keep him or her in good shape for learning. So you dance to music for a few minutes in order to refresh yourself for returning to the business of learning the higher calculus. These alongside goings-on I will refer to as *multi-stranded activities*.

Within holistic methods that are inside the learning, that relate to the content of the lessson, there are those that are organized into some coherent cycle with an underlying rationale, like various versions of the *experiential learning cycle*. There are also those which simply lie side by side without some integrating sequence, and these I will refer to as *multi-stranded learning*.

Among holistic activities not directly to do with the content of the lesson, there are those which directly bear upon the emotional effects of learning. So I may invite students to break off from learning and explore what emotional processes it has been generating within them: they may report these or portray them in sound or movement or a group sculpture. An extension of this is to invite students to take time out from working on a subject to do some emotional work on blocks to learning which they are encountering.

There are three other things that holistic learning of a subject could imply. First, it might mean that in learning the subject, I learn how it directly affects all the different aspects of myself. So in studying astronomy I may learn how it directly affects me spiritually and in other ways. Second, I learn how it is interdependent with a whole range of other subjects. So I may learn how astronomy and theology (or physics, or ...) have had a bearing on each other during different epochs. Third, I may learn a main subject always alongside one or more different subjects that are somehow complementary to it.

Learning how to be a whole person, personal development, differentiates itself into several interconnected domains. The first is the intrapersonal, what goes on within the psyche, and this includes attending to what is repressed, what is relatively underdeveloped, and what is entirely undeveloped but not repressed. The second is the interpersonal sphere of face-to-face interactions; the third is the cultural realm of social institutions, their roles, beliefs, norms and values; the fourth is the ecological zone, interaction with the planetary environment; and the fifth is what I call the transplanetary sphere, more often called transpersonal, the domain of the psychic and the spiritual.

I shall argue in the next chapter that learning to be a whole person involves learning to initiate change in all these interacting areas.

These five domains can all involve learning in the classroom or group room, but flow beyond that to be grounded, through action inquiry, in learning in the world.

Below is a brief resumé of the distinctions made so far. The main ones are represented in Figure 3.1.

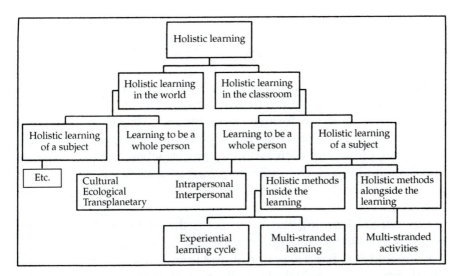

**Figure 3.1**  *Holistic learning tree*

1. **Holistic learning in the world, in living and in working.**
2. **Holistic learning in the classroom or group room.**
3. **Holistic learning of a subject or skill.** This yields:
   - **Inside the learning.**   Holistic methods are used to learn the content of a subject or skill: they are the means of learning it. Here we have the distinction between the experiential learning cycle and multi-stranded learning.
   - **Alongside the learning.**   Holistic, multi-stranded activities are not directly to do with the content of the subject or skill but are interspersed throughout the lesson to minister to various aspects of the whole person and to keep him or her in good shape for learning. This, I suggested, can extend to exploring the emotional effects of learning, and doing work on emotional blocks to learning.
   - **Domain impact.**   The student learns how the subject or skill directly affects the different aspects of his or her being.
   - **Domain interdependence.**   The student learns how the subject or skill is interconnected with a whole range of other subjects or skills.

- **Domain complementarity.** The student learns a subject or skill alongside one or more other subjects or skills that are complementary to it.
4. **Learning how to become a whole person.**  This is explored in Chapter 16. It involves attention to the intrapersonal, the interpersonal, the cultural, the ecological and the transplanetary domains.

## Holistic Learning and Experiential Learning

I consider that holistic learning is wider than and includes experiential learning in the classroom or group room. The latter is a basic part of the former, but the former raises broader issues about what a whole person is, what aspects of personhood are encompassed. Experiential learning, both in theory and practice in current educational method, involves minimal notions of what a whole person is; whereas holistic learning asks critically what this minimal model leaves out.

Experiential learning theory rests on the philosophic distinction between knowledge by acquaintance, that is, through encounter and meeting and first-hand experience, and knowledge about, or propositional knowledge, which is indirect and does not require any acquaintance with what the propositions give information about. William James (1890) made the distinction clearly and it has continued to be central in philosophy, psychology and educational theory. Kolb (1984) discusses it in detail in his account of experiential learning.

Traditional non-experiential learning is information-bound, all to do with indirect knowledge, knowledge about X, Y or Z. The student listens to lectures to acquire information, reads books and articles for more information, memorizes all this, reflects on it, writes about it in essays and talks about it in tutorials. It is non-stop description, abstraction, ideation, and judgment mediated by the written and spoken word. And none of this is grounded in personal experience. The student is locked into a horizontal round of propositional knowledge with no vertical depth in knowledge by acquaintance. The only exceptions are in science subjects which include experimental work in the laboratory.

Experiential learning breaks out of this and makes sure that at some point – *whatever* the subject – the student is involved in direct experiential knowledge, knowledge by acquaintance. This means the student has personal encounter with things, procedures, persons or places that are pertinent to the subject, either literally or symbolically, has inward reactions to them and may take outward action in relation to them. Such encounter, reaction and action may be immediate, by means of some structured experience within the learning situation; or it may be recollected from past personal experience verbally or graphically or by movement or some kind of dramatic portrayal. The student then reflects on this first-hand experience, and so turns it into learning (Boud et al, 1985).

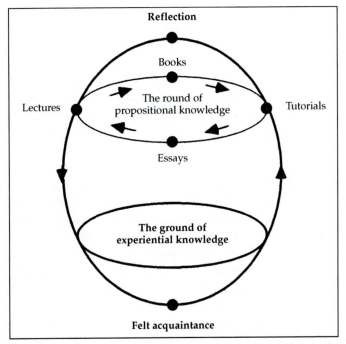

**Figure 3.2**　*Experiential grounding of the propositional round*

Figure 3.2 shows the traditional round of propositional knowledge grounded in experiential knowledge by the use of the experiential learning cycle, applied by exercises interspersed during lectures and tutorials.

Experiential learning is holistic in this significant sense that it integrates within the learning process perception, inner reactions such as emotion and imagination, outward action, and reflection. Its primary dynamic is the movement between the poles of first-hand personal encounter – knowledge by acquaintance – and reflection. Experiential learning is the process of being sensitively tuned in to that encounter and then reflecting on it.

Holistic learning certainly includes this minimal core model of the whole person, but it asks what is left out of this minimal model. What about intuition, psychic and spiritual capacities? How does whole personhood function, and what does this imply for integrated learning? What distinguishes the egoic individual from the whole person and what difference does this distinction make to our understanding of the learning process?

## The Generally Acceptable Model of a Whole Person

The minimal core model which experiential learning people use is itself an extraction from what I call the generally acceptable model of a whole person. This is a workable model for most people in our culture, including psychologists, educators, novelists and the person on the street. It consists of a pool of generally accepted beliefs about what a whole person includes. So we get a combination of: perception, memory, imagination, dreaming, thinking, intuition, movement, choice, intention, will, action, sensation, bodily needs and desires, social needs, emotion, interests. Underlying all this is the basic tripartite paradigm of the structure of the person in the Western tradition, which can be traced back to Plato: cognition, conation and affect – thinking, willing and feeling (Allport, 1958; von Eckartsberg, 1981). And in the background there are composite notions like those of person, self, subject, character, disposition and temperament.

While most professionals would probably find everything on the list intellectually acceptable, they will make different sorts of selections from it to suit their different purposes. What is clearly off the generally acceptable list is anything to do with subtle energy and subtle bodies, with extrasensory perception and other psychic abilities, and with transpersonal or spiritual dimensions of the person.

Experiential learning people tend to boil the generally acceptable list down to a minimal core. Kolb (1984) has it reduced to feeling, perceiving, thinking and behaving. But he does not define feeling; and emotion, intuition and imagination are excluded from his basic fourfold set. I have given elsewhere (Heron, 1992: 193-197) a detailed critique of Kolb's theory, which is really just a model of experiential learning derived from positivist scientific inquiry: we reflect on experience, generalize from these reflections then test the implications of these generalizations through further active experience.

Others condense experiential learning simply into experience and reflection; or to experience, reflection and action (Henry, 1989). 'Experience' here certainly means perception, and may include other things depending on the experience in question. On the one hand, these minimal accounts are convenient for pioneering experiential learning, for getting ideas of it out and about; and for introducing change with a minimum of resistance. On the other hand, their shallowness misses the depth of personhood and its potential learning power.

## Avant-garde Models of the Whole Person

Our culture being what it is, the generally acceptable account of the whole person is secular and humanist, including only biological and psychosocial realities. Avant-garde models go beyond this to include at least a transpersonal, that is, a spiritual, dimension. Thus Jung (1977) works with sensation, feeling, intuition and thinking from the general list, and adds among other archetypes in the collective unconscious the archetype of the self, which is not the ordinary self on the general list, but a deep spiritual centre whence proceeds personal integration and transformation. Assagioli (1965) enlarges Jung's selection from the general list to include: desire, sensation, feeling, imagination, intuition, thinking, the (ordinary) self and the will. Then to avoid all the contradictory things Jung bundles into the collective unconscious, he separates the unconscious from the super-conscious – which is the home of the transpersonal or higher self. The basic selections of these two theorists are shown in Figure 3.3.

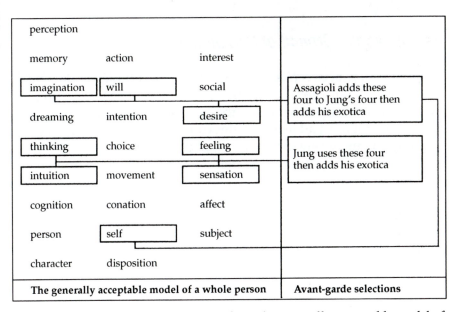

**Figure 3.3**   *Avant-garde selections from the generally acceptable model of a whole person*

These are two popular avant-garde models, as also are those derived from Hindu and Buddhist psychology. Swami Rama in the Hindu tradition has a model of the lower mind, *manas*, that integrates sense impressions, interacting with memory, *chitta*, and the separate subject or ego, *ahankar*. Beyond this is the higher intuitive mind, *buddhi*, the locus of wise discrimination and the will. And beyond all this is the Self, *Atman*, the universal witness consciousness, the blissful sheath (Swami Rama et al, 1976).

What is noticeable about these three models, two occidental and one oriental, is that the spiritual dimension of the person, called by all of them the Self, or transpersonal self, is portrayed as different from the various other component parts of the person such as perception, memory, feeling, the will, and is quite different from the everyday self of the general list. It is as if, when you are in an ordinary state of mind, the spiritual self is something you are outside of, or do not know about, or have to find, or meditate or develop into. To get to it you have to go from one psychological place to another of quite a different kind. There is also the implication that you probably need a guide or a guru to help you make the journey.

In the theory of the person I have put forward (Heron, 1992), this separation between the spirituality of persons and their everyday psychological functions is done away with. In the next section I give a brief overview of this new theory.

## Feeling as the Ground of Personhood

The distinction between feeling and emotion is quite fundamental, but general confusion abounds. In ordinary usage, 'feeling' is frequently used as a synonym for 'emotion'; it is also used as a synonym for almost all mental states from bodily sensations to subtle intuitions. In more considered usage, philosophers and psychologists have used the word 'feeling' or 'felt' to indicate how we apprehend the world. So William James says that it is 'through feelings we become acquainted with things' (James, 1890, Vol 1: 221); and other philosophers talk about the felt qualities of the world. Kolb (1984) also allocates feeling to the apprehension of concrete experience. But none of these people says what this feeling is that enables us to apprehend things. The word is used, it seems quite aptly, but the meaning is left tacit, a concept shrouded in experiential vagueness.

My view is that while emotion is to do with the fulfilment or frustration of our individual needs and interests in the forms of joy, surprise, anger, grief and so on, feeling is a term I reserve for the capacity of the person to participate in wider unities of being, to indwell what is present through attunement and resonance. Through feeling I become at one with the content of experience, and at the same time know my distinctness from it. This is the domain of empathy, indwelling, participation, presence, resonance, and such-like (Heron, 1992: 16).

Lawrence Hyde is about the only writer I know who made a clear distinction between the more intense, agitated character of emotion and the creative aspect of feeling by which 'we place ourselves in communion with what we find outside ourselves'. He variously called this empathy, heterocentric evaluation, and identification with the being of things 'in the mode of love' which at the same time enhances our own sense of identity (Hyde, 1955).

Koestler (1964) came close in his valid distinction between self-assertive emotions and participatory emotions, but the notion of feeling was never separated out from the latter. Empathy, from the German *Einfühlung*, feeling into, has been with us for a long while; but its conventional definition implies some special kind of state we need to get into in order to be empathic. In Chapter 12 I suggest how 'empathy' needs to be redefined to rescue it from the idea of self-bound projection.

My point about feeling, as I have defined it, is that it does not have to be discovered. You do not have to make a special psychological journey to find it. Nor does it have to be pulled like a rabbit by meditative magic out of an internal hat. It has only to be noticed as an integral part of everyday living as a distinct being in a multiple world. It is through feeling that we meet our different worlds and engage in resonant transaction with them.

Feeling is a necessary condition of ordinary perception. It attunes us to the manifold of beings which perceptual imagery clothes. We do not know that our imagery is imagery of anything, unless our participative feeling tells us of our distinctness-in-union with what there is. The subject-object split which comes from the conceptual layer in perception – the restless seeing of things as objects of different named sorts out there separate from us – may cause us to disattend from the grounding level of feeling our world, to such a degree that it seems to disappear from consciousness. But the felt acquaintance is always necessarily there.

It is feeling which distinguishes between dreams and waking life, because by its nature it is attuned to the differentiation of being into different kinds and levels of particular. So feeling authorizes intuition to understand dream images as portrayals of our inner life, and as distinct from the perceptual world of life awake. Feeling, in short, enables us to engage with and participate in our various experiential realities, to differentiate them from each other, and to know that we are distinct from any one of them even while being in a unified field with it.

This capacity for feeling is the ground of personhood, is that in which all other psychological functions are latent and out of which they emerge. It is the guiding entelechy of personhood, the formative principle and potential which can be evoked to shape our inner development. It is a profound and immediately accessible spiritual principle, the manifestation of divine life immanent within the psyche. I must refer the reader to *Feeling and Personhood* (Heron, 1992) for further details to enlarge this summary account of a comprehensive theory.

## The Up-hierarchy Model of the Whole Person

I see the whole person as compounded of four basic psychological modes – the affective, the imaginal, the conceptual and the practical. Each of these is composed of two polar and interdependent functions, a participatory one which makes for unitive interaction with a whole field of being, and an individuating one which makes for experience of individual distinctness. Stating the participatory first and the individuating next, the affective functions are feeling and emotion, the imaginal are intuition and imagery (imagery includes perception, extrasensory perception, memory and imagination), the conceptual are reflection and discrimination, the practical are intention and action. Reflection and discrimination correspond to Piaget's formal operational and pre-operational thinking (Flavell, 1963).

In terms of whole person dynamics, I think there is a basic, ground process going on in which the affective mode as feeling has all the other modes latent within it, and they emerge out of it in what I call an up-hierarchy form. An up-hierarchy works from below upwards, like a tree with roots, a trunk, branches and fruit. It is not a matter of the higher controlling and ruling the lower, as in a down-hierarchy, but of the higher branching and flowering out of, and bearing the fruit of, the lower. The basic features of an up-hierarchy are these:

- What is higher is tacit and latent in what is lower.
- The lowest level is the formative potential of higher levels.
- The higher levels emerge out of the lower.
- There are many different possible forms of emergence.
- The higher levels are a reduced precipitate of the lower.

- The higher levels are a focused consummation of the lower.
- Each level has a relative autonomy within the total system.
- What is lower grounds, supports and nourishes what is higher.

So the human psyche functions as an up-hierarchy grounded on feeling, the capacity for resonance with being and participative attunement to other beings. Out of the affective mode emerges the imaginal mode, including the imagery of imagination, memory and perception. From the imaginal proceeds the conceptual mode, the domain of thought and language; and this is the basis for the development of the practical mode, the level of intention and action. Figure 3.4 depicts the up-hierarchy with the participatory and individuating modes at each level.

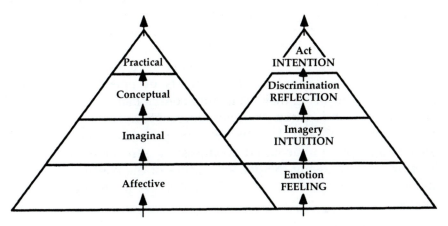

**Figure 3.4**　*The up-hierarchy of psychological modes*

Especially significant for learning is the view that the patterned fields of the imaginal mode are the source of all subsequent conceptualization. Hence the importance for the student of dwelling in the imaginal mode before explicit conceptual work, in order to make the latter easier and more fruitful. This view has been thoroughly worked out in *Feeling and Personhood* (Heron, 1992) and I must again refer the reader to this for the details.

## The Self and the Whole Person

Another basic distinction I make is between the self or ego and the whole person (in *Feeling and Personhood* I use the term ego). I construe the self as a relatively separate contraction, within the practical mode, of the individuating functions of emotion, imagery (mainly perception and memory), discrimination and action. This is illustrated in Figure 3.5. The self is over-identified with these; at the expense of the participative functions of feeling, intuition, reflection and intention and is an activist usurper working in relative dissociation from them. Not absolutely of course, since the self also uses the participative functions both tacitly and exploitatively to serve its own interests.

The self, which is busy not noticing its ground in participative feeling, identifies with its subjectivity as split off and separate from the objects of the world. Having this kind of a self seems to be a precondition of becoming a whole person. And a whole person in terms of this model is one in whom the individuating functions, previously contracted into the self, are brought into fully conscious integration with their participative correlates: emotion and feeling, imagery and intuition, discrimination and reflection, action and intention.

A self never attains total closure. First, it has tacitly to feed off the participative functions even while denying them any conscious role. Second, there are spontaneous moments of openness when the deeper functions bring their fruits into consciousness, as at times of interpersonal and group communion, contemplation of art and nature, creativity and free expression, peak experiences. Third, there is the option of acquired openness: the self can learn to create apertures for accessing the deeper reaches of the psyche. Figure 3.5 shows an open self that has cultivated access to the participatory modes.

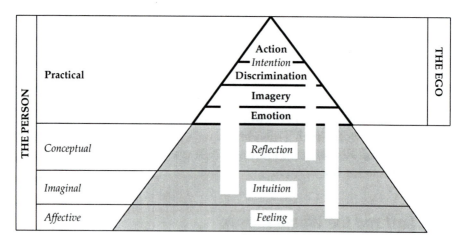

**Figure 3.5**   *The open self (ego)*

## *Open Self and Whole Person Learning*

What all this means for learning is that we need to distinguish between two kinds of holistic learning. There is a more limited sort to do with the self and which involves mainly the individuating functions of emotion, imagery, discrimination and action. There will be some shafts going down into the participatory functions of feeling, intuition, reflection and, of course, intention. I will call this open self learning, a first step in holistic learning.

Then there is the full-blown holistic version, which I call whole person learning and which explicitly integrates in the learning cycle both the individuating and the participatory modes: emotion and feeling, imagery and intuition, discrimination and reflection, intention and action. Open self and whole person learning, as I use the terms, are two forms of holistic learning about some subject. Whole person learning in this sense is still distinct from learning how to be a whole person – a wider notion which is not subject specific.

Open self and whole person learning about a subject involve experiential learning methods which make sure that at some point the student is involved in felt acquaintance. He or she has personal encounter with things, procedures, persons or places that are pertinent to or symbolic of the subject, and has inner and outer responses to them. Such encounter may occur now within the learning situation through some kind of special exercise; or it may be recollected from past personal experience. The student then reflects on this first-hand experience, and by doing so turns it into learning. I shall give details of open self and whole person experiential learning cycles in Chapter 14.

## *Closed Self Learning*

Traditional non-experiential learning is self-bound, often involving a very closed self. The learner, moving around between interest, boredom and fear (of falling behind, failing exams, being disapproved of) listens to teachers, reads books, tries to discriminate the presented content, to memorize it and to rehearse it in practice using the written or the spoken word. What is involved here is a closed circuit of the individuating self functions used in a restricted way: limited emotion, perceptual imagery, memory imagery, intellectual discrimination, and action as writing and speaking.

The learner's emotional base is suppressed and narrow, not in any way attended to by the teacher, and is a disconcerting *ad hoc* mix of conflicting positive and negative emotion. The imagery is reduced: perception is restricted to listening to teachers and looking at books, and memory is confined to the content of these perceived images. Intelligence is only involved in grasping the minimal conceptual geography of the topic; and action is exclusively word-oriented. So the individuating functions themselves, especially emotion, perception and action, are underdeveloped and inadequately integrated. And the propositional knowledge involved in learning has no experiential grounding in direct, felt acquaintance.

Traditional learning starts to shift out of this closed self format towards a minimal open self format to the extent that it includes more than mere intellectual discrimination of content and requires the student to engage in active reflection on this content, applying rules (Piaget's concrete operational thinking) or thinking in terms of possible or hypothetical relationships (Piaget's formal operational thinking). You can arrange all subjects in secondary and higher education on a continuum from mere discrimination (the individuating function of the conceptual mode) to advanced reflection (the participatory function of the conceptual mode), depending on the nature of the subject, the level at which it is being taught, and how it is being taught. But there is still the absence of experiential grounding: only science subjects that include experimental work in the laboratory have any base in perception and action.

Traditional methods at most open up the closed self by sinking a shaft down into the participative mode of reflection. The critical question is how valid an account of the world such reflection can yield when it is developed without other interconnected shafts being sent down into the grounding participatory modes of intuition and feeling, and without integrated development of the individuating functions of emotion, perception and action through the inclusion of experiential activities and exercises. Forms of open self and whole person learning are proposed in Chapter 14.

# *4 The Group Dynamic*

This chapter explores a concept basic to all facilitation, whatever dimension or mode is involved. By the group dynamic I mean the combined configuration of mental, emotional and physical energy in the group at any given time; and the way this configuration undergoes change. I will look at stages of the group dynamic; sketch in some of its positive forms; give considerable attention to the negative forms, and outline the role of the facilitator in dealing with them; and finally consider some further dimensions of group dynamic theory.

## *Stages of the Group Dynamic*

There is no reliable rule about how the dynamic will develop and unfold through the history of a group. The configuration of its energies can take many different forms, both positive and negative. The positive forms are usually attained after a passage through the negative forms. This attainment will depend on the objectives of the group, its programme, its membership, and the role of the facilitator. Later in this chapter I consider seven kinds of positive form: task-oriented, process-oriented, expressive, interactive, confronting, personal work oriented, charismatic. And three kinds of negative form: the educationally alienated, the culturally restricted and the psychologically defensive.

Although the total history of the group dynamic is variable, depending on the factors I have just mentioned, one can pick out four more obvious phases, so far as the shift from negative to positive forms is concerned. There is a cyclic flow of energy, as through the four seasons of the year from the time of the winter solstice.

1. **The stage of defensiveness.** This is usually at the outset of a group. Trust is low, anxiety is high, the group dynamic may get locked into one or more of the three restricted forms — educationally alienated, culturally restricted, psychologically defensive — described later in this chapter. *Wintertime:* the ground may be frozen, and the weather stormy or overcast.

2. **The stage of working through defensiveness.**   The group is now under way, trust is building, anxiety is reducing, as the facilitator is busy with the kind of strategies presented in this book. A fresh culture is being created. *Springtime:* new life starts to break through the surface crust.

3. **The stage of authentic behaviour.**   The group is deep into its real destiny. Trust is high, anxiety is a spur to growth and change, inner and outer conflicts are owned and resolved, light is grounded in an acceptance of shadow. There is openness to self and others, risk-taking, working, caring and sharing. There is flexibility in moving between different strands of learning. Leadership is shared, with a good balance of hierarchy, co-operation and autonomy. Authentic behaviour has many varieties and can include any of the positive forms of the group dynamic – task-oriented, process-oriented, expressive, inter-active, confronting, personal work oriented, charismatic – described in the next section below. *Summertime:* there is an abundance of growth, and the sun is high.

4. **Closure.**   As the group draws to a close, the members gather in and review the fruit of their learning, and prepare to transfer it to life in the wider world outside. At some point in this process separation anxiety will loom up – the distress at parting after such trust and depth of interaction. It can slip the group back into defensiveness unless dealt with with awareness – firstly by accepting that the end is nigh, secondly by dealing with any unfinished business, thirdly by celebrating each other and what has gone on, fourthly by saying a warm, friendly farewell in the group and one-to-one. *Autumn:* the fruit is harvested and stored, the harvesters give thanks and go their way.

## *Positive Forms of the Group Dynamic*

The whole purpose of this book is to help these forms come into being. The facilitator's concern is to enable them to emerge through the *Sturm und Drang* of the negative forms.

1. **Task-oriented.**   The group is outgoing, busy with planning, working on a project, practising some particular skill, busy with a structured exercise, undergoing some experience, exploring some issue, engaged in theoretical study. Members co-operate in learning, in problem-solving and decision-making.

2. **Process-oriented.** The group is ingoing, examining its own psychosocial process, seeking to understand how it is functioning.
3. **Expressive.** The group is active with celebration and creative expression in word, art, music, song or movement.
4. **Interactive.** Group members are engaged in interpersonal work and feedback, giving and receiving impressions, sharing attractions and aversions, withdrawing and owning projections.
5. **Confronting.** Members are engaged in creative conflict resolution, in supportive confrontation.
6. **Personal work oriented.** Individual members are taking time for personal growth work. Each one has a turn, working in pairs or small groups, or with you in the presence of the whole group. This work covers a wide spectrum, from cognitive and analytic self-discovery, through emotional disclosure, regression and catharsis, to transmutation and transpersonal development.
7. **Charismatic.** The group is attuning to psychic and spiritual energies, entering altered states of consciousness and action, engaged in ritual, expressive spirituality, silent meditation.

Where the positive forms abound, group members have adaptability in moving between different strands of learning and experience. Similarly, the facilitator has flexibility in moving between the six dimensions, and has the right balance of hierarchy, co-operation and autonomy. In more general terms, these seven positive forms can be seen as the outcome of three main influences:

1. **Cultural liberation.** Avant-garde ideas, practices, norms and values from the growing edge of the surrounding culture that come into the group via the facilitator and forward-thinking group members.
2. **Educational confluence.** Different strands and kinds of learning, interacting and alongside each other.
3. **Psychological openness.** The willingness of group members to open up to the challenge of change and growth. These are shown in Figure 4.1 below.

These three influences are interdependent, and there is a certain progression through them. Cultural liberation – the influence of innovative thought and practice from outside – manifests through the ideas and skill of the facilitator, which generate educational confluence – holism in course design and method. This in turn sets the scene for the psychological openness of course participants. The facilitator, through command of the educational process, mediates between cultural progress and individual learning and growth.

**Figure 4.1**    *Influences on positive forms*

## Negative Forms of the Group Dynamic

The counterparts to this positive triad are three main kinds of negative form, each with sub-varieties. These are shown in Figure 4.2. They interlock, affecting and influencing each other. You could say they are three different but overlapping perspectives on the same basic phenomenon: a block, a rigidity, a restriction in the dynamic of the group, so that learning is distorted or held back.

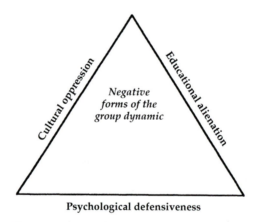

**Figure 4.2**    *Influences on negative forms*

1. **Cultural oppression.**   Group behaviour is restricted by oppressive norms, values and beliefs that flow into it and permeate it from the surrounding culture.

2. **Educational alienation.**   The group is limited to just one kind of learning objective. Its dynamic becomes contracted, cut off from other kinds of being and learning.
3. **Psychological defensiveness.**   Group behaviour is distorted by the various anxieties of participants. Present and past distress floods the group dynamic, throwing it into rigid, defensive forms.

Oppressive beliefs and practices from the culture are manifest in the limited and alienating educational model used within the course, and both set the scene for the psychological defensiveness of course participants. I will now consider each of these three factors in more detail.

## Cultural Oppression

### The Cultural Context

The participants of the group are enrolled from the surrounding culture. They bring with them, embedded in their attitudes and behaviour, many of the restrictive values and norms of that culture. Unless confronted and transformed, these will become the tacit values and norms of the group. I will select one prevailing cultural value and two prevailing cultural norms.

1. **Competitiveness.**   The culture fosters the value of competition – for profit, possessions, pleasure, status, competence and power.
2. **Emotional closure.**   The culture has a powerful norm of controlling and suppressing emotions of all kinds. It accepts only a limited expression of positive emotions and expects the total repression of distress emotions.
3. **Charismatic inhibition.**   The culture has another powerful norm of controlling and suppressing the innate spiritual presence of each person, along with their subtle senses and energies.

All these will pervade the group in its early stages and will impose a related set of social restrictions on behaviour in the group.

### Socially Restricted Forms of the Group Dynamic

There are many of these. I identify some of the more obvious ones that can all occur in a group of beginners. They are less likely in an advanced group, although one can never count on this.

1. **Rigid contribution hierarchy.**   By a contribution rate, I mean the degree to which any one person speaks in the group. A number of

high contributors emerge fairly swiftly, verbally dominating the proceedings. There are others with a medium contribution rate and a residual number who are low contributors or who never say anything at all.

A contribution hierarchy of high, medium and low contributors will function with great persistence and lack of awareness, unless broken up. A variety of discussion procedures can achieve this break.

2. **Power struggles.**  A contribution hierarchy can also turn into a decision hierarchy, in which high contributors struggle with each other to railroad through their preferred choices. Democratic decision-procedures are needed to deal with this.

3. **Gender bias.**  This is changing in the surrounding culture, but is still extensive, and can invade the group. Men speak and act first, often interrupting women without realizing, verbally elbowing them out of the way. Women's needs, perspectives and initiatives are ignored or suppressed and the women let this happen.

4. **Compulsive task-orientation.**  There will be a strong compulsion to fill unscheduled or process-oriented time with some clearly defined, easily identified and familiar kind of task.

5. **Emotional and physical isolation.**  There is a very strong tacit norm that people keep emotionally buttoned-up and physically entirely separate. Self-disclosure about certain kinds of personal information and emotion is taboo, as is any kind of touching or holding of other people.

6. **Spiritual and subtle occlusion.**  Everyone will tend, consciously or unconsciously, to practise being absent, non-existent, as a spiritual being, with subtle senses and energies.

These socially restricted forms yield somewhat to consciousness-raising at their own level. Helping group members to become aware of these and other cultural invasions is an important part of the learning process. They interact intimately, however, with the psychological defensive forms, which are discussed below, so both forms need to be dealt with alongside each other.

## Educational Alienation

### Learning Objectives of the Group

What the group is for, that is, what its members have come together to learn and do, will influence the configuration of group energies. Different objectives will have different effects. A comprehensive account of learning objectives can be derived from seven basic areas of human experience, and their combinations.

1. **Economic/practical.** The objective of the group is to learn some technical or manual skills for application in productive or service occupations, or in allied hobbies.
2. **Intellectual/theoretical.** The group is busy with intellectual learning of either pure or applied knowledge.
3. **Political/organizational.** The group is learning human relations, decision-making and other skills for managing and changing social, economic and political structures.
4. **Aesthetic.** The group is learning skills in imaginal understanding and expression, in artistic creation or interpretation.
5. **Personal/interpersonal.** The group is learning skills in both personal development and in interacting with other people.
6. **Transpersonal.** The group is learning skills in entering transfigured states of being – psychic, charismatic, meditative and spiritual states.
7. **Sensory/physical.** The group is learning skills in sensory and perceptual awareness, in embodied participation in the world.
8. **Combined.** The group is combining two or more of the above sorts of learning objectives.

Each one of the first seven on its own can have different effects on the group dynamic. But these effects have a common underlying form: they each involve some sort of alienation. It is not that this alienation is necessarily going to occur. But there is a tendency for it to happen where the learning objectives of the group are single-stranded.

## Alienated Forms of the Group Dynamic

Alienation is to do with dissociation, fragmentation, separation, being cut off, indifferent, remote and estranged. It can occur within a person, as self-alienation, when that person becomes identified with some aspect of the self and cut off from other aspects. It can occur between people, so that people relate to each other in a closed, restricted and estranged kind of way. And it can occur within a whole group, so that the group energy is locked into some restricted way of being or doing that is cut off from other ways. To clarify: the alienation of A from B, means that A is developed in a way that excludes and is cut off from the development of B.

Here is just a sample of alienated forms. More can be derived from the list of learning objectives above.

1. **Alienation of intellect.**   In a group pursuing only intellectual objectives, the group dynamic can suffer alienation. The mental activity in the group gets cut off from lived encounter with emotional, social and physical realities, interactions between people become excessively cognitive and emotionally dead or indifferent. Talk is all in terms of generalities and events considered in the abstract, far removed from personal experience.

2. **Alienation of affect.**   In a group committed to personal and interpersonal development objectives, the reverse kind of alienation can occur. The group gets immersed in a turgid emotional life of shared experience, cut off from the exercise of reflection and thought, and so does not understand or make enough sense of what is going on. Interaction is in terms of immediate emotional experience, far removed from more comprehensive perspectives.

   The dynamic in both the above kinds of group may also become quite dissociated from the spiritual dimension of being.

3. **Alienation of spirit.**   Groups that pursue purely transpersonal learning objectives, may engage in spiritual practices and share personal spiritual experiences, but in the process become alienated from adequate intellectual discrimination, from participative decision-making, from emotional realities and from authentic interpersonal openness.

4. **Alienation from the body.**   Each of the above three kinds of group may in their different ways and to differing degrees become alienated from the body, its energies, sensations and impulses, its need to be owned, identified and enjoyed as an expressive form of the psyche – mind, emotion and spirit – in space, and its sensory and perceptual participation in the world.

A group with a single-stranded set of learning objectives is prone to an alienated dynamic. Once it has launched itself unawarely on only one kind of learning, it will get stuck there. It makes sense to design an experiential group with composite, multi-stranded objectives, so that it may develop a non-alienated dynamic. This means, for example, combining practical, intellectual, personal, interpersonal, sensory and transpersonal objectives in the same group. One of these may be the primary strand of learning, with the others acting as complementary strands.

Educational alienation, therefore, is to be dealt with primarily at the stage of course design. This is supported by effective facilitation in switching between different strands of learning as the course unfolds.

The overall goal is holistic learning, many threads interweaving, or, to change the metaphor, confluent education – many streams running side by side with interconnecting channels. In this way, the physical body, the energy system, the emotions, the intellect, the imagination, the will and their spiritual ground can be integrated and developed in varying combinations in the process of growth and learning.

## Psychological Defensiveness

### The Anxieties of Participants

The dynamic of a group is strongly influenced by the anxieties of its participants. Such collective tension obscures the route to experiential learning. At the outset of a group, there is an abundance of disquiet just below the surface of the group dynamic. This anxiety is of two immediate kinds: existential and archaic. I consider two other sorts of anxiety later on.

1. **Existential anxiety.** This anxiety arises out of the immediate situation of being in the group. The participant at the start of an experiential learning course has, to a greater or lesser degree which partly depends on their experience of the method, an identity crisis. This has three interconnected components which reinforce each other, in the individual and collectively.
   - **Acceptance anxiety.** Will I be accepted, liked, wanted? Or will I be rejected, disliked and unwanted? Here the person's need to love and be loved is at risk.
   - **Orientation anxiety.** Will I understand what is going on? Will I be able to make sense of this situation, so that I can find some kind of identity within it? Here the person's need to understand and be understood is at risk.
   - **Performance anxiety.** Will I be able to do what I have come to learn? Will I be competent or incompetent? Will I be able to control the situation to meet my needs? Here the person's need to act and choose, the need for mastery and personal power, and their need to be chosen, is at risk.

   These are all perfectly normal and healthy fears. On their own, if modest, they may act as spurs to fulfilment, motivating members, respectively, to find acceptance and relationship with others, make sense of their experience, and perform well in the given tasks. If this is so, then their influence on the group dynamic is positive and benign, helping to create a co-operative, meaningful and constructive climate. But if they become stronger, they may distort the group dynamic into relatively minor defensive forms that can impede learning.

However, existential anxiety may also be compounded by archaic anxiety. Either the existential anxiety becomes very strong and triggers the archaic or it is high because the archaic is already running into it. The group dynamic may then be flooded by more fear than anyone can handle. The behaviour of participants is distorted into major defensive forms, the compound anxiety being displaced into unaware, maladaptive attitudes that entirely block learning and growth.

2. **Archaic anxiety.**    This anxiety is the presenting symptom, on the fringe of consciousness, of the repressed distress of the past – the personal hurt, particularly of childhood, that has been buried and denied so that the individual can survive emotionally. The undischarged pain of this much earlier and more radical identity crisis, is precipitated toward the surface, stirred up by the existential anxiety of being in the group, and beyond this by certain threatening issues, which I discuss in the next section.

Archaic anxiety represents three interconnected forms of repressed distress which all have their roots in traumatic childhood situations and their elaboration by later experiences of hurt and oppression:

- **Repressed grief.**    The hidden pain of not having received and not having been able to give enough love: the pain of emotional rejection, deprivation and neglect.
- **Repressed fear.**    The hidden panic of having felt that one's whole identity is being threatened by overwhelming situations one cannot understand, and therefore cannot control or resist.
- **Repressed anger.**    The buried rage at the interference with one's liberty, one's freedom to explore oneself and the world in the light of one's own imagination, needs and interests.

There are less and much more severe forms of these three. Most people seem to carry around some degree of each. This is because we live in an emotionally repressive culture, in which social conditioning requires children to learn to suppress, ignore and eventually deny their personal hurts – rather than find healing through catharsis and awareness training (Heron, 1990a, 1992).

On top of the deeper repressions of grief, fear and anger, there is a much more accessible kind of archaic distress – embarrassment, which is basically a conditioned fear of what people will think if they find out about the real you. It acts as a powerful inhibitor of the underlying pain.

## Threatening Issues

There are certain threatening issues which arise at different stages of a group's history. In the early stages of a group, these issues will tend to be more disturbing than in later stages. They are threatening not only because they generate existential anxiety, but even more so because they can stir up archaic anxiety which then starts to run into and reinforce the existential disquiet. These issues are typically to do with:

- Authority and control.
- Conflict and aggression.
- Intimacy and contact.
- Love and care.
- Sexuality and gender.
- Identity and purpose.
- Disclosure and expression.
- Truth and honesty.
- Mastery and competence.
- Knowledge and ignorance.
- Psychic awareness and spirituality.

Such themes, when they arise at a certain time and in a certain way in the group, may resonate with the earliest, most vulnerable and often traumatic experiences of early life.

Then archaic anxiety comes to the fore, triggered directly by the threatening issue itself, or by a build up in the existential anxiety which that issue arouses. When the archaic is on the move, and tangles with the existential, the total charge of tension can become disabling. The group dynamic is distorted into certain typical defensive forms. Existential anxiety on its own, when strong enough, can also generate these forms, but in a much less severely distorted form.

## Defensive Forms of the Group Dynamic

There seems to be a collusion, a contagion, an unconscious kind of triggering mediated by subliminal cues, so that at times the whole group is locked in the defensive mode. The defence is against both the threatening issue, and the provoked anxiety with its underlying existential and archaic agendas.

The group dynamic can then have three defensive forms which can be mutually reinforcing and which can co-exist – in different subgroups – at the same time.

1. **Submission.** Group members displace their anxiety into a family of distorted passive behaviours. They may become compulsively dependent on the group leader, or any rival leader, blindly following, seeking permission. They may show signs of withdrawal and shut-down, of powerlessness, loss of identity and of compulsive guilt. They are inwardly isolated, alienated, and constrained by tacit norms that inhibit intimacy, emotion and contact.

2. **Flight.** The anxiety is displaced into compulsive flight from the real issues emerging within the life of the group. The indications of such flight are: irrelevant theorizing and generalizing; jocularity; gossip about trivialities; persistently talking about the world outside the group; 'rescuing' someone from the brink of real personal work and self-disclosure; compulsive questioning of someone in the group; retreating into a collusive pair with some other group member; insisting on a clear task, a programme, a conventional goal.

3. **Attack.** The anxiety is displaced into compulsive attack. The group leader is resisted, his or her proposals rejected, his or her authority, relevance or competence challenged. One or more group members may compete in a rival bid for leadership; or become locked in mutual aggression. Some group member may be scapegoated – irrationally blamed, invalidated, criticized, accused, labelled and stereotyped. The room and other physical facilities may be continuously complained about. Any positive change in the dynamic may be interrupted and wrecked. Good energy is mocked.

Figure 4.3 shows in broad outline the conceptual model of defensive forms. It simplifies the total process, of course. In reality, there are not just three vertical lines of influence as the arrows suggest, but an interlocking network of influences. Nevertheless, the arrows do pick out primary dynamic connections.

It is important to make a distinction between acute and chronic defensive forms. Acute ones are products of existential anxiety only, and have little or no significant resonance with past pain. Chronic defensive forms result from a strong charge of archaic anxiety which boosts the existential. The acute ones are much less distorted than the chronic, and will yield more readily to interruption than the chronic.

The role of the facilitator, among other things, is to help group members unlock themselves from these defensive forms, and so create a different kind of group dynamic. However, before considering this role, we must note that the facilitator can be involved in a special way in defensive forms. This brings us to transference.

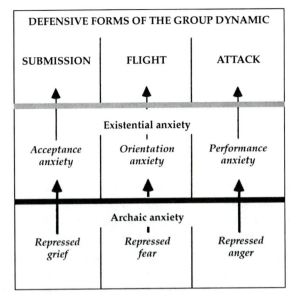

**Figure 4.3**  *Psychological defensiveness*

## *Transference*

When transference occurs, participants unconsciously transfer to the group leader, from the hurt child within, hidden and repressed feelings about a parent or some other important authority figure from the past.

1. **Positive transference.**  One or more group members unconsciously project on to the facilitator the frozen need and longing for the good parent they never had. This may lead to submissive forms of defensiveness, such as dependency, following and permission-seeking in relation to the facilitator. A positive transference can be put to work and used to motivate learning and growth for a period. But sooner or later the persons concerned need to withdraw – and perhaps be helped to withdraw – the projection, see it for what it is, and assume the attitudes of their own authentic adulthood.
2. **Negative transference.**  One or more group members unawarely project the distorted fear and anger about the bad parent they actually had. This can result in aggressive defensiveness that attacks the facilitator, such as active resistance, denigration, sabotage and rivalry. A negative transference always tends to make learning more difficult as long as it is in place, and where it is particularly strong in someone, the facilitator may need to work intensively with the person concerned, so that he or she can

identify the projection and withdraw it, after being helped to release some of the underlying distress.

3. **Acute transference.**   Group members may temporarily undergo an acute transference, positive or negative, at some early stage of the group. It causes them to slip into defensive behaviour for a while, but as things proceed, and with a little facilitation, they move out of it quite readily.

4. **Chronic transference.**   This fastens relentlessly on to the facilitator, and may need special and sustained attention to resolve. It may be positive or negative.

5. **Universal transference.**   The process of unaware projection of emotions that belong to the past, on to some one or more persons in the present, is one of the most persistent phenomena in the dynamic of a group, and, indeed, in society at large. It goes every which way, not just from member to leader, but from member to member. In this case, it widens out beyond feelings for parents and authority figures. Any kind of repressed distress about anyone from the past can be unawarely projected on to some present person, who is thus unconsciously appointed to be the current scapegoat for past ills.

   This blind scapegoating is also a defence against facing and owning and dealing with the hidden pain. Hence a strong projection will not want to let go of its victim, and may powerfully resist being seen for what it is. The deeper the hurt, the more relentless is the projection.

6. **Counter-transference.**   The unaware projection of hidden distress from the past may also proceed from the facilitator to one or more group members, or even the group as a whole. This is so-called counter-transference. Once your facilitation gets tangled up with your own blindly projected distress, it degenerates. It submits to group pressure, or takes flight from what is really going on, or verbally attacks and blames people. The group dynamic rapidly goes down the drain. One basic indicator of good facilitators at work is that they keep relatively clear of their own past unfinished business while on the job. This is one of the most important criteria of their emotional competence (Heron, 1992; Postle, 1991).

## The Role of the Facilitator

The dynamic of the group is grounded in the life of emotion and feeling. Hence in Chapter 11, which deals with the feeling dimension,

I look in more detail at ways of managing the dynamic directly at the affective level. However, while it is controlled through impact on the emotion and feeling of group members, this impact can also be made indirectly through the other dimensions. The whole of the rest of this book is about different ways in which you, the facilitator, can influence it. But when it is locked into negative forms, here are some of the basic things you can do to move it on. This list anticipates strategies that will be dealt with in more detail later.

1. **For cultural restrictions**
   - **Consciousness-raising.**  You seek to raise people's consciousness about contribution rates, power struggles, gender bias, task compulsion, emotional isolation, charismatic inhibition. You confront the restriction by identifying it and pointing it out.
   - **Interruption.**  Having pointed out the restriction, you interrupt both its active and its passive forms by devising procedures and exercises that break it up; or by asking those involved to practise alternative behaviours on the spot.
2. **For educational alienation**
   - **Holistic course design.**  You can create a multi-stranded curriculum with learning objectives of complementary kinds. Your design combines different kinds of learning which involve and integrate different aspects of the whole person.
   - **Effective switching.**  You manage effectively the switch from one strand of learning to another. This is to do with the choice of switch – from what to what; the timing of the switch – making it when it is needed; and the manner – helping people to adjust.
3. **For psychological defensiveness.**  Many of the items below can also deal with cultural restrictions, where these are simply forms of psychological defensiveness in society at large.
   - **Culture-setting.**  At the very beginning of the group, you gently manifest charismatic, distress-free authority in declaring values of warmth, support, trust and safety as the basic culture of the group. You affirm the worth and rights of persons.
   - **Permission-giving.**  Again, with distress-free authority, you clearly give permission for  people to be vulnerable, to uncover and heal their hurts.
   - **Growth ground-rules.**  To help members to overcome the more obvious defensive behaviours, you propose a clear set of ground-rules: speaking in the first person singular, addressing others directly, and so on.

- **Honouring choice.** You make it clear that every group member has a right to choose when to lower their defences, and to choose when to do some personal work. You respect this in practice, and never pressure anyone.
- **Conceptual orientation.** You give a short theoretical input on the nature of existential and archaic anxiety, and the ways they can distort the group dynamic into distorted forms.
- **Confronting.** You raise consciousness about particular, current processes: issues being avoided, defensive and distorted behaviours – which include transference, i.e. projection on to you, and between group members.
- **Emotional switching.** You deftly propose some activity that interrupts the defensive block by switching emotional energy from it, and into some other way of being. Restoring a light and positive climate, when things get too heavy.
- **Laughter.** Keep the group bursting into laughter at regular intervals. This discharges the conditioned fear we call embarrassment, and so reduces the tendency of the dynamic to get locked into defensive forms.
- **Lowering the cathartic threshold.** You introduce structured exercises, such as those involving breathing and body work, that interrupt body–mind defences and bring the underlying distress up for discharge and healing.
- **Individual work.** You work with an individual in front of the group, with everyone's attention and support, showing that the release of emotional hurt is healing and restorative. This includes work on projections on to you and between group members.
- **Group autonomy.** Not everything is to be dealt with by facilitation. The group also needs times to spot its defensive forms on its own, and find its own ways of interrupting them and getting into a working phase.

## Extensions of Group Dynamic Theory

The threatening issues which I listed earlier are those that are most immediately involved in the dynamic of any face-to-face human group, and the anxieties to which they give rise – existential and archaic – are the bedrock of any group dynamic theory, in my view. But I believe there are two other kinds of anxiety, aroused by two other kinds of threatening issue that are more wide-ranging.

1. **Cultural and planetary anxiety.** The sorts of concerns which give rise to this are: Is the society in which I live making the most of its human and physical resources? Is it a just society? Does it acknowledge fully human rights? What can I do about human rights abuses in so many parts of the world? What can I do about the deaths of millions of children each year, and the sufferings of so many more?

   Can we cross the divide between rich and poor nations? Can we stop the expropriation of profits from underdeveloped economies? Will we destroy our planet by nuclear holocaust? How do we reduce defence budgets? Can we master the population explosion and global food shortage? Are we taking care of our planet, preserving and fostering our total environment? Can we halt the decimation of species and habitats?

2. **Transcendental anxiety.** The sorts of concerns which give rise to this are: Is there a god? What is my relation with such a reality? What is my destiny? How have I come into being? Who or what has made me? Am I created continuously? What is the ground of my identity? Who am I? Is my soul saved, or lost, or neither?

   What happens to me after death? Am I surrounded by another world? What is its impact upon me now? What are the great reaches of transcendental creation? Are there invisible powers and presences? How do I contact them?

One view of these two kinds of anxiety is that they provide the parameters within which existential and archaic anxiety arise. Thus the threatening issues which give rise to existential and archaic anxiety are subordinate to the wider concerns, which give rise to cultural/planetary anxiety and transcendental anxiety. These further anxieties may distort the group dynamic into the following distinctive defensive forms, which will need attention in their own right.

## Conventional Inertia

Cultural and planetary anxiety, when unowned and unprocessed, may displace into a fixation and rigidity of conventional attitudes and behaviour, a defensive clinging to the status quo, a contraction and closure on local established social structures and practices. This is the same as the *cultural oppression* already discussed and suggests one possible source of it, along with the contribution of psychological defensiveness to societal rigidity.

### Transcendental Contraction

Transcendental anxiety, when unowned and unprocessed, may displace into separatist alienation, the illusory belief and attitude that the everyday self is separate from the world, from things and other people, from other dimensions of being, and from universal consciousness-as-such. Ordinary consciousness is focused on everyday choice and on the beliefs that service such choice. It contracts around these individual-centred concerns with a rigid, unyielding separatist illusion. It is closed to the unitive vision, the sense of dwelling in the whole, in its subtle and pervasive energies.

### Beyond Contraction

Looked at as positive stimuli, cultural/planetary anxiety and transcendental anxiety offer two very fundamental and complementary challenges.

- The challenge of shaping a new kind of society, both locally and globally, which cares for the planetary environment and manifests social justice.
- The challenge of living awarely within the conscious experiential field of a multi-dimensional universe.

Both these challenges provide an exhilarating context for the future development and application of experiential learning.

## Transpersonal Influences on the Group Dynamic

The group dynamic can become transformed and transmuted by opening it up to subtle forms of energy and spiritual influence, by various forms of attunement, meditation, ritual, song and chanting, invocation and evocation, sacred dance and movement, sacred postures and other procedures. This takes us into the domain of the charismatic group. Movement into this field is increasingly an option today as more people learn to slough off the charismatic inhibition pervasive in the culture (Heron, 1996b, 1998a).

This tendency is also reinforced by the participative world-view that is currently emerging (Merleau-Ponty, 1962; Bateson, 1979; Reason and Rowan, 1981; Spretnak, 1991; Heron, 1992, 1996a; Varela et al, 1991; Skolimowski, 1994; Reason, 1994; Abram, 1996). Here are three closely related group dynamic principles which I believe are well grounded in participative experience:

1. **Unified affective field.** At the level of basic feeling, which I distinguish from emotion (see Chapter 3), and define as the capacity for mutual participation with other beings through empathic resonance, a group can learn consciously to access a shared experiential field of harmonic resonance. This can provide a deep ground, a generous backdrop, for owning and processing the emotional currents and turbulence that may surge through the field, and for enhancing the learning activities that occur within its aegis.

   It can also be called a shared experiential *spatial* field, as explained further in Chapter 12. Experiential space is the inner felt sense of space as a form of consciousness and life. It is a medium for human communion; it is the 'ocean of shared feeling … where we become one with one another' (Alexander, 1979: 294).

   It is valuable for facilitators to resonate with this field at their own feeling level to establish a radical, dynamic basis out of which images and concepts of appropriate interventions can emerge.

2. **Holonomic focus.** The holonomic principle, thought by radical physicists, systems theorists, and others to be a universal property of nature (Capra, 1983), asserts that the whole being is coded or enfolded in each of its parts. The whole body is genetically coded in each of its cells. The whole hologram is represented in any part of the holographic plate. The whole of the implicate order of the universe is enfolded in any part of the explicate universe (Bohm, 1980).

   In an integrated, open and committed group, communion is holonomic. It infuses the personal distinction of each member with the collective compenetration of all. The whole group is coded within the resonant attunement of each person within it. Thus the destiny of the whole group can manifest at a particular time through the individual perspective of one person. The group is represented by one of its members, who will contribute in a way that focuses the learning of all.

   The facilitator can be sensitive to this phenomenon and be alert to make way for it when it is about to manifest. The facilitator too, is a holonomic focus for the energy, needs and concerns of the whole group. Feeling and tuning in to the shared experiential field is a way of enabling that to become evident.

3. **Open window.** When a group either intentionally or spontaneously enters a unified affective field, it is *as if* it creates an open window onto a more interior kind of worldspace, with the felt sense of discreet communion with presences within it. The potential of this kind of opening calls for careful experiential inquiry (Heron, 1998a).

# 5 The Planning Dimension

Detailed presentation of the core model of this book, the dimensions and modes of facilitation, begins in this chapter with the planning dimension.

In Chapter 2, I introduced the notion of the facilitator's political authority, which in its old-fashioned form means that the teacher just makes a taken-for-granted decision that he or she will unilaterally plan the students' learning programme in all its aspects. I suggested that new-style political authority is much more subtle, sophisticated and empowering, because it is exercised at higher-order levels of decision-making. It means that you, the facilitator, make a unilateral decision about who will plan the programme as a whole, or different parts of it: whether you will do the planning, or the students and you, or the students on their own. And at a more subtle level, it means that you make a unilateral decision about who will take the decision about who will plan the programme. Will you alone decide whether to involve students in the planning? Will you consult with the students and make a conjoint decision with them about whether you, they and you, or they alone plan all or different parts of the programme? Or will you delegate to the students the decision about who will plan what?

In this chapter I propose to go over all this again more comprehensively and in more detail. In facilitation training courses, I find that it takes some time for trainees to get a clear working conceptual grasp of these different *levels* of decision-making and of the different *decision-modes* that can be exercised at each of them. Also to grasp that however much you consult students, at some level you make a unilateral decision to do so. It takes much longer for facilitators to work awarely and intentionally with the levels and modes, and apply them appropriately in the real world of training.

So for you, the new-style facilitator, trying only to shift one level up, the question is: what is the programme of activities for the group, and who will decide what it is? In some specialist skills training for beginners, it may be appropriate that much of the programme is planned and decided by you alone. But as group members take these skills on board, then at some point they have a claim to be consulted about further planning. The more autonomous they become in the mastery of a new range of skills, the more they know about how they need to develop them in the future.

In other groups, such as those for in-service further training, it may be appropriate to adopt consultative planning from the outset, because the participants have a good understanding of what they need to learn, and their experience needs to be honoured. From the standpoint of your specialist knowledge, you also have an important perspective on what experienced professionals need to learn. So you and they negotiate to get your respective bits of content into the programme.

When to plan for the group, plan with the group, or give space to the group to plan on its own? It depends on the sort of group – its learning objectives; the length of the group – how long it lasts; the level of learning and experience of group members; and the stage in group development – whether early, mid-term, or later on.

Whenever you consult a group about its programme of learning, you are implicitly asking its members to identify their personal learning needs and goals and so to make sure that the programme will fulfil them. You may want to make this process explicit, and precede any planning consultation with an exercise in which each person assesses their own learning needs. Please bear this in mind when you read the words 'consult' or 'consultation' below.

## Planning Overview

If we consider the total educational process, there are six key areas for planning:

1. **Objectives.**   These are learning outcomes and give an account of what group members will acquire from the course: the main sorts of insight, knowledge, skills, changes of state and being to be developed.
2. **Programme.**   This is the content of learning, designed as a timetable for realizing the objectives.
   - It includes all the *topics* and activities in each of the different strands of the curriculum. Each strand will contain certain basic sorts of topic and activity, and within each sort, a detailed set of contents.

- The programme distributes the topics over *time*. There are several aspects to this: the total length of the programme; the total number of hours for each sort of topic; the sequence of topics, those which come before, those which come after; and those which run concurrently, side by side.
- It will also indicate the teaching and learning *methods* involved, allocate some of the human and physical *resources* for learning, and possibly show when various kinds of *assessment* will occur. So it overlaps with the next three items.

3. **Methods.** These are the teaching and especially the learning methods. In Chapter 2, when discussing tutelary authority, I mentioned several of these: open learning, active learning, real learning, peer learning, multi-stranded curriculum, contract learning, resource consultancy, guardianship. And there are also, of course, the interrupted lecture, the seminar and the one-to-one tutorial.

4. **Resources.** These include human resources: staff, other students, professionals and people with specialist knowledge and skills in the community. And physical resources: books, journals, laboratory equipment, writing materials, drawing and painting materials, computers, e-mail, Internet, study rooms, libraries, museums, professional institutions, and so on.

5. **Assessment.** This is to determine whether group members have realized the learning objectives through participation in the programme. It requires criteria of competence or achievement, a method for applying these criteria to the learners' performance, and a way of deciding the final assessment outcome.

6. **Evaluation.** This is to evaluate the facilitator's style and the educational effectiveness of all the above five elements and of how they are interrelated.

If we take the three decision-modes of hierarchy, co-operation and autonomy – you, the facilitator, decide unilaterally for the group, decide bilaterally with the group, and delegate decision-making to the group – then we have the table of options shown in Figure 5.1.

There are very many ways of combining the decision-modes going across the table. Thus you alone may decide on the learning objectives and on the course programme, co-operate with the group in designing and implementing assessment procedures, and let the group alone do the course evaluation. There are also many ways of combining the decision-modes within one column. So some parts of the course programme you plan alone, some parts you plan with the group, and some parts the group plans on its own; some

| | Objectives | Programme | Methods | Resources | Assessment | Evaluation |
|---|---|---|---|---|---|---|
| **Hierarchy** You alone | | | | | | |
| **Co-operation** You with group | | | | | | |
| **Autonomy** Group alone | | | | | | |

**Figure 5.1** *The three decision-modes and the elements of the educational process*

teaching/learning methods you decide on alone, some you decide with the group, and some the group determines for itself; and so on. Combining options both across and within columns gives you enormous scope in the politics of educational decision-making. Modern educational method has barely begun to tap the potential of this table.

What now follows is *a basic map of political options* for you as facilitator of learning. Figure 5.2 shows the seven ways of using the decision-modes, singly and in various combinations. It applies to the six educational areas, both to the components of each area and to the whole set of areas. So remember that 'all' and 'some' in the table below refer to items both across columns and within columns in the previous table.

| | | Hierarchy | Co-operation | Autonomy |
|---|---|---|---|---|
| 1. | | *You decide all* | | |
| 2. | | *You decide some* | *You with group decide some* | |
| 3. | | *You decide some* | *You with group decide some* | *Group decide some* |
| 4. | | *You decide some* | | *Group decide some* |
| 5. | | | *You with group decide some* | *Group decide some* |
| 6. | | | *You with group decide all* | |
| 7. | | | | *Group decide all* |

**Figure 5.2** *Seven ways of using decision-modes in planning*

Let us consider this table in relation to the six fundamental elements of the educational process: objectives, programme, methods, resources, assessment and evaluation. Row 1 is the traditional, authoritarian model of education: staff decide everything – what the students shall learn, how they shall learn it and whether they have learnt it. Row 7 is the peer self-help model of education, with an entirely autonomous, self-directed student body. If there are any teachers and facilitators, they are hired by, and under contract to, the students.

Rows 5 and 6 are dubious: they imply that absolutely everything is up for negotiation and, in row 5, delegation. But if everything really is negotiable, you do not stand for anything, have no educational model to offer. If you have really thought through the matter, there will be some aspects of the educational process which will be non-negotiable because they exemplify values and principles to which you are committed. These aspects define the sort of educational model you are dedicated to realize.

Thus your model may include significant student participation with staff in educational decision-making. And your commitment to this makes it a non-negotiable principle, stated in the course prospectus, to which new students are invited to subscribe. You are not open to people on your course negotiating you back into traditional authoritarian, unilateral decision-making about everything.

Row 3 is the most comprehensive educational model. It combines all the decision-modes, and provides the greatest scope for the effective facilitation of learning. It represents the view that hierarchy – in certain forms, at certain stages and applied in certain areas – is a necessary condition for the embryonic development of self-determination. This is the paradox: that people need to be led to freedom, to be guided and enabled to be autonomous.

Row 3 allows for enormous variation with respect to what goes in each column. It can accommodate a progression from high staff involvement in educational decision-making, to minimal involvement; and innumerable different ways of making this progression.

## Levels of Decision-making

We now return to the different levels of decision-making involved in planning the programme of learning. I introduced these levels in Chapter 2 and sketched them in again at the opening of this chapter. Here is a readily accessible figure relating the four decision-levels to the three decision-modes.

## Level 1

**Managing this learning activity.** This is the ground-floor level of deciding how to structure and manage the learning that is about to happen in the classroom now. Will you alone manage the activity, will you manage it in co-operation the group, will you delegate it to the group to self-manage, or will you use each of these in relation to different aspects of the activity?

## Level 2

**Planning the programme of learning.** This is the level of planning the timetable of learning for the whole course or some substantial part of it. Who will decide on the plan? Will you alone do the planning, will you do it in co-operation with the group, will you delegate it to the group, or will you use each of these in relation to different aspects of the plan?

## Level 3

**Deciding who plans the programme of learning.** This is the first higher-order decision-level. It involves deciding whether you alone decide who at level 2 plans the programme, whether you co-operate with the group in deciding who at level 2 plans the programme, whether you delegate it to the group alone to decide who at level 2 plans the programme, or whether there is a mixture of these with regard to different broad areas of planning.

## Level 4

**Deciding who decides who plans the programme of learning.** This is the second and final higher-order decision-level. At this level you alone decide who at level 3 decides who plans the programme. So at level 4 you decide unilaterally whether at level 3 you alone decide who at level 2 plans the programme, or whether this is done co-operatively by you with the group, or delegated to the group, or some combination of these is used.

Figure 5.3 shows the fundamental anatomy of power and control options for you, the facilitator, and the group. Level 4 is where your political authority ultimately resides. Unilateral decision-making at this level is unavoidable. On each of the other three levels, any one, or any two, or all three decision-modes may be used. So over the three levels below level 4, innumerable different decision-mode patterns may be used.

| DECISION-MODES → <br><br> DECISION-LEVELS ↓ | HIERARCHY <br> Direction <br> Facilitator does it <br> FOR people | CO-OPERATION <br> Negotiation <br> Facilitator does it <br> WITH people | AUTONOMY <br> Delegation <br> Facilitator gives it <br> TO people |
|---|---|---|---|
| **Level 4** <br> deciding who decides who <br> plans the programme of <br> learning | | | |
| **Level 3** <br> deciding who plans <br> the programme of <br> learning | | | |
| **Level 2** <br> planning the <br> programme of <br> learning | | | |
| **Level 1** <br> managing <br> this learning <br> activity | | | |

**Figure 5.3**   *The four decision-levels and the three decision-modes*

To take one simple pattern: as facilitator, you decide directively at level 4 to negotiate with group members at level 3 about who will plan the programme, and this negotiation may result in the planning at level 2 being done partly by you alone, partly by you with the group, and partly by the group alone, and these plans may similarly include a mix of decision-modes in the management of day-by-day learning activities.

If the number of patterns is narrowed down by combining any one, and only one, decision-mode from each of the three levels below level 4, then we get 27 simplified forms of power and control for facilitator and group. It is a useful imaginative exercise for a facilitator to reflect on some of these forms, and evaluate what they would mean in reality, as an aid to acquiring command of the overall model. But in reality, of course, more than one decision-mode may be used at any of these three levels.

## Refining the Decision-modes

If you examine all the interventions given later in this chapter, you will find that each of the three main decision-modes has two basic forms. I present them here as a convenient overview – to provide orientation and perspective. And I will describe them as applied within level 2, planning the course programme.

## Hierarchical Mode

1. **Autocratic direction.** You decide on the programme without consulting group members about their proposals for the programme.
2. **Consultative direction.** You decide on the programme after you have gathered in the proposals of group members, based on their needs and interests. The final decision is yours: it may or may not take into account the suggestions you have heard.

## Co-operative Mode

3. **Negotiation.** You bring your strong facilitative concerns to the negotiating table and decide on the plan conjointly with the group, seeking agreement, and, where necessary, mutual compromise, between your proposals and group members' proposals.
4. **Co-ordination.** You act as chairperson to the group planning meeting, prompting, guiding and helping the group to make a collective plan. You are not negotiating a plan with the group, but facilitating its emergence – under your touch – from the group. This is much more group-centred than negotiation, and is on the boundary with the autonomous mode.

## Autonomous Mode

5. **Functional delegation.** Either by direction or by negotiation, you delegate to individual members different planning functions, and to the group as a whole a procedure for integrating these strands into a collective plan.
6. **Contractual delegation.** Within the broad terms of a contract (outlined in terms of time-span and main objectives) determined either by direction or negotiation, you delegate all detailed planning to group members, to manage in their own way.

   Note: delegation is necessarily set within limits determined by either direction or negotiation. Absolute delegation means that the facilitator has abandoned his role: the group has become a small political autonomy.

## *Autonomy: Delegated or Seized*

Sometimes, of course, the group will not have power delegated to it, but will seize its autonomy. Either the group is ready for this autonomy, that is, sufficiently skilled and aware, or it is not ready, still unskilled and unaware. And either the group wants to exercise this autonomy in a good direction (as you see it), or in a bad direction.

So there are four possibilities: the group is ready for a good autonomous goal, unready for a good autonomous goal, ready for a bad autonomous goal, and unready for a bad autonomous goal. The third one of these is odd and unlikely: a skilled and aware group is not likely to want to go in a bad direction – but it is still a possibility. You, the facilitator, should rapidly support the first of these four, strongly confront the relevant parts of the other three, and if the group insists on going ahead, let them do so, but then move in to sort out the confusion when the trial exposes the error.

## *A Decision-mode and a Decision-procedure*

It is important not to confuse a decision-mode with a decision-procedure. The former refers to the way you, the facilitator, use your power: do you decide for the group, or with the group, or delegate the decision to the group? These are the three decision-modes of hierarchy, co-operation and autonomy. A decision-procedure is a method used for making a collective, group decision: the decision is based on unanimity, or some form of majority vote, or consensus, or gathering the sense of the meeting. I say more about these different decision-procedures later in this chapter in the section on co-operative interventions.

If your decision-mode is hierarchical, i.e. you are being directive, you will not use decision-procedures at all. If you are in the co-operative mode, making some decisions with group members, you and they will use a decision-procedure. And if in the autonomous mode you have delegated some decisions to group members, they on their own will use a decision-procedure.

## *Apollonian and Dionysian Planning*

By Apollonian planning, I mean the kind of planning implied so far in this chapter: the detailed structuring of future time with a programme of learning. Such planning creates a well-defined, temporal map of the course.

It may cover different periods. If the course is for one year with three terms, then a long-range plan covers the whole year, a medium-range plan one term, and a short-range plan one week.

Dionysian planning, by contrast, is impromptu, often improvisatory, responding flexibly and imaginatively to the presence of the group, to its feel and mood and thrust, as well as to the purpose of the course. The Dionysian plan unfolds itself step by step, from one learning activity to the next; and each activity can be chosen by a different decision-mode and executed by a different decision-mode.

So you directively choose one activity, which is managed autonomously by the group; then by negotiation you and the group choose the next activity, which is managed by you directively; and so on. Dionysian planning gives you maximum scope for weaving a creative path around the decision-levels table (Figure 5.3 above), choosing decision-modes at each level as these seem to be appropriate for the unfolding dynamic of the group.

The Dionysian planner will certainly have the overall objectives in mind; will have a thorough mental grasp of the range of relevant topics, methods and resources; and will probably have a variety of alternative programme outlines in mind. But the actual plan emerges, unfolds, one activity at a time, as the realities of the developing situation make one option feel more fitting than another for the next step.

Some facilitators go through three stages. At the start of their career, when insecure, they create and implement complete Apollonian plans. As their experience, skill and confidence build, they continue to make Apollonian plans, but use them as guidelines only, feeling free to rearrange the schedule in the light of the developing dynamic of the group. In the fully mature stage, they are able, when appropriate, to come to the group pregnant with all the possibilities and options, each successive activity being born in the Dionysian mode.

Apollonian planning is good for in-service further training groups, based at the outset on consultation and negotiation, and where there is a good deal of job-relevant subject-matter to be covered. What such a plan lacks in flexibility can be compensated for by blocking in only a very broad outline long-range, and making the detail short- to medium-range, with further planning done in stages.

Dionysian planning is good for special skills-building where there is a strong emotional and personal growth dimension, such as co-

counselling training for beginners. It gives scope for charismatic command of the group dynamic by the facilitator, giving a secure framework within which beginners can be guided into self-directed catharsis. For non-beginners, a much more consultative Apollonian short- to medium-range framework may be appropriate.

The two kinds of planning can be combined in different ways. Thus an Apollonian plan can include longer or shorter periods blocked in for Dionysian planning to be done either by direction, negotiation or by delegation. The Dionysian facilitator can at a certain point in the course break out into the Apollonian mode. There is plenty of scope for interweaving the two.

## The Planning Dimension: Hierarchical Mode

You here choose for the group: you direct the planning of the group's learning, making decisions for the learners at level 2 in Figure 5.3. You decide unilaterally, in whole or in part, on the programme, its integration of topics, timing, methods, resources and assessment; on the learning objectives that underlie the programme; and on when and how to conduct a periodic evaluation, a review of its effectiveness. Such hierarchical planning can be either Apollonian or Dionysian. In some of the figures below, I will only include the most immediate components of programme planning: topics, timing, methods, resources and assessment.

If you are a hierarch at level 2, you may or may not have been one at level 3. You are always a hierarch at level 4. If you are a hierarch at level 3, you may or may not be one at level 2 – see intervention 6 below. The first four interventions below are all at decision-level 2, the basic planning level.

1. **Total directive planning.**  You are a complete hierarch, planning all aspects of the course programme by yourself, using either intervention 3 or intervention 4 below. But your programme may provide for all three decision-modes – direction, negotiation and delegation – to be used in managing the planned learning activities at level 1. If Dionysian, your planning will be piecemeal and episodic; if Apollonian, it will apply to longer periods.
2. **Partial directive planning.**  You are a hierarch only when planning some aspects of the course programme, using 3 or 4 below; other aspects you plan through negotiation or by delegation. So you are involved in some selection within all three rows of Figure 5.4. See also Figure 5.2.

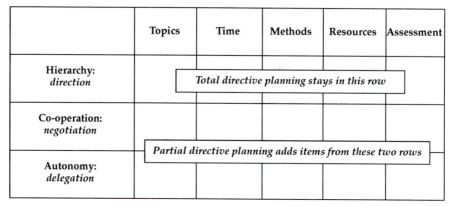

**Figure 5.4**    *Total and partial directive planning*

3. **Autocratic directive planning.**    You make your planning decisions without consulting group members about their ideas
   beforehand. You do not first seek their programme proposals
   and their evaluations of your ideas. You may, however, seek relevant information only from the group prior to devising your plan.
   This is the sort of information needed for you to make sound
   decisions. So you may ask each member to give you a list of self-
   assessed personal learning needs and goals, which gives you
   some basis for determining the learning objectives which will
   underlie you plan.
   - **Without rationale.**    You present your plan without giving any
     supporting reasons for it, and its advantages over other alter-
     natives.
   - **With rationale.**    You present your plan and give supporting
     reasons and stress its advantages.
4. **Consultative directive planning.**    You make your planning decisions after you have consulted the group members who will be
   affected by them. You gather in their programme proposals and
   opinions. Lists of individual learning needs are pooled and used
   by group members to come up with their own timetable design.
   You genuinely consider these views, but the final version of the
   plan is yours – it may or may not take into account what group
   members have suggested.
   - **Facilitator-centred.**    You disclose in full your provisional plan
     first of all. Then you elicit the group's views, which will
     include evaluations of your proposals and alternative
     timetable designs. You make a decision on the final plan after
     considering reactions to your ideas.

- **Group-centred.** You elicit the group members' programme proposals, after stating the broad area for planning, before putting forward your own proposals in full; then make your final version of the plan. This is useful if you want to get a full range of views which are not constrained by any prior statement of yours.

There is a clear distinction between consultative direction and negotiation and it is important that your group understands the difference between them, and knows which one you are using. The former is hierarchical: you retain the right to regard or disregard the views you have elicited from group members, making up your own mind finally. The latter is co-operative: you commit yourself to take into account the views of the group, and to work out an agreed decision with them.

5. **Directive planning review and control.** You set your criteria for success in implementing your plan, gather in data in the light of these criteria, evaluate the success, and modify the plan or its implementation accordingly. You do all this directively: group members only provide relevant data, perhaps by filling in a questionnaire you have designed. This is a directive form of course evaluation.

6. **Decision-mode directive choice.** Here we are at decision-level 3: the level of choosing the decision-mode to be used in planning. You decide directively, for the group, what sort of decision-mode you are going to use when planning the programme. That is, you decide who will do the planning: whether you alone, you with the group, the group alone, or some mixture of these with respect to different aspects of planning. So, as a level 3 hierarch, you may or may not choose to be a level 2 hierarch. See Figure 5.5 below.

This directive choice may be either autocratic or consultative (interventions 3 or 4 above); but the decision-mode it finally chooses is made by you and you alone, and is not up for negotiation.

At this level you can also directively choose a co-operative or autonomous decision-mode for planning the review of planning, given in its hierarchical form in 5, above.

7. **Decision-mode mastery.** The above model can now be extended to give you comprehensive mental mastery of the power-structure involved in facilitating an experiential learning group. First a reminder of the four different levels at which decision-modes can be applied.

| | LEVEL 3<br>D-mode for choosing | LEVEL 2<br>a d-mode for planning | LEVEL 1<br>a d-mode for learning |
|---|---|---|---|
| Autocratic<br>direction | *Decision-mode directive choice is in one of these two spaces* | | |
| Consultative<br>direction | | | |
| Negotiation | | *The choice made will be in one or more of these six spaces* | |
| Co-ordination | | | |
| Functional<br>delegation | | | |
| Contractual<br>delegation | | | |

*Hierarchical choice by autocratic direction or consultative direction of which decision-modes – direction, negotiation/co-ordination, delegation – to use in planning the course programme – which interrelates topics, time, methods, and resources, assessment. Methods will include decision-modes to be used in the learning activities.*

**Figure 5.5**   *Decision-mode directive choice*

- **Level 4.**  Making a directive choice to use a decision-mode to choose a decision-mode to be used in planning the programme.
- **Level 3.**  Using a decision-mode to choose a decision-mode to be used in planning the programme.
- **Level 2.**  Using a decision-mode to plan the programme. This will include choosing decision-modes to be used in learning activities.
- **Level 1.**  Using a decision-mode in managing the learning activities. When the group members are busy with some exercise, are you directing them, or collaborating with them, or are they managing it on their own?

These levels and the full range of choices that can be made are shown in Figure 5.6. So a tick in the second box down in the level 3 column means that you have hierarchically decided (at level 4) to negotiate with group members (at level 3) about which decision-modes to use for planning (at level 2) the course programme. If there are also ticks in the second and third boxes in the level 2 column, this means that your negotiation with the group at level 3 resulted in an agreement that some part of the planning would be negotiated with you, and the rest would be delegated to group members. And if, finally, there is a tick in the bottom box of the level 1 column, this means that the programme resulting from both the negotiated and the delegated planning includes only the use of delegation (student autonomy) in the management of all learning activities.

Figure 5.6 is in this hierarchical section of the chapter since it brings out clearly that your ultimate political authority of making unilateral decisions about the learning process resides inescapably at level 4. This is the level at which you choose whether and how and when to empower learners to take charge of their own learning destiny.

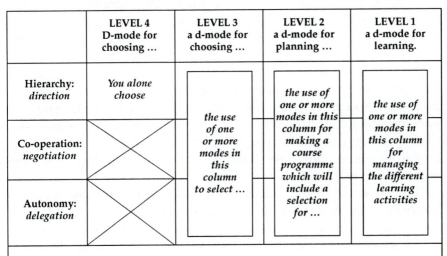

| | LEVEL 4<br>D-mode for<br>choosing ... | LEVEL 3<br>a d-mode for<br>choosing ... | LEVEL 2<br>a d-mode for<br>planning ... | LEVEL 1<br>a d-mode for<br>learning. |
|---|---|---|---|---|
| Hierarchy:<br>direction | *You alone*<br>*choose* | | | |
| Co-operation:<br>negotiation | | *the use*<br>*of one*<br>*or more*<br>*modes in*<br>*this*<br>*column*<br>*to select ...* | *the use of*<br>*one or more*<br>*modes in this*<br>*column for*<br>*making a*<br>*course*<br>*programme*<br>*which will*<br>*include a*<br>*selection*<br>*for ...* | *the use of*<br>*one or more*<br>*modes in*<br>*this column*<br>*for*<br>*managing*<br>*the different*<br>*learning*<br>*activities* |
| Autonomy:<br>delegation | | | | |

*At level 4 you alone choose to use one or more modes in level 3 to choose one or more modes in level 2 for use in planning the course programme – which interrelates topics, time, resources, methods and assessment. The planning of methods will include one or more decision-modes to be used in level 1 in managing the various learning activities.*

**Figure 5.6** *Decision-mode mastery*

It will take a good hierarch to help a group master and put to good use the subtleties and complexities of the empowering structure which this table lays bare.

## The Planning Dimension: Co-operative Mode

You plan the course programme, in whole or in part, with the group. You are committed to negotiate, to take into account and seek agreement with the views of group members in constructing the programme – its integration of topics, timing, methods, resources and assessment. Decisions at level 2 are collaborative; you have abandoned any claim to final unilateral control. But you press strongly the claims of your own point of view. Where you and the group differ strongly, you seek compromise rather than unilateral surrender.

Remember that not everything is negotiable. As I said earlier, there will be some aspects of the educational process which will be nonnegotiable because they exemplify values and principles to which you are committed. These aspects define the sort of educational model you are dedicated to realize. Hence it is important that people know what the value profile of this model is, as a basis for joining the group.

There is, within the co-operative mode, an important difference between negotiating with the group and co-ordinating the group, i.e. chairing a group planning meeting. In the former you put forward your own proposals, dialogue with the group about theirs, and collaborate in devising a conjoint outcome. The latter is more groupcentred: your profile is lower and you don't put forward your own proposals. You are helping the group make their plan, but you still have considerable influence on the outcome through the chair, by raising relevant issues for the group to consider. Both are in the cooperative mode, but co-ordination is at the boundary with the autonomous mode

There is another important difference, already discussed above, between a decision-mode and a decision-procedure. By a decisionmode I mean whether the facilitator is exercising power in the hierarchical, co-operative or autonomous modes – that is, by direction, negotiation or delegation. By a decision-procedure I mean the way in which a collective decision is made – by the group as a whole – by voting, or other examples I give below. It applies only in the cooperative and autonomous modes.

So co-operative decision-modes can now be used in five ways, which can be described in terms of decision-levels.

- **Level 3.**   Co-operative choice of a decision-mode to use in planning.
- **Level 2.**   Co-operative planning of the course programme.
- **Level 2.1.**   Co-operative choice of a decision-procedure to be used in co-operative planning.
- **Level 1.**   Co-operative management of a learning activity.
- **Level 1.1.**   Co-operative choice of a decision-procedure to be used in the co-operative management of a learning activity.

The first eleven interventions below are all at decision-level 2, the basic planning level.

1.  **Total co-operative planning.** All the major aspects of planning – the integration of topics, timing, methods, resources and assessment – are agreed between you and the group and all major programme decisions reached by conjoint negotiation or co-ordination. A programme entirely decided by negotiation may, however, in its choice of learning methods, include all the decision-modes for managing different kinds of learning activity.
2.  **Partial co-operative planning.** Only some aspects of planning are decided by conjoint negotiation or co-ordination. Others are decided by direction or delegation: you are involved in some selection within all three rows shown in Figure 5.7. See also Figure 5.2.

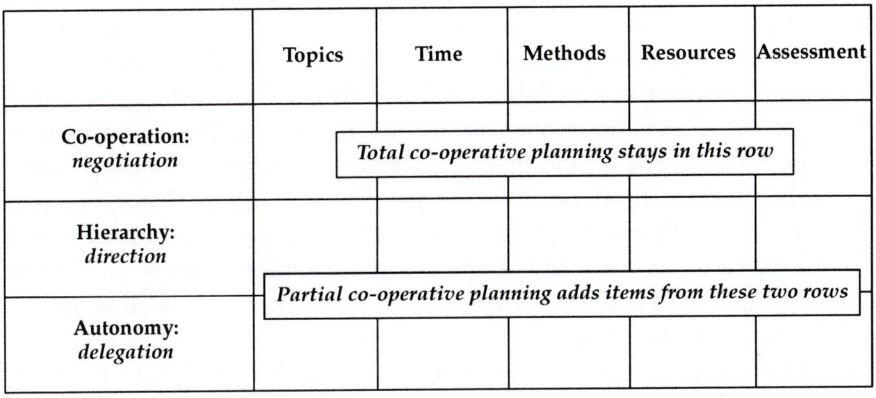

|  | Topics | Time | Methods | Resources | Assessment |
|---|---|---|---|---|---|
| **Co-operation:** *negotiation* | | *Total co-operative planning stays in this row* | | | |
| **Hierarchy:** *direction* | | | | | |
| **Autonomy:** *delegation* | *Partial co-operative planning adds items from these two rows* | | | | |

**Figure 5.7** *Total and partial directive planning*

3.  **Facilitator-centred negotiated planning.** This creates a group *learning contract*. You first propose your version of the course programme, then invite group members to propose their modifications of it, and negotiate with them until the final version is agreed. This can well be preceded by people writing out lists of self-assessed personal learning needs and objectives.
    - **Strong form.** You present a fully detailed programme for the group to consider. Then they negotiate with you on their additions, deletions and modifications..
    - **Weak form.** You give only broad outlines of a programme for the group to consider. Then they negotiate with you on this, and you with work them to fill it in. This is close to 4, next.

4. **Group-centred negotiated planning.** This also creates a group *learning contract*. A learning contract is one that is evolved co-operatively between tutor and students, facilitator and group members. It outlines a programme of learning including topics, time, methods, resources and assessment. It is also a good idea if it builds in periodic reviews (evaluations) of the whole contract. You first invite group members to propose their version of a course programme, then propose your modifications of it, and negotiate with them until a final version is agreed. This can be preceded by people writing out lists of self-assessed personal learning needs and objectives.
   - **Strong form.** You ask the group to present a fully finished programme for negotiation.
   - **Weak form.** You ask the group for a broad outline only, which you then fill in together with them.

5. **Group-centred co-ordinated planning.** This is a third approach to making a group *learning contract*. You are not nego-tiating a course programme with group members, but simply co-ordinate their decision-making. You will need to agree some form of decision-procedure, as in 10 below. You act as chair-person to group members' planning meetings, helping them clarify their final version of a programme. As chairperson, you are still influential, you can prompt the group, raising task and process issues for the members to consider. This is still more group-centred than group-centred negotiation. It is close to the autonomous mode.

6. **One-to-one negotiated planning.** You and one group member or student negotiate an individual *learning contract* over a speci-fied time for that person. The negotiation can be facilitator-centred or member-centred, as in 3 and 4 above. The plan includes an interim review of progress with possible modifica-tion of the contract in the light of this, and a review, at the end of the specified time, of the degree of success in implementing the contract.

   Note. Remember that any learning contract, whether group or individual, may include within it all the decision-modes, applied to the management of different kinds of learning activity. So it can be agreed in the contract that some learning activity is directed by you, some is in collaboration with you, and some is self- or peer directed and autonomous.

7. **Co-operative programme review and control.** You agree with the group on a set of criteria for success in implementing, and hence for evaluating the effectiveness of, a group learning

contract; and on ways of gathering in relevant data that will provide a basis for the evaluation. After some period of implementation, you together consider the data and seek a consensus evaluation. As a result you may renegotiate the contract, and make agreed changes in it. This is collaborative evaluation of a learning programme after collaborative planning of it. Of course, you can also have collaborative review of a programme after directive, or autonomous, planning of it.

8. **Open door negotiation and renegotiation.** You are available on an ad hoc basis to negotiate filling gaps in the original programme, or to make impromptu plans for an extended programme, or to renegotiate old plans not suited to members' goals and needs and the developing context of learning. This can be preceded by:

9. **Renegotiation clause.** You encourage shared leadership by building in a collaboration clause from the start of the group. This clause states: It is in principle open to anyone at any time to seek to negotiate any change in the learning programme, and to ask for an appropriate time to conduct this negotiation. Of course, this clause is given scope in a co-operative review as in 7 above. Equally, the clause may empower someone to call for such a review.

10. **Decision-procedure negotiation.** You seek agreement with the group on how to reach a final decision, for example in 5 above, group-centred co-ordinated planning. First of all, the group will need to understand the range of decision-procedures:
    - **Unanimous vote.** A decision is reached when everyone votes in favour.
    - **Percentage majority vote.** A decision is reached when the majority vote reaches a certain percentage of those voting.
    - **Simple majority vote.** A decision is reached when the majority vote is over a half of those voting.
    - **Consensus.** The most acceptable solution for all. A decision is reached when the minority agrees that its views have been heard and understood and yet still rejected; and when it assents to abide by the majority view it dislikes the least.
    - **Gathering the sense of the meeting.** There is no formal vote. After a full airing of views, the chairperson gathers the sense of the meeting into a proposed decision. If there is expressed dissent from this proposal, the discussion continues. The chairperson then gathers the sense of the meeting into a second proposal. This process continues until the gathered sense is assented to. Someone else may gather

the sense of the meeting, and put it to the chair; especially if the sense is eluding the chairperson. Note that final assent here may include both positive assent and negative assent, the latter being a willingness to accede to a still disliked proposal.

You and the group will have to use a decision-procedure in deciding which decision-procedure to choose for use in co-operative planning. You just have to go for one, in order to avoid the lurking infinite regress of deciding which one to use in deciding which one to use, etc.

11. **Discussion-procedure negotiation.** All the above decision-procedures presuppose that they have been preceded by some good discussion-procedure, which ensures that everyone has a say, that no-one overtalks and dominates and that no clique railroads through its views. To create a co-operative discussion culture in which high contributors do not dominate the proceedings constraining the others to be medium or low (or nil) contributors, you can:

- Raise consciousness of the issue by giving the group feedback on its pattern of contribution rates.
- Invite everyone to be responsible for managing contributions equitably: by speaking out, by reaching out to bring each other in and draw each other out, by practising restraint if one is a compulsive and competitive high contributor.
- Negotiate the use of a round, especially for an important issue, in which each person takes a turn to express their views on it.
- Negotiate the use of the ground-rule that no-one speaks twice until everyone has spoken once.
- Negotiate the use of procedures such as: no-one speaks until handed the mace by the current speaker; no-one speaks until sitting in a fish-bowl in the centre of the group, and no-one stays there talking with the others in the bowl for too long.
- Negotiate the use of three subgroups, one of high contributors, one of medium and one of low contributors.

12. **Decision-procedure review and renegotiation.** After a period of using an agreed decision-procedure, you review its use with the group, and renegotiate to continue its use or to change to some other procedure.

13. **Decision-mode co-operative choice.** Here we are again at decision-making level 3, as in 6 under the hierarchical mode. This is the level of choosing the decision-mode to be used in planning. So really this intervention comes first, before all the

ones above. See Figure 5.8 below. You decide by negotiating with the group, what sort of decision-mode you are going to use when planning the course programme. This negotiation may be facilitator-centred, in which you press the claims for some decision-mode first; or it may be group-centred, where you ask the group members to put forward their case for a decision-mode before you do. You present the range of decision-modes – autocratic or consultative direction, negotiation, co-ordination and the two forms of delegation – and negotiate with the team which one or more of them to use in planning the course programme.

| | LEVEL 3<br>D-mode for choosing | LEVEL 2<br>a d-mode for planning | LEVEL 1<br>a d-mode for learning |
|---|---|---|---|
| Autocratic direction | | | |
| Consultative direction | | | |
| Negotiation | *Decision-mode co-operative choice is in one of these two spaces* | *The choice made will be in one or more of these six spaces* | |
| Co-ordination | | | |
| Functional delegation | | | |
| Contractual delegation | | | |

*Co-operative choice by negotiation or co-ordination of which decision-modes – direction, negotiation/co-ordination, delegation – to use in planning the course programme – which interrelates topics, time, methods, and resources, assessment. Methods will include decision-modes to be used in the learning activities.*

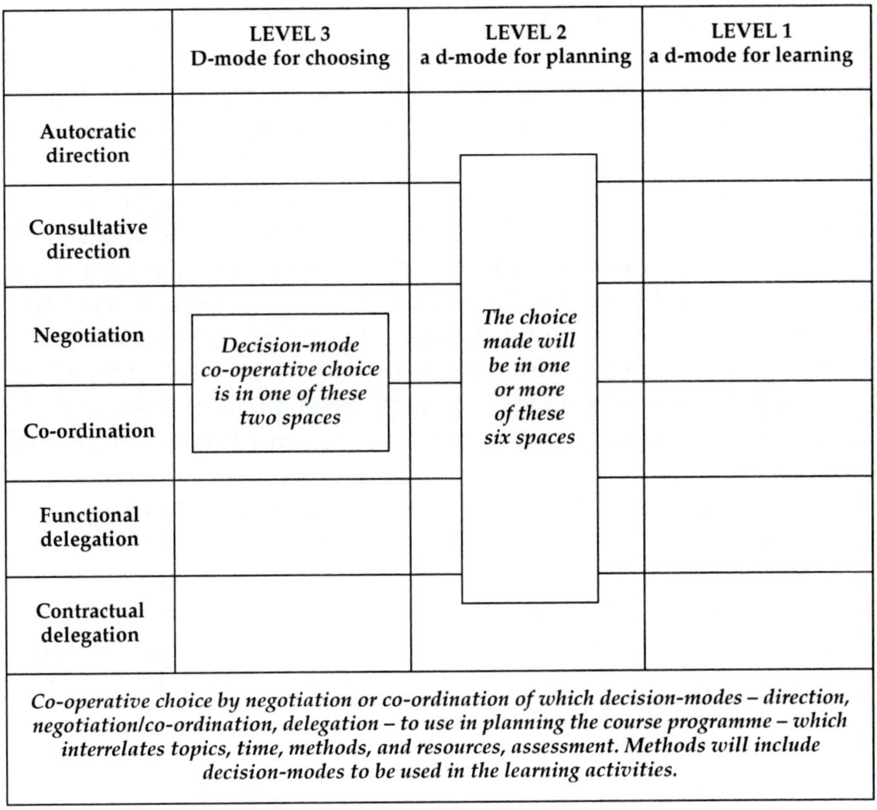

**Figure 5.8** *Decision-mode co-operative choice*

14. **Decision-mode review and renegotiation.** You invite the whole group to review with you the effectiveness of some decision-mode that is currently in use for planning. This may lead on to renegotiating the mode. Or the review may take place after the planning is over, and so may influence the choice of decision-mode for future planning. Whereas in number 7 above

you and the group evaluate a programme, in this item you evaluate together the effectiveness of how decisions about the programme are being made, whether by hierarchy, co-operation or autonomy, or some combination of these.

## The Planning Dimension: Autonomous Mode

Here you are getting out of the way, affirming the group's need to do its own planning and to sort out issues of power and control in deciding what to do. The planning of the course programme, in whole or in part, is delegated to the group. The decision to delegate some planning to the group is, of course, made at decision-level 3, and is either made directively by you, or by negotiation with the group, or by the group on its own. In the last two cases, you will have decided at decision-level 4 to adopt these strategies at decision-level 3. For a reminder about these levels, see Figure 5.3.

Sometimes, to repeat the important point made earlier in this chapter, the group will not have planning delegated to it, but will appropriate its autonomy. Either it makes a mature claim for independence, rooted in skill and knowledge; or it tries to seize its power when it is not ripe enough. It is wise to support and encourage the former, and resist and confront the latter. However, if group members insist in going ahead with their premature seizure of power, let them do so, and later you can help to sort out the confusion when the trial exposes the error.

Another point is that you can delegate a chunk of planning to the group as a whole, and let the members sort out who does what, and how they work together. This I call contractual delegation. Or you can delegate particular planning functions to individuals and also a procedure whereby they can readily integrate their strands into a collective plan. This I call functional delegation. I discuss these two below.

A special case of delegation is in a training the trainers' group, where you delegate your own role to one person in the group for them to practise being a facilitator of course design. So their task is to manage a part of real planning of the training that is to take place in the group. Your delegation can say what decision-mode to use, or not.

1.  **Total delegated planning.**  All aspects of programme planning are decided autonomously by group members, using 3 or 5 below. You play no part in the process. You become redundant

as a facilitator in the planning stage. The group becomes an autonomy, a totally self-directed peer planning group. If the plan itself excludes your having any facilitative role in the learning activities, then you have been given the boot, and your career with this group is over. However, the plan may programme you to facilitate some of the learning activities, using the decision-modes of direction or negotiation. But you can't do any of this unless you agree to it, so negotiation, if only tacit, comes back in here.

2. **Partial delegated planning.**   Only some aspects of course planning are delegated for the group to decide, using 3 or 5 below, while others are done by direction or negotiation. 1 and 2 are shown in Figure 5.9.

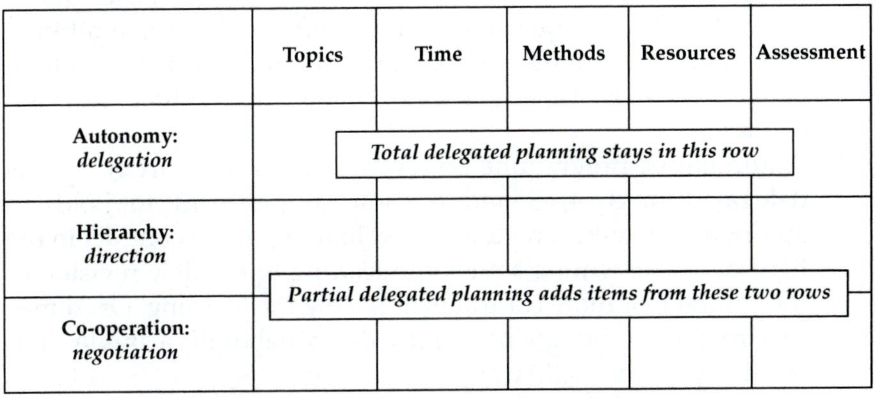

| | Topics | Time | Methods | Resources | Assessment |
|---|---|---|---|---|---|
| **Autonomy:** *delegation* | *Total delegated planning stays in this row* | | | | |
| **Hierarchy:** *direction* | | | | | |
| **Co-operation:** *negotiation* | *Partial delegated planning adds items from these two rows* | | | | |

**Figure 5.9**   *Total and partial co-operative planning*

3. **Contractually delegated group planning.**   You define with the group, by direction or negotiation, a whole block of learning in terms of its main objectives and the overall time to be taken for it; or in terms of some other broad parameters. Within this outline contract, all programme planning is undertaken by group members on their own. They decide who does what and how they work together. This generates the autonomous peer group learning contract.

4. **Contractually delegated individual planning.**   Here you define with one individual, by direction or negotiation, a whole block of learning in terms of its main objectives and the overall time to be taken for it; or in terms of some other broad parameters. Within this outline contract, all planning is undertaken by the individual alone, in their own way. This generates the autonomous individual learning contract.

5. **Functionally delegated group planning.** By direction or negotiation, you delegate to different individuals in the group different planning functions, i.e. responsibility for planning different aspects of the course programme. And to the whole group you delegate an integrating procedure whereby it can bring these strands together and plan collectively. There will have to be some outline contract about overall time and range of learning; so this item puts more structure into 3, above. This is the semi-autonomous peer group learning contract.

6. **Functionally delegated individual planning.** By direction or negotiation, you delegate to one individual responsibility for planning a personal learning programme. You also delegate a procedure for effective planning which that person can follow. There will have to be some outline contract about overall time and range of learning; so this item puts more structure into 4, above. This is the semi-autonomous individual learning contract.

7. **Autonomous programme review and control.** Part of what is delegated in 3, 4, 5 and 6, is a commitment to hold an autonomous interim review, an evaluation, of the contract in the light of implementing some of it, leading to possible revision of the contract, or more control over pacing the learning. Of course, this review could go back into the collaborative mode, and involve you, the facilitator.

8. **Trainee–trainer delegation.** You delegate your own role to one group member, to practise facilitation on some real chunk of programme planning that is needed for the current group – which, of course, will be a training the trainers' group. You may specify in the delegation what decision-mode the trainee is to use in facilitating the planning; or you may leave it to the trainee's own judgment. Remember you can also delegate to someone the practice of Dionysian planning. A more limited kind of trainee–trainer delegation is to ask someone to take over facilitating the selection and use of some decision-procedure to co-ordinate group planning.

9. **Planning initiative clause.** You have delegated to group members the right to take unilateral initiatives – changing the existing programme and creating contingency plans – as emerging learning needs and interests require. This clause may be attached to a plan made by any decision-mode. It may pervade the whole ethos of the team as a form of self-directing facilitation.

10. **Autonomous participation clause.** You affirm at the outset of the group, with occasional reminders if necessary, a strong participants' autonomy clause. This states:

'Whenever I or anyone else proposes an activity, please feel free to participate or not participate in it, according to your own judgment about whether it seems relevant and appropriate to your own needs and interests. You are under no pressure from me and hopefully no-one else in the group to engage in any activity which you do not freely choose. Your right to abstain from participation will be fully respected.'

When a member double-binds about joining in some activity, that is, appears to be saying both yes and no in different verbal and non-verbal ways, then you can confront the person until an unequivocal choice is made. If the choice is finally no, then you instantly accept and respect this. No-one should be constrained to engage in any activity to enhance their growth.

An autonomy clause, clearly stated in principle, and fully honoured in practice, is in my view an essential moral component of an experiential learning group. It is also psychologically effective. When members really feel they can say 'no', they may discover a more powerful motivation within to say 'yes'. Persons are only fully respected when, among other things, they have the right to dissociate. If the dissociation is purely defensive, rooted in avoidance, persons still have the right to hold on to their defences as long they choose. And again, saying a fully defensive 'no', loud and clear, often creates the space for saying a risk-taking 'yes' at a later date.

11. **Dionysian autonomy phase.** If you are busy with Dionysian, step-by-step planning, one activity generating the next, then for a certain length of time you make no planning interventions of any sort about what the group is going to do. Nor do you facilitate the choice of decision-modes and decision-procedures. No prompts, no guidance, no reminders or consciousness-raising: you keep entirely silent about planning and decision levels. You announce the start of an autonomy phase, and explain its rationale: a time for the group to practise autonomous Dionysian planning – or to go Apollonian if they wish. This strategy still allows you to make interventions on the other dimensions.

12. **Going out.** One dramatic way of underlining any kind of autonomous planning in the group, is for you to go out of the room when it is going on. This has the advantage of preventing the group from trying to fall back on your resources, or being

dependently distracted by your presence. The disadvantage is that you get no insight into difficulties encountered.

13. **Autonomy lab.** This overlaps with item 12, autonomous mode, the structuring dimension, Chapter 13, but I give the fullest account of it here. A whole workshop, or major part of a workshop, is devoted to this strategy. You are only a resource, alongside all other resources (other participants, books, tapes, computers, CCTV, etc.), and only do anything when asked by participants to meet some specific learning need (Harrison, 1973). All planning is self- or peer directed, and you are not involved in facilitating it at any point. It is also entirely Dionysian and multiple, with many different short-term plans emerging alongside each other all round the room.

The planning sequence is: first autonomous decision-making by each participant about personal learning needs and how to meet them, and then some co-operative decision-making with others with similar learning needs. Group members exercise total initiative and autonomy in deciding what their learning needs are, how to meet them, in what order and with whom. Everyone has the challenge of structuring their own learning experience, pacing and changing it, through negotiation with others. Here are some useful guidelines for setting up an effective autonomy lab:

- To be really effective, the lab needs to go on for several hours at least.
- Before the lab each person, including you, prepares a legible list of what they want to get from or with others, and what they have to offer to others. Each list bears its author's name.
- The lab starts with all these lists posted up. Everybody studies them all, prior to going around, talking to people to find out more about what's on them. Then people start to negotiate meeting their needs or responding to the needs of others. These spontaneous negotiatons go on all around the room in small clusters.
- It is important to have a ground-rule that no-one deals with their own anxiety by trying to organize the whole event for everyone else.
- There is a large sheet on which people enter the various agreed events, with their title, facilitator (if there is one), location, time frame, names of participants, and whether open to others to drop in.
- There is an appointed space where, at any time during the lab, people can meet and negotiate further events.

- When not being called upon as a resource, you go around meeting your own learning needs, taking initiatives, co-operating with others, and so on. You may or may not feel it appropriate to have a proviso here, that you will give up doing your own thing, if some person or small group want to call upon you as a resource.

However, you are not the only, or even the primary, resource. The point about an autonomy lab is that it is a peer teaching as well as a peer learning situation. Everyone is a potential resource for everyone else. Thus at the outset each person needs to identify what knowledge, skills and experience they have to offer, as well as what it is they want to learn.

This is one of the most profitable kinds of learning experience. It is the most total form of delegation on the part of you, the facilitator. Within the lab, autonomy becomes the primary value, and provides the ground for effective co-operation between group members. You function as a facilitator only under contract to fully autonomous learners – a contract which they initiate and define.

14. **Planning to transfer the learning.**  Group members take time, in pairs or small groups, to support each other in setting up goals and making action-plans that will transfer what they have learned within the group to their work and personal life outside the group. This can be made a regular feature of long-term day-release courses, with each person reporting back to their support group on how the transfer went.

15. **Claiming power.**  This, of course, is not an intervention of yours, but it requires a response. The group want to take over the planning and do it independently, either before you have made any proposals about the matter, or after you have decided on a hierarchical or co-operative mode of planning. As I wrote in the introduction to this section on the autonomous mode, either the group makes a mature claim for independence, rooted in skill and knowledge, or it tries to seize its power when it is not ripe enough. It is wise to support and encourage the former, and resist and confront the latter. However, if group members insist in going ahead with their premature seizure of power, let them do so, and later you can help to sort out the confusion when the trial exposes the error.

# 6 The Meaning Dimension

This chapter continues detailed exposition of the core model of the six dimensions and three modes of facilitation. This second dimension is concerned with giving meaning to and finding meaning in the experiences which group members are having – individually, in particular interactions, in small group learning activities and in the group as a whole. Your concern here is with how the participants make sense of what is happening and acquire understanding.

## Four Forms of Understanding

Understanding is the core of learning. To learn something is to understand it, to retain that understanding, and to be able to express it effectively. If the focus is all on retention with little understanding, then we get mere rote learning, or learning by heart. If the focus is all on understanding with no retention, we get flashes of insight which fade as soon as they light up and have no power to kindle future thought or behaviour. To learn properly is to understand and to rehearse that understanding, take charge of it, so that it becomes influential from its base in the memory. And this is consummated in relevant expression of what has been learnt.

As with learning, there are four kinds of understanding. I state them in a learning cycle sequence, as distinct from the epistemological hierarchy of the four kinds of learning given in Chapter 1 (see Chapter 15, Figure 15.3, showing the learning cycle and the hierarchy together).

1. **Conceptual understanding.** This is understanding that something is the case, evident in and expressed in statements and propositions.
2. **Imaginal understanding.** This is understanding configurations in form and process, evident in and expressed in the symbolism of

line, shape, colour, proportion, sequence, sound, rhythm, movement; and, toward the interface with conceptual learning, in the metaphorical, evocative and narrative use of language, as in the work of the poet, novelist and dramatist.

3. **Practical understanding.**  This is understanding how to act, how to do something, evident in and expressed in some practical skill.

4. **Experiential understanding.** This is understanding by encounter, by direct acquaintance, by entering into some state of being. It is manifest and expressed in and through the process of being there, face-to-face with the person, at the event, in the experience.

I use the term experiential learning as a shorthand for the process of interweaving these four sorts of understanding in such a way that they make a relatively permanent change in a person's behaviour and state of being. The basic way to interweave the four is to use an experiential learning cycle, and I introduce a version of this under the structuring dimension in Chapter 13, and other varieties in Chapter 14.

Imaginal understanding is often neglected in accounts of the learning process, yet it is clearly central in, for example, mediating between conceptual understanding and practical understanding. If someone explains to me in conceptual terms what to do in order to swing a golf club correctly, I have intuitively to convert this into an imaginal understanding of the whole configuration of stance and movement involved, as a basis for building up my practical skill.

## Areas of Understanding

Understanding can be applied in three ways, which are: understanding the task, understanding the group process, and, jumping up a level, understanding either of these. The task may mean some subject matter, an interpersonal skill, a piece of personal growth work, or whatever. Group process refers to what is going on within and between people, where this is not itself part of the task. Jumping up a level means understanding what is involved in getting to understand the task or the process: upper-level learning about ground-floor learning. If we put the four forms of understanding with the three areas, we get the table shown in Figure 6.1, below. It provides a map of 12 different ways in which participants in an experiential learning group can make sense of what is going on.

|  | Task | Group process | Learning process |
|---|---|---|---|
| Conceptual understanding |  |  |  |
| Imaginal understanding |  |  |  |
| Practical understanding |  |  |  |
| Experiential understanding |  |  |  |

**Figure 6.1**   *Forms and areas of understanding*

Most of the interventions below relate to conceptual understanding and to imaginal understanding in one or other of the three areas. The occasion of their use will be in the feedback and reflection phases of a structured exercise using the experiential learning cycle, or in reflective episodes about the whole development of learning in the group.

Practical and experiential understanding come under the structuring of learning activities, which is the subject of Chapters 13 and 14.

## The Meaning Dimension: Hierarchical Mode

The basic strategy here is for you to make sense of what is going on for the group, or one or more persons in it. You give meaning to events, illuminate them, either by taking time out to provide relevant information and theory, or a rationale of group dynamics and experiential learning, or by making a particular interpretation of some episode, in the midst of it or just after it, or by some form of demonstration or presentation.

You may be expounding some subject matter relevant to a task, or giving feedback on the execution of a task. You may do all this in the imaginal as well as in the conceptual way.

After you give your interpretation or information, whether to the whole group or to one or two people only, you have a choice. You can continue to be the hierarch, and leave it there to hover and make its impact, without any follow-up; or you can shift over into the cooperative mode and elicit reactions, views and comments, alternative perspectives – and work with the group in seeking to understand what has gone on.

1.  **Theoretical input.**   Your input may present in conceptual form any kind of information relevant to current learning. In a skills

training group, the input may give the conceptual background and descriptive modelling of behaviour to be practised in some structured exercise.

You may present some theoretical model of what goes on in experiential groups, maybe with some of the research findings about different aspects of such groups. The model may use group dynamic, psychodynamic, sociodynamic or transpersonal concepts, or some mixture of these. The input may be at the start of the group, during it, or at the end of it. It will be followed by question and answer. The purpose of the input is to provide members with some basic conceptual orientation which they can use to make sense of the group process. It gives a general framework; it isn't aimed at particular persons or particular episodes.

Theoretical inputs can be enriched by interweaving them with one or more varieties of imaginal input, including flip charts and other visual aids.

2. **Imaginal input.**   With respect to the task, the group process or the learning process, you seek to evoke imaginal understanding through the use of one or more of the following methods.

   ● **Metaphor.**   The imaginative use of myth, metaphor, allegory, fable and story to convey meaning.
   ● **Instance.**   You describe an illustrative incident, or dramatic case study, from real life.
   ● **Resonance.** You recount associations and memories evoked by what is going on, in order to find meaning through resonance with the form of other situations, which may be from some quite different field.
   ● **Presentation.**   You present non-verbal analogies in the form of graphics, paintings, music, mime or movement.
   ● **Dramaturgy.**   You combine metaphor with presentation in a creative piece of theatre.
   ● **Demonstration.**   You show in your own behaviour, both verbal and non-verbal, what it is you mean: you model a skill in action, positively showing it well done, and negatively showing how it can degenerate.
   ● **Caricature.**   You give feedback to someone by mimicking their behaviour and caricaturing – in a kind way – the salient features to which you wish to draw their attention.

All this is to help participants get an imaginative grasp of basic configurations of form and process in the area of concern. In a skills training group, any of these methods can be used to help the trainees create an imaginal model of the behaviour that is to be practised.

3. **Video shows.**   You make a direct appeal to imaginal understanding by showing a video that exhibits some behaviour you want to convey. The video demonstrations can use caricature and selective emphasis to get their point across.

4. **Handouts.**   You provide these to back up the sorts of input given in 1, 2 and 3 above. They include all kinds of written material, diagrams and other graphics, reproductions of paintings, music discs, video and audio tapes.

5. **Attributive interpretation.**   You attribute simple psychological meaning to some current piece of behaviour in the group, in terms of intention, motive, desire, wish, emotion, thought, and any other such everyday mental concepts.

   The attribution may be to what is overt in the behaviour, for example to help A notice the behaviour of B – 'A, B has just clearly shown that he wants to get to know you better' – or it may be to what is covert in the behaviour, to help people become more aware of their own process – 'There seems to be a great deal of anger implicit in this exchange of views'. It may be directed at the group as a whole, but is more likely to be aimed at some interactive sub-group, or an individual member.

6. **Psychodynamic interpretation.**   You give meaning to some current episode in the group in psychodynamic terms. It is more theory-laden than a simple attribution. It is always aimed at particular persons and particular behaviour.

   - **Present process.**   The interpretation deals only with the current state of the psyche in terms of some theoretical model. You may interpret some behaviour in terms, for example, of the Jungian four functions and their current dynamic interaction. You may interpret a defensive form of behaviour only in terms of existential anxiety (see Chapter 4).
   - **Present and past process.**   This kind of interpretation identifies current behaviour as a distortion due to unfinished emotional business from the past, with those involved acting out maladaptive survival mechanisms of early life, adopting various defensive behaviours in the group to avoid issues that stir up buried, painful trauma. Here, therefore, you interpret these behaviours in terms of archaic anxiety reinforcing the existential.

7. **Sociodynamic interpretation.**   You give meaning to what is going on in more sociological terms, and seek to raise group

consciousness about: how decisions are or are not being made; how issues of authority and leadership are shaping events; how tacit norms constrain behaviour; how members attain identity by informal allocation of roles; how contribution rates, hierarchies and pecking orders become established; communication networks; subgroups and conflict; and so on. Again, these interpretations are aimed at specific events and persons.

8. **Holonomic interpretation.** You make sense of what is going on in terms of the holonomic principle (see Chapter 4). You propose that the concerns of the whole group are now manifest through the individual perspectives of one person, that the group is represented by one of its members, whose contribution focuses the learning of all.

9. **Participative interpretation.** You identify the current state of being in the group as one of entrainment, that is, of mutual participation through empathic attunement, a shared experiential field of harmonic resonance, a deep engagement in the ocean of shared feeling (see Chapter 4). You may want to point out that this experiential field shades off into a tacit penumbra of apparently limitless extent.

10. **Open window interpretation.** You make sense of some happening in terms of an opening to: the influence of the ancestors, spirits, presences; the effect of occult forces or the play of archetypal powers from other dimensions of being; extensions or shifts in experience of space or time; the awakening of kundalini in the psychic body; sudden episodes of extrasensory perception or psychokinesis; encounter with deeper aspects of human destiny and the human condition; and so on.

11. **Imaginal interpretation.** Each of the above from 5 to 10 can also be presented in different imaginal forms by using one or more of metaphor, instance, resonance, presentation, dramaturgy, demonstration and caricature, as these are defined in 2, above. This direct appeal to imaginal understanding of form can be used alone, or with conceptual interpretation. It can give insight on several levels at once.

12. **Conceptual feedback on an exercise.** Where structured exercises are being used for skills building or personal growth or anything else, then you give direct descriptive and evaluative feedback to the participant who has just taken a turn. This feedback may overlap with some of the kinds of interpretation given above, but will have special reference to the particular purpose of the exercise. Negative feedback is usefully followed by an immediate rerun of the exercise.

13. **Imaginal feedback on an exercise.** You can use mimicry and caricature in live demonstration as feedback, showing in your own behaviour how the form of the trainee's action has gone awry. There are all the other imaginal devices of metaphor, instance, resonance, presentation and dramaturgy as in 2, above.

14. **Micro-cue feedback.** This is used in structured exercise feedback. It is aimed at the small details of unaware and distorted behaviour: a turn of phrase, a tone of voice, an inflection, a gesture, a posture. You make a simple attributive interpretation: stating how each small item reveals a certain state or attitude of mind. You can give imaginal feedback by caricaturing the trainee's micro-cues in your own behaviour.

    Micro-cue feedback, followed by immediate trainee reruns, is very important in the reshaping and fine-tuning of behavioural skills.

15. **Facilitator explanation.** You explain what you are doing, have done, or are about to do, as facilitator, and why. This can apply at any level of your decision-making: selecting a decision-mode for planning, planning, facilitating some piece of learning; and, more widely, to anything you are doing on any of the six dimensions. This is a powerful aid to learning in facilitator training courses. You make meta-comments, illustrating how a method or skill you are teaching is manifest in what you are here and now doing in facilitating the training.

16. **Review of the learning process.** You throw light on how the learning is being managed or is proceeding in the group. You can do this by descriptive statements, to aid conceptual understanding, or by the imaginal devices presented in 2, above. As a hierarchical intervention, that is, one that does not lead into a sharing of perspectives within the group, it will probably occur quite early on in a beginners' group.

17. **Unilateral assessment and evaluation.** These have a public form and a private form. In the public form, you give to group members your assessment of their learning performance, without involving them either in the selection of criteria or the act of assessment. This exclusion of the learner from the process of assessment is educationally unsound, and out of date today. So also is unilateral course evaluation, in which you alone give to the group your judgement on the effectiveness of course design and methods, your own style, and other matters to do with the course as such. However, the private form, which involves silent and unspoken assessment and evaluation, is something that any competent facilitator will be busy with at

regular intervals, as part of her or his self-monitoring and reflection on facilitative actions.

## *The Meaning Dimension: Co-operative Mode*

You do not give your meaning to what is going on, but alert members to something that is happening in the group, some aspect of its task or process, and prompt them to seek out and give their own meaning to it. You may then add your view, as one idea among others, without necessarily claiming special status for it. You invite group members to participate with you in the generation of understanding. Whether the whole group, a sub-group, or just one person, is the focus, the idea is for you encourage a pooling and sharing of perspectives, including your own.

The first interventions below prompt group members, as something is happening, to give their own interpretation to it. You, therefore, choose the behaviour that is to be interpreted, but invite the group to make the first interpretations. There is a hierarchical element in the choosing and pointing out, but the primary thrust of the intervention and its intent is co-operative. You are seeking to elicit an exchange of ideas between you and the group.

1. **Describe behaviour.**   You simply make a descriptive comment about some observable piece of behaviour, without attaching any kind of interpretation to it, or without asking anyone to interpret it. 'We have been discussing this for an hour'; 'We are all sitting with our arms crossed'; 'Peter, you never look at Jane when you speak to her'. This may lead to some airing of views, in which you can join, about what the described behaviour signifies.

2. **Indicate behaviour.**   This is the same, except that you don't pick out the observed behaviour verbally, but non-verbally, by gesture, touch, the direction of the gaze, or by mirroring it in action.

3. **Invite conceptual interpretation.**   You ask a question whch draws attention to something that is happening and which invites someone to make sense of it, to give it a meaning. You then engage in a discussion with the group about any one or more interpretations that have been offered.

   - The question you ask can be nonspecific or specific about the happening. It can also be nonspecific or specific about what sort of interpretation is being prompted.

If you say 'What is going on in this group right now?', you are being nonspecific about what behaviour you are pointing to, and about what sort of interpretation you are seeking. If you say 'Is our physical behaviour being constrained by some tacit norm?', you are being more specific on both fronts. So there is here a whole spectrum of prompts, from those that are very open-ended to those that are very closed round one piece of behaviour and seek out one precise interpretation. The range of possible interpretations include all those described under the hierarchical mode:

- Attributive, psychodynamic, sociodynamic, holonomic, participative, open window.

4. **Invite imaginal interpretation.** Here you ask a question which draws attention to something that is happening and which also invites someone to make sense of it in a specific imaginal way:

   - **Invite mythic interpretation.** Ask group members to be creative in the use of metaphor, allegory, phantasy, fable or story, to give an account of some task or process issue and generate imaginal understanding of it.
   - **Invite interpretation by resonance.** Invite group members to share any associations and memories evoked by what is going on in the group, in order to find meaning through resonance with the form of other situations.
   - **Invite presentational feedback.** You invite one or more group members to give imaginal meaning to what has just been going on, by symbolzing it non-verbally in movement, a group sculpture made out of body postures, vocal sounds or instrumental music, a painting or drawing.
   - **Invite dramaturgical feedback.** You ask participants to improvise a mime or spoken drama which portrays some current task or process issue.
   - **Invite mimicry feedback.** Invite one or more group members to mimic and caricature some piece of behaviour that one or two people are busy with, so that there is a variety of imaginal showings of the behaviour. It is essential that mimicry and caricature are benign and not malicious.

You may be moved to participate in any of these imaginal expressions. You join in the general discussion which follows. Feedback on these expressions may lead over into a sharing of verbal interpretations, including yours; so the group moves from imaginal to conceptual understanding.

5. **Facilitating self-discovery**. Working co-operatively with a group member, picking up on their cues, and prompting a response as in 1, 2, 3 or 4 above, you invite just one person to make sense of their personal experience. You may complement this by inviting feedback from other group members, and by giving some yourself.

6. **Collaborative feedback and reflection in the whole group.** After autonomous self- and peer feedback and reflection within a small group exercise, you invite all the small groups to come together for further sharing with each other and with you. This yields more learning and gives you the opportunity to discuss issues that arise from the sharing and to negotiate what to sharpen up in the next round of practice.

7. **Collaborative group process review.** You invite the group, every once in a while, to look back on a whole phase of its activity and to identify and evaluate the various aspects of its process. You may prompt by raising different categories for consideration, drawn, for example, from Chapter 4 on the group dynamic; and from aspects of your own facilitator style, its use of dimensions and modes. You may share your own views among views that are put forward by the group and lead into a general discussion on the dynamic of the group. This can be both verbal/conceptual and by any of the imaginal devices described in this chapter. Conceptually, the review can be developed into model- and theory-building based on the group's own process.

8. **Collaborative learning task review.** Together with the group, you periodically take time out to review the learning tasks the group has undertaken, to reflect on what is being learnt, how it is being learnt and whether it is being learnt. This evaluation overlaps with 7, co-operative programme review, co-operative mode, planning dimension, Chapter 5.

9. **Collaborative assessment.** This can be applied at stages during, and at the end of, a particular strand of learning, such as facilitator training. You agree criteria of competence with the group. Group members use these for self- and peer assessment. You then use them to assess the group members. Finally, you and they negotiate a final assessment. This is a combination of self-, peer and facilitator assessment of learning performance. You will need to give group members a structure for doing this, and train and supervise them in the early use of it. The basic stages are:

- **Negotiated criteria-setting.** You talk and negotiate with group members until you all agree on a few basic criteria of competence, relevant to the skill being assessed. This is facilitator-centred if you present your criteria first, before negotiation, and group-centred if participants present all their criteria first. For a full discussion, see Heron (1988).
- **Self-assessment.** Each individual assesses their own competence, in front of their peers and of you, dealing with strengths and weaknesses in the light of each criterion.
- **Peer assessment.** Group members take it in turns to assess – in the light of each criterion – the competence of the person who has just completed their self-assessment, with special reference to overstated, understated or omitted strengths and weaknesses in the self-assessment.
- **Facilitator assessment.** You now take your turn in assessing the same person's competence in the light of the criteria, also with special reference to overstated, understated or omitted strengths and weaknesses in the self-assessment and in the peer assessments of that person.
- **Revised self-assessment.** The same person takes a further turn to revise their self-assessment, taking into account peer assessments and the facilitator assessment.
- **Optional: negotiated final self-, peer and facilitiator assessment.** In this optional extra, you negotiate a final assessment with the person, if your facilitator assessment dissents from their revised self-assessment. The use of this option depends on the subject matter. If it is a personal growth that is being assessed, you may judge that self-asssessment is primary and the sequence should end with the revised self-assessment. If more external and technical skills are being assessed, there is a case for more facilitiator influence and control through your negotiation in the final assessment. You may or may not consider it appropriate to bring in the peers to contribute to this final negotiation.

Each stage requires a precise time allocation, and pacing and time-control need to be well managed. The outcomes for each person can be used to generate action plans for further learning.

If you take a turn along with everyone else in the self- and peer assessments of competence in the selected skill, if you omit the part about commenting on peer assessments, and if you don't claim more weight for your reviews than for anyone else's, then you have effectively merged collaborative assessment into self- and peer assessment, autonomous mode (see below).

10. **Collaborative course evaluation.**   This combines 7 and 8 just above and is applied to the whole course. You and the group collaborate in devising a set of procedures for evaluating the whole course, your own role and your use of the six dimensions and three modes, the objectives of the course, the content of the programme, the use of time, the effectiveness of the methods for the learning about the topics, the group processes, the assessment methods, and so on.

   • The evaluation procedures can include: filling in collaboratively designed questionnaires, filling in a few basic categories on public wall charts, open discussion, fishbowls on selected issues, the use of any of the imaginal methods described in this chapter, and so on.

11. **Co-operative inquiry.**   You initiate, and invite the group to participate with you in, a co-operative inquiry. This is a form of person-centred research, in which everyone involved moves between two roles:

   • As co-researchers, the inquirers generate the thinking that conceives, designs, manages and draws conclusions from, the research.

   • As co-subjects, they engage in the action and experience which are the focus of the research.

For an overview of co-operative inquiry, see Chapter 7. For a fuller account, I refer the reader to two basic texts (Heron, 1996a; Reason, 1988).

   Any group using an experiential learning cycle systematically, is already engaged in an incipient form of co-operative inquiry. Both methods move cyclically between phases of reflection and phases of action. What co-operative inquiry adds is the focus on systematic inquiry, which takes understanding into issues of valid knowledge. This makes it more rigorous in method, including the use of a whole set of procedures to enhance the validity of the inquiry process and of its findings as they emerge.

   Co-operative inquiry could be used as an advanced stage of experiential learning. Thus when a basic set of skills has been learnt, then the whole conceptual framework which they express – or, more manageably, some feature of it – can be taken into a co-operative inquiry.

   In a co-operative inquiry, you start out as the initiating researcher and facilitator; but once the group has internalized the method, you become peer, and all facilitative roles in the inquiry process are rotated among group members.

## The Meaning Dimension: Autonomous Mode

Here making sense of what is happening is autonomous and self-generated within the group. This may be done within one or more structures recommended by you as options to be taken up autonomously whenever needed. Or the structures may be delegated by you as part of your facilitation of a training session. But inside this structure, group members are on their own, and meaning is self-generated.

More generally, in terms of the ongoing history of the group, there are times when you intentionally give no information, no views on issues, no interpretation of events, nor do you elicit from members their own views about some issues you think relevant, or their interpretations about something you have seen. You do nothing that alerts people to the meaning of current issues and events. You leave this entirely to the group members, as and when they feel moved to do so.

1.  **Self- and peer feedback and reflection.** This is the reflection phase in a structured exercise, using the experiential learning cycle, and delegated by you to autonomous small groups for skills. A key part of the structure is that each person, after taking their turn at practice, gives feedback to self, then receives feedback from peers. After feedback, the behaviour is rerun until everyone is satisfied that it is on track. After self- and peer feedback on all the turns, then the small group reflects on the issues that have emerged, distilling further learning from the experience.

    This self- and peer feedback and reflections is the central place where meaning is generated autonomously. It is always done in the small practice group, before coming back for wider sharing in the large group and with you. Of course, the autonomous feedback may incorporate concepts given by you in introducing the exercise: but when this happens, or whether and how it does, is all the domain of group autonomy.

2.  **Self- and peer learning groups.** These are small groups for those who are working individually or for those who are doing some task collectively, as a team. In either case, they may be busy with what was agreed in the various learning contracts discussed in 3, 4, 5 and 6, co-operative mode, planning

dimension, Chapter 5. For cognitive tasks, people can brain-storm and discuss ideas; share resources, references and infor-mation; share work in progress and final drafts for feedback and discussion. For skills building, they can use the cycle of practice, feedback, reflection and more practice.

3. **Self- and peer imaginal groups.**   These are small groups for autonomous learning in which members use the full range of imaginal methods – metaphor, instance, resonance, presenta-tion, dramaturgy, demonstration, caricature – to deepen their understanding of topic, skill or process. These groups may be the same as those in 2, functioning intermittently in the imaginal way, and so moving between conceptual and imaginal ways of making sense.

4. **Self- and peer supervision groups.**   These are a little different. Participants meet at intervals in small groups and take it in turns to share some current learning problem, to do with task or process issues or both. Immediately after their turn, each person receives comment, opinion, feedback and suggestions on what has been shared from the other group members, and then makes a final statement taking account of all this, including some action plan for dealing with the problem. Both conceptual and imaginal sorts of understanding can be applied. For a full discussion of peer supervision and support groups, see Chapter 9.

5. **Self- and peer learning resources.**   You provide, and support group members in providing, facilities for individual, self-directed learning, and/or peer learning in small groups: libraries, handouts, books, articles, audio-visual aids, CCTV, computer-assisted and computer-managed learning prog-rammes, computer access to the Internet, self-rating question-naires and inventories, written or taped instructions for structured exercises (task or process oriented) in small groups.

6. **Autonomous group process review.** You delegate to members, in small groups, the opportunity to do their own review of recent whole group process, looking back to identify and evaluate its various aspects. It is for them to choose relevant categories of analysis and evaluation. It may then be fruitful for the small groups to come together and share with each other and with you, leading to a general discussion, in which case we are back in the collaborative mode.

7. **Autonomous learning task review.**   You delegate to members, in small groups, the opportunity to do their own review of the learning tasks the group has undertaken, to reflect on what is

being learnt, how it is being learnt and whether it is being learnt. Again, as in 6, it may then be fruitful for the small groups to come together and share with each other and with you, leading to a general discussion, in which case we are back in the collaborative mode.

8. **Self- and peer assessment.** In small groups, each member assesses their own competence in skills or other learning, with feedback from peers. This refers back to a whole lot of work done, and is for use at infrequent intervals and at the end of a course. You will need to give group members a structure for doing this, and to train and supervise them in the early use of it, until they become effectively self-directing. The basic stages are:

- **Autonomous criteria-setting.** Group members agree, on their own, on a few basic criteria of competence relevant to the skill being assessed.
- **Self-assessment.** Each individual assesses their own competence, in front of their peers, dealing with strengths and weaknesses in the light of each criterion.
- **Peer assessment.** Group members take it in turn to assess – in the light of each criterion – the competence of the person who has just completed their self-assessment, with special reference to overstated, understated or omitted strengths and weaknesses in the self-assessment.
- **Revised self-assessment.** The same person now takes a further turn to revise their self-assessment, taking into account peer assessments.
- **Optional: negotiated self- and peer final assessment.** In this optional extra, the peers negotiate a final assessment with the person, if they dissent from the revised self-assessment. The use of this option depends on the subject matter. If it is personal growth that is being assessed, it seems that self-assessment is primary and the sequence should end with the revised self-assessment. If more external and technical skills are being assessed, there is a case for more peer influence and control through their negotiation in the final assessment.

Each stage requires a precise time allocation, and pacing and time control need to be well managed. This is a rigorous and demanding procedure which visibly matures those who apply themselves to it.

It can be used entirely on its own, as described, with you the facilitator absent, or with you sitting in but not participating at all (except in early stages for supervision of the procedure). It is also, of course, in modified form, a component within 9, collaborative assessment, co-operative mode, in this chapter. In each case, every participant can use its outcomes to generate an action plan for further learning.

9. **Autonomous course evaluation.**   You delegate to members, in small groups, the opportunity to do their own evaluation of the whole course, or of a major part of it. It is for them to choose relevant categories of analysis and evaluation procedures. This combines 6 and 7 above, and may consider the outcomes of 8. It may then be fruitful for the small groups to come together and share with each other and with you, leading to a general discussion, in which case we are back in the collaborative mode.

10. **Autonomous co-operative inquiry.**   As in 11, co-operative inquiry, co-operative mode, in this chapter, except that it excludes you, the facilitator. The group rotates the facilitator role among its members from the outset. This would be at an advanced stage in a group's history, after it had learned to do co-operative inquiry with you.

11. **Peer review audit.**   This is self- and peer assessment applied to professional work in the world: it can be used on day release, in-service professional development training groups. The purpose of peer review audit is for professionals in an entirely self-directed way to generate and maintain standards of excellence in performance on the job.

    It will usually be done by a small group of those doing the same kind of work. The group will need some training and supervision by you to acquire the competence to do this exercise effectively on its own. The method is discussed in detail in Chapter 8. See also Heron (1982). The stages, in brief outline, are as follows:

    ● **Analyse job.**   The group members break down the work into its component parts, and choose one part of it to audit.
    ● **Agree criteria.**   They decide on a small number of basic criteria of what it is to do that part of the work well.
    ● **Devise self- (and peer) assessment.**   They work out a way of sampling their daily work of this kind, of assessing it in the light of the agreed criteria, and of keeping some record of these self-assessments. Where people work together, the self-assessment can be extended to include some form of peer assessment on the job. These first three stages can all be done in one meeting of the group, on the day release course.

- **On the job self- (and peer) assessment.** They get on with their professional work for an agreed period of days or weeks using the self-assessments (with peer assessments where possible, although it usually isn't practicable), on work samples, and keeping records of all these.
- **Feedback on assessment.** The group have a second meeting on the day release course and each one takes it in turns to share the self- and peer assessments on her performance with the rest of the group. Each presenter gets feedback on his self-assessment from the other group members, being confronted on understated or avoided weaknesses, and on overstated strengths, and supported on understated or omitted strengths. Subtle insight and skill is needed here, since the feedback is based on what comes over in the presentation of the self-assessment and in the data it contains. The presenter then reviews her overall self-assessment in the light of this feedback. This may lead over into a personal action-plan to take account of the findings.
- **Planning the next cycle.** The group members now decide whether to start a second cycle continuing to assess performance on the same part of the job. If so, they review the criteria, methods of sampling, assessment and record-keeping, the amount of time spent on the job between feedback meetings; and they may modify some of these. If not, then they choose some other part of the job and go through the whole procedure on that.
- **On the job self- (and peer) assessment etc.** This process can continue indefinitely. In practice, a group will prefer to use it for a certain number of cycles, then apply the learning for quite a long period without further audit.

Peer review audit is the most rigorous kind of peer support group for professional practice. Several other kinds of peer support group of a more accessible kind are described in Chapter 9.

12. **No interpretation phase.** You stop giving interpretations or prompting the group to interpret. You open the space for group members to generate their own meanings. This sort of interpretative absence can be unannounced, or you can stay that you are going to do it and, perhaps, for how long it will continue.
13. **Autonomous monitoring of meaning.** In this extension of the initiative clause (see 9, autonomous mode, planning dimension, Chapter 5) into the meaning dimension, you have created a

climate of shared leadership, in which group members spontaneously give meaning to what is happening, alongside your
management of this dimension

14. **Trainer–trainee delegation.** You appoint one person in the
group, or in each of several sub-groups, to exercise the interpretative role over a period of group interaction. Afterwards other
members give their feedback on the interpretations. This, of
course, is an exercise in a training the trainers' group.

15. **Self-generated insight.** Some systems of growth and therapy
(e.g. primal therapy, co-counselling) believe that the only really
authentic interpretations of a psychodynamic kind are those that
arise spontaneously within the individual in the course of their
personal growth work. This work may be actively facilitated,
but you, the facilitator, never make any interpretations, and
make sure space is given for the client to verbalize self-
generated insights as they arise. So your facilitation, especially
with respect to release of emotion, is hierarchical and co-operative. But so far as meaning is concerned, only client insights
count.

# 7 Co-operative Inquiry

This chapter, which outlines the salient features of the participative research method of co-operative inquiry, is the first of three chapters which expand on particular interventions given in the previous chapter on the meaning dimension. Co-operative inquiry appears there as item 11, co-operative mode, and item 10, autonomous mode.

## Definition of Co-operative Inquiry

Co-operative inquiry involves two or more people researching a topic through their own experience of it, using a series of cycles in which they move between this experience and reflecting together on it. Each person is co-subject in the experience phases and co-researcher in the reflection phases. The defining features of co-operative inquiry are:

- *All* the subjects are as fully involved as possible as co-researchers in *all* research decisions – about both content and method – taken in the reflection phases.
- There is intentional interplay between reflection and making sense on the one hand, and experience and action on the other
- There is explicit attention through appropriate procedures to the validity of the inquiry and its findings.
- There is a radical epistemology for a wide-ranging inquiry method that can be both informative about and transformative of any aspect of the human condition accessible to a transparent body-mind, that is, one that has an open, unbound awareness.
- There are as well as validity procedures a range of special skills suited to such all-purpose experiential inquiry.
- The full range of human sensibilities is available as an instrument of inquiry.

## *Participation and Inquiry*

The following tables set out the structure of participation in social science research. Table 7.1 shows the two main kinds of participation and the different degress to which the researcher and the research subject can be involved in them. The next three tables show how these kinds and degrees apply, respectively, to co-operative inquiry, traditional quantitative research, and traditional qualitative research. For full details, see *Co-operative Inquiry* (Heron, 1996a).

**Table 7.1**    *Kinds and degrees of participation*

|  |  | Researcher | Subject |
|---|---|---|---|
| **Political participation:** | A | Full | Full |
| involvement in research | B | Full | Partial |
| thinking & decision-making | C | Full | Nil |
| **Epistemic participation:** | D | Full | Full |
| involvement in experience & | E | Partial | Full |
| action being researched | F | Nil | Full |

**Table 7.2**    *Full form co-operative inquiry*

|  | Researcher | Subject |
|---|---|---|
| **Participation in decisions** | Full | Full |
| **Participation in experience** | Full | Full |

**Table 7.3**    *Traditional quantitative research*

|  | Researcher | Subject |
|---|---|---|
| **Participation in decisions** | Full | Nil |
| **Participation in experience** | Nil | Full |

**Table 7.4**    *Traditional qualitative research*

|  | Researcher | Subject |
|---|---|---|
| **Participation in decisions** | Full | Partial |
| **Participation in experience** | Partial | Full |

## Outcomes of Co-operative Inquiry

Four main kinds of inquiry outcome, corresponding to the four forms of knowing, experiential, presentational, propositional and practical:

- Transformations of personal being through engagement with the focus and process of the inquiry.
- Presentations of insight about the focus of the inquiry, through dance, drawing, drama, and all other expressive modes: these provide imaginal symbols of the significant patterns in our realities.
- Propositional reports which (1) are informative about the inquiry domain, that is, they describe and explain what has been explored, (2) provide commentary on the other kinds of outcome, and (3) describe the inquiry method.
- Practical skills which are (1) skills to do with transformative action within the inquiry domain, and (2) skills to do with various kinds of participative knowing and collaboration used in the inquiry process.

## Topics of Co-operative Inquiry

The first half of the list relates to informative inquiries, which have propositional outcomes which describe and explain what is going on, or presentational outcomes which portray it.

- Participation in nature: from molecules, minerals and galactic clusters to microbes, protoplasm and all life forms in the biosphere.
- Participation in art: from sculpture and painting to theatre and song.
- Participation in intrapsychic life: from sensations and moods to elevations and ecstasies.
- Participation in interpersonal relations: verbal and nonverbal, from one-to-one encounters and face-to-face groups, to structured large groups meetings.
- Participation in forms of culture: from environmental and economic arrangements to education and politics.
- Participation in other realities and altered states of consciousness: from telekinesis and extrasensory perception to cosmic consciousness and unitive awareness.

The second half of the list covers items for transformative inquiries, which have practical or skills outcomes, including their effects.

- Transformation of the environment: from local to planetary ecology; from architecture to permaculture.
- Transformation of social structure: social practices and rituals; organizational development; economic and political transformation; liberation of the disempowered and disadvantaged and of their oppressors; a self-generating culture.
- Transformation of education: from birth to death; including self-directed learning, peer and holistic learning.
- Transformation of professionalism: professional skills; peer review audit; creating a culture of competence; deprofessionalization, delegation and facilitation.
- Transformation of personhood: personal growth skills, interpersonal and transpersonal skills.
- Transformation of life-style: ranging from intimacy and domicile to occupation and recreation.

## *An Outline of Inquiry Stages*

### *Stage 1*

The first reflection phase for the inquirers to choose:

- The focus or topic of the inquiry and the type of inquiry.
- A launching statement of the inquiry topic.
- A plan of action for the first action phase to explore some aspect of the inquiry topic.
- A method of recording experiences during the first action phase.

### *Stage 2*

The first action phase when the inquirers are:

- Exploring in experience and action some aspect of the inquiry topic.
- Applying an integrated range of inquiry skills.
- Keeping records of the experiential data generated.

### *Stage 3*

Full immersion in stage 2 with great openness to experience; the inquirers may:

- Break through into new awareness.
- Lose their way.
- Transcend the inquiry format.

## Stage 4

The second reflection phase; the inquirers share data from the action phase and:

- Review and modify the inquiry topic in the light of making sense of data about the explored aspect of it.
- Choose a plan for the second action phase to explore the same or a different aspect of the inquiry topic.
- Review the method of recording data used in the first action phase and amend it for use in the second.

Subsequent stages will:

- Involve, including the first, from five to eight full cycles of reflection and action, with varying patterns of divergence and convergence, in the action phases, over aspects of the inquiry topic.
- Include a variety of intentional procedures, in the reflection phases, and of special skills in the action phases, for enhancing the validity of the process.
- End with a major reflection phase for pulling the threads together, clarifying outcomes, and deciding whether to write a co-operative report.
- Be followed by post-group collaboration on writing up an agreed form of report.

Figure 7.1 shows the four stages of the inquiry cycle, for a full form inquiry, in which everyone is fully involved as both co-researcher and co-subject, and in which people interact with each other in the action phase, hence the stage 2 arrows are both within each participant and between participants.

## Extended Epistemology and the Inquiry Cycle

Figure 7.2 shows an up-hierarchy (what is below grounds and supports what is above) of the four forms of knowing which precisely mirrors the up-hierarchy of the four forms of learning shown in Figure 1.1., Chapter 1.

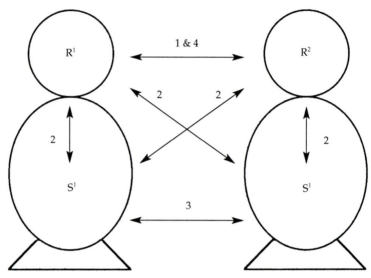

R¹, R² ... Rⁿ = participants as co-researchers
S¹, S² ... Sⁿ = participants as co-subjects

**Figure 7.1**   *Four stages of the inquiry cycle*

Experiential knowing – imaging and feeling the presence of some energy, entity, person, place, process or thing – is the ground of presentational knowing. Presentational knowing – an intuitive grasp of the significance of patterns as expressed in graphic, plastic, moving, musical and verbal art-forms – is the ground of propositional knowing. And propositional knowing – expressed in statements that something is the case – is the ground of practical knowing – knowing how to exercise a skill. This relationship can also be expressed as a circuit, as in Figure 7.3.

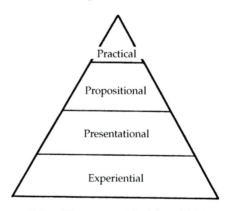

**Figure 7.2**   *The pyramid of fourfold knowing*

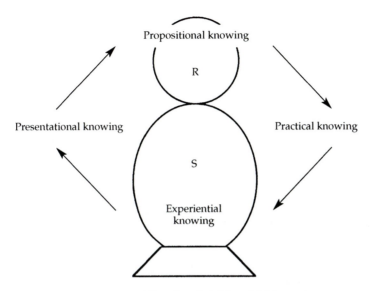

**Figure 7.3**   *The circuit of fourfold knowing*

Figures 7.4 and 7.5 show the circuit applied to co-operative inquiry, in which the participants move to and fro between phases of sense-making in terms of presentational and propositional knowing and phases of action inquiry in terms of practical and experiential knowing.

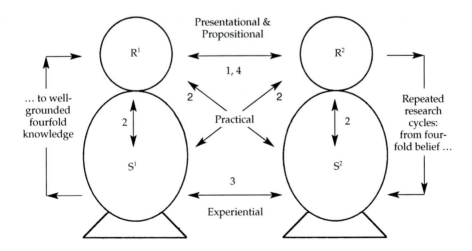

**Figure 7.4**   *Four cognitive modes and stages of the inquiry cycle*

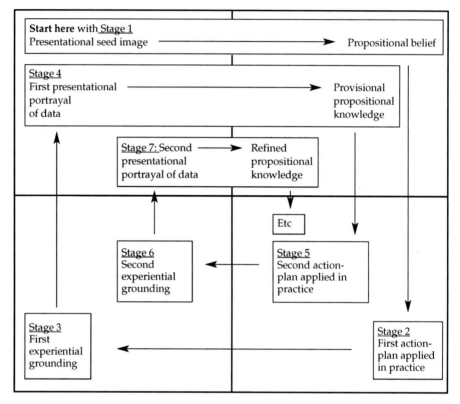

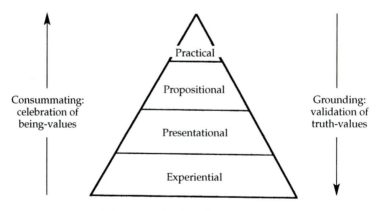

**PRESENTATIONAL**                              **PROPOSITIONAL**

**Start here** with Stage 1
Presentational seed image ——————————————→ Propositional belief

Stage 4
First presentational ——————————————→ Provisional
portrayal                                        propositional
of data                                          knowledge

Stage 7: Second ——→ Refined
presentational          propositional
portrayal of data       knowledge

Etc

Stage 6                 Stage 5
Second                  Second action-
experiential            plan applied in
grounding               practice

Stage 3                                          Stage 2
First                                            First action-
experiential                                     plan applied
grounding                                        in practice

**EXPERIENTIAL**                                **PRACTICAL**

**Figure 7.5**    *Four cognitive modes and stages of the inquiry cycle*
*(version 2)*

Consummating:                    Practical                    Grounding:
celebration of                                                validation of
being-values                     Propositional                truth-values

                                 Presentational

                                 Experiential

**Figure 7.6**    *Bipolar congruence*

Figure 7.6 illustrates two complementary forms of congruence between the four forms of knowing. Going up the pyramid, the upper forms of knowing progressively consummate the lower in terms of the values of human flourishing. Going down the pyramid, the lower forms ground the upper in terms of truth-values.

## *Special Inquiry Skills*

The first group relate to radical perception in informative inquiries where the purpose is to be descriptive and explanatory of the inquiry domain.

- **Being present.** This is to do with empathy, with meeting and feeling the presence of people and a world. The skill is about harmonic resonance and attunement, participating in the inner experience of people and the mode of awareness, the prehension, of things. It is indwelling the inward declaration made by the being of the other. It is necessarily associated with the next.
- **Imaginal openness.** This is to do with being receptive to the meaning inherent in the total process of shaping people and a world by perceptually imaging them with sensory and nonsensory imagery. I enact and participate in their appearing and intuit its meaning. The skill is about imaginal grasp, the intuition of pattern meaning.
- **Bracketing.** This is to do with managing the conceptual labels and models embedded in the process of perceiving people and a world. The skill is about holding in abeyance the classifications and constructs we impose on our perceiving, so that we can be more open to its inherent primary, imaginal meaning.
- **Reframing.** This is to do with the conceptual revisioning in perceiving a world. With this skill we not only hold in abeyance the constructs being imposed on our perceiving, we also try out alternative ones for their creative capacity to articulate an account of people and a world. We are open to reframing the assumptions of any conceptual context or perspective.

The second group relate to radical practical transformative inquiries where the purpose is to engage in some action that seeks change within its domain.

- **Dynamic congruence.** This is about practical knowing, knowing how to act. The skill goes way beyond ordinary competent action.

It means being aware, while acting, of the bodily form of the behaviour, of its strategic form and guiding norms, of its purpose or end and underlying values, of its motives, of its external context and supporting beliefs, and of its actual outcomes. At the same time it means being aware of any lack of congruence between these different facets of the action and adjusting them accordingly.

- **Emotional competence.** This is the ability to identify and manage emotional states in various ways. These include keeping action free from distorted reactions to current events that are driven by the unprocessed distress of earlier years; and from the limiting influence of inappropriate conventions acquired by social conditioning.
- **Non-attachment.** The ability here is to wear lightly and without fixation the purpose, strategy, form of behaviour and motive which have been chosen as the form of the action. This is the knack of non-attachment, not investing one's identity and emotional security in the action, while remaining fully intentional about it and committed to it.
- **Self-transcending intentionality.** This skill involves having in mind, while busy with one overall form of action, one or more alternative forms, and considering their possible relevance and applicability to the total situation.

## *Validity Procedures*

The purpose of these procedures is to free the various forms of knowing involved in the inquiry process from the distortion of uncritical subjectivity, that is, a lack of discriminating awareness.

- **Research cycling.** If the research topic as a whole, and different sub-wholes and parts singly and in combination, are taken round several cycles of reflection and action, then experiential and reflective forms of knowing progressively refine each other, through two-way negative and positive feedback.
- **Divergence and convergence.** Within the action phase of any one cycle, or as between the action phases of two adjacent cycles, the co-inquirers can diverge over different parts or sub-wholes of the topic, or converge on the same part or sub-whole, or on the whole. This gives rise to innumerable combinations of divergence and convergence which, expressed through research cycling, can enable all forms of knowing to articulate the research topic more thoroughly.

- **Reflection and action.** Since reflective and experiential forms of knowing refine each other through cycling to and fro between reflection and action phases, this effect also depends on getting a right balance between these two phases, so that there is neither too much reflection on too little experience, nor too little reflection on too much experience.

- **Aspects of reflection.** Within the reflection phase, there is a balance between presentational (expressive or artistic) ways of making sense and propositional (verbal/intellectual) ways. And within intellectual ways, there is balance between four mental activities: describing, evaluating descriptions, building theory, and applying what has been learned in one cycle to the management of the next.

- **Challenging uncritical subjectivity.** This is done with a simple procedure with authorizes any inquirer at any time to adopt formally the role of devil's advocate in order to question the group as to whether one of several forms of uncritical subjectivity is afoot. These forms include: not noticing, or not mentioning, aspects of experience that show up the limitations of a conceptual model or programme of action; unaware fixation on false assumptions implicit in guiding ideas or action plans; unaware projections distorting the inquiry process; lack of rigour in inquiry method and in applying validity procedures.

- **Chaos and order.** This is not so much a procedure as a mental set which allows for the interdependence of chaos and order, of nescience and knowing. It is an attitude which tolerates and undergoes, without premature closure, inquiry phases which are confused and disoriented, ambiguous and uncertain, conflicted and inharmonious, generally lost and groping. These phases tend in their own time to convert into new levels of order. But since there is no guarantee that they will do so, they are risky and edgy. Tidying them up prematurely out of anxiety leads to pseudo-knowledge.

- **Managing unaware projections.** The group adopts some regular method for surfacing and processing repressed templates of past emotional trauma, which may get unawarely projected out, distorting thought, perception and action within the inquiry. The very process of researching the human condition may stir up these templates and trigger them into compulsive invasion of the inquiring mind.

- **Authentic collaboration.** Since intersubjective dialogue is a key component in refining the forms of knowing, it is important that it manifests through authentic collaboration. One aspect of this is that group members internalize and make their own the inquiry method so that they become on a peer footing with the initiating researchers. The other aspect is that each group member is fully and authentically engaged in each action phase and in each reflection phase; and in each reflection phase is fully expressive, fully heard, and fully influential in decision-making, on a peer basis with every other group member.

## Three-stranded Initiation of a Co-operative Inquiry

The person initiating a co-operative inquiry needs to foster three things:

- The initiation of group members into the methodology of the inquiry so that they can make it their own.
- The emergence of participative decision-making and authentic collaboration so that the inquiry becomes truly co-operative.
- The creation of a climate in which emotional states can be identified, so that distress and tension aroused by the inquiry can be openly accepted and processed, and joy and delight in it and with each other can be freely expressed.

The first of these is to do with cognitive and methodological empowerment, the second with political empowerment, and the third with emotional and interpersonal empowerment. Initiating researchers need some skills in all these three ways of empowering others. The combination is familiar to the whole person educator whose analogous concern is to facilitate:

- Self-directed learning by students of some content and method.
- Increasing student participation in all aspects of educational decision-making: the objectives, topics, resources, methods, programme and pacing of learning; the assessment of learning, and the evaluation of the course.
- Integration of cognitive with emotional and interpersonal aspects of learning.

# 8 Peer Review Audit

This chapter elaborates on peer review audit, introduced as item 11 in the autonomous mode of the meaning dimension in Chapter 6, where it is defined as self- and peer assessment applied to professional work in the world. I suggest there that it can be used on day release, in-service professional development training groups, and that its purpose is for professionals in an entirely self-directed way to generate and maintain standards of excellence in performance on the job. Beyond its introduction on a day release course, its ongoing role is within organizational life, where its adoption can be fostered by the manager as facilitator of work-enhancing human resource development.

## Autonomous Meaning of Work

I suggest that the manager as facilitator selects mode-dimension combinations to create a managerial style that progressively moves toward more delegation and employee autonomy: increased self- and peer determination. To foster the autonomous mode on the meaning dimension means delegating knowledge and data-gathering, interpretation, feedback, reflection and review to people; so that making sense of what is going on, giving work meaning, is autonomous, entirely generated by them. One way for the manager to promote this kind of delegation is to train people to run their own peer review audit groups. Members of such groups give meaning to their work by a form of self-directed quality control of job performance.

Peer review audit is a radical kind of peer supervision whereby a small group of people in the same profession or team come together in regular meetings to develop and apply standards of professional competence (Heron, 1982; Kilty, 1978, 1980). It is quite different from peer supervision with a critical incident focus – described in the next chapter – which works with case content material and on-the-job issues, and tacitly assumes job definition and criteria of competence. Peer review audit works at a prior level: it deals directly with job definition and makes explicit criteria of competence.

The procedures are simple enough. The group defines the job and analyses it into its major component parts. It takes one such part of the job and devises a basic set of criteria for competent practice in that part. It then works out a way in which group members can use those criteria to self-assess their on-the-job competence and can keep a record of this self-assessment. Members go off and apply this self-assessment to their professional practice in the chosen part for an agreed period. Then they meet again to present their self-assessment records and to listen to, and take account of, peer feedback on them. In the light of all this they review and revise the criteria used, also the self-assessment method used and the way of recording it, and issues of competence in the chosen area of work. They may launch into a second cycle assessing the same part of the job. Sooner or later they will choose to move on to another part of their work, dealing with it in the same way, starting with defining it and devising criteria of competent practice of it, and so on.

What we have here is a form of professional development, a strategy of continuing education, and a method of collaborative action inquiry into professional practice. It can be used with any professional group; and I have introduced it to doctors, dentists, teachers in higher education, co-counselling teachers, managers, management trainers, group leaders, behavioural science researchers, and others.

## Commitment to Excellence

Every profession is faced with the big issue of how to maintain standards of competence. Keeping up to date with information and technical advances, and acquiring new skills, through ongoing education and training play an important part. But sooner or later there has to be some kind of review of what the professionals are doing and how they are doing it. Centralized generation and control of standards by means of re-examination, or by roving inspectors who sit in at the workplace, is one method. It suffers from 'big brother syndrome': centralization of this kind can lead to rigidity, dogmatism, narrowness and authoritarianism. It lacks a proper regard for individual professional flair and judgment. By undermining these important qualities, it can lead to conformity and playing safe among the rank and file.

The other method is for the professionals themselves to review what they are up to. For in the last analysis it is personal commitment to excellence on the job that is crucial. This commitment cannot be imposed, it can only be self-generated. It is a matter of intrinsic motivation, of being fired by the deep satisfaction of doing good work. Peer review audit provides a supportive network of colleagues, and a procedural framework, within which this kind of personal motivation can flourish.

## Education for the Professions

There is however a major anomaly in our current methods of educating professional people. I have long argued that a fully educated person is, among other things, an awarely self-determining person, in the sense of being able to set objectives, to formulate standards of excellence for the work that realizes those objectives, to assess work done in the light of those standards, and to be able to modify the objectives, the standards or the work programme in the light of experience and action; and all this in discussion and consultation with other relevant persons. And many people, I find, agree that this sort of action competence is indeed what we can reasonably expect of an educated professional.

Unfortunately, the educational process in most of our main institutions of higher education does not prepare students to acquire this kind of self-determining ability For the staff in these institutions unilaterally decide student objectives, work programmes and assessment criteria, and unilaterally do the assessment of student work. This goes on until graduation, so that fledgling professionals are undereducated so far as the *process* of education is concerned. They have had no experience in setting objectives, planning a work programme, devising assessment criteria, or in self-assessment; nor have they acquired any skills in doing any of these things co-operatively with others (Heron, 1988).

What this all means is that many professional people have emerged from an educational system which has not equipped them with the basic self-determining and co-operative competencies that are required for the effective practice of peer review audit. For this form of audit is all about setting criteria for oneself and with others, practising self- and peer assessment. So training and preparation are needed, which is why I am devoting a whole chapter to the method, with considerable discussion of the facilitation issues involved at each stage.

Of course, the education system is slowly changing. A growing minority of places of higher education in some countries are introducing more student autonomy in learning (Boud, 1988). But there is still a long way to go before the majority of places use a process of learning that is truly educational.

The medical profession in the UK was caught out by the anomaly to which I have referred. In 1976 it published a high level report on Competence to Practise, in which it recommended to itself a form of audit based on self- and peer assessment – peer review audit – as the most appropriate method of audit for mature professional people. It rejected any kind of audit imposed from on high by some centralized body of medical authorities, and for the same sorts of reasons which I have given above. The problem was, and still is, how to act on this given that doctors emerge from a highly authoritarian educational system, unilaterally and centrally controlled by staff. The result has been something of a developmental stalemate.

Peer review audit, then, needs a training programme, a whole workshop devoted to it. I use a two-day block followed two weeks later by another day. This gives an opportunity to go through the whole procedure slowly, taking plenty of time to look at all the relevant issues along the way. The two-week gap is for people to go off and do their self-assessments on the job; and they return to present them on the final day.

## Peer Assessment

There are two major issues about the whole process that I must cover before going through it in detail. Many professional people will consider it impractical to take time out during the working day to visit colleagues from the audit group and do on-the-job peer assessment of their work. So in many peer review audit groups, the peer assessment is done on the presented self-assessments, not on the actual work to which those self-assessments refer. This is still immensely fruitful as we shall see.

Where it is possible for people who do the same sort of job in the same organization and building to sit in from time to time on each other's work and do on-the-job peer assessments, this is all to the good; and I refer to this option in discussing the stages where it applies. Even so, it is still secondary to and supportive of, and does not replace, the main point and power of the method, which is self-assessment.

## Practice and Outcomes

The other important point is the distinction between assessing practice, what the professionals do and how they do it, and assessing outcomes, the effects of their practice on their clients, on the social system, on the natural world, or on any physical artefact. Are we to look at what the doctor does, or at the effects of this on the patient? It might seem that patient outcome is the final test of medical competence. But only to a degree, since the effectiveness of many medical practices depends significantly on patient co-operation and self-help. Outcome studies may report ambiguously on both medical intervention and patient self-determination, and indeed on other unsuspected variables.

So with some other professions. There is no correlation between teachers' lecturing skill and students' examination performance, presumably because many students compensate for poor lectures by private study. Generally speaking, where the outcome of professional practice is to do with effects on other persons, there is likely to be this kind of ambiguity. Where the effect is on a physical product, as in architecture and engineering, then outcome studies are reliable. Houses and bridges either stand up or collapse, and if they collapse under normal circumstances then faulty design is the cause.

Many professional groups that use peer review audit will be in one or other of the many helping professions. They will probably be wise to assess both practice and outcomes, the exact mix depending on the profession and the practicalities of gathering in assessment of outcomes in the time available. Some of the ambiguity about client outcomes can be dealt with by asking the clients themselves to report on outcomes through questionnaires and interviews. Clients can also, of course, give vital feedback on practice, since they are often at the immediate receiving end of it.

Finally, there is the possibility of peer review audit groups which include both the professionals and some of their clients. There can then be a conjoint audit of both practice and outcomes.

I now present the various stages of the audit. The first three stages are all done at the first meeting, stage 4 is on-the-job application of the audit, stages 5, 6 and 7 all occur at the second and peer review meeting, stage 8 is the second cycle of on-the-job application, and so on. Figure 8.1 illustrates the whole procedure.

## Stage 1.  Select an Area of Practice to Assess

The group members break down their professional work into its component parts, and choose one part of it, or sub-part, to audit. This is first of all an exercise in job definition, an exercise valuable in its

| STAGES OF PEER REVIEW AUDIT | TRAINING AUDIT | SECOND CYCLE etc |
|---|---|---|
| Stage 1 Select area of practice<br>Stage 2 Agree on criteria<br>Stage 3 Devise self-assessment method | 2 days maximum<br>Half-day<br>minimum | |
| Stage 4 Assessment on the job | 2 weeks | 4 weeks |
| Stage 5 PEER REVIEW<br>        Presentation: 12 minutes<br>        Questions: 3 minutes<br>        Peer assessment: 6 minutes<br>        Devil's advocate: 6 minutes<br>        Positive feedback: 5 minutes<br>        Review and plan: 5 minutes<br>Stage 6 Review of audit procedures<br>Stage 7 Plan second cycle<br>        If same area, refine Stage 6<br>        If new area, Stages 1, 2, 3 | 1 day | 1 day |

**Figure 8.1** *Stages of peer review audit and time allocations*

own right. The job may need to be analysed into sub-parts or even sub-sub-parts in order to get down to an area that can be effectively assessed.

Thus a group of dentists defined their work as fourfold: clinical practice, staff management, administration, legal and financial matters. Clinical practice was further subdivided into examinations, X-rays, fillings, extractions, etc., and at this level a choice for assessment could be made.

Then the group need to select one area of practice to assess. The basic rule here is for everyone to choose the same area, so that members can pool their wisdom in defining criteria of competence for it, and get the full benefit of comparing and contrasting their performance in it. The dentists mentioned above started their first cycle with 'fillings'; another group of dentists selected 'long-term patient care over eight years'; training officers chose 'managing staff in the immediate office'; health education officers chose 'managing time on a daily basis'; doctors chose 'keeping medical records'.

## *Facilitation*

In a training group everything depends on getting a good start, so the selection of the area of practice to assess is crucial. Here are some things to remember.

- Job definition analysis can be done by a group brainstorm on a wall-chart, then you facilitate a group discussion which gets it into some compact final form; or by each member doing their own analysis first, then the results are compared, debated and collated. Keep the thing going into parts, sub-parts or sub-sub-parts until the group gets to assessable items.
- Members may need some prompting about job definition areas that a narrowly conventional approach might exclude, such as emotional self-management, interpersonal skills, or ecological control. At the same time, unless there is a special eagerness to do so, the first two of these are not the obvious candidates for a first run at assessment on-the-job. Something less close to psychological base might be better for getting the feel of the method.
- People can usually only manage to assess one area of practice at a time. Covering several areas at once is unwieldy in criteria-setting, in on-the-job assessment and in reporting back. So resist any unrealistic proposal of this kind from the group.
- Useful guidelines for people in choosing an area are: that it is manageable for assessment; that it has a fair amount going on in it; that it excites interest and curiosity as a vehicle for assessment. There is also: its importance, that is, how much it is a key part of the job; close to this, but not the same, is whether it is symbolic of, a marker for, other areas of practice (as with 'keeping medical records' for doctors); and whether it is currently undergoing some crisis of change or stasis.
- The job analysis and the selection of an area can run together. In other words, the group breaks the job up into certain major parts, selects one of these, then converts this into its sub-parts, and chooses one of these for the assessment. It may be too fatiguing for the group to do the whole job analysis covering all parts and sub-parts.

## Stage 2. Agree Criteria of Competent Practice for the Selected Area

Group members now decide on a set of basic criteria of what it is to do good work in the selected area of practice. First they have to generate some criteria, then choose which ones to use. The basic rule here is to limit the final number that will be used to an absolute maximum of six, while three or four would be quite acceptable. To have a large number of criteria to apply in on-the-job assessment in the midst of a busy professional life, or at the end of a long working day, is unrealistic. The whole format of this method has to be compact so that the motivation to use it is enjoyed and undimmed.

Dentists who wanted to assess 'fillings' used as criteria: cleared decay, retention, no ledges, supported enamel, lining, contouring. Training officers who wanted to assess their competence in 'managing staff in the immediate office' devised the following criteria: setting objectives with staff; agreeing standards with staff; agreeing time-scale with staff; balancing monitoring of staff with staff autonomy; consulting staff prior to generating policy; supporting staff.

## Facilitation

Because mainstream higher education still does not educate and train people to generate criteria for their own work, this stage needs a lot of attention, with trainees being given much support on various issues. People often seem to enter a sudden mental fog when asked to generate criteria of competence for what they do. The culture has conditioned them to be punitively judged, and the distress about all this clouds the mind for a while, until they start to get a feel for what it is to be creatively and happily self-assessing. Here are some of the main issues to consider.

- I usually recommend that group members first write out individual lists of criteria for the chosen area of practice. This gets them in the way of thinking about criteria. Then these lists can be presented all together on a wall-chart for everyone to see and discuss. Then the thing can go any one of three ways. People can stick with their own individual criteria; or they can collate and edit these until they all agree on a consensus list so that everyone is using the same; or they can agree that each person can use any three or four from the total unedited pooled list, so they may use some of their own and some of other members. The more technical the practice with physical outcomes as in dentistry, architecture, engineering, the more important it is to have consensus criteria; the more socially interactive the practice, the stronger the case for the mixed model, the third way, which seeks to balance the claims of idiosyncratic personal values with the claims of the collective wisdom of the group. This issue can be debated within the group. As usual, it is best to support whichever way seems to motivate people the most. It can always be modified in a later cycle of the audit.

- Criteria occupy a simple kind of logical structure which is hierarchical. Ask a dentist what good clinical practice is and he will say good examinations, good X-rays, good fillings, good extractions, etc. Ask what a good filling is and he will say good retention, good contouring, etc. Ask what good retention is … and so it goes on. A good outcome is defined by a sub-set of outcomes, and each good sub-set item is defined by a further sub-sub-set of outcomes, etc. Similarly, a good practice is defined by a sub-set of good practices, and each good sub-set item is defined by a further sub-sub-set of practices, etc. And the hierarchy can go on endlessly into the minutiae of good outcomes or good practice.
- Group members need to grasp this basic structure and accept that for the purposes of doing an effective audit, they need to come to a resting place quite soon in the hierarchy and just assume as tacit the criteria for doing well the sub-practices or sub-outcomes they have chosen as criteria for doing well the main area of practice or outcome they want to assess. Thus the dentists assessing fillings, using as criteria the outcomes of cleared decay, retention, no ledges, supported enamel, lining, contouring, intuiting the more detailed evidence for each of these things being in good order. What is interesting about all this is that the assessment ultimately rests on an *intuitive feel for a good pattern* in the practices or outcomes used as criteria.
- There are practice criteria and outcomes criteria. The former are about what the professionals do and how they do it; the latter are about the effects of their practice on their clients, on the social system, on the natural world, on the physical artefact. I discussed this important distinction in an earlier section, where I suggested that it is probably wise to audit both practice and outcomes where possible. The dental group that wanted to assess their work on fillings used only outcomes criteria to do with the end-result in the mouth of the patient, such as cleared decay, proper retention, etc. But they could and perhaps should have used equally important practice criteria to do with the sequence of working, the tools to use, etc.
- Outcomes criteria are related in a special way, *other variables notwithstanding*, to standard good practice criteria. If the practice is good, the outcomes are good. But this relation is asymmetrical. For it does not follow that if the outcomes are good then the standard good practice criteria must have been applied. The same good outcomes, or even better ones, may be the result of some total innovation in practice that departs radically from the standard. However if the outcomes are bad, then we can conclude

that at any rate the standard good practice was not followed. So if only outcomes criteria are used, we either know, with negative outcomes, that standard good practice was not used, or we do not know, with positive outcomes, whether standard practice or innovative practice was used. Try to use both outcomes and practice criteria.

● Where the outcomes criteria are defined by professionals in terms of the reactions of other people, then it makes sense at some point for the professionals to ask those people whether they agree that such responses are for them a sign of good practice. Such agreement is a meta-outcome criterion: it is a higher order outcome criterion for choosing first-order outcome crtieria.

## Stage 3.  Devise a Self-assessment Method for Practice On-the-job

I call this a self-assessment schedule. It is both a method for assessing myself in the selected area of practice, on-the-job, according to the chosen criteria; and it is a way of recording this self-assessment so that I have some clear data to bring to the next peer review meeting. If the area of practice is one that has a lot of different instances, like a dentist doing fillings, then the method needs to include some form of sampling the practice, otherwise continual assessment will overwhelm the job. It is also valuable, wherever possible, to buttress the self-assessments with assessments from relevant others.

The dentists assessing fillings did the assessment over 20 working days before the next peer review meeting. Each day they self-assessed two fillings immediately after completing them. These fillings were chosen 'at random' by the dental nurse, but only after they were done. Each dentist had a sheet with horizontal rows for the two fillings for each of the 20 days, and the six criteria (cleared decay, retention, no ledges, supported enamel, lining, contouring) in vertical columns. For each filling they entered a rating between 1 and 5 under each criterion: 3 was a minimal acceptable standard, 5 was excellent and 1 was 'lousy'. After the ratings there was a space for notes on any special features of the filling or comments that would help the dentist remember it. This sheet was the basis for presenting their self-assessments at the peer review meeting.

The training officers assessing their competence in 'managing staff in the immediate office' kept a daily diary of staff management activities with sufficient detail to key in their memory to the events that occurred. Variations they proposed were: record only pertinent activities; record everything and underline pertinent activities; record both what you do and what you do not do. At the end of each daily entry in the diary they scored themselves, for each of the criteria they had chosen out of the pooled group list, on a rating scale from 1 to 5: 1 was very low competence, 3 was medium competence, 5 was very high competence. Each rating had an explanatory note attached saying why it was pitched where it was. An optional extra, depending on personal preference and local circumstance, was to ask one or more of the staff being managed to assess the training officer, using the same criteria and rating scale, over the whole period of the on-the-job assessment. All this data was brought to the next peer review meeting.

After this stage members disperse to do their on-the-job assessments, so at the end of this stage they need to decide over what period they will do these before the follow-up review meeting. And if any members of the group are going to be available for each other as peer on-the-job assessors, then the planning of this needs to be agreed.

## *Facilitation*

There are several design issues in devising an effective and workable self-assessment schedule for use on the job. It is as well to have a good grasp of them when assisting a training group to work through this stage.

- While self-assessment is primary and cannot be replaced by assessments from others, the latter are powerful adjuncts to the former. So encourage people where possible to use on-the-job assessments of their work by peers, by other staff and by clients. On-the-job assessment by peers means that a professional equal, ideally one of the peer review audit group, is present during the relevant work and assesses it on the spot, using the agreed criteria and rating scale. Other staff doing different kinds of work in the same team can give vital assessments under certain criteria; and so of course can clients, who are perhaps the most under-used, primary source of feedback for all professionals. Other staff and clients can also be consulted about the criteria they are being asked to use and may well want to propose modifications that represent their perspectives more fully.
- If the professionals do a lot of the sort of work they want to assess, then they have to assess samples of it. Too much sampling and assessing is a distraction from working, so the whole audit

becomes self-defeating. On the other hand, too little sampling and assessing and the audit loses validity. So the potentially conflicting claims of the work and the audit have to be reconciled. In the early stages it is better if the claims of the work have precedence over those of the audit. If too much rigour, time and energy goes into the audit, people will rapidly lose motivation to sustain it. It is better for a group to devise a modest schedule of sampling and assessing, so that it has a good chance of being applied in a continuous way. As well as the frequency of sampling being modest, the recording and scoring needs to be simple and accessible.

- Who chooses the sample? If you choose it after the event, you can bias your sampling by choosing only the best instances. If you choose it before the event, you can boost the event by making sure you perform well. The latter option seems best. To choose the sample before doing the work brings out the virtue of running a self-assessment schedule, which is that of itself it promotes good practice. Those interested in some more 'random' selection can do something like the dentists, who asked the dental nurse to choose the work to be assessed after it had been completed. But even here the virtue still works, since if any piece of relevant work may be called to account and you do not know which, you will be that bit more diligent with each of them.

- The assessment can be done immediately after the work has been done, or later in the same day on the basis of memory. It all depends what sort of work it is. Leaving assessment until the day after or longer is hazardous, unless there are good audio or video tapes, or comprehensive descriptive notes or recorded data. One approach is to keep good descriptive notes of relevant instances in a daily diary, then assess a whole batch of such instances after a few days, dealing with each one in turn.

- The use of a rating scale for each of the chosen criteria is really a way of marshalling an intuitive feel for a good or bad pattern in the instance of it. Or, to put it another way, it is an intuitive way of applying the next but tacit and unformulated sub-set of criteria. It is important to stress again that, however elegant the self-assessment schedule and the analysis of the criteria, in the last anaylsis the whole thing comes down to an *intuitive feel for a good pattern* at the workface of practice and outcome.

## Stage 4.  Assessment of Practice On-the-job

Group members now disperse back to work to apply the self-assessment schedules on-the-job for an agreed period before meeting again for the peer review. Dentists assessing fillings chose 20 working days, training officers looking at managing staff in the immediate office opted for 7 working days. In a training audit this period will usually be decided in advance by the facilitator and the institution organizing the event.

### Facilitation

The main issue is how long this period of on-the-job self-assessment is to last. If it is too short, there is no time for the virtuous effect on practice to build up momentum, and no adequate sample of behaviour is taken. If it is too long, then commitment to sustain the audit may falter through lack of peer support and stimulus. Less than a week seems too short, and more than four weeks seems too long – at any rate for an early stage of audit.

## Stage 5.   Peer Review: Self-assessment Presentations

This is in many ways the most critical part of the whole procedure. The whole group meets and each member takes it in turn to share with the others his or her on-the-job self-assessments and any additional assessments from peers, other staff or clients. Each presenter gets feedback from the other group members, being confronted on overstated, understated or avoided weaknesses, and on overstated, understated or omitted strengths. Interpersonal skill is needed here in giving feedback that is both honest and respectful, and avoids either pussyfooting or clobbering. The presenter then reviews his or her overall self-assessment in the light of this feedback; this may lead over into a personal action-plan to take account of the findings.

   A group of teachers in higher education, in a peer audit training programme, used the following format for each person in their peer review. This is a standard format but clearly there can be many variations of it. The teachers were working in sub-groups of five or so.

### Part 1.  Presentation (12 minutes)
The presenter describes the activity being audited, the criteria used, the self-assessment method and frequency and method of sampling

used, how thoroughly or forgetfully the auditing was done; and then shares an overview of his or her on-the-job self-assessments, and assessments by peers, other staff and clients, using charts, scores, notes and anecdotal material to demonstrate and support stated strengths and weaknesses. He or she may also identify relevant enhancing or distorting circumstances; and close with some general estimate of his or her current level of competence with respect to the area of practice under audit. This is done from a designated place in front of the group. The peers give sustained, warm, empathic and uncompromising attention, without comment at this stage.

### Part 2.　Clarifying questions (3 minutes)

The peers then ask any questions which help them understand more fully what has been said, which clear up obscure parts of the presentation, or which open up important and relevant but unstated information. There is no feedback at this stage.

### Part 3.　Peer assessment (6 minutes)

Any peers present who made on-the-job assessment of the presenter's work, using the same self-assessment schedule, now give details of it, also using charts, scores, notes and anecdotal material to demonstrate and support stated strengths and weaknesses. If it was not possible for the presenter to get on-the-job peer assessment of this sort, then this stage is omitted. If this stage is included, it is still followed by stage 4.

### Part 4.　Devil's advocate (6 minutes)

Where there is no peer assessment stage this is the central part of the peer review, so far as peer feedback is concerned. The ground-rule here is that the peers can amplify the least doubt, unease or uncertainty, as well as put forward obvious doubt, unease or uncertainty, about the presentation. The title 'devil's advocate' gives permission for this amplification, which gives this stage its effectiveness. It is a subtle assessment of the self-assessment presentation, and can be extremely telling in what it picks up. It is a stage in its own right and is not just there to compensate for the absence of any on-the-job peer assessment. What the peers are listening for here and amplifying in their feedback are: what has been overstated, understated or omitted, and this in relation to both strengths and weaknesses. So the peers need to remember and tune in for these six categories: overstated strength, understated strength, omitted strength, overstated weakness, understated weakness, omitted weakness. The evidence for them will be either obvious or lurking in either the manner or the content of the presentation. And the manner is just as important a source of evidence as the content.

The presenter listens to all this without any comment or reply, dissociating from any temptation to get into defensive, self-justifying reply. His or her task is to use great discrimination, discarding what is misconception or projection, taking on board what is telling and perceptive, even if uncomfortable; and in this way mentally refining his or her original self-assessment.

### Part 5.  Positive feedback (5 minutes)

Here the peers give their unqualified appreciation and affirmation of what they genuinely valued about the presenter, the manner of presentation, the format of the presentation, and the quality of the work being reported on.

### Part 6.  Presenter's review and action plan (3 minutes)

This time is optional. Some presenters will simply want to digest the whole experience and will not yet be ready to express any review or devise an action plan. Others may want to take this time to revise their self-assessment in the light of the feedback, and to make some action plan about how they want to modify their future practice in the area that has been assessed.

### Facilitation

There is a host of issues in the above set of six stages, and I shall only mention some of the major ones.

- The above sequence takes either 29 or 35 minutes, depending on whether there is any peer on-the-job assessment available. So with a group of five, we are talking here of two and a half to three hours of extremely intense and concentrated work. Groups have shown a remarkable commitment to sustain this, because of the rewards and challenges involved. But there needs to be a time-keeper for each presenter; and the time-keeper will also facilitate the pacing, reminding the presenter of how much time is left during any stage, and prompting the person to keep to basic data and not get overwhelmed by detail. If there are eight people in the group, it will be essential to have a break of 20 minutes or so after four of them have taken a turn.
- It is usually relevant for the presenter to say something about his or her thoroughness in doing the self-assessment. It is good to encourage people to have a ground-rule of being entirely open

and honest about this; and to encourage people to take their turn no matter how loose or forgetful their auditing was. It is easy enough for the clamour of work and consequent fatigue to drown out the claims of self-audit, and people need support and affirmation through this stage.

- Remind both presenters and peers to keep an eye on the six categories: overstated strength, understated strength, omitted strength, overstated weakness, understated weakness, omitted weakness. Remind peers to keep an eye out for them not only in the content of the presentation (what the person says about work incidents, about the criteria and using them, about the self-assessment method and data), but in its manner, that is, the selection and use of language, the tone of voice, facial expression, posture and gesture, the emotional undertow of what is being said, hints of unfinished business from the person's past, etc. And remind presenters that our competitive and emotionally repressive culture conditions us through insecurity both to make false claims about our performance, and to be self-deprecating about our real strengths.

- Both in the peer assessment round and in the devil's advocate round (stages 3 and 4) it is essential for people to learn to give feedback in a manner that is not punitively judgmental, that is free of malice or hurtful attack, and that is fundamentally respectful and supportive of the person to whom it is addressed. This is a basic interpersonal skill: to avoid mollycoddling and evasion on the one hand, destructive sledgehammering on the other, and find that high ground between them that combines love with a statement of the unequivocal and the uncompromising. The facilitator with a training audit group can interrupt every distorted bit of feedback and invite its author to rephrase it until he or she gets it clean and feels what it is like to say it clean. Given clean feedback, it is important for the devil's advocate round to become rigorous and exacting, for the feedback to include references to manner as well as content of presentation, and to confront the presenter as much with intimations of understated and omitted strengths as about anything else.

- When people give positive feedback in stage 5, it is useful if they can keep a balance between appreciating the work reported on, the manner of presentation, the format of the presentation, and the qualities of the whole person.

- While this peer review sequence is a central and dramatic part of the whole audit procedure, it is the facilitator's task to remind people that it is designed to affirm the primacy of self-assessment while making the fullest use of the discriminating assessment of others. The purpose of peer feedback is not to cow the presenter into conformist submission, but to provide a powerful crucible in which he or she can refine his or her self-assessment, and to enhance personal commitment to excellence.

## Stage 6.  Review of Audit Procedures

As a lead-in to this review, it is a good idea if everyone in turn gives a more detailed account of their use of the audit procedures, especially during the on-the-job audit. This was covered briefly at the opening of the self-presentations, but now is the time to go into it more thoroughly. This is a self-assessment now of one's past self-assessment competence on the job. How often did you remember, or forget, to do whatever your schedule required? If you forgot, did you try to catch up by doing self-assessments in a batch rather than one by one at the time as you should have? How thorough was your recording and scoring? How honest was it? What difficulties were found in applying the criteria, and in using the schedule? Did motivation and commitment stay the course or not? Did you notice any good or bad effects on daily practice of using the procedures? Do you want to keep on doing this?

On the basis of these disclosures, group members now review all the relevant procedures. These are: the criteria used; the method and frequency of sampling; the method of self-assessment; the method of assessment from others; the method of record-keeping; the amount of time spent on the job between meetings; the self-presentation procedure at the follow-up meeting. They may propose changes to some of these or not as they judge fit.

It is valuable for the group to do this review before members decide whether to continue to audit the same area of practice as before, or whether to change over to look at another part of their work. This is the decision the group makes next.

### Facilitation

This stage is a meta-audit of the basic audit and is important to do before continuing any further with the basic audit.

● Group members need an opportunity to share openly not only their successes and failures in using the method, but also what they make of it in terms of interest and usefulness, and whether indeed they want to go on with it. This is done in the opening part of stage 6. This is the personal experience part of the meta-audit.

- In reviewing all the methods used, the group moves on to the procedural part of the meta-audit. Sometimes people have difficulty shifting from assessing their work to assessing how they have been assessing their professional work, and keep slipping back from the latter to the former. Then the facilitator needs to keep re-routing them.

- In revising the methods, the members are effectively making them their own. Too many modifications rapidly introduced will probably mean a degeneration. For people will be avoiding the challenge and discipline of the original model, whose rationale they have not fully grasped. I have not yet encountered this. On the contrary, participants seem to be invigorated by the rigour of the model and are anxious to preserve its basic format.

## Stage 7.  Planning the Second Cycle

Group members now decide whether to continue to audit the same area of practice chosen for the first cycle or whether to select some new area. If they proceed with the same area, then they will only need to refine the revisions already made in stage 6 to the criteria, the method of sampling and frequency of sampling, the method of self-assessment, the method of assessment from others, the method of record-keeping, the amount of time spent on the job before the next review meeting.

If they opt for some new area of practice to assess, then they go through stages 1 to 3 again, no doubt a lot quicker than the first time, since people will by now be familiar with the logical geography, and some of the self-assessment methods devised for the first area will transfer over to this second area of practice.

At this stage, the training officers assessing their competence in 'managing staff in the immediate office' decided to continue auditing the same activity but homing in on aspects of it which the self-assessment presentations had highlighted as needing more attention. This meant they refined and focused more sharply their account of the activity and modified the original criteria accordingly. They kept to the same on-the-job self-assessment schedules.

### Facilitation

We are now coming up against issues of time management, so I will mention this issue first.

- Stages 5, 6 and 7 are all being done at the same meeting. Stage 5, if done in a presentation group of not more than five people, takes from two and a half to three hours, effectively a whole morning. Stages 6 and 7 can take an hour each, so we are talking a whole day or two half-day sessions here. I will return to issues of time management further on.
- The more basic issue in stage 7 is to do with convergence and divergence. If the group continues to converge on the same area of practice cycle after cycle, it masters that area thoroughly, but at the expense of integration with mastery of other areas. If on the other hand the group diverges at each cycle from one different area to another, the mastery of all areas is integrated, but minimally since each area is minimally mastered. Every group has to solve this equation according to its own situation and preferences. One solution is to add a new area of practice at each cycle, while continuing on a skeletal audit from the previous cycle, so with every cycle you are doing a major and a minor audit. Another is to do two cycles for each area, and every few cycles do a global audit (see below). It is all a matter of ingenuity and enterprise to work out a suitable formula.

## Stage 8.  The Second Cycle of On-the-job Self-assessment

The group is now busy on the job, auditing either the same area of practice as on the first cycle, or a different area. An indefinite number of cycles is now under way, involving some formula for balancing convergence and divergence, mastery of parts with mastery of the whole.

### Facilitation

The single main issue here is for how long a peer group runs an audit, before taking a break to lie fallow and let the effects of the prior audit phase work as an unstructured creative yeast. Each group will decide this on their own account, according to local variables. But the principle seems clear that peer review audit needs to be run in phases with significant non-audit periods in between.

## Peer Review Audit and the Experiential Learning Cycle

It is instructive to construe the audit cycle in terms of the primary and secondary experiential learning cycles discussed in Chapter 14. The secondary cycle starts with stages 1, 2 and 3 of the audit in the conceptual mode, analysing the job, devising criteria and a self-assessment schedule. It includes stage 4 which goes into the practical mode, working on the job.

Stage 4 in turn contains the on-the-job self-assessments which constitute a series of primary cycles. These include the practical mode of the job, at the heart of which is the audit in the affective and imaginal modes, involving the feel for a good pattern at the workface, and the conceptual mode for the self-assessment scoring, and so back to work in the practical mode.

The primary cycles continue throughout stage 4, until there is a return to the secondary cycle in the conceptual mode with stages 5, 6 and 7. Figure 8.2 illustrates the sequence, and brings out the sophisticated nature of peer review audit as a form of action inquiry and action learning. The bedrock of the whole process is the feeling for a good pattern of practice and/or outcomes.

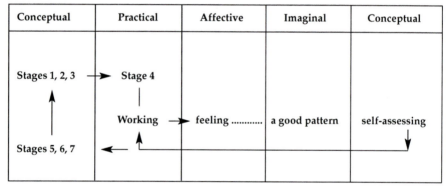

| Conceptual | Practical | Affective | Imaginal | Conceptual |
|---|---|---|---|---|
| Stages 1, 2, 3 → Stage 4 | | | | |
| ↑ | Working → feeling .......... | | a good pattern | self-assessing |
| Stages 5, 6, 7 ← | ↑ | | | ↓ |

**Figure 8.2**    *Peer review audit and the experiential learning cycle*

## Further Issues

### Training

For reasons stated in the opening section of this chapter, people need initiating into peer review audit through a training programme. I use a two-day block for stages 1, 2 and 3, with a two-week gap for stage 4, on-the-job audit, followed by a one-day session for stages 5, 6 and 7. Once trainees start on stage 8, the second cycle, they are on their own, although they can always call in their original trainer as a consultant for occasional sessions.

### Time management

To get an audit started, it needs a minimum of a half-day session, to take people through stages 1, 2 and 3. I have launched audit programmes with a half-day session, but on a full training programme I prefer an opening two-day block so as to have plenty of time to create the right climate, to take each of the first three stages slowly and consider all the issues, and to do other back-up exercises. Once an audit gets going, it needs a whole day or two half-day sessions, between cycles of on-the-job self-assessment. Half a day is for the presentation of self-assessments, the other half for reviewing the methods used and preparing for the next cycle. If each cycle is four weeks, then peer review audit means a day a month. See Figure 8.1.

### Time discipline

Every stage and part of a stage needs a clear time allocation and the group needs to be disciplined in keeping to its time boundaries. The job of time-keeper can be rotated round the group. The time-keeper can also be responsible for pacing things, for moving the group along so that it covers all the relevant ground in the time allocated.

### Process discipline

The group needs to monitor its use of feedback, especially during the devil's advocate round in stage 4, and make sure that it is clean. The role of process guardian can be rotated round the group if people feel the need for it.

### Size of the group

Two people can do an effective peer review audit, although of course they are short on peer variety and peer feedback. Eight is probably a maximum number, especially for the presentation of self-assessments. With 20 or so people on a training programme, I usually work in groups of five.

### Composition of the group

The basic premise is that the group consists of peers from the same profession. But there are important variations. You can have a hierarchical group within the same profession; for example, a group of hospital doctors that includes a consultant, senior registrar, registrar and junior house doctor; or among teachers, the head, the deputy head, a head of department, a senior teacher and a junior teacher.

Another radical variation is to have mixed practitioner-client audit groups. The professionals audit what they do, and their clients audit what they do in response to what the professionals do. But they work together through all the stages, contributing to each other's different content. There can thus be a very effective conjoint audit of both practice and outcomes.

### Comparable audit groups

Several peer review audit groups within the same profession can run concurrently, and for a time independently. Then they can meet in inter-group exercises to compare and contrast: job definitions, practices identified and chosen for audit, criteria used, central issues of practice to emerge, and so on. In this way a profession can explore its own developing culture: the constancies and variations in values, norms and practices. The intergroup session can also compare the various audit methods used: sampling methods, self-assessment schedules, the use of assessment from others, record-keeping, time on the job between meetings, self-assessment presentation procedures, stages of the audit, and so on.

### Co-operative inquiry

Peer review audit as it stands is a form of peer group action inquiry in the sense in which I have used this term in previous chapters. As such it can readily be included within the format of a full-blown co-operative inquiry – into professional standards, competence, culture and practice. Co-operative inquiry, outlined in Chapter 7, does research with people, not on them. All those involved are both co-researchers in devising, reflectively managing and drawing conclusions from the research, and also co-subjects in experiencing and doing whatever it is that the research is about. They cycle several times between reflection as researchers and action as subjects, and use a variety of validity procedures to keep themselves clear of consensus collusion and other hazards of the method.

I and others have written about this kind of non-alienating research at length elsewhere, advancing central arguments for it and reporting examples of it (Heron, 1996a; Reason, 1988, 1994). Peer review audit is a collaborative action inquiry which cycles between reflection at group meetings and action on the job: it is already ripe for inclusion in the co-operative inquiry format.

### Process commendation

The point of peer review audit is lost if the standards generated and confirmed by one group for itself are used to dictate professional behaviour to any other group or the profession at large. The process is more important than any prescriptive products, and it is this process which is to be commended to other groups within the profession, so that they can generate their own dynamic standards.

### Global audit

I have stressed the importance for beginners of not taking on more than one area of practice, so that they are not over-taxed in getting to grips with the basics of the method. But once they have done so over a few cycles, then they can consider the possibility of the occasional global audit, which I mentioned in stage 7 above as a way of balancing the claims of convergence and divergence. A global audit takes the whole job as the area of practice, and treats each of its main parts as criteria of competence. It then uses the principle of intuitive feel for a good pattern in scoring performance under each criterion on, say, a five-point scale. This audit uses very broad brush-strokes in keeping diary notes of performance, and in self-assessment of that performance. It is too imprecise for the beginner, but can be very fruitful after someone has mastered the more precise format by looking at a small part of the job.

# 9 Peer Support Groups

This chapter describes several different kinds of peer support group, alluded too at the end of item 11 on peer review audit, autonomous mode, meaning dimension, Chapter 6. It develops the theme of facilitator authority being used to enhance the emergence of self and peer determination in an independent group that, once launched, runs indefinitely without any dominant facilitator. Such a group is a forum within which people can find and give their own meaning to their professional and personal lives. Hence it is within the autonomous mode on the meaning dimension. It combines whole person learning with autonomy in the learning process, allied with co-operative empowerment from peers.

## The Concept of a Peer Support Group

I use 'peer support group' as a generic term for any kind of group in which people meet on a regular basis to help each other develop their personal or professional lives in the world. It is peer run, with an agreed structure within which members may rotate time-keeping and other roles, and has no permanent leader. The structure can be reviewed at intervals and revised in the light of consensus experience. In the previous chapter I discussed one special kind of peer support group – peer review audit – and there are many more of less rigorous format which can have a liberating and transformative influence. In this chapter I review just a few of these.

In our emotionally repressive, competitive society, in which competence anxiety abounds amid mutual fear and suspicion, people need encouragement and guidelines to start peer support groups. Hence the case for including the experience of an appropriate kind of group towards the end of a training programme. The facilitator can propose an initial format, have people try it out, then gather in feedback afterwards and in this context raise consciousness about the various issues involved in running it effectively.

The argument for peer support groups runs as follows:

- Persons are only persons in active relation with other persons.
- Persons develop holistically in learning relations with other developing persons in reference to real-life situations.
- A culture or sub-culture ceases to be oppressive when its members meet in small groups to revise its norms, values and social practices in their individual and collective lives, personal and professional.
- A liberating culture is one which is self-generating and self-renewing through such autonomous, whole person, peer learning and inquiry.

Peer support groups can deal with personal life, professional issues, or the interface between the two. When they deal with professional issues, I call them peer supervision groups: these will usually have members from the same profession, to get the benefit of insider know-how. But there is also a case for the occasional mixed profession group, where, in effect, other members will give an intelligent lay person's view of what the focal member presents. I have known experienced doctors benefit greatly from lay feedback on situations of deep professional concern.

The agenda of peer support groups can cover difficulties, problems and thorny issues; or affirm joys, successes and creative achievements. It may uncover what is past, examine what is current or prepare for the future. It is invariably committed to transformation, either in the sense of enhancing the value that is present, or manifesting the value that is absent. And it may use imaginal techniques, analytic techniques, emotional techniques or practical techniques.

## *Running a Peer Support Group*

Here are a few suggestions, based on my experience, for setting up a peer support group:

- Meetings can be for 2 to 3 hours every 2 to 3 weeks.
- With a membership pool of 15 people, an average of 8 or more may attend at each session.
- Those who want a turn say how much time they each need and negotiate with each other until the times for the turns fit the total time available. Turns may be of different lengths to meet people's

differing needs. Not everyone who attends a given meeting may need or want a turn
- The person who takes a turn says how he or she wants to divide the time and to use each portion, and asks another member to keep time and call out when each portion is up. It works best if people keep to the discipline of their overall time, although they may want to rearrange the size of the portions once they get going.

The group may want to allow time for a short opening and closing ritual, and, before the closing ritual, a few minutes for a brief process review of how the session has been for everyone, including any ideas for modifying the procedure. And after ten sessions or so, the group will need a whole session for an extended review of the method, of its strengths and weaknesses, possibly leading to major or minor revisions of the whole format.

## Helpful Ground-rules for a Peer Support Group

Here are some suggestions for ground-rules that help to bring the group process alive:

- Be co-operative, supportive, and non-competitive.
- Find strength in the acceptance and disclosure of your growing points, where you are vulnerable, unknowing and unskilled. Avoid any kind of window-dressing and image-building in what you present.
- Listen fully to others and attend to what they say and how they say it and how they are being and what they are doing when they say it.
- Give both positive and negative feedback with an equal sense of the worth of the person to whom either is addressed.
- When giving negative feedback, make sure it tells the truth with love, and is free of either evasive pussyfooting, or punitive sledge-hammering.
- Give the group a committed priority in organizing your time; and attend the group whether you need to take time in it for yourself or not.

I now give a selection of peer support group methods which I believe are particularly valuable. I start with those that have a professional focus, including one on the professional/personal interface, and I call these peer supervision. I move on to those that are concerned with

personal life, and I call these peer unfoldment. There is nothing especially sacrosanct about the various formats, and while they have been
tried and tested, new groups may well want to introduce creative
variations to suit their own needs and interests. For an account of a
range of methods that peer support groups could incorporate see
Huczynski (1983).

## Peer Supervision: Critical Incident Focus

Members bid for time, and each one who takes a turn divides it into
three portions. The whole procedure is given in summary form in
Figure 9.1. Suppose it is your turn, then:

| STAGE 1 | STAGE 2 | STAGE 3 |
|---|---|---|
| | Your peers take it in turn to comment on any one or more of the following: | You choose to do one or more of the following: |
| You present a critical incident/issue | The other<br>Your intervention<br>The relationship<br>The wider context<br>Your presentation<br>Their inner reactions<br>Similar experiences<br>Relevant information<br>Practical strategies<br>Invitation to work | Review opening presentation<br>Make an action plan<br>Personal development work<br>Projected rehearsal |

**Figure 9.1**    *Peer supervision: critical incident focus*

### Stage 1

You lay bare some critical issue from recent or current professional
practice, something that exposes you to your limitations, that
presents a challenge.

### Stage 2

You hear a statement from each of your peers, listening carefully and
without entering into any dialogue with them, except to ask the occasional clarifying question. Suppose you have described some recent
problematic encounter with a client, then your peers can comment in
any one or more of the following ten ways:

- They may raise an issue about what the client has said or done, or not said or not done; and in general about the client's state and situation.
- They may focus on your interventions in relation to the client.
- They may attend to the relationship and the process between you and the client, including all aspects of transference and counter-transference.
- They may deal with wider contextual issues to do with the organizational and cultural patterns of oppression within which you and the client are set.
- They may comment on how you have presented the problem, the story-line, the choice of language, the tone of voice, the non-verbal manner, and draw some inference from this about what you are carrying from the encounter, or what you are mirroring about the encounter with the client, or about the wider context.
- They may disclose their own images, fantasies, thoughts, emotions, of a kind that seem to have been irrationally stirred up by what you are saying, and present this as their reception of something unaware going on in you, in your relation with your client, or with the wider context.
- They may share their own experience of a similar kind so that you may learn something from it by way of comparison and contrast.
- They may offer some relevant piece of information, or refer you to some useful article, report or book, or suggest you talk to a colleague or friend of theirs.
- They may offer policies or practical strategies for you to consider using on yourself, your client or the process between you and your client, or in relation to the context.
- They may invite you to do some piece of personal work on yourself, or some skills practice through role play, here and now in front of the group.

## Stage 3. You Can Do One or More of the Following Four Things

- You can review your opening presentation in the light of what your peers have said, and note which of their comments you need to take on board, after discriminating selectively amongst them. It is important that this does not degenerate into a defensive rejection of those you do not want to accept.
- You can make an action plan, in which you commit yourself to try out certain behaviours in future incidents of the sort you have been presenting.

- You can engage in some piece of personal development work pertinent to the issue, either self-directed or facilitated by a member whose competence you respect.
- You can practise some relevant skill through the use of a short role play, trying out interventions that you were unable to make and that would be useful in the sort of situation you reported. This is called projected rehearsal.

### Facilitation

Here are some useful tips for the facilitator to remember when introducing and monitoring the process as part of a training programme.

- It is helpful if group members are familiar with the ten different sorts of statements they can make, given above. Each member needs to get more and more skilled in using the whole repertoire; and the members as a team need to balance the various sorts when giving feedback to the one who is taking a turn. In this way the feedback will be multi-perspectival, giving an in-depth reflection of what has been presented. Peter Hawkins and Robin Shohet (1989) have written a comprehensive book on supervision which is full of fruitful ideas which peer supervision groups can use.
- Comment and feedback of any sort is contaminated and offensive when it includes words such as 'ought', 'should' and 'must'. Suggesting practical strategies, no. 9 on the list, needs to be free of any kind of patronage.
- A key issue throughout the whole procedure is how much the presenter is (a) caught up in rigidities and compulsions that are run by unresolved distress from the past, (b) held up by limiting conventional assumptions derived from a rigid social system, and (c) the victim of simple ignorance and lack of skill, or (d) involved in some combination of these. Peer feedback that can help raise consciousness supportively about these matters is useful.
- When people take their turn as presenter, they need to give some thought to the length of each of the three stages, and to have some idea of what might be best for the final stage. A piece of personal work or the rehearsal of a skill at the end may need more time than a selective taking on board of what the peers have said. Over several turns, there is a tendency to avoid these two action methods by always choosing the verbal summing up. The group needs to have a clear contract and commitment about the relevance and importance of the action methods.

- It is a good idea for people to be flexible about how they divide their overall time. On different occasions they may want to allocate very different proportions to the three stages. They may also want to rearrange the stages, for example, presenting a problem first, then doing some personal work or a skills building role play, then gathering in feedback from their peers.
- Members may want to record their peers' comments on audiotape, or to ask someone to act as scribe and write down what they say.
- Diana Cortazzi and Susan Roote developed a model of illuminative incident analysis for a group of staff who work together as a team. The team members choose a critical incident in which they have all been involved, each person represents this with a drawing, then takes it in turn to exaggerate the drawing in order to probe the attitudes and actions of those involved (Cortazzi and Roote, 1975).

## Peer Supervision: Good News Analysis

In this group, members bid for time and divide their time into three parts.

### Stage 1

You present some piece of your own professional practice that went well: you describe what happened first, and then seek to identify what factors contributed to your success. There are four sorts of factor here:

- What is going on in your client.
- What is going on in you the practitoner.
- What is going on in your client–practitioner interaction.
- What is going on in the wider social contexts of which either or both of you are part.

### Stage 2

The peers can now give:

- Supportive feedback on the manner of presentation.
- Supportive feedback in terms of subliminal impacts, images, thoughts, sensations, energy movements, that occurred in them during the presentation.

- Their affirmation of and agreement with the presenter's account of contributing factors.
- Their opinion about what other factors may also have contributed to the presenter's success.

## Stage 3

You say anything else you need to say after the peers have spoken, and you again affirm and celebrate what you have done and what you have shared.

## Facilitation

The idea of this group is to get learning, motivation and uplift out of good news. When introducing this experience within a training programme, the facilitator needs to alert people to several issues.

- It is important that the exercise is entirely free of subtle competitive window-dressing and image-building, with members tacitly vying with each other to parade their successes. So it is as well to encourage them to enjoy the celebration of genuine competence in a spirit of mutual support, and to eschew the displacement of insecurity into aggressive accounts of real competence or bolstered reports of pseudo-competence.
- One way a group can control for this is to have a fallback devil's advocate procedure. If members feel that the manner of a presentation is aggressive-competitive or its content is phoney, they put on a special hat such as a sombrero, kept ready in the wings. This announces that they are about to speak as the devil's advocate. They then give their confronting feedback. Anyone else who supports the feedback, takes the hat and says so. Anyone who disagrees says so, in this case without the hat. The presenter does not respond to any of this, but listens attentively, taking on board what he or she needs to hear, and continues the presentation modifying it or not as he or she thinks appropriate in the light of the feedback.
- Some members may be uncertain and diffident about their successes, or feel they have to be able to report a big piece of good news, a real triumph of skill or caring or creativity. A good ground-rule here is that effective micro-events are as important to share as valuable macro-events.

Good news analysis complements critical incident focus (covered in the previous section), so sessions of the latter can be interspersed with some sessions of the former, or vice versa; or a group could experiment with alternating between the two. What is clearly important is that peer supervision groups do not fall foul of the idea that all learning and development comes from processing mistakes and confusions. The affirmation and analysis of success is extremely potent in generating further growth.

## Peer Supervision: Actual Practice

This is a good model for counsellors and psychotherapists, although demanding. It has four main stages.

### Stage 1

The group members agree on a basic set of criteria for assessing the competent practice of one-to-one psychotherapy and write these up on a wall-chart. A set of six criteria works best, because it is manageable for feedback rounds (see below). The set may include things like: not falling foul of counter-transference; giving space for client self-direction; commanding a suitable range of interventions; and so on. Reaching agreement on this set may take up the whole of the first meeting.

### Stage 2

At the next meeting, one of the group starts the thing off by saying he or she wants to be the first client. This means being a real client, with something real to work on. As in the market place this client chooses any one of the other members to be their therapist. It is a ground-rule of the group that when chosen for this role you do not demur.

### Stage 3

The therapist member works with the client member for 30 minutes. It is best to have a standard time for this, so that it applies to everyone taking a turn as therapist. This means that all therapists and clients have parity of opportunity. Half an hour gives both of them enough time to make some useful headway, while giving space for perhaps two other 30 minute sessions at the same meeting.

## *Stage 4*

Immediately after the session, the therapist gives him or herself feed-back in the light of the agreed criteria, then the client gives the thera-pist feedback in the light of the criteria, and then everyone else in the group does so. In each case the person giving this feedback looks at both strengths and weaknesses under each criterion. The therapist may want to take notes of all this, or appoint a scribe to do so, or record it on audiotape. The therapist just listens to the feedback and does not respond or comment, but can ask clarifying questions. After all the feedback has been given, the therapist may simply want to digest it, or may want to revise his or her original self-assessment and say which bits of feedback he or she is particularly aware of needing to take on board.

This whole process is then repeated perhaps another two times in the same meeting, with each self-appointed client choosing a different therapist from among the group. Sometimes just two sessions in a meeting will be quite enough for the time and energy available.

As well as a brief process review at the end of each meeting, there will be the periodic whole meeting process review, at which the set of criteria and the format are reappraised and perhaps modified.

## *Facilitation*

This kind of peer supervision is rigorous and exacting. It generates considerable anxiety among members until the group is under way and gets used to the exposure. Here are some of the main issues that can arise.

- The therapist's self-assessment can sometimes degenerate into blaming the client for being a bad client. There needs to be a ground-rule that the client or other group member will interrupt this when the therapist, or anyone else in their feedback, slips into it. While it is impossible for no reference at all to be made to what the client was saying and doing, in general the full focus of the feedback needs to be about the therapist's performance. In one group of this kind I was in, the first therapist to take a turn got into blaming the client through sheer anxiety.
- The complementary degeneration to that of hunting down the client, is for group members to scapegoat the bad therapist and attack someone in an overdetermined way for evident incompe-tence. What is needed here is supportive and uncompromising

consciousness-raising about the weakness, not displacement of group members' distress into destructive punishment.

- There is a further degeneration of tacit consensus collusion to the effect that 'I will be gentle with your performance so that you will be gentle with mine'. Feedback praises good points under each criterion and plays down or ignores the bad points. The meeting becomes anodyne with an excess of mutual approval. This needs to be exposed and interrupted.

- The short process review at the end of each meeting can be used to check to what extent, if any, these three degenerations occurred during any of the feedback sessions.

- This form of peer supervision is, in effect, a sort of short-term peer review audit (discussed in detail in the previous chapter) which combines self-assessment with immediate peer assessment on work done. But the work done is a one-off on someone in the group, whereas a real peer audit group of therapists would be assessing work done over a period of some weeks with regular clients. So I think this is best classified as a radical form of peer supervision.

## Peer Supervision: Veridical Report

This model was developed by a group of medical practitioners which I initiated into peer supervision in West London and proved to have great staying power. Its virtue, and the learning derived from it, depend on its simplicity and the integrity of the participants. I will describe it in medical terms, but it can be applied by other professions.

One basic clinical entity, such as hypertension, or low back pain, or middle-ear disease, is stated in advance as the topic. At the meeting you take turns to state exactly and truthfully what you actually do in such a case. The ground-rule here is that you are ruthlessly honest and report veridically what you practise in the privacy of your consulting room. This is a warts and all account: it includes intuitive or improper shortcuts, obsessive over-caution, deviations from or elaborations of standard procedure, innovations and eccentricities and alternatives, as well as conventional routines.

Other members can ask clarifying questions about what you have reported, but they do not pronounce judgment on it or give an opinion about it. Both in the reporting and the questioning it is a foul to use the words 'should', 'ought' or 'must'. And the word 'foul' is called out by anyone or everyone if any of these words are used.

What is going on in such a group is that as the different and absolutely veridical reports are presented side by side, each member is making comparisons and contrasts among all of them, and especially with his or her own. What this leads to, for each person, is a significant tacit reappraisal of standards of competent practice in relation to the clinical entity being reported on. But each person comes away with an idiosyncratic set of revised standards. Of course, standards are not always revised; existing ones may simply be confirmed.

### Facilitation

The effectiveness of this group as a form of peer supervision entirely depends on the fullness of the veridical reports. When I attended a process review of the medical group that had been using this model for some time, it became clear how members had soon discovered that if the reports degenerate into window-dressing and false image-building, the whole thing loses impact, becoming soporific and pointless. It was their high standard of honesty that had given the group its long life.

## Peer Supervision: Projected Rehearsal

This is a good model for people who are embarking on a phase of innovation in their professional practice, such as teachers in higher education who want to introduce holistic learning or more student self-direction into their classes, or traditional verbal therapists who want to start using client-centred action methods. What they need is an opportunity to overcome the anxiety of trying out something new and to build up confidence and finesse in doing it. This is where projected rehearsal comes in. It involves practising actual professional behaviour in a role play with one's peers.

It is also a good model for those who are introducing change at the political level, that is, proposing innovation at committee and board meetings or individually to senior (or junior) staff. And, of course, it is of benefit to anyone who has mismanaged some past critical and recurrent situation, and wants to practise competent ways of handling it in the future.

Once this group is under way, each meeting will open with report-back time for accounts of what has been carried through from previous role plays into real-life action. This is followed by the main part of the meeting, which is practice time for rehearsal in new role plays. After bidding for practice time, each protagonist in turn goes through the following procedure.

## Stage 1

Divide your time into three parts: the first is for your proposal and feedback on it; the second is for your role play enactment and feedback on it; the third is for final review and reflection, and a practical commitment to real-life application. The second period is the main one and needs to be the longest. Appoint a time-keeper to move you on from part to part.

## Stage 2

You outline what you wish to practise now, with whom you will apply it in your future work and your reasons for wanting to do all this. Then sketch out a provisional role play design.

## Stage 3

Your peers give you feedback and comment on these intentions. They may endorse what you have said, or build on your design. They may explore the reasons you have given, or the wider contractual and contextual issues. They may raise issues of appropriateness on behalf of the recipients of what you intend. They may suggest revisions of what you wish to practise or of the role play design.

## Stage 4

You digest all this, take it on board or not as you are moved, make a final statement about your role play design and what you are going to do in it; then coach group members to play the roles of the real-life recipients.

## Stage 5

You do the role play and if you feel at all dissatisfied with any part of your performance, immediately halt the play and keep re-running that bit, with feedback from your peers on each re-run, until you and your peers are happy with it. Your peers too can halt the play, propose feedback and a re-run, as soon as they see you throw away your power and slip verbally or posturally into anxiety, insecurity and defensiveness.

## Stage 6

Your time-keeper now moves you on to the final stage of review, reflection and commitment. You review the whole practice and reflect aloud upon it, then hear your peers do the same, and let this lead into a group discussion of the central issues.

## Stage 7

You make a closing commitment to follow through on this practice in real-life in a specific situation on a stated date; and to report back on how it went at the next meeting after that date.

The next meeting opens with report-back time in which each person who has something to report takes a minute or two to do so and to listen to whatever the peers are moved to say. Sometimes members may want to replace their practice time with an extended report-back time because they got in a tangle when trying something out on the job and need to get clear about it, in which case they can use the critical incident format given above. Another model is to alternate a projected rehearsal meeting with a whole meeting of report-back – using the critical incident format – on real-life application.

## Facilitation

When running a projected rehearsal session in a training programme, there are some key points for the facilitator to underline.

- The main learning is in the practice, especially the re-runs based on perceptive feedback. Encourage people to learn the art of multiple re-runs, often on quite small areas of behaviour – a phrase or a sentence and its associated vocal and non-verbal manner – in which personal power is lost and thrown away. The protagonist keeps the re-runs going and modifies them until he or she feels what it is like for that bit of behaviour to carry authentic personal power rather than lose it. Also exhort people to learn to notice those verbal and non-verbal cues – in themselves and in others – in which the loss of power is evident, so that they can give effective feedback.
- It is always best if protagonists give feedback to themselves first, so they get used to self-observation and self-assessment and do not become dependent on the perceptions of others for their self-knowledge. Even when you, as facilitator or peer, interrupt role

plays because protagonists have given away power in a phrase, you still ask them first what they notice about what they have just said and done, before you give your perception of it.

- The important thing is to make sure the biggest block of time is devoted to the actual performance of the role play, and to move people on promptly from stage 1 of talking about it, to stage 2 of doing it. Newcomers especially will put off the challenge of learning through action by discussing the issues involved, the background factors and everything else that delays the moment of experiential reckoning. This changes once people have come to terms with the risks involved and are exhilarated by the outcomes.

- What is usually at stake when someone is contemplating introducing innovation in the classroom or anywhere else is their projected anxiety about being rejected by the recipients. Once their behaviour when introducing the innovation is in the grip of this anxiety, then it makes the anxiety self-fulfilling: the behaviour is so off-key and disempowered that it produces rejection. Chapter 12 on charismatic training deals with this issue in depth and many of the methods described there need to be applied in projected rehearsal. Basically, people need to learn in action to put their personal power forth in a manner that elicits excitement and positive anticipation in recipients.

## Peer Supervision: Confession Dinner

This is another classic medical model, which I have developed for any profession.

### Stage 1

The group members meet for a meal.

### Stage 2

When it is over and the group is entirely alone without possibility of interruption, a bell is rung and there is silence.

### Stage 3

Anyone who is moved to do so rises to their feet and makes confession of just one item, which may be anything from among the following sorts of misbegotten behaviour.

- **Gross professional negligence.** This is about mistakes made, whether from ignorance, inadequate skill, carelessness, laziness, self-interest, irresponsible delegation, fatigue, illness, irrational compulsion, drunkenness, addiction or any other inadequacy. This covers both neglecting to do something vitally important for the client's welfare, and doing something entirely mistaken: in both cases with unpleasant consequences for the client. There is clearly a gradient here. In the medical case, it runs from the unnecessary removal of the patient's appendix to the unnecessary loss of the patient's life. And each profession will have its range from the minor to the major disaster.
- **Gross professional misconduct.** While the previous item is about negligence or error within the occupational task, this one is about stepping right outside the bounds of the role into abuse of the client. There is verbal abuse, denigrating, criticizing, swearing and yelling at the client; physical abuse, hitting and kicking the client or causing other grievous bodily harm; sexual abuse, from seduction through harassment to rape; mental abuse through false information, false doctrine, rejection, threat, exploitation of transference, malicious hypnosis or suggestion, overcontrol and domination; financial abuse through devious extraction of money, gifts and property.
- **Gross unsolicited behaviour.** Here the professional is within the occupational role, but doing major things to or for the client without the client's consent, approval or knowledge. This is a basic infringement of the client's right to self-determination and to be consulted about every important action being taken on their behalf.

## *Stage 4*

After the statement, the bell is rung three times followed by a short silence while everyone takes in what has been said. Then there is a round of applause, which is intended to affirm the person who has spoken for owning and bearing witness to their malfeasance.

The same person may declare any number of items, but each is dealt with separately, followed by the bell, silence and applause, before the next one is announced.

There is no discussion about or comment on any confession that is made by anyone, either at the meeting or afterwards at any time. Everyone takes an oath to this effect at the opening meeting. The only exception to this is at a periodic process review meeting when the whole procedure is reviewed and perhaps modified. One issue that may arise at such a meeting is whether what people are confessing to is appropriate and falls within the guidelines given above or within whatever other guidelines the group has given itself. Particular confessions may well have to be mentioned as evidence in making one's point in such a discussion. Also at issue may be how members are making their confession, and again instances may need to be cited.

The purpose of having a dinner first is to create an ambience of solidarity and mutual support, but any other group activity that has this effect could equally be used.

### Facilitation

The main issues in setting this up or recommending it are to make sure people follow the central ground-rules: there are no eaves-droppers of any kind when the confessions start; there is no comment at any time by anyone about any confession; each confession, even from the same person, is followed by the bell, the silence and the applause; members stand to make their statements. The group can appoint one of their number to be the manager of all this throughout the session, and to interrupt any infringements.

## Peer Supervision: the Personal/Professional Interface

This is a group in which professionals can explore the interaction between their personal and professional lives, issues at the interface. One format to use is the 'critical incident focus' described above. Another is to adapt 'healing the memories' below, and work on the wounded child within the professional helper: perhaps the most radical and far-reaching approach.

## Peer Unfoldment: Life-style Enhancement

I now move on to consider peer support groups that focus on personal development issues in the widest sense, although it is important to stress that such issues can include all work-related matters. This first one on life-style enhancement is perhaps the most broad-ranging.

## Stage 1

At its first meeting, the group generates a wall-chart that covers all the main life-style areas. It may want to pin this up in the meeting room as a general backdrop to its procedure. A life-style map will cover something like the following main categories, although every autonomous group will come up with its own and different version.

- **Socio-economic.** Place and type of residence; money and finance; occupation and career planning; social roles/class; cultural minority status; nationality.
- **Interpersonal.** Friendship, acquaintanceship, colleagueship; intimacy, nurturance, sexuality; gender; parenting; cohabitation; family of origin.
- **Basic self-care.** Social support networks; body care, health and hygiene; pleasure, fun and recreation; enriching the imagination; coping with emotional and physical trauma.
- **Extended development.** Continuing education and training (personal development, interpersonal skills, technical skills, professional competence, hobbies/interests, academic study); creativity and expression; cultural pursuits; social and political action; ecological and planetary concern; psychic and spiritual unfoldment.

Some groups may prefer to do without a life-style map, since any map makes each item look too cut off from everything else, whereas in reality all aspects of a life-style interact.

## Stage 2

At the next meeting the group will start with those who want it bidding for time. When presenting, you divide your time into three parts, and in the first part choose any area of life that you want to enhance by developing or changing it. You describe your situation saying what is going on, how active or inactive you are in the area, how satisfied or dissatisfied, how liberated or oppressed, and whether you want to leave it as it is, modify it or change it dramatically, and in what way you want to modify or change it. The area can be chosen because there is some problem or deficiency in it; or because it appears to be entirely placid and contented. In other words, you can start with difficult terrain or challenge easy ground. You may also want to adventure into new territory and talk about entering some life-style area that you have never gone into before.

## Stage 3

The next part of your time is for peer feedback to which you listen without comment except for asking the occasional clarifying question when you do not understand properly what is being said. Your peers can comment on many things about your account:

- Your attitudes and actions in the area.
- The other people involved.
- The processes going on between you and them.
- The circumstantial factors.
- The wider social and cultural context.
- Your positive and negative assessment of the situation.
- Your account of wanting to change it or not.
- What is implicit in the manner of your presentation.
- What subliminal impacts, images, emotions and energies they were receiving during your presentation.
- Their own related kind of experience.
- Any relevant information.
- A pertinent strategy for you to consider.
- A proposal for some action method for you to use in your final part.

## Stage 4

The final and third part of your time as presenter is to have a final review of the issues in the light of what has been said, or to make an action plan, or to do some personal development work that is evoked by the presentation, or to use a role play to practise some behaviour pertinent to changes you want to make. The last two of these may need more time than the first two, so it is well to have a sense, when dividing your time at the beginning, of how you want to use the last part of it. You can also combine two or more of these if there is enough time.

## Facilitation

This three-stage procedure mirrors that of critical incident focus in peer supervision for professionals, as in Figure 9.1, but with some additional items the peers may comment on. The same sorts of useful tip are relevant for the facilitator to remember when introducing life-style enhancement as part of a training programme.

- It is helpful if group members are familiar with the many different sorts of statements they can make when giving feedback. They are listed above in the account of stage 3. Each member needs to acquire skill in using the whole repertoire; and the members as a team need to balance the various sorts when giving feedback to the one who is taking a turn. In this way the feedback will be multi-perspectival, giving an in-depth reflection of what has been presented.
- Comment and feedback of any sort is contaminated and offensive when it includes words such as 'ought', 'should' and 'must'.
- A key issue throughout the whole procedure is how much the presenter is (a) caught up in rigidities and compulsions that are run by unresolved distress from the past, (b) held up by the oppressive conventional assumptions of a rigid social system, and (c) the victim of simple ignorance and lack of skill, or (d) involved in some combination of these. Peer feedback that can help raise consciousness supportively about these matters is useful.
- When people take their turn as presenter, they need to give some thought to the length of each of the three stages, and to have some idea of what might be best for the final stage. A piece of personal work or the rehearsal of a skill at the end may need more time than a selective taking on board of what the peers have said. Over several turns, there is a tendency to avoid these two action methods by always choosing the verbal summing up. The group needs to have a clear contract and commitment about the relevance and importance of the action methods.
- It is a good idea for people to be flexible about how they divide their overall time. On different occasions they may want to allocate very different proportions to the three stages. They may also want to rearrange the stages, for example, presenting a life-style issue first, then doing some personal work or a skills-building role play, then gathering in feedback from their peers.
- Members may want to record their peers' comments on audiotape, or to ask someone to act as scribe and write down what they say.

## Peer Unfoldment: Celebration, Affirmation and Visualization

The purpose of this group is to build on strengths and accentuate the positive. Everyone takes equal time. There is no bidding for time, or some people 'not needing' time. The commitment is that you always take a turn, especially when you don't feel like it. Each person's turn proceeds in three stages which are paced over the time available.

## *Stage 1*

You celebrate, without negative qualification of any sort, what is going well for you currently in your life, or what recent event was good news, or what remoter past event was good news. You may mention several events, but you keep to one basic theme, so the events are all instances of the same theme. Everyone applauds.

## *Stage 2*

You frame the same theme into a strong verbal affirmation, a positive direction for your life now and in the future, and repeat the affirmation slowly, aloud, several times, varying the language until you get it feeling right. Everyone applauds.

## *Stage 3*

You visualize and describe out loud very precisely and clearly a future event in your life which thoroughly fulfils this theme. Everyone in the group says together 'This will be so'.

## *Facilitation*

When taking people through this for their first time, remind them that life is full of large and small jewels, buds or seed-pods of experience that often seem to get left by the wayside, their potential unfulfilled, their promise prematurely abandoned or swept aside in the pressure of the day. Remind them also that every day has hints of what it could be, if the fullness of personhood within were creatively manifest.

- Interrupt, and train group members to interrupt with a friendly but clear signal, any drift into negative qualification in stage 1. In the same way make sure that the affirmations and the visualization, stages 2 and 3 respectively, are free of any such qualification. This means the presenter keeps revising the same statement until it is free of both verbal and non-verbal detractors.
- Some members may be diffident about good news in their lives, or feel they must report a big piece of good news. A good ground-rule here is that very small positive happenings and choices are as

important to affirm as the large ones; or even more important because of their hidden potential. So too with long-past events.

- Occasionally by the principle of opposites, strong unqualified celebrations and affirmations may flip the presenter into distressed memories from his or her personal past. It is definitely not the purpose of the method to induce this kind of flip, nevertheless it can sometimes occur. If this is a minor flip with not much charge on it, it is best to ignore it and just refocus the mind on the positive statements. If it is a major flip, with the presenter already in catharsis, then it makes sense to go with it and clear it. Co-counselling training, or the equivalent, can be useful here (see under 'healing the memories' below). After clearing it, then the presenter gets right back on track with the celebration, affirmation or visualization. Those in the group with appropriate skills can rotate the role of cathartic facilitator, whose job it is to take the presenter through the release until it is appropriately cleared for that time.

- In order to keep the exercise free of insecure posturing and deluded self-inflation, the group can be trained to use a devil's advocate procedure. If members feel that the manner of a presentation is posturing or deluded, they put on a special hat such as a sombrero, kept ready in the wings. This announces that they are about to speak as the devil's advocate. They then give their confronting feedback. Anyone else who supports the feedback, takes the hat and says so. Anyone who disagrees says so, in this case without the hat. The presenter does not respond to any of this, but listens attentively, taking on board what he or she needs to hear, and continues the presentation modifying it or not as he or she thinks appropriate in the light of the feedback. This method has to be handled with great skill. It degenerates badly when it is used by someone in the group who is too distressed to acknowledge a genuine celebration.

## Peer Unfoldment: Projected Rehearsal

This is the same procedure as that given above under 'Peer supervision: projected rehearsal'. Here it is used to practise behaviour for some impending event in one's personal life that is felt to be challenging, threatening, demanding, or whatever. It can be used by both women and men to practise being assertive in future situations where they are likely to lose personal power or give it away.

## *Peer Unfoldment: Healing the Memories*

This is a group in which people support each other in healing the wounded child within. In an emotionally repressive society, the wounded child within each adult is a universal phenomenon, and an increasing number of practitioner-theorists acknowledge this point (Miller, 1987). Many people go to a psychotherapist to deal with this, but one of the problems of professionalizing the process of healing – with resultant imbalance of roles and power – is that the therapy situation can only too readily reproduce the original abuse all over again.

Another approach has been the use of peer self-help psychotherapy groups. The one that I have most experience of, and can vouch for, is co-counselling as practised by groups affiliated to Co-counselling International (Heron, 1998b). This is the method I would recommend for a peer support group working with the wounded child. Those who want to use it will need to go to a basic co-counselling training, which is available in most main centres.

Co-counsellors work in pairs, taking it in turns to be client and counsellor. Thus in a two-hour session, for the first hour A is client and B is counsellor, and for the second hour they reverse roles. Co-counsellors are trained in a range of simple strategies which undo the repressive barrier holding down memories of childhood trauma and distress, and provide for the reliving of the memories and the discharge of the distress. So there occurs the catharsis of grief through crying and sobbing, fear through shaking and trembling, anger through harmlessly directed storming sounds and movements, embarrassment through laughter. The point of this release is the spontaneous insight which follows it, leading to a re-evaluation of the hurtful childhood situation that caused the distress, and a reap-praisal of one's current life free of projected hidden trauma. This combination of old pain released and restructuring insight gives a person more inner freedom to live their life less driven by the compulsions of the wounded child within.

The techniques are used by the client in a self-directed way, as much as by the counsellor on the client. And this strong affirmation of the possibility and practice of client self-direction, saves co-counselling from some of the abuse problems of traditional one-way therapy, where techniques tend always to be in the hands of the therapist.

A peer support group using this method can break up into co-counselling pairs for a series of shorter or longer sessions, with changes of partners for each session. Sessions can be on whatever each client wants and needs to work on; or in some sessions the clients in every pair can work on the same theme. Another powerful option is for the group to stay as a whole and each person in turn takes an equal amount of time to work on what they want, or on an agreed theme. Each client can choose to work in an entirely self-directed way, or with just one other chosen person as counsellor. In either case, the rest of the group give intense, sustained supportive and silent attention.

### Facilitation

The major facilitation issues affecting a group of this sort will have been dealt with at the basic co-counselling training. They relate to the techniques used, the roles of client and counsellor, different contracts between client and counsellor, the importance of equal time, never more than one counsellor when clients take turns in a group, the quality of attention in the counsellor, the balance of attention in the client, and so on. The peer support group can rotate at each meeting the role of facilitator whose sole job is to co-ordinate group decision-making about how to structure the total time available.

## Peer Unfoldment: Invoking the Empowering Future

Healing the wounded child redeems the past; its complement is a form of peer support which invokes the empowering future. It is helpful if members of this group happen to have done some co-counselling training or are otherwise competent in regression work; but it is not at all essential, for this group looks entirely to the future. Members can either work in pairs taking equal turns to be invoker and witness, or can take equal turns as invoker in the whole group with everyone else being witnesses.

What the invoker does is to assume a strong psychic and spiritual affinity with quite specific creatively advanced and worthwhile future events, and the people involved in them. These events are well beyond the likely span of the invokers' earthly lives. So the invoker chooses a time well into the future, say 300 years hence, when things will be very different from now, but not so different that the imaging power falters with doubt and uncertainty. He or she tunes in and feels this time ahead, and then starts to allow the images that form, whether visual, auditory or kinaestheic, to become more and more distinct by describing them fully. What is being described is a real situation with real people in a real environment in a real part of time and space on this planet. It just happens to be in the future.

Towards the end of their time, the invoker describes how her or his current life can be empowered by drawing into it, and shaping it with, some of the liberating and creative aspects of the future scenes just envisioned.

## *Facilitation*

What this exercise needs is that people have faith in their ability to feel the future and in their imaging power. So it is as well for the facilitator introducing this method in a training session to affirm clearly both these competencies in everyone present.

- Encourage invokers to go with their imagery, however slight and faint, and to describe it immediately. The description fosters the imagery, and the imagery empowers the description. Once this mutual enhancement takes off, remarkably clear scenes will come before the mind's eye or ear or kinaesthetic sense.
- Occasionally by the principle of opposites, envisioning a positive future may flip the invoker into distressed memories from his or her personal past. It is definitely not the purpose of the method to induce this kind of flip, nevertheless it can sometimes occur. If this is a minor flip with not much charge on it, it is best to ignore it and just refocus the mind on the future. If it is a major flip, with the invoker already in catharsis, then it makes sense to go with it and clear it. This is where co-counselling training can be useful. After clearing it, then the invoker gets right back on track and is off into the future again.
- The witness gives abundant supportive attention to the invoker, and makes no comment on and asks no questions about what the invoker describes as long as the invoker is going well. But when the invoker falters, seems to lose faith in the images and slows down the description, then the witness can ask questions that help to develop the flow of imagery and descriptions. Otherwise the witness only bears witness.

# *10 The Confronting Dimension*

This chapter returns to a detailed account of the core model of the six dimensions and three modes of facilitation. It considers the third dimension, the confronting aspect of facilitation, which is to do with how to raise consciousness about resistances to, and avoidances of, things that need to be faced and dealt with. Because of such resistance and avoidance, there is a block, a rigidity, a restriction in the dynamic of the group, so that learning is distorted or held back.

## *Sources of Rigidity*

What the nature of the resisting and avoiding is, takes us back to Chapter 4. There I looked at three negative forms of the group dynamic, each giving a different perspective on resistant rigidity in the group. I will mention them again briefly here, and add two further sources of such blockage.

1. **Educational alienation.**   If the group is limited to just one kind of learning objective, then its members can become rigid and alienated in their way of being: intellect cut off from emotions and the spirit; emotions cut off from the intellect and the spirit; the spirit cut off from both intellect and emotions; etc.
2. **Cultural oppression.**   Group behaviour is constrained into resistant blocks by oppressive norms and values which members bring with them from the surrounding culture.
3. **Psychological defensiveness.**   Group behaviour is seized into distorted, defensive forms by an uprush of existential and archaic anxieties – arising, respectively, from unowned present and past distress – which are stirred up by issues arising simply from being in the group, and from what happens in the group
4. **Underdevelopment.**   Group members lack knowledge, competence and cultivated awareness – in the area of some special skills,

or about group process, or about the learning process, or all of these. Such ignorance creates its own kind of blind, resistant inertia.

5. **Easy street.**   Group members go for the soft option, the familiar ground, the comfortable and the convenient. This is basically an avoidance of risk-taking, the preference for no challenge: the lotus-eating, pleasure-seeking rigidity.

Of course, these five processes overlap and reinforce each other. But there are times when each one of them can appear quite noticeably in its own right, even though one or more of the others will be somewhere in the background.

## *Elements and Purposes of Confrontation*

When you, the facilitator, want to confront any of these five processes, there are three things about which you can raise group members' consciousness, and there is a purpose you may have in mind in addressing each of them:

1. **The issue.**   You want the group members to become aware of the threatening issue being avoided, so that they can address it and move the learning into it. In Chapter 4, I gave the following list of such issues:
   ● Authority and control.
   ● Conflict and aggression.
   ● Intimacy and contact.
   ● Love and care.
   ● Sexuality and gender.
   ● Identity and purpose.
   ● Disclosure and expression.
   ● Truth and honesty.
   ● Mastery and competence.
   ● Knowledge and ignorance.
   ● Psychic awareness and spirituality.
2. **The rigid avoidance behaviour.**   You also want them to become aware of one or other of the defensive forms of behaviour that is doing the avoiding, so that they can see it for what it is and abandon it for a more adventurous form. In Chapter 4, I gave the following account of such behaviours:
   ● **Submission.**   Group members displace their combined existential and archaic anxiety into a family of distorted passive

behaviours. They may become compulsively dependent on the group leader, or any rival leader, blindly following, seeking permission. They may show signs of withdrawal and shut-down, of powerlessness, loss of identity and of compulsive guilt. They are inwardly isolated, alienated, and constrained by tacit norms that inhibit intimacy, emotion and contact.

- **Flight.** The anxiety is displaced into compulsive flight from the real issues emerging within the life of the group. The indications of such flight are: irrelevant theorizing and generalizing; jocularity; gossip about trivialities; persistently talking about the world outside the group; 'rescuing' someone from the brink of real personal work and self-disclosure; compulsive questioning of someone in the group; retreating into a collusive pair with some other group member; insisting on a clear task, a programme, a conventional goal.

- **Attack.** The anxiety is displaced into compulsive attack. The group leader is resisted, his or her proposals rejected, his or her authority, relevance or competence challenged. One or more group members may compete in a rival bid for leadership; or become locked in mutual aggression. Some group member may be scapegoated – irrationally blamed, invalidated, criticized, accused, labelled and stereotyped. The room and other physical facilities may be continuously complained about. Any positive change in the dynamic may be interrupted and wrecked. Good energy is mocked.

- **Conventional inertia.** Cultural and planetary anxiety, when unowned and unprocessed, may displace into a fixation and rigidity of conventional attitudes and behaviour, a defensive clinging to the status quo, a contraction and closure on local established social structures and practices.

- **Transcendental contraction.** Transcendental anxiety, when unowned and unprocessed, may displace into separatist alienation, the illusory belief and attitude that the everyday self is separate from the world, from things and other people, from other dimensions of being, and from universal consciousness-as-such. Ordinary consciousness is focused on everyday choice and on the beliefs that service such choice. It contracts around these individual-centred concerns with a rigid, unyielding separatist illusion.

3. **The source.** Then you want them to identify the source of that behaviour, so that they have more command over it. In the previous section, just above, the following five sources are defined. They can overlap and feed each other.

- Educational alienation.
- Cultural oppression.
- Psychological defensiveness.
- Underdevelopment.
- Easy street.

You can focus on one or other of these three elements – the issue, the rigid behaviour, the source – or on all of them. They are interdependent. Sometimes it is enough to mention the first one. Raising awareness about the issue that is being avoided breaks the block, resistance ceases and members take up the challenge. It may not be necessary to deal with the other two things.

At other times members may have clearly to identify the rigidity and become aware of its source, before they can dislodge themselves from it. In the more extreme case, some resistant behaviour may be so rooted in, for example, archaic distress, that you have to take time out to do personal growth work on this source before you can get any behavioural shift toward the issue. However, confrontation per se is concerned with effecting a behavioural shift by consciousness-raising alone.

## The Process of Confrontation

You need to be respectful and affirmative of persons while being uncompromising about the issue and the rigid behaviour. The ideal is to tell the truth with love, without being the least judgmental, moralistic, oppressive or nagging. You are not attached to what you say: you can let it go as well as hold firmly and uncompromisingly to it.

Because you know the confrontation may be received by group members as something of a shock, the thought of delivering it may make you anxious. If this perfectly normal present-time anxiety gets compounded by archaic anxiety – from old, unfinished confronting agendas of your own past – then all this may distort your confronting behaviour in one of two directions, as shown in Figure 10.1.

At one extreme, you may soft-pedal the delivery, skirt round the issue, and shirk unmasking fully the rigid behaviour; or at worst, you may simply not make the confrontation at all. At the other extreme, you may become heavy-handed, bludgeoning the group in a punitive way.

The first is avoidance behaviour, the second attack behaviour. Both are distortions coming out of your compound anxiety, from which you have not managed to free your intervention.

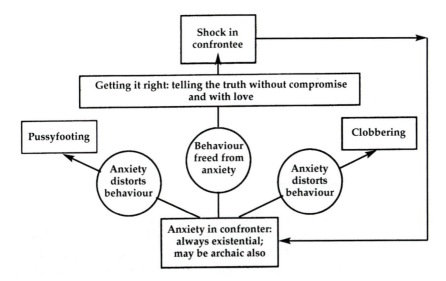

**Figure 10.1** *The process of confrontation*

The challenge is to get it right. Too much love and you collude. Too much power and you oppress. When you get it right, you are on the razor's edge between the two.

## Confronting and Meaning

In several of the interventions below, the confronting and meaning dimensions directly overlap. The strategy – an interpretation – is of the same sort as one in the meaning dimension, but it is also used to shock and awaken people out of their unaware, rigid state.

Nevertheless, the two dimensions are distinct. Many interpretations and other interventions on the meaning dimension have no, and are not intended to have any, confronting impact. Making sense of experience is much wider that uncovering defensive states of mind and behaviour.

## Cycles of Expansion and Contraction

While the group is moving from the stage of defensiveness to the stage of authentic behaviour, as described in Chapter 4, it will go through typical cycles of expansion and contraction. When the initial rigidity is successfully confronted and the underlying issue faced, then the group process expands in a phase of open learning. After a while, another kind of rigidity comes to the fore, the group process contracts, and the cycle is repeated.

So the need for confronting interventions is periodic. There are phases when the climate needs to be safe and supportive to maximize learning, and at these times it is inappropriate to confront. If you do so, you are getting lost in some counter-transference, or misjudging the state of the group dynamic.

## One-to-group and One-to-one

This dimension corresponds, for the group, to one-to-one confronting in my six category intervention analysis, as presented in *Helping the Client* (Heron, 1990a). Please note in that book I call unaware, distorted and defensive behaviours and attitudes, and the issues to which they relate, 'agendas'. Also note that in the one-to-one context with which that book deals, threatening issues will not arise in the same sort of way that they do in a group. For the individual client in a one-to-one setting, many agendas will arise because they are an issue for that person in their current everyday life. However, transference, which I discuss in Chapter 4 of this book, is a process that occurs in both one-to-group and one-to-one settings.

The two contexts also become similar if a group goes in for much personal growth work per se, independent of group-related issues. A very wide range of individual agendas indeed may then come forward. The facilitator and the person working are effectively in a one-to-one setting and the six category analysis of confronting applies.

## The Confronting Dimension: Hierarchical Mode

Here you directly interrupt the rigid behaviour, and point to the issue which that behaviour is busy avoiding. You do this in such a way that those concerned may take up the issue, and thereby show some awareness of their avoidance.

You are doing this to people and for people, entirely in the hierarchical mode. Any particular unilateral confrontation is by definition unsolicited. It points to something the group is unaware of, and so cannot ask to be helped with. But it is legitimated by the implicit warrant of your role. It is the sort of thing a facilitator is expected to do. This warrant, for any given group and its objectives, does have limits, however, and you need to be clear in your own mind what these limits are.

Give time, after a confrontation, for people to assimilate the shock of it and to explore their reactions to it. Interrupt any return to compulsive avoidance and denial. Help people own their defensive process and see it for what it is.

If only one or two group members are involved, you may wish to move over into the co-operative mode, gather in feedback from other people in the group and have a general sharing of views.

1. **Confronting interpretation.**   You interrupt the resistant behaviour – of one or some or all of the group – and identify it as a way of not dealing with some issue. This is done in a manner that is supportive of the persons concerned, uncompromising about the behaviour.
   - **Issue focus.**   You may say: 'I think we are all avoiding issue X.' So you go straight for the avoided issue, without focusing on how it is being avoided. The immediate challenge of the issue may loosen people from their resistant block.
   - **Avoidance focus.**   You may say: 'I think this behaviour Q is a way of avoiding something.' You spotlight the process of resistance. You may do this for its own sake, to facilitate learning about human behaviour, or you may not be clear what the issue is, although the avoidance of something is obvious. Alternatively, you may sense what the issue is, but judge that it is too heavy to go for it straight away. So you start with the avoidance first, then move on to the issue.
   - **Source focus.**   You may say: 'I think cultural norm F is invading the group, getting us stuck in behaviour Q as a way of avoiding something.' You identify the avoidance behaviour, but the main focus is on where it comes from. You judge it is important first to raise consciousness about the source of the resistance. You may then go on to the issue that is being avoided.
   - **All of it.**   You may say: 'I think cultural norm F is invading the group, getting us stuck in behaviour Q as a way of avoiding issue X.' This is the full-blown confronting interpretation. This may be the one that raises consciousness to the point of addressing issue X. But if it seems it would be too much to cope with, then proceed gradually, as above.

The kinds of interpretation used in the above examples are attributive and sociodynamic. Confronting interpretations can also be psychodynamic, holonomic, participative and open window. See items 5 to 10, hierarchical mode, meaning dimension, Chapter 6.

2. **Imaginal confrontation.** You give a representation of the avoided issue, the avoidance behaviour and its possible source, in part or in whole, in one or other of the imaginal forms – metaphor, instance, resonance, presentation, dramaturgy, demonstration and caricature. See items 2 and 11, hierarchical mode, meaning dimension, Chapter 6. For example:

- You make up a poem, a fable or fairy tale about what is going on. *Metaphor.*
- You tell them about similar predicaments that have occurred in other groups. *Instance.*
- You recount your associations and memories evoked by what is going on, in order to evoke meaning through the form of other situations, which may be from some quite different field. *Resonance.*
- You portray the situation non-verbally in posture, gesture, movement and sound; or by a drawing *Presentation.*
- You portray the situation in an improvised piece of theatre, playing all the parts. *Dramaturgy.*
- You re-enact as accurately as possible the defensive behaviour that has occurred. *Demonstration.*
- You re-enact the situation caricaturing its the salient features. *Caricature.*

3. **Objective confrontation.** The interpretations in 1 can be delivered in an 'objective' form, as a straight declaration of what is going on in the group. But it is still supportive: non-punitive and non-moralistic. It is given as information to be used; not as condemnation and heavy-handed judgment.

4. **Subjective confrontation.** The interpretations can also be given in a more diffident, 'subjective' mode: 'For what it is worth, right or wrong, my impression is that …'. This version may express a real uncertainty about the content of the interpretation, or it may be used to gain a hearing about a very sensitive issue. Again, it is supportive and non-punitive.

5. **Confronting theory.** You present some general ideas which raise consciousness about personal or group defensiveness. For example, aspects of the group dynamic theory raised in Chapter 4. You may then apply the ideas to current or recent defensive events in the group.

6. **Confronting action.** When confronting one or more persons, or the group as a whole, you propose an action – doing or saying something – that challenges and interrupts the defensive behaviour in those concerned. There are two versions:
   - **Issue focus.** The action brings people directly to grips with the issue they have been avoiding. So you may ask them to declare attractions directly to those for whom it is felt.
   - **Source focus.** The action takes people into the source of the avoidance. You could, therefore, ask them to declare their fear of owning and dealing with such attraction – and make associations between this fear and events in their past history. Or you propose that they do some active body work to loosen up archaic distress that is being avoided.

7. **Contractual confrontation.** This confrontation invokes an explicit contract group members have made with you and with each other – about learning objectives, learning methods, decision-making methods, your role, values of the group culture, ground-rules of interaction within the group, ground-rules of group discipline (such as time-keeping, smoking, etc). The contract is invoked to interrupt behaviour that is both breaking the contract and avoiding some issue. You challenge the offenders to abide by the contract and address the issue, or to give good reason for renegotiating the contract. In the extreme case, you can add the third alternative, which is for the offenders to leave the group if they are unwilling to adopt either of the first two alternatives.

   The great advantage of having an explicit and fairly comprehensive contract, agreed early on in the group, is that it both disarms a certain amount of defensive behaviour in advance; and it provides an effective tool, if appropriately invoked, for dismantling any defensive behaviour which cuts across it.

8. **Skills feedback confrontation.** In a skills training group, a trainee may have great difficulty in acquiring a new piece of behaviour, through some combination of habit, inertia, lack of awareness, social embarrassment and deeper levels of defensiveness. With a light and loving touch, you keep homing in with feedback on the bits of behaviour that go wrong, keep modelling how to do them, and keep the trainee rerunning the practice until it starts to come right. This purely behavioural feedback and remodelling can be effective without going into the dynamics of defensiveness.

9. **Disagreeing and correcting.** This is the traditional cognitive kind of confrontation, in which you disagree with what is being

said and correct it. You interrupt, and raise consciousness about, errors and confusions of understanding. This needs to be followed by a co-operative discussion that leads either to final agreement or respectful disagreement.

10. **Discharge confrontation.** Free from any explicitly stated attack, invalidation or negative feedback, you discharge fully in sound (no words) and movement your pent-up anger and frustration generated by blocking and avoidance behaviour in the group. A radical but effective strategy if the situation merits it and provided you can enter into a constructive, caring interaction with those concerned immediately afterwards.

## The Confronting Dimension: Co-operative Mode

You work with the group and its members to raise consciousness about avoided issues, resistant behaviour and its sources – by prompting people to do this to some degree for themselves. You invite and ask them, consult them and compare and share views with them.

When only one or some of the group are involved, you ask them first, then gather in views from the non-involved, and finally add your own. This is followed by general discussion. An important and special case is when it is your own behaviour that needs confronting.

1. **Invite a confronting interpretation.** Where some or all of the group are resistant and blocked, you invite those concerned to come forward with their own account of the threatening issue, or of the avoidance behaviour, or of the source of this behaviour, or of some combination of these. You then ask for the views of the others. You may then add your own view as one among many. This is collective and co-operative consciousness-raising. The verbal form of this intervention, when addressed to those concerned, is: 'I would like to suggest that you consider whether you are avoiding any issue now; and if so, what it is, how you may be avoiding it, and what the sources of that avoidance may be.' You may need to deal with these four points – whether, what, how, why – progressively and gradually rather than all at once.

2. **Invite imaginal confrontation.** Ask group members to use one or other of the imaginal forms to portray the avoided issue, the avoidance behaviour and its possible source, and so

generate intuitive understanding of these. You participate in creating the portrayal, and have a discussion about it with everyone afterwards. So you and group members may do one or other of the following:

- Co-operate in creating a myth, fable or fairy tale about what is going on. *Metaphor.*
- Share with each other similar predicaments that have occurred in other groups. *Instance.*
- Recount associations and memories evoked by what is going on, in order to find meaning through the form of other situations, which may be from some quite different field. *Resonance.*
- Portray the situation non-verbally in an interactive dynamic sculpture of posture, gesture, movement and sound. *Presentation.*
- Portray the situation in an improvised piece of theatre. *Dramaturgy.*
- Re-enact the defensive behaviour all over again as accurately as possible. *Demonstration.*
- Re-enact the situation caricaturing its the salient features. *Caricature.*

3. **Confronting questioning.** This is a more head-on technique. You can put a straight, direct question that interrupts the resistant behaviour, and asks those concerned to raise their own consciousness about it. Aiming the question is in the hierarchical mode, but the main intent of the question is co-operative: to prompt, encourage, and elicit; to invite the recipient to participate in uncovering the learning.

- **Issue focus.** Your question asks the group or person to identify the issue that is being avoided: 'What are issue are you busy not addressing?' The thrust of this question can be framed in many different ways.
- **Avoidance focus.** Your question asks whether the behaviour you have interrupted has some evasive function: 'Is the way you are speaking and holding yourself right now a way of avoiding something else?'
- **Source focus.** Here your question asks about the origins of the resistant behaviour: 'Where does this way of avoiding the issue originate?'
- **All of it.** Your question puts it all together: 'Is what you are saying and doing a way of avoiding something; if so, what issue you not dealing with; and what is the source of the avoidance?'

4.  **Contractual query.** You put a question to those whose unaware behaviour is breaking a contract made with the group – about learning objectives, learning methods, decision-making methods, your role, values of the group culture, ground-rules of interaction within the group, ground-rules of group discipline (such as time-keeping, smoking, etc). – and thereby also avoiding some issue: 'What are you avoiding by breaking your agreement with the group to…?'

5.  **Competence query.** In skills training practice, your question for the trainee who can't get it right is: 'Can you identify exactly what it is you do that keeps you off track?' Or: 'What precisely do you need to do to get it right?' After you get an answer, you can ask other members of the practice group to give their feedback and comment. If the trainee gets clear about what to do to get it right, then he or she reruns the practice until it comes right.

6.  **Cognitive query.** For someone in a state of mental error, confusion or contradiction, you ask: 'Is that really how you understand it?' Or: 'What is it you are busy trying not to understand?'

7.  **Putting them to the group.** Where one or two or more members are locked unawarely in some avoidance behaviour, you invite others in the group to confront what is going on. Several overlapping confrontations may be given, to which you may or may not add your own. This, too, is co-operative and collective consciousness-raising, in which the recipients are invited to participate.

8.  **Descriptive confrontation.** You simply make a descriptive comment about the avoidance behaviour, without attaching any kind of interpretation to it, or without asking anyone to interpret it. 'You have spent 20 minutes criticizing this room.' This may, or may not, lead to some airing of views by group members about whether the described behaviour is avoiding something, and if so, what, and maybe even why.

9.  **Indicative confrontation.** This is the same as 7, except that you don't pick out the avoidance behaviour verbally, but non-verbally, by gesture, touch, the direction of the gaze, or by mirroring it in action.

10. **Distract and interrupt.** You distract people from, and also cut right across, their unaware avoidance behaviour, and so indirectly raise in them a question mark as to what it is all about. You may do this in many different ways: by a change of topic or activity, by totally shifting group attention to someone else, by moving very close to those involved, by touching them in a friendly way, etc.

11. **Conflict resolution.**   A special case of avoidance behaviour is when two group members become locked in unproductive conflict. If raising their consciousness about the avoided issue does not get them out of it, then you may invite them to participate in a conflict resolution exercise which you facilitate. The first thing is to free them from their emotional fixation so that they can understand each other's point of view and deal with the issues, rather than hysterically defend their ground. There are three classic techniques. They are given in order of depth of intervention.

   - **Controlled discussion.**   You umpire an exchange of views with two rules: each person makes only one point at a time; and each restates the other's point to the other's satisfaction before making a point in reply. This takes the heat out of the discussion, and starts listening and relating.
   - **Role reversal.**   You umpire an exchange of views. When the tension rises, have the pair reverse roles, and switch chairs, so that they represent fully their opponent's point of view. Then switch them back to themselves. Repeat until the debate moves towards rationality and resolution.
   - **Hidden agenda counselling.**   Ask each person what it is they really need from the other. Do this by asking them to address an empty chair as if it were the other person and complete several times the question 'What I really want from you is…'. This may uncover some hidden agenda – projected personal and private unfinished business with someone from the past – that is nothing to do with the real issues and the actual situation.

   The second thing is to adjudicate co-operative problem-solving. Take the pair through a problem-solving cycle.

   - **Diagnosis.**   Prompt them to state the problem clearly and agree the degree to which each of them is responsible, and what the other causes, if any, are.
   - **Treatment.** Help them to identify possible solutions, assess each one in terms of its probable outcomes, choose one of them, and make an appropriate action plan to implement it.
   - **Follow-up.**   Invite them to contract to meet at a future date and review the action taken, its effectiveness in dealing with the problem, and the current status of the problem.

## The Confronting Dimension: Autonomous Mode

Here you do not work in the confronting mode either directly, or indirectly by prompting, but create a climate of safety, support and trust, so that the challenge to dismantle defences occurs independently within the group or the individual. It may be that structures given by you enable group members to practise self- and peer confrontation. So we have:

1. **Structured peer confrontation.** You set up a structured exercise in which participants confront each other in small groups. The confrontation may relate to issues that have been avoided, to how they have been avoided and from what source, whether earlier in the large group, or currently in the small groups. Or the exercise may build up confronting skills by role playing imaginary scenarios.

2. **Structured self-confrontation.** You set up an exercise in which each person takes it in turns, in small groups, to confront themselves about what issues they are currently avoiding, how they are avoiding them, and what the source of the avoidance seems to be. Again this can relate back to the large group, or currently to the small group. This exercise can be done with or without peer feedback on each self-confrontation.

3. **Devil's advocate.** You establish a ground rule whereby it is open to anyone at any time to announce they are going to assume the role of devil's advocate. They put on a special hat, or hold a 'mace', to indicate they are in the devil's advocate role. They may then expose hidden issues, avoidance behaviour and possible sources of it. This piece of theatre enables the devil's advocate to raise a confrontation issue more in a spirit of inquiry and creative challenge. All kinds of doubts, uncertainties and uneasinesses about the group dynamic can be dealt with in this way, without the advocate fully identifying with them or officially holding them. The theatre also places the listeners at some distance from what is being said so that they can consider it more carefully.

4. **No confrontation phase.** You stop confronting or prompting the group to confront. You wait to see if group members will generate their own confronting. This phase can be (a) unannounced, or (b) you can say that you are doing it and for how long.

5. **Tense silence.** An unannounced and impromptu autonomy phase, in which you respond to mounting tension within the

group with silence, waiting for the group to implode into confronting its own process. This is a special case of 4 (a).

6. **Self- and peer confrontation group.**   The group is run in such a way that all the confrontation is done by self or peer and never by you. You make it explicit that you will function on the other dimensions but not on the confronting dimension. This model presupposes that you have already included in the group programme some demonstration of and training in confronting strategies. This is a substantial version of 4 (b).

7. **Autonomous monitoring of avoidance.**   In this extension of the initiative clause (see item 9, autonomous mode, planning dimension, Chapter 5) into the confronting dimension, you create a climate of shared leadership, and encourage group members to exercise their right to take unilateral initiatives in which group members spontaneously confront avoided issues and resistant behaviour, alongside your management of this dimension.

8. **Backing off.**   When two or more persons, or the group as a whole, are highly defensive and are resisting dealing with your confrontation, you suddenly drop it entirely, and switch over to some quite different matter. The effect is to increase the internal pressure toward self-confrontation – about the abandoned issue – in those concerned.

9. **Self-confrontation only.**   You create a climate of safety and support in the group, with a ground rule that there is no person-to-person, and no person-to-group, confrontation, but only internal, self-confrontation. This presupposes that group members have had some kind of training, in purely self-directed personal development work, and that each one is very sharp at interrupting their own projections onto others.

10. **Trainer–trainee delegation.**   You appoint one person in the group, or in each of several sub-groups, to exercise the confronting role, with feedback on the intervensions afterwards from other members. This, of course, is an exercise in a training the trainers' group.

11. **Confrontation resources.**   CCTV with playback is a resource which the group can use on its own to confront its own process. Individuals too can use it on their own to confront their own more personal defensive behaviour, evident in frame-by-frame exposure of micro-cues. Self-rating instruments, and question-naires for the group, can also be used.

*Concluding note.* Psychological somnambulism is a chronic habit in human behaviour: the tendency to fall asleep in interactions with others without awareness of one's behaviour, its effects and its motives. Hence we need, with much supportive rigour, to help each other wake up from time to time.

# 11 The Feeling Dimension

Continuing with details of the core model, this chapter is all about the fourth and feeling dimension of facilitation. While I call it the feeling dimension, it is concerned with the management of both feeling and emotion, and emotional processes are frequently at the forefront of this management. However, feeling is the unitive ground of these processes, so I use it to name the dimension.

As I made clear in Chapter 3, I make a basic distinction between feeling and emotion. Feeling is participatory affect, emotion is individualizing affect. Feeling is the capacity of a person to participate in wider unities of being, to indwell what is present through attunement and resonance. Through feeling a person becomes at one with the content of experience, and at the same time knows her or his distinctness from it. This is the domain of empathy, indwelling, participation, presence, resonance, and suchlike (Heron, 1992: 16). Emotion is to do with the fulfilment or frustration of our individual needs and interests in the forms of joy, surprise, anger, grief and so on.

In Chapter 4, I defined the group dynamic as the combined configuration of mental, emotional and physical energy in the group at any given time and the way this configuration undergoes change. Emotional energy is very much the immediate thrust of the dynamic. For you, the facilitator, a central question is how to handle the emotional life of the group. One key to this handling is to be open to the ground of participative feeling in the group. So first, several sections on emotional processes, then a key section on feeling and the group dynamic, before an account of the various interventions.

## Positive Emotional Processes

There are at least seven basic constructive emotional processes, each requiring awareness. One or more of them will be at the heart of the group dynamic when authentic behaviour of one sort or another – as outlined in Chapter 4 – is going on. Each of them is healthy, valid and appropriate in its proper context.

1. **Identification.**   A person knows what emotional state they are in and can identify the emotions involved, can experience them, and owns them.
2. **Acceptance.**   A person both identifies/experiences/owns their emotions and accepts them.
3. **Control.**   A person awarely controls their emotional state, without either denying it or suppressing it, in order to accomplish some task, or interact appropriately with other persons.
4. **Redirection.**   A person awarely directs an aroused emotion into a channel other than its normal outlet. Thus a person who is angry about an interruption of their activity, may for good reason choose to direct the energy of the anger into some vigorous game.
5. **Switching.**   A person awarely chooses to change an emotional state by switching attention off it and its context, on to some other activity and outlook which generate a different emotional state. As a result of switching, one sort of emotion gives way to a different one. You can switch laterally, from an emotional state on the ordinary level of consciousness to another state on the same level; or you can switch vertically, from a state on the ordinary level to a state on a higher level of consciousness.
6. **Transmutation.**   A person awarely chooses to sublimate and refine an emotional state so that it is internally transformed. This is the psychological alchemy of turning base metal into gold. A basic method is to reconstrue a situation, cognitively restructure it, so that you see it in a new light, which transforms your emotional response to it. Another is to hold the light of awareness intently and constantly within a negative emotional state, until its dross is transfigured.

    Let me underline the difference between redirection, switching and transmutation.
    - **Redirection.**   The emotion continues to be present, but its energy is given some alternative outlet to the one it would normally seek. So anger is redirected into competitive sport rather than let out in protest at being interrupted.
    - **Switching.**   The emotion falls into the background because some other emotion is intentionally generated in the foreground. So the anger recedes because choosing to attend some quite different situation and outlook brings exhilaration to the fore.

- **Transmutation.** The emotion internally changes its nature and becomes a different emotion: the frequency of its energy is entirely altered. So anger, by the transformative, focused action of consciousness, becomes peace.
7. **Catharsis.** A person awarely chooses to discharge distress emotions – grief, fear, anger – through, respectively, tears, trembling, high frequency sound and movement. The painful emotion is released from the mind and body; and this generates spontaneous insight into its origins and subsequent effects.
8. **Expression.** A person awarely gives verbal and physical expression to their emotions, to celebrate, affirm and bear witness to the joy and drama of their unique existence.

Experiential learning, in its affective dimension, is concerned to help people acquire skills in the exercise of all these processes, shown in Figure 11.1.

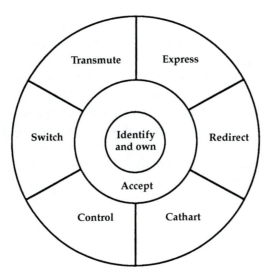

**Figure 11.1** *Positive emotional processes*

## Negative Emotional Processes

There are eight, roughly corresponding, negative emotional processes:

1. **Alienation.** A person is cut off from their emotional state and cannot identify what it is. Asked about their emotions, they will talk about their thoughts.

2. **Suppression.**   A person identifies their emotional state only enough to subject themselves to instantaneous social inhibition.
3. **Fixation.**   A person is stuck in some emotional state, either fascinated by it in a morbid way or sunk in it with depressive inertia. Their awareness is a slave of the state and cannot (or, more properly, feels unwilling to make the effort to) move out of it.
4. **Displacement.**   A distress emotion is displaced unawarely into some action that is maladaptive, socially inappropriate and disturbing, or into some negative attitude toward the self. The distress emotion involved is usually also repressed.
5. **Distraction.**   Emotional states fluctuate in a disoriented way because the person is being chaotically distracted by one stimulus after another, coming from some mixture of the mind and the external world.
6. **Degradation.**   An emotional state is debased into a lesser or lower or more negative one, by indulging in it in a distorted way.
7. **Dramatization.**   A distress emotion is displaced into pseudo-catharsis. The outlet has elements of the hysterical or the rigid. The distress slips out of the true cathartic channel, and distorts itself on the way out.
8. **Repression.**   Distress emotions are pushed out of consciousness and their presence in the mind is denied. Then we have the return of the repressed in distorted form. Most of the so-called defence mechanisms are a combination of repression and 4, displacement.

Experiential learning, in its affective dimension, is concerned to help people acquire skills in identifying all these negative processes, in interrupting them, and in transforming their energy and integrating it with positive processes.

## The Role of Pathology

There are psychotherapies that aim to clean you up. Their goal is to get rid of the pathology, the distress, the misbegotten behaviour, and restore you to fully integrated, healthy human functioning. There have been Reich's genital character, Janov's post-primal man, the rational distress-free human of re-evaluation counselling – and so on.

There are others, however, which see the dark side of human nature as a complement to the light, and seek to accept and include it, reclaiming its energies from rejection, denial and hostility. Thus the concept of integrating the shadow in Jungian psychology (Jung, 1964). And Hillman, in his archetypal psychology, sees the tendency of the soul continuously to pathologize its existence in different areas, as the leading edge of its growth. It generates new patches of disturbance in order to deepen its maturity (Hillman, 1975).

The distinction is roughly that between perfectionism and holism – which could also be called organicism. The former seeks to get rid of the chaos and create a being without disorder. The latter seeks to integrate and transform the dross, acknowledging it as a continuous source of growth, creating a developing whole being, not a perfect one.

Holism sees intermittent chaos as the fertile soil of new levels of organization and order. My own view of these two ideologies is that perfectionism is itself a pathology – a defence against holism.

## Emotion and the Group Dynamic

The positive emotional processes, listed above, will be present in differing combinations at the heart of the group dynamic when it is in one of its seven basic positive forms, described in Chapter 4: task-oriented, process-oriented, expressive, interactive, confronting, personal work oriented, charismatic.

And the negative emotional processes listed above will be present in differing combinations when the group dynamic is in one or more of the five negative forms I have so far considered: educationally alienated, culturally restricted, psychologically defensive, underdeveloped, and in easy streeet. These were last defined in Chapter 10.

The group dynamic is always a mixture of positive and negative emotional processes, positive and negative forms. This is its necessary destiny. To refer back to the stages of the group dynamic described in Chapter 4, the third, summertime stage of authentic behaviour is never free of negative emotional processes.

On the contrary, these provide an important part of the humus for nourishing its growth. It is just that, compared to earlier stages, the balance of negative and positive is different. In the early stages, the negative processes and forms tended to block the positive; in the third stage, the negative are used like fuel to kindle growth and empower the positive.

## Feeling and the Group Dynamic

Again, a reminder that I use the term 'feeling' to mean the capacity of the person to participate in what is here and now, to indwell what is present through attunement and resonance. Through feeling I know unity with the content of experience, and at the same time know my distinctness from it. This is the domain of empathy, indwelling, participation, presence, resonance and suchlike.

In Chapter 4, I introduced the notion of the *unified affective field* as a fundamental dimension of the group dynamic. At the level of basic feeling, persons have a capacity for mutual participation with other beings through empathic resonance. A group can learn consciously to access this shared experiential field of harmonic resonance with each other. It can provide a deep ground, a generous backdrop, for owning and processing the emotional currents and turbulence that may surge through the field, and for enhancing the learning activities that occur within its aegis.

The group can thus open to share experiential space, the inner felt sense of space as a form of more-than-human consciousness and life. It is a medium for radical human communion, the 'ocean of shared feeling ... where we become one with one another' (Alexander, 1979: 294). It is valuable for facilitators to resonate with this field at their own feeling level to establish a radical, dynamic basis out of which images and concepts of appropriate interventions can emerge.

## *The Feeling Dimension: Hierarchical Mode*

You take charge of the affective dynamic of the group, directing its process and deciding how the emotional life, and participative feeling, of the group will be handled. You think for the group, judging what ways of managing emotions, and opening to feeling, will suit its members and its purpose best. This means that you identify what the current affective dynamic is, and decide whether to stay with it and extend or deepen it, or change it.

1.  **Instruction: identify, own and accept.**   In the very early stages of a group, especially with beginners in emotional education, you will need, when people show signs of alienation and suppression of emotion, to instruct and advise them to identify, own and accept their emotional states.
2.  **Attributing emotion.**   As an alternative, you attribute to one or more group members an emotional state which is unnoticed by them. This is the same as attributive interpretation, item 5, hierarchical mode, meaning dimension, Chapter 6. It may also be a confronting attribution; or it may not, since not every case of someone not noticing their emotions is defensive – it may be just be a conventional lack of awareness.

3. **Projection alert.** You alert the group, early in its history to the pervasive dynamic of unconscious projection, the hidden emotional traffic between people: positive and negative transference (see Chapter 4) flowing unawarely between group members, and between members and you. This is also a confronting, consciousness-raising intervention. It is central to working with the emotional dynamic of the group.

4. **Instruction: aware control.** As emotions come up in a group and need to be processed, not everyone can do this work at the same time. You will need to instruct people to learn the art of conscious control: to identify and own the emotions, not to suppress or repress or displace them, but to put them awarely on hold, while they wait their turn, or play some other part in the proceedings.

5. **Giving permission for catharsis.** At an early stage in the group's history, you announce with benign authority that catharsis is acceptable, human and healing. You clearly give permission for catharsis to occur, encourage members to accept it when it arises, and give a rationale of its benefits. This permission-giving is directed at the hurt child within – who really needs to hear support and encouragement for the discharge of its pain. This is a basic hierarchical strategy.

6. **Lowering the cathartic threshold.** Here you take the whole group toward catharsis, by proposing an activity which releases emotional distress in some group members, and lowers the threshold of release in all. The activity may be to do with breathing and body work, with the use of psychodrama, with deep reverie and active imagination. You explain beforehand what the exercise is intended to achieve, and reinforce your permission-giving statements. Actual cathartic work with an individual, I consider below under the co-operative mode of the feeling dimension.

7. **Transmutation.** You propose work on emotional states by transmutative methods in which you are directive, for example, in a guided fantasy using archetypal symbols. For further details of transmutation and transmutative interventions see *Helping the Client* (Heron, 1990a).

8. **Expression and celebration.** You propose and direct an activity, for one or more members, or for all the group, as a means of expressing, symbolizing, celebrating their state of being. It may include affirmations, validations and appreciations. It may be song and music making, dance and movement, drawing and painting, story telling, dramaturgy: imaginal

methods will be to the fore. The expression may celebrate one's own state of being, someone else's, relationships, art, nature, work, humanity, the planet or other realities. It may involve interpersonal declarations and explorations. This expression of emotion may not only be celebratory but also in the minor key: elegiac, dramatic. It may be defiant, bold, and so on. It may be in the charismatic and spiritual domain.

9. **Switching.** You take charge of this process, and do it for the group. This is one of the most basic of all interventions for altering the group dynamic. Your intention is to change the being, the emotional state of the group, or of one or more persons in it, by proposing some verbal or non-verbal behaviour that switches attention away from the current state and generates another one. You may suggest a task or change of task, a structured skills building exercise, a theory session, some process analysis, a verbal round, a set of movements, body work, hyperventilation, an active game, a song, a dance, a shout, a break, a ritual, a meditation, group attunement and so on.

Switching may be used to take the group from negative to positive states. Within positive states, it may be used to shift the dynamic, either way, between passive and active states, cathartic and outgoing states, low and high energy states, transcendental and grounded states, task and process states, intellectual and experiential states, task states of different kinds and so on. Special cases of switching are opening and closing a group, starting and ending a day or a session.

Switching aids confluent, holistic learning, prevents alienation and sustains positive emotional arousal as a basic motivation for learning. Holistic learning means creating equipoise between different kinds of learning. This requires multiplicity, variety and complementarity or contrast – the play of opposites – all in good measure. So there is a balance of several, varied and contrasted activities – within one strand and as between diverse strands of the curriculum. You use switching to orchestrate this balance.

Note that while switching can use several interventions listed in this and other dimensions, not every use of these same interventions is for purposes of switching. They may be used to sustain or develop a state of being, not change it.

Table 11.1 presents a range of options for switching, arranged under affective, imaginal, conceptual and practical strands of learning.

**Table 11.1**   *Items for switching*

| | | |
|---|---|---|
| *Affective strand emotion* | • Building self-esteem and affirming self.<br>• Appreciation from and to others.<br>• Co-operation and mutual support<br>• A confident emotional climate.<br>• Positive emotional associations.<br>• Creative expression of positive emotion in song, dance, movement,music, art, drama, story-telling,games.<br>• Verbal expression of positive emotion.<br>• Exploring emotional and interpersonal processes underlying the task. | • Identifying, owning and accepting emotional states.<br>• Redirecting, switching and transmuting emotional states.<br>• Removing emotional blocks to creativity and learning.<br>• Clearing projections from and to others.<br>• Interrupting the displacement and acting out of past distress.<br>• Healing the memories: catharis of past distress. |
| *Affective strand: feeling* | • Physical and mental relaxation:<br>• Participative attunement with people, processes, nature, presences.<br>• Opening and closing, holonomic and special purpose rituals.<br>• Invocations, evocations and benedictions.<br>• Use of bells, gongs, candles, incense, robes. | • Sacred postures, dancing, chanting and singing.<br>• Celebration, praise, worship, high prayer, meditation of all kinds.<br>• Charismatic training and exercises. Inner transmutation exercises.<br>• Sharing peak experiences.<br>• Making music, listening to music.<br>• Appreciation of colour and form. |
| *Imaginal strand: intution and imagery* | • Perception, memory, imagination: visual, auditory, kinaesthetic, tactile.<br>• Pictures, graphics, movement, mime, sound, music. Film, TV.<br>• Story, allegory, myth, metaphor and analogy. Poetry.<br>• Role play, dramaturgy, caricature.<br>• Cases, instances, demonstrations.<br>• Symbolic imagery. | • Associated imagery and resonant experiences.<br>• Brainstorming, synectics, lateral thinking, creativity training.<br>• Use of the voice: timing, tone, rhythm, inflection, speed, volume, pauses.<br>• Extrasensory perception, psi capacities and use of subtle energies.<br>• Insight, intuition, divination |
| *Conceptual strand: reflection and discrimination* | • Reading, writing and talking.<br>• Phenomenological descriptions, maps.<br>• Loose or tight conceptual framework.<br>• Free or directed association of ideas.<br>• Divergent or convergent thinking.<br>• Deductive thinking: contradiction and necessary implication.<br>• Causal thinking: cause and effect, causal laws and theories.<br>• Systems thinking: mutual influence: | • Dipolar thinking: interdependence of opposites.<br>• Contextual thinking: interpretation as a function of culture and history.<br>• Problem-solving.<br>• Practical thinking: for this end, do that.<br>• Ethical thinking: moral judgements.<br>• Evaluative thinking: judgements of worth and value.<br>• Conjecture: potentials and possibilities. |
| *Practical strand intention and action* | • Intentionality: long term and short term goals, means and ends, options and outcomes, action plans and programmes.<br>• Visualizing the future.<br>• Doing: exercise of the will, action, direction of the execution.<br>• Discussion/decision-making methods.<br>• Organizational restructuring. | • Body-work and bodily exercises.<br>• Breath-work and breathing exercises.<br>• Subtle energy work and exercises.<br>• Structured exercises of all kinds.<br>• Skills: technical, aesthetic, intrapsychic, interpersonal, transpersonal, psychic, political, organizational, ecological, economic, technical, psychomotor. |

The supposition in using any of these items as part of a multi-stranded programme is that some of them will be inside, part of, learning something, and some of them will be alongside, a break from, the learning. This gives great freedom to the facilitator to explore, through switching, the use of holistic learning without being tied down by any strict format.

10. **Active charisma.**    You manifest your presence, your charismatic way of being in and through the up-hierachy of empowerment, as described in Chapter 12. This means entering into the fullness of your presence, letting this shape the tone and timing of your voice, your use of language, and your strategic purposes. In this way you empower both yourself and your participants through whatever intervention you are making. See Figure 11.2.

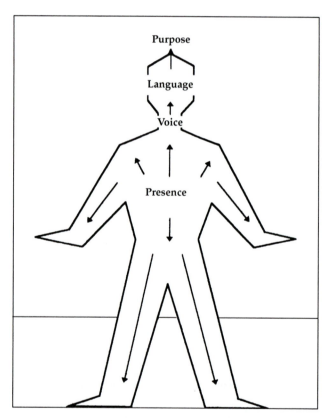

**Figure 11.2**    *The up-hierarchy of empowerment*

11. **Use of experiential space.** You consciously enter, and facilitate from, the tacit shared experiential space of the whole group, compenetrating with everyone in it, working with the dynamic effects of interpersonal geometry – of different spatial relations between you and individuals or the group as a whole. See Chapter 12.

12. **Creating a unified affective field.** I described this field in Chapter 4. You lead the group in establishing a shared experiential fields of harmonic resonance with each other, akin to establishing mutual brainwave entrainment. You may want to do this at the start of the day's session to provide a ground for the unfolding emotional process, and for all other kinds of learning. You can do it in a variety of ways. Here are three:

    - **Tibetan bowl.** Stroke the rim of a Tibetan bowl with a wooden stick to generate a sustained tone. Invite everyone to tune in to this tone in silence, or to make a tone that is harmonic with it.

    - **Mutual presencing.** Invite everyone to sit close and comfortably and link hands, right over left, relax physically and mentally, and enter a state of mutual awareness of each other's presence and of the presence of the group as a whole.

    - **Lean ritual.** A lean ritual is free of any explicit theology, and uses the primal meaning of basic words and gestures. Thus the group stand in a circle with arms reaching upward and say 'Above', then kneel to touch the ground and say 'Below', then cross their hands over the heart and say 'Within', finally reach out to take the hands of those on either side and say 'Between'. Innumerable versions of a lean ritual can be designed. Lean ritual generates a subtle sense of shared sacred space.

13. **Charismatic leadership.** You take the group into various altered states of consciousness and transfigurations of personhood through any one or more of a whole range of methods of transformation involving the use of sound, movement, posture, music, verbal expression, and various forms of intentional awareness training. For one characterization of this range see *Sacred Science* (Heron, 1998a). It also includes charismatic training, as detailed in Chapter 12. This initiative presupposes the assent of the group, and opens up the group dynamic to the influences of a vast sphere of subtle energies and spiritual awareness.

## *The Feeling Dimension: Co-operative Mode*

You work with the group, eliciting, prompting, encouraging and indicating different ways of managing emotions, and of opening to participative feeling and creating a unified affective field. You are not managing the affective dynamic of the group for the group, but facilitating co-operative management – you with them.

1. **Acting into owning.**   One or more group members are invited by you to say or do something which enables them to identify and own unnoticed emotions.
2. **Consensus about the affective dynamic.**   You prompt the group, by some questions, to identify its affective state. Is the emotional dynamic positive, outgoing and task-oriented, or inward, brooding and process-oriented, or locked in negative emotional states, or near the release of authentic distress, or something else? Is the group open to participative feeling? Is it subtly attuned to wider reaches of awareness and being? You share your views and co-operate in an emerging consensus.
3. **Negotiating the affective process.**   You invite the group to choose the positive process which it needs to use, either to sustain its current dynamic or to change it. You discuss with the group whether it is time to identify, control, redirect, switch, transmute, cathart or express emotions. You share your view as one among many. You may need to prompt the group, remind them of possibilities, including entry into participative feeling and a unified affective field. But the outcome is a shared choice.
4. **Negotiating the affective method.**   After agreeing on the process, you then negotiate with the group on the method it will adopt to switch, cathart, express or whatever you have chosen to do. Again, you may need to prompt the group with a reminder of the range of options, before you and they choose one together. This intervention is also a co-operative one on the structuring dimension.

   The decision-procedure, in 2, 3 and 4 here, will usually be one in which you 'gather the sense of the meeting' after a sufficient number, including yourself, have spoken. These three strategies need a light touch, keeping the business elegant, not ponderous and protracted.
5. **Negotiating a switch.** This has already been included in 3 and 4, but it is worth separating out since switching (see item 9 under the hierarchical mode above) is so basic. You discuss with the group whether a switch is appropriate and if so agree with the

group what sort. Does the group need to work with emotional process, participative feeling, intuition and imagery, thinking and discrimination, or intention and action, including sensory awareness? See Table 11.1.

6.  **Individual cathartic work.**   You invite one person to do some cathartic work, releasing emotional pain, in the middle of the group, supported by group energy and attention and facilitated by you. This always involves co-operation between you and the individual concerned, since it is based on their freely given assent and choice, and proceeds by a subtle midwifery from you that interacts with cues the person is already emitting.

    This person may already be on the brink – tearful, or trembling, or tense with anger – triggered by something going on in the group. Or they may simply report (whether casually or more substantially) on some problem or difficulty, while still cut off from the underlying distress. If the person gives a double message, of both wanting and not wanting to do the work, keep putting out the invitation until an unequivocal 'yes' or 'no' is forthcoming. If the final response is 'no', then respect this: no-one should ever be pressured into catharsis. Each person must choose and has a right to choose the moment for lowering their defences.

    The work, of course, may involve other growth processes as well as or instead of catharsis. Good individual work is a co-operative dialogue between the client following your leads, and you following the client's cues. It needs rounding off with affirmative, supportive comment from other group members.

7.  **Working with content cues.**   When doing individual cathartic work, you work with content cues – what the person is saying; and with process cues – how they are saying it and what is going in their bodies while they are saying it. This micro-facilitation is at the heart of the co-operative enterprise of item 6, individual work. I give here some of the basic techniques for working with content cues. This means working with what a person is saying, with their stated difficulty, with meaning, story-line and imagery. For a more detailed account of these, for other techniques, and for a discussion of the issues involved, see my *Helping the Client* (Heron, 1990a). In the list below I shall refer to those who are doing the work as 'clients'.

    - **Present tense description.**   Interrupt analytic talking about a problem, and ask clients to describe – in the present tense as if it is happening now – a specific, traumatic and critical incident, evoking it in literal detail by recall of sights and sounds and smells, of what people said and did.

- **Psychodrama.** As the distress comes to the fore through the use of literal description, invite clients to re-enact the incident as a piece of living theatre, imagining they are in the scene and speaking within it as if it is happening now. Ask them to express fully what was left unsaid at the time, and to say it directly to the central other protagonist in the scene. Catharsis can powerfully occur at this point.

- **Shifting level.** When clients are making a charged statement to the central other protagonist – such as 'I really need you to be here' – in a psychodrama about an incident later in life, you quickly and deftly ask 'To whom are you really saying that?'. They may then very rapidly shift level to a much earlier situation and become, for example, the hurt child speaking to its parent. Often the catharsis dramatically intensifies.

- **Earliest available memory.** Simply ask clients for their earliest available memory of an incident typical of a current difficulty, and work on that with literal description and psychodrama. Depending on how it goes and how early it is, you may get them to shift level inside that psychodrama too.

- **Scanning.** When clients identify a current problem, ask them to scan along the chain of incidents, all of which are linked by the same sort of difficulty and distress. They evoke each scene, then move on to the next, without going into any one event deeply. This loosens up the whole chain.

- **Slips of the tongue.** When a word or phrase slips out that clients didn't intend to say, ask them to repeat it a few times, and to work with the associations and/or process cues. This invariably points the way to some unfinished business.

- **Contradiction.** Ask clients to use words, tone of voice, facial expresson, gesture, posture that lightly and clearly contradict, without qualification, their self-deprecating statements and manner. This interrupts the external invalidation the child within has internalized to keep their distress suppressed, and rapidly opens up into laughter, followed, if you are quick on the cues, by deeper forms of catharsis.

- **Validation.** As the distress comes up, gently and clearly affirm clients, their deep worth, the validity of their pain, their need for release, how much they deserves this time, support and care.

- **Free attention.**   If clients are sunk in their distress, ask them to recount some recent pleasant experiences. This will generate some free attention, without which catharsis cannot occur. Go on to the other techniques.
- **Association.**   Work with clients' spontaneous, unbidden associations. These include what is on top at the start of a session; the sudden surfacing of an earlier memory while working on a later one; the extra bits of recall that come up to illuminate a remembered event. The thoughts and insights that arise during a pause in catharsis and as it subsides are important. This re-structuring of awareness is the real fruit, not just the release itself.
- **Integration of learning.**   After a major piece of cathartic work that has generated a good deal of insight and re-evaluation, prompt clients to formulate clearly all they have learnt, and to affirm its application to new attitudes of mind, new goals and new behaviours in their life now. At this point cathartic work finds its true raison d'être.

8. **Working with process cues.**   This means working with how clients are talking and being, that is, with tone and charge and volume of voice, with breathing, use of eyes, facial expression, gesture, posture, movement.
   - **Repeating distress-charged words.**   Ask clients to repeat words and phrases which carry a distressed emphasis, several times, and louder, and perhaps much louder. This will start to discharge the underlying distress, or bring it nearer the surface. This is particularly potent at the heart of a psychodrama, when clients are expressing the hitherto unexpressed to some central other protagonist from their past.
   - **Exaggerating distress-charged movements.**   Ask the client to repeat and also exaggerate small involuntary agitated movements until they become large and vigorous, then to add the sounds and words that go with them. This too will start to discharge the underlying distress, or bring it nearer the surface.
   - **Amplifying deepening of the breath.**   Ask the person who quite suddenly and unawarely breathes in deeply, to continue deep and rapid breathing, making a crescendo of sound on the outbreath. This may release deep sobbing, or screaming and trembling, or a discharge of anger.
   - **Mobilizing distress-locked rigidities.** Ask clients to become aware of some bodily rigidity, exaggerate it to let the distress energy pile up in the lock, then to throw the energy out in

vigorous movement, finding appropriate sounds and words. So a tight fist and rigid arm is first exaggerated into even greater tension, then converted into rapid thumping on a pillow. You will need to encourage clients not to throttle back the sound, and, behind that, the long-repressed words.

- **Acting into.** When clients are already feeling the distress and want to discharge it, but are held back by conditioned muscular tension, you suggest they act into the feeling, that is, create a muscular pathway for it, by vigorous pounding and sound for anger, or trembling for fear. If they produce the movement and sound gymnastically, then often real catharsis will take over.

- **Physical pressure.** When clients are just struggling to get discharge going, or have just started it, or are in the middle of it, you can facilitate release by applying appropriate degrees of pressure to various parts of the body: pressure on the abdomen, midriff or thorax, timed with the outbreath; pressure on the masseter muscle, some of the intercostals, the trapezius, the infraspinatus; pressure on the upper and mid-dorsal vertebrae timed with the outbreath, to deepen the release in sobs; pressure against the soles of the feet and up the legs to precipitate kicking; extending the thoracic spine over the practitioner's knee, timed with the outbreath, to deepen the release of primal grief and screaming; and so on. The pressure is firm and deep, but very sensitively timed to fit and facilitate the cathartic process. Anything ham-fisted and ill-attuned is destructively intrusive.

- **Physical extension.** As clients are moving in and out of the discharge process, you can facilitate the release by gently extending the fingers, if they curl up defensively; or by gently extending the arms; or by drawing the arms out and away from the sides of the body; or by extending an arm while pressing the shoulder back; or by gently raising the head, or uncurling the trunk; and so on. All these extensions are gentle and gradual, so that the client can choose to yield to them and go with them.

- **Relaxation and light massage.** This is an alternative mode of working on physical rigidity. You relax the person and give gentle, caressing massage to rigid areas, or a gentle pulsing vibration, as in holistic pulsing. Catharsis and/or memory recall may occur as muscle groups give way to the massage.

- **Physical holding.** You reach out lightly to hold and embrace the person at the start, or just before the start, of the release of grief in tears. This can greatly facilitate the intensity of sobbing. Can be combined with aware pressure on the upper dorsal vertebrae at the start of each outbreath. Holding hands at certain points may facilitate discharge. When discharging fear, the person can usefully stand within your embrace, and your fingertips apply light pressure to either side of his or her spine.
- **Pursuing the eyes.** By avoiding eye contact with you, clients are often also at the same time avoiding the distress feelings. You gently pursue their eyes by peering up from under their lowered heads. Re-establishing eye contact may precipitate or continue catharsis.
- **Regression positions.** When process cues suggest either birth or pre-natal material, you can invite clients to assume pre-natal or birth postures, start deep and rapid breathing and wait for the primal experiences to rerun themselves. This may lead into deep and sustained cathartic work in the primal mode. If so, you need to keep leading the person to identify the context, to verbalize insights, and at the end to integrate the learning into his current attitudes and life-style. Regression positions may also be less ambitious like lying in the cot, sitting on the potty, sucking a thumb, etc.
- **Seeking the context.** When clients are deeply immersed in process work and in catharsis, you may judge it fitting to lead them into the associated cognitive mode, asking them to identify and describe the event and its context, to verbalize insights, to make connections with present-time situations and attitudes. This crosses over to work with content.
- **Ending a session.** At the end of a cathartic session, it is necessary for you to bring clients back up out of their cathartic regression into present time, by chronological progression at intervals of 5 or 10 years, by affirming positive directions for current living, by describing the immediate environment, by reciting simple lists, by looking forward to the next few days, and so on.

9. **Individual charismatic work.** You invite one person to do some charismatic work in the middle of the group. It may involve charismatic training, see Chapter 12, or co-creating/ primary theatre, see item 3, autonomous mode below, supported by group energy and attention and facilitated by you. Again, this always involves co-operation between you and the

individual concerned, since it is based on their freely given assent and choice, and proceeds by a subtle midwifery from you that interacts with cues the person is already emitting.

10. **Over the shoulder.**   In a training group for facilitators, when a trainee is practising facilitating the individual work of someone else in the group, you sit a little to the side and behind the trainee, prompting, monitoring and rearranging their interventions. This is a training dialogue in the co-operative mode and needs a deft and light touch.

11. **Co-creating a unified affective field.**   Or a sacred space. See item 12 above, under the hierarchical mode, and in Chapter 4. A good co-operative way to create such a space, is for you and the group to co-design a lean ritual (see item 12 above), using the primal metaphoric meaning of basic words, gestures and postures, and objects such as flower, leaf, key, bell. The group, through you and three or four members building on and modifying each other's proposals, will quickly get a feel for a well-rounded lean ritual. Have a couple of practice runs, with feedback, which may lead to one or two more changes.

12. **Co-operative inquiry in the spiritual and the subtle.**   You initiate a co-operative inquiry into some kind of spiritual or subtle experience. For co-operative inquiry, see item 11, co-operative mode, meaning dimension, Chapter 6; and Chapter 7. For a typology of spiritual and subtle experiences, and accounts of co-operative inquiries in this field, see *Sacred Science* (Heron, 1998a).

## The Feeling Dimension: Autonomous Mode

In this mode you give the group space to manage its own affective dynamic. You delegate this work to be self-directed in various forms within the group. Such delegation will have been preceded by a significant amount of relevant training.

1. **Self and peer individual work.**   Working in pairs or in small groups, people take equal time in turns to be the self-directed client, doing personal growth work on their own internal affective dynamic. In both pair work and small group work, each client can either be entirely self-directed, without anyone else being the facilitator; or can ask their partner, or one (and only one) group member, to be an occasional facilitator. All this presupposes there has been training in what to do in both client and facilitator roles.

There are two basic dimensions to this affective work, which are interdependent and can lead over into each other, although the client may choose to attend primarily to one:

- **Emotional processing.** The client is dealing with distress emotion by catharsis and/or transmutation; and expressing and celebrating positive emotional states. Co-counselling, as practised in Co-counselling International, is a classic example.
- **Participative feeling.** The client, at the level of basic feeling, is unfolding and expressing her or his capacity for mutual participation with other presences, both human and more-than-human (in nature and supernature), through empathic resonance. I call this co-creating, and outline one version of it in *Sacred Science* (Heron, 1998a). I also call it *primary theatre*, see item 3 below.

2. **Spontaneous dynamic peer groups.** You set up small peer groups to sit and give each other attention through eye contact, and wait and watch how the group dynamic comes alive, its energy moving about unpredictably and spontaneously, touching different people at different times to cathart, transmute, express, celebrate, or whatever. Work is self-directed, with no-one in the facilitator role. Emotional processing ebbs and flows interwoven with participative feeling and attunement. Such a group presupposes that its members have a certain baseline of emotional competence and skill in participative attunement. This is a more free-flowing, unstructured, Dionysian version of 1 above. Individual work is not timed, and not everyone may take a turn.

3. **Primary theatre in charismatic peer groups.** You initiate small groups in which each person is equally open to respond in movement, speech, sound and song to the spontaneous promptings of their immanent, indwelling spiritual energy. The process can be Dionysian: unstructured, spontaneous, interactive. Or it can be Apollonian, with each person taken equal time for a turn, with the supportive attention of the rest of the group. This sort of group attends primarily to participative feeling, although emotional processing is by no means excluded. My version of primary theatre is based on certain basic principles:

- Each person has their own original relation with creation.
- Revelation is now, in immediate present experience.
- Spiritual authority is within.

The premises of the method are:

- Posture, gesture, movement and sound are for humans the primary language of a participative relation with what there is.

- Spoken metaphor is the verbal elaboration and celebration of that language.

In primary theatre a person explores, reveals and celebrates, in these non-verbal and verbal ways, their original relation with creation.

4. **Autonomous expression and celebration.**   You create a climate in which group members spontaneously express and celebrate positive affect in their own way, at their own chosen time.
5. **Autonomy lab.**   This is one of the most powerful ways in which group members can get a feel for managing their own personal dynamic in the context of the dynamic of various sub-groups and of the autonomy lab as a whole. For a full account of what goes on in an autonomy lab, see item 13, autonomous mode, planning dimension, Chapter 5.
6. **No affective facilitation phase.**   You announce a phase in which you will not manage the affective life the group, but leave members to identify the dynamic and decide whether to stay with it or what process to use to change it.
7. **Autonomous monitoring of the affective dynamic.**   In this extension of the initiative clause (see item 9, autonomous mode, planning dimension, Chapter 5) into the feeling dimension, you create a climate of shared leadership, in which group members spontaneously identify the affective dynamic and propose changes in it, alongside your management of this dimension.
8. **Trainer–trainee delegation.**   You appoint one person in the group, or in each of several sub-groups, to manage the affective dynamic and follow it up with feedback on their facilitation from other members. This is used for training trainers.

# 12 Charismatic Education and Training

In the previous chapter on the feeling dimension, I listed an intervention called 'active charisma', items 10, hierarchical mode. And it is in the context of this dimension that it is most appropriate to go into the nature of charisma or personal power, since it is to do with awakening our capacity for participative feeling, as I have defined it in this book. I introduced the concept of charismatic authority briefly at the beginning, and then again at the end, of Chapter 2. I launch this chapter with a brief reminder of Weber's use of this notion.

## Charisma, Personal Power and Presence

According to the *Shorter Oxford English Dictionary*, the word 'charism' is from the Latin *charisma* and means 'a favour specially vouchsafed by God; a grace, a talent'. In New Testament Greek it means the gift of grace. It was introduced into sociology by Max Weber to refer to an 'extraordinary quality' in persons which gives them a unique and magical impact on others. He distinguished between individual charisma which arises from personal qualities, and the charisma of office which comes from a sacred role.

Weber used the concept in his theory of authority, which included three possible types of legitimacy in a society: traditional, charismatic and legal–rational. If a society becomes too restricted by tradition, change is usually only possible when past customs are challenged by a charismatic leader whose legitimacy derives from his or her personal qualities. Charisma thus has revolutionary power. But when the leader has achieved change it has to be secured by setting up legal–rational legitimacy through an administrative system. Secondary persons are endowed with the authority of the leader through the symbols of their office, and so we have the 'routinization of charisma' (Gerth and Mills, 1984).

What I mean by charisma is personal power. I do not mean by such power the ability to control and dominate others, to be a source of oppression. I mean the very opposite: the ability to be empowered by one's own inner resources, the wellspring within, and the ability thereby to elicit empowerment in others.

A component of charisma is presence. Persons have presence when there is something about their posture and demeanour – their way of being within their bodies and within space of a room – that draws the attention of those around. Personal power is presence in action, set into motion through dynamic interaction with others.

Presence is to do with participative awareness manifest through physical bearing. The person is in conscious command of how he or she is appearing in space and time. There is a full, felt and intentional participation in being embodied. This awareness with command is not distracted by any internal emotional agitation, or by what is going on in the external environment. Charisma – personal power or dynamic presence – is about conscious command of the self in and through the various sensory modes, in active participative relations with other people. I will call these psychophysical modes, since the mind is always involved with them, either in conscious use, or in a half-conscious forgetful state.

A pioneer of conscious use of the self through postural rearrangement was F. M. Alexander, an Australian actor who discovered he could improve the functioning of his larynx by controlling involuntary movements of his head and neck. He developed this into the Alexander Technique (Alexander, 1969; Barlow, 1973; Brennan, 1991; Thame, 1978). His celebrated injunction 'head forward and up' was part of a whole system of unlearning bad postural and motor habits before learning new ones.

While there is some overlap between the Alexander Technique and what I have to say in this chapter about charisma and dynamic presence, my approach is more radical, based on a clear distinction between experiential space and physical space.

My account of dynamic presence makes it behaviourally accessible to anyone. The notion of charisma is demystified and revealed as the birthright of every person who takes the trouble to practise it. In the next section I give a summary account of the psychophysical modes of relating to others, before moving on to deepen the account of presence.

## *The Psychophysical Modes of Relating to Others*

Figure 12.1 illustrates the primary psychophysical modes of interpersonal encounter. To call these modes of relating to others 'psychophysical' is to say that they are never merely physical, but always informed by greater or lesser intentionality and awareness. They are forms of mental and personal as well as physical expression.

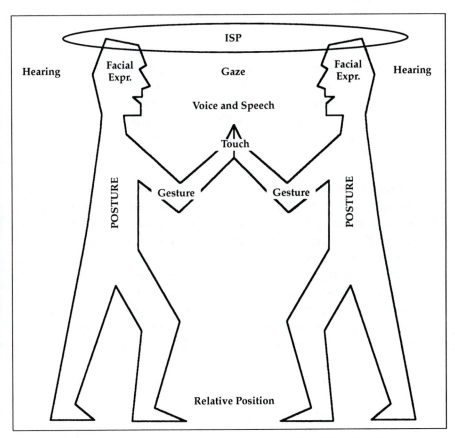

**Figure 12.1** *The psychophysical modes of relating to others*

1. **Posture.** Posture or bearing is about how people hold their trunk, limbs, head and neck as a whole when standing, sitting or reclining. When taken into motion, posture becomes carriage or gait. Posture says a lot about a person's way of being in a world: their relation with the ground, the heavens and the immediate environment, including other people.
2. **Gesture.** I have in mind here primarily the use of the hands and arms; but this can extend to include movements of the

trunk, head and neck, and occasionally a foot. Hand and arm gestures can be purely expressive: they convey their own kind of presentational meaning, as an aesthetic accompaniment to the conceptual meaning of the spoken word. Or they can be indicative, and have a functional purpose: to beckon, halt, point, outline, and so on. Some indicative gestures may also be expressive.

3. **Facial expression.**   The face can be in repose, as when looking at the world, or listening attentively to another person; or it can be animated as when talking and active in conversational exchange, or in emotional arousal. Facial expression depends on how the muscles of the jaw, mouth, nose, eyes and brow interact. It is a potent indicator of a person's mental and emotional state.

4. **Relative position.**   There are three dimensions of the position of one person relative to another. The first is distance: they can be near or far, from being close up to being at the other end of the room. The second is height: they can be above or below or at the same level; for example, one standing when the other is sitting, or both sitting. The third is orientation: they can be face to face; beside on the right or on the left, and either facing the same way or opposite ways; face to back, or back to back. These three dimensions can combine in innumerable ways.

5. **Voice.**   By voice I mean the paralinguistic aspects of speech, that is, how a person speaks as distinct from what they say. This includes physical tone or timbre, volume, pitch, rate of speech, rhythm of speech, use of inflection and emphasis, use of silence and pauses, emotional tone. The variations and combinations of these provide a powerful non-verbal vocal language, which can be used to influence strongly what is being said.

6. **Speech.**   This covers what a person says, the meaning of the words used. It also refers to how language is used: the choice of words and grammatical structures.

7. **Hearing.**   Hearing has three aspects: listening to how the other speaks, to the various dimensions of voice; listening to what they are saying, to the content of their speech; and listening to the linguistic structure of their speech, that is, the choice of words and of grammatical structures.

8. **Gazing.**   I refer here to the use of the eyes, which is twofold. I can look at your behaviour, that is, at your posture, gestures, facial expression, relative position. Or I can look into your eyes, which, if they are looking into mine, will involve mutual gazing. Mutual gazing may be less or more mutual. One person may be dominant in the gaze, the other transfixed into temporary

passivity and submission; or both persons may be equally engaged in projecting and receiving. In the latter case, mutual gazing is one form of immediate encounter with another human being. It enables true meeting to occur, since both persons are in simultaneous, reciprocal contact. I gaze at and receive your gaze, which is gazing at and receiving mine. Four acts are interacting all at once. We participate in each other as distinct beings.

9. **Touch.**   I may touch you in the dominant mode, when you are entirely passive and receptive, as when I lay my hand on your shoulder. Or we may touch each other with full reciprocity as when we shake hands. This last is the other form of immediate encounter between human beings: I give my touch and receive your touch while you do the same. Four processes interact simultaneously. Again, we participate in each other as distinct beings.

10. **Smell.**   There are gender differences here. Assuming basic hygiene, women are more aware than men of intrinsic biological smell. In ordinary social intercourse, this is not a channel of communication that is highly significant at the conscious level. Nevertheless, there may be strong subliminal influences which have an effect on behaviour. Also the use by both sexes of deodorants, by men of after-shave lotions, and by women of perfumes, may influence mutual perceptions and appraisals.

11. **Taste.**   As a mode of relating to others, taste is normally restricted to intimate, erotic encounters.

12. **Intrasensory perception.**   By intrasensory perception, ISP for short, I mean a non-sensory apprehension of the other's mental and emotional state, which is interwoven with sensory apprehension but cannot be reduced to it. Thus the gaze is mediated by the eyes, but is not the eyes. Personal touch is mediated by tactile sensation but is not identical with it. Feeling the experiential space of one's body is mediated by the proprioceptive system, but is not identical with it. Feeling the energy field of the other is not the same as observing their posture and is not an inference from it, but a non-sensory apprehension interwoven with it. In all these instances, intrasensory not extrasensory perception is afoot. ISP is symbolized in Figure 12.1 by the inclusive circle over the two people, and it can be imagined as extending down to interpenetrate all the modes of relating.

The basic distinction in this list is between speech – the use of language to convey meaning – and all the other non-verbal modes including voice. Thomas Reid, the Scottish philosopher of common sense, likewise distinguished between the artificial language of words and the natural language of 'modulations of voice, gestures and features'. These latter signs, he held, are naturally expressive of our thoughts and it is by them we give force and energy to our use of words. Words 'signify but do not express, they speak to the understanding, but the passions, affections and the will hear them not; these continue dormant and inactive until we speak to them in the language of nature to which they are all attention and obedience'.

Reid also thought that the 'vocabulary' of natural language, that is, what non-verbal signs mean, is everywhere the same and intelligible without having to be learnt. The knowledge of it is latent in the mind and a precondition of being able to develop verbal language (Reid, 1764). For more recent work on the relation between verbal and non-verbal language see Abram (1996) and Heron (1992, 1996a).

In primary theatre, the psychophysical modes, other than speech, are for humans the primary language of a participative relation with what there is. Through exploring and expressing this language, a person reveals and celebrates their original relation with creation. The addition of verbal metaphors elaborates the primary non-verbal language (see item 3, autonomous mode, feeling dimension, Chapter 11). Primary theatre is a good foundation for charismatic training.

## *The Experiential Body and the Physical Body*

The most basic of the psychophysical modes of relating, since it is the ground of all the others, is posture – how you hold and carry yourself and occupy your space. This spatial disposition, or physical attitude, is informed by a mental attitude which is conveyed to attentive observers. This bodily manifested state of mind reveals a great deal of information about persons: their fundamental orientation of being within their world, how they feel about themselves and what is around them. And it makes a statement to other people about all that.

When you use total body posture awarely, you do so by feeling where every part of your body is in relation to every other part, and where the whole is in the airy space around, and in relation to the ground, the horizon and the sky. This feeling is organized as your inner body-image, and as we shall see later, it is a feeling which extends out to participate in wider reaches of experiential space. Your inner body-image must be distinguished from your outer body-image. The latter is derived from what you look like from outside: from what you can see of yourself, from mirror images and from feedback from others about your appearance.

The inner body-image is the one you live in. You inhabit it when you stand and sit and move and lie down. It is your *felt sense* of how you are distributed in space, grounded on the earth and open to the sky. It is mediated by integrated kinaesthetic and proprioceptive imagery. I shall call it the experiential body: the body known in terms of inner feeling and experience. The outer body-image, known by your looking and by the perception of others, I shall call the physical body. Figure 12.2 illustrates the difference between the two.

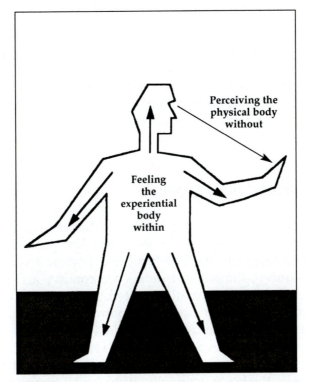

**Figure 12.2**  *The experiential body and the physical body*

The experiential body, as well as providing immediate inner experience of your physical body and its disposition in space, is also a form of consciousness. I am talking in non-Cartesian terms here: consciousness as spatial extension. The mind pervades and is manifested in the space of the experiential body. When you are fully aware throughout the experiential body, upholding physical bearing with that consciousness, then you manifest personal presence.

It is clear that the experiential body is spatially extended awareness. If it were not so we could have no inner knowledge of how the physical body is disposed in space. It is also clear that the experiential body interpenetrates and is distinct from the physical body. The interpenetration guarantees awareness and control of physical location. The distinction between the two is evident in the fact that while you can prod and slap my physical leg and measure it, you cannot do the same to my extended felt sense of where that leg is. You can stick a pin in my body, but not in my experience of my body.

Deriving from the distinction between the experiential body and the physical body is the distinction between experiential space and physical space. Experiential space is known by indwelling it, by feeling it from within and as a whole, simultaneously in all its parts. Such indwelling is in principle illimitable, of unknown potential range. Physical space is known perceptually, serially in terms of piecemeal views, perspectives and orientations, through vision, hearing, touch and by moving from one part of it to another. Experiential space complements physical space, interpenetrating it and enhancing it with a four-dimensional all-at-once grasp of its three dimensions.

## The Experiential Body in Stasis

Many facilitators are crouching unawarely, forgetful and half-asleep, in their experiential bodies and their physical posture shows the unmistakable signs of this. The head and jaw are too far forward, stature is reduced, the anterior thorax too concave and withdrawn, the pelvis and thighs posturally negated. Such a person is about to talk too much, exhibits anxious overcontrol and is missing a lot of what is going on in the group energy field around.

In this condition, the experiential body is in stasis. In conventional pathology, stasis is a stagnation or stoppage of the circulation of any of the fluids of the body, especially of the blood in some part of the blood-vessels. By analogy, there is a stagnation or stoppage of awareness in the experiential body. Some parts of it have very low level of awareness: the felt sense there is almost asleep. In other parts, awareness comes and goes in an irregular fashion here and there. This state of affairs is portrayed in Figure 12.3.

When you are crouching in this way in your experiential body, your awareness in it is reduced and disjointed, occurring in disconnected pockets. So if you are dimly slumped in a chair with ankles crossed, and head jutting forward, you have a low level oscillating awareness of lumps of yourself here and other parts there. To take this sort of stasis into the facilitator role is to have little or no presence and to appear mainly as a talking head.

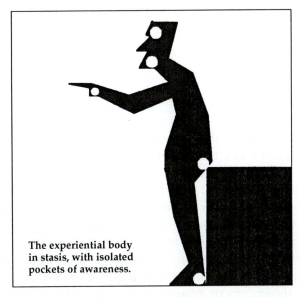

The experiential body
in stasis, with isolated
pockets of awareness.

**Figure 12.3** *The experiential body in stasis*

## The Experiential Body in Presence

Charisma or dynamic presence occurs to a remarkable degree simply when people arouse themselves from inner slumber and occupy the total experiential body with full consciousness. What is distinctive about this awareness is that it is holistic. It occurs all at once. It is a concurrent knowing of where all the parts are and of their integrated volume, their gesture in space. It is not an external, perceived, perspectival knowing of form, but an internal, felt, simultaneous grasp of a total three-dimensional pattern. It is living geometric awareness of one's place in space.

Head, neck and spine are arranged in such a way that there is a subtle unifying sense of lift and levity running through the whole. There is an expansive lengthening and widening of the back. Pelvis, thighs and legs are grounded in awareness of the floor below. This harmonious integration of levity and gravity is managed from the *hara*, the vital centre in the abdomen just below the level of the navel. F M Alexander had the idea of what he called the primary control – 'the head, neck, back relationship' – for co-ordinated posture (Brennan, 1991: 21). The martial art of Aikido goes further and brings out the role of the *hara* as the organizing centre for this and all other relationships in the experiential body, so that there is a felt sense of it as a liberated integrated gesture in space, encompassing a free flow of subtle energy.

When a person does this very simple act of using the will to be synchronously aware within the whole experiential body, then he or she has moved from an ordinary, slouched and impotent state, to an altered, commanding and potent state of being. It is as if the experiential body, thus aroused as a fully extended form of consciousness, radiates its subtle energy, permeating those around and subliminally eliciting their attention. It also means, of course, that the person is ready to feel the spatial, energetic and social field beyond the confines of his or her physical body. The facilitator in this state is poised at the verge of pervasive interpersonal empathy. It is also as if in this state a person refracts something of his or her archetypal nature, *ipsissimus* or *ipsissima* (his verymost self, her verymost self).

A facilitator who is experientially aware throughout his or her posture, who feels its totality, the complete gesture it makes in space, exhibits unmistakable presence. This is the foundation of charisma. And, as if the will is the rotating knob on a rheostat, you can increase or decrease the energy of awareness, the conscious charge, within the felt experiential body, and so enhance or reduce the charismatic impact.

## From Presence to Personal Power

In the opening section to this chapter, I defined personal power in two overlapping ways. First, as the ability to be empowered by one's own inner resources, the wellspring within, and the ability thereby to elicit empowerment in others. And second, as dynamic presence, presence in action, set into motion through active relation with others. You can manifest total presence when in the company of others, yet not engage in any kind of explicit social intercourse. When you start to interact with others, you can either take your presence into personal power, or disappear into conventional social behaviour.

Personal power is rather like the original light of the soul taking charge of its earthly location and its human relationships. Our whole culture runs a strong tacit taboo which conditions people to bury such a propensity and keep it repressed, and to feel diffident and embarrassed when invited to manifest it. This awkwardness, hidden behind conventional social behaviour, is very strong. So the move from being silently present to actively manifesting personal power is a challenge.

In terms of the psychophysical modes of relating, what is called for is the integration of posture, gesture, facial expression including the gaze, with relative position, hearing, voice and, of course, speech.

Human beings are multi-modal beings and have a great facility for integrating many different psychological and interactive modes in one effortless performance, even if much of the time they do this forgetfully and half-asleep from the point of view of personal power. So it is not the integrated mastery that is difficult, but the release from embarrassment and conventional comatose habit.

## The Up-hierarchy of Empowerment

What is needed is a radical strategy for releasing the inner wellspring so that people are inwardly empowered, and feel both the exhilaration of this and the rapport with others that it engenders. This strategy is provided by the up-hierarchy of empowerment, which is the key to charismatic authority and can readily be turned into dynamic experience.

An up-hierarchy works from below upwards, like a tree with roots, a trunk, branches and fruit. It is not a matter of the higher controlling and ruling the lower, as in a down-hierarchy, but of the higher branching and flowering out of, and bearing the fruit of, the lower. The basic features of an up-hierarchy are these:

- What is higher is tacit and latent in what is lower.
- The lowest level is the formative potential of higher levels.
- The higher levels emerge out of the lower.
- There are many different possible forms of emergence.
- The higher levels are a reduced precipitate of the lower.
- The higher levels focus and consummate the lower.
- Each level has a relative autonomy within the total system.
- What is lower grounds, supports and nourishes what is higher.

It is my belief that the developed human psyche functions as an up-hierarchy, in which the grounding level is that of feeling, construed as the capacity for resonance with being and participative attunement to other beings. Out of this affective mode emerges the imaginal mode, including the imagery of perception, memory and imagination. From the imaginal proceeds the conceptual mode, the domain of thought and language; and this is the basis for the development of the practical mode, the level of intention and action. This view has been thoroughly worked out in other books (Heron, 1992, 1996a) and I must refer the reader to them for the details.

When this up-hierarchy model is applied to the empowerment of the psychophysical modes of relating to others, then we have the following levels. In terms of a spatial metaphor, level 1 is *below* level 2 and so on, and power and influence proceeds from below upwards.

## Level 1

The grounding level is that of feeling the fullness of your presence, as already described. You are experientially extended, all at the same time, throughout your posture, feeling its totality, the complete gesture it makes in space. This feeling of presence in your posture will integrate with it your gestures, facial expression including the use of the gaze, your position relative to the other, and your listening, and will extend to pervade empathically the total presence of the group and of members within it. This feeling is the well-spring of the up-hierarchy, the source out of which all the other stages emerge. It is a matter of standing tall, generous and expansive within the space of the world.

## Level 2

Allow this integrated feeling of personal and interactive presence to shape when and to whom you speak, the whole pattern of the timing and tone of your voice and of the phonetic sound you make. Voice, remember, is to do with how you speak, as distinct from what you say. By the timing of your voice, I mean a combination of the following: the speed at which you speak, the rhythm of your speech, the use of inflection and emphasis, and the use of pauses and silences. By the tone of your voice, I mean mainly the emotional tone, but include also physical tone or timbre, volume and pitch. And by the pattern of sounds you make, I mean literally the shape of the noises, the phonemes, that come out of your mouth. The idea at this stage is to let the total pattern of timing, tone of voice and phonetics well up out of feeling fully present as described in level 1.

## Level 3

Now let the timing and tone of voice and pattern of sound of level 2 shape the choice of words and grammatical structures, the linguistic pattern you use. And let this in turn influence what you say, the ideas and information, judgements and opinions you put forward.

## Level 4

Finally, allow your intentions and purposes in relating to the other to be shaped and moulded by the cumulative impact of all the prior levels of the up-hierarchy.

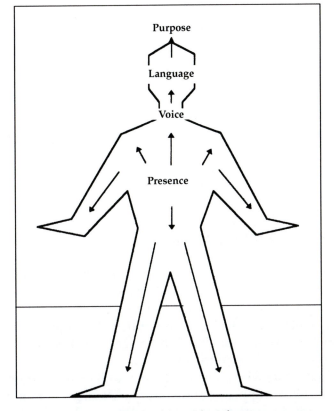

**Figure 12.4**   *The up-hierarchy of empowerment*

Figure 12.4 shows the up-hierarchy of empowerment. In this figure, 'presence' refers to everything in level 1, 'voice' to the timing, tone and sound of voice in level 2, 'language' to both the choice and meaning of words in level 3, and 'purpose' to the intentions involved in relating to the other at level 4.

This is, of course, a complete reversal of the conventional approach to relating to another person. The normal thing is to have some purpose in mind in approaching the other, to let this shape the content of what you are going to say, which in turn will select the words and linguistic structures, which will influence the tone, timing and sounds of voice; then posture, gesture, facial expression and relative position will adapt accordingly. This is the normal down-hierarchy influence in human interaction.

I am not suggesting that this down-hierarchy is to be abandoned. It is too habitual, too ingrained in social intercourse for that. And it is the necessary complement to the up-hierarchy. What I propose is that the facilitator disattend from it, and empower him or herself with conscious use of the up-hierarchy, and learn how empowering it is for the other to be the recipient of that conscious use. In a later section I discuss the integration of the two hierarchies.

For purposes of clarity in the exposition, I have described the four levels of the up-hierarchy as if they follow one after the other in a temporal sequence: first you do this and then the next and so on. But this is obviously not what actually happens. While level 1, that of postural presence, clearly comes first in time, the other levels come all at once. What the up-hierarchy is pointing to is an order of influence, what is simultaneously grounded in what. It indicates whence and how the empowerment proceeds.

## Integrated Postural Presence

Level 1 of the up-hierarchy is as I have said the grounding level. I characterized it as being 'experientially extended, all at the same time, throughout your posture, feeling its totality, the complete gesture it makes in space', and described it further in the earlier section on 'The experiential body in presence'. Let me say here what this does not mean in postural terms.

Many facilitators who have not done any charismatic training tend toward the following postural distortion. The neck is taut, the head and jaw are pushed too far forward and down, the masseter muscle of the jaw is sometimes too tense; the back is reduced in length; the chest is concave and the heart area negated and disowned; the lower abdomen and the whole of the pelvic area and upper thighs are disregarded, by a buried position in a chair, with legs inertly crossed. The same distortions continue when the person stands – neck taut, head and jaw forward and down, the stature reduced, chest caved in, and the lower body energetically alienated. It is virtually impossible to get awareness and presence going with this posture. The experiential body of the person concerned is in chronic stasis.

Some trainees need physically rearranging to discover the power latent in their presence. So I gently move the chest forward inviting the person to extend the thoracic spine a little, spread the chest and move the heart forwards and *offer it to the group*. This makes the head and jaw less cantilevered, more appropriately forward and up, aligns, lifts and liberates the spine and neck, widens the back, and interrupts the compulsion anxiously to talk too much in clock time. Then I invite them to sit upright grounded on the chair with legs uncrossed, feet earthed and thighs apart, to own the whole of the lower half of the body, letting its energy enrich their presence, and to organize the total gesture in space from the lower abdomen. It is very noticeable how simply getting into this postural re-alignment will by itself dramatically alter how a person uses their voice and what they say in their speech.

The heart is full of psychophysical energy and so is the pelvis. These energies need to be the ground for the energies of the throat and the head in integrated postural presence. People need quite a lot of encouragement to open up and evoke these energies and get them going in manifest presence and personal power.

Postural presence, being dynamic and holistic, will integrate with it your gestures and facial expression including the use of the gaze, since these things are all integral parts of the experiential body. It will also integrate your position relative to the other, and your listening, and I deal with these in the next section.

## Pervasive Interpersonal Empathy

When the experiential body is fully awake as an extended form of consciousness, the person is thereby attuned to the whole of the immediate spatial and social environment. To be entirely here now is also to be entirely there now. Presence at the centre of where you stand in the world yields attunement at the periphery. To feel from within the total gesture your body is making in space means also that your awareness goes beyond that gesture: it interpenetrates holistically the spatial field around you. You are aware of your position in relation to others, and you are aware of others – not simply perceptually but by a subtle interpenetration of their own experiential space. You are in a state of pervasive interpersonal empathy. You are listening to others.

In the literal sense of 'listening' you are hearing what people are saying and how they are saying it: you are attending to speech and voice in others. In an extended and metaphorical sense, you are 'hearing' how they are being in their own experiential space. You are resonating with them, attuning to them, feeling their way of manifesting themselves in the moment. We call this rapport.

Egan in his fourth edition of *The Skilled Helper* writes of 'social-emotional presence' by which he means giving full attention to the client, combined with verbal and non-verbal behaviour which indicates 'a clear-cut willingness to work with the client'. This is backed up by an awareness of one's body as a source of communication, and by what he calls 'microskills' which include facing the client squarely, adopting an open posture, leaning forwards or backwards to enhance responsiveness to the client, maintaining good eye contact, and being relatively relaxed in these behaviours. He thinks this microskills level is 'the most superficial level of attending' (Egan, 1990: 108–111). This last is surely a mistaken view, mainly because Egan has not penetrated to the heart of presence – which is how a person simultaneously feels his or her total gesture in space. It is this whole way of being here now, which extends out to embrace the client, that is the foundation of rapport.

What underlies rapport is the fact that experiential space, the holistic space of the experiential body which we feel all at once, extends to interpenetrate surrounding space in order to be able to know the gestures being made in that space. To know from within the total shape your body is making in space, means that you also know the spatial field around it from within. This capacity to feel the 'within' of space around us, and so to feel interpenetration and resonance with the experiential space of other beings, is, I believe, a fundamental capacity of human personhood (Heron, 1992; Abram, 1996). We are inherently empathic, resonating, attuning, spatially interpenetrating beings. We can know each other through this subtle compenetration – shared participation in experiential space – as well as through perceptual encounter in physical space. What our culture does is to fixate our attention on the latter and suppress our capacity for the former.

A deeper view is that:

- There is one universal experiential multispace, the presence of a cosmic consciousness interpenetrating, upholding and including physical space.
- Each person is a local and limited experiential space within it.
- There is in reality no gap, no barrier between the immediate experiential space of individual personal presences, nor between them and the experiential multispace of cosmic presence.

In face-to-face shared rapport there is compenetration of presence, a mutual indwelling by each of his or her own and the other's experiential space. There is participation in one common experiential field with two distinct foci. Sometimes the rapport may be more consciously one-way, as with facilitators doing one-to-one counselling or working intensively with one person in front of a group. In this case their felt participation in the experiential space of the other is the ground for their practice of active empathy. It heightens their ability to attend not just to the meaning of what is being said, but also to how it is being said – the tone of voice, choice

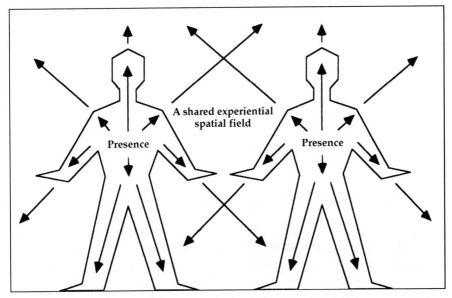

**Figure 12.5** *A shared experiential spatial field*

of language, emotional emphases and inflections, redundancies and slips of the tongue. And it enables them to notice all the bodily cues – the rate and depth of breathing, use of eye contact, facial expression, rigidities or labilities of gesture and posture – which reveal how the person is being, both consciously and unconsciously. Figure 12.5 illustrates a shared experiential spatial field.

Huxley (1963) thought that empathy was strictly a metaphysical impossibility because, he said, we are all private island universes, yet he also held it was necessary and possible by inference or feeling into others. This conflicted and confused view is quoted by Egan (1990: 123) and seems to be echoed by Margulies (1984: 1030) who writes of empathy as a 'negation of self' and thinks it 'involves a kind of self-aggression'. Theodor Lipps thought our belief in the existence of other minds is based on an empathic projection of self into the physical manifestations of others. And generally empathy is defined as a projection of self into the feelings of others. The word itself was coined by Vernon Lee in 1904 and used by Titchener as a translation of the German *Einfühlung*, 'feeling into'.

I think empathy is much better defined as an immediate felt apprehension of the psychophysical states of others. It is a participative kind of direct knowing. It involves neither inference, nor a projection of self into the feelings of others, if this is meant to imply that we assume the form of those feelings and thus know them only indirectly. Max Scheler's account of our knowledge of other minds as direct perception, in which we see a complex whole consisting of the physical expression and what it expresses, comes nearer the truth of the matter. He argues cogently against inference and self-projection theories of how we know that other minds exist (Scheler, 1954).

I suspect that the reduction of empathy to a kind of self-bound projection is all to do with the experiential body being in stasis, with a lack of cultivation of the total feeling of one's gesture in the surround of experiential space. For it is this which yields felt participation in the experiential space of other people.

## *Dynamic Interpersonal Geometry*

Rapport – compenetration with people in experiential space – means that you the facilitator are fully aware of your position relative to everyone else in the group. It also means you are free to move around within this shared inner space using its dynamic interpersonal geometry, suffused by subtle currents of life and mind.

The group is seated in a circle; you are aware of its shape, of where you and your chair are in relation to each person. You may remain seated. You may stand in front of your chair or behind it. You may move to the centre of the circle or across it to one or more persons. You may move round the circle on the outside of it and stand at various points beyond its perimeter. You may swap chairs with one person in order to sit beside another. You may work with someone standing, sitting or kneeling in front of them, on their right or their left side, very close or more distant.

All these options and many more open up as forms of enriching the facilitation process. They all have primary meaning, in terms of the original language of creation. The impulse to use shared experiential space within a group in these ways comes from within that space. It moves you with its own dynamic currents. I cannot give rules or guiding principles for doing it. Remember that you are moving primarily in the 'within' of space, the felt sense of the shared experiential space of the group, and only secondarily in the physical space of visual perspectives. If you stay in this 'within' of space, people will feel subliminally what you are about, and will be subtly liberated by it.

## *Clock Time and Charismatic Time*

In the sequential account of the up-hierarchy, I suggested that what is born, at level 2, out of the integrated presence of level 1, is the timing of speech, which as well as the rate at which you speak includes the rhythm of your speech, the use of inflection and emphasis, and the insertion of pauses and silences. For the facilitator there are two basic sorts of speaking time: clock time and charismatic time.

Clock time is rapid speech time, the one used in most teaching and most conversation. It conveys information, belief, evaluation and opinion in fairly long bursts delivered non-stop. It tends to be verbally dense, fast, loaded with information, somewhat urgent and in a subtle way over-tense. Most facilitators use it most of the time, since it is the norm for the culture.

One reason why it is urgent and over-tense is because it is being used to displace anxiety about facilitator performance. Another less obvious but equally important reason is that it is also being used, unconsciously, as a defence against the possibility of moving into a totally different way of speaking – in charismatic time.

Speech in charismatic time is deep rhythm speech. The use of the voice is imaginatively shaped and moulded out of the speaker's living presence. It is born out of his or her conscious grounding, being fully here in the space of the world. It is much slower than clock time use of the voice, contains clear rhythmic inflections and the intentional insertion of pauses and silences. A pause is a momentary cessation of speech in the interests of rhythm and emphasis. A silence is a longer pause pregnant with intention and awareness, entirely free of all urgency or tension, and allows both the sound and the meaning of what has been said to resonate fully within the listeners.

The tone of voice is warmer, richer, deeper, more mellow. With the slower more rhythmic delivery, the altered tone and the use of well-timed silences, the choice of words becomes more basic, the language becomes richer in imagery, tinged with the poetic. The listener is more deeply engaged with the content. He or she is imaginatively involved in what is being said, has time to understand and assimilate it and get interested. In short, the listener starts to feel empowered.

The rapidity of clock-time speech, and its inability to use intentional silence, serves in general social intercourse to displace a good deal of continuous tension. Facilitators, as I have said, use it for the same purpose and therefore tend to say too much for too long. This is inevitable if the purpose of speaking at an unconscious level is to relieve anxiety. So facilitators need both to reduce the overall amount they say in clock time, and to learn to speak, as appropriate, in charismatic time.

For a facilitator to say everything in charismatic time would become unbearably pompous, and tedious for the listeners. But to

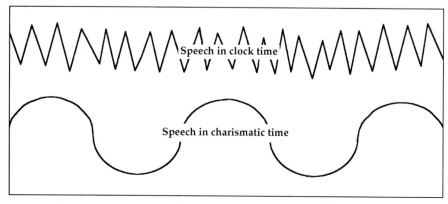

**Figure 12.6**    *Speech in clock time and in charismatic time*

say everything in clock time, which is the current norm, leaves everyone impoverished and unempowered, as if there is a hidden conspiracy, to which all are subservient, that the depths of human reality shall be ignored. What is needed is a facility for moving between the two kinds of speech, which are symbolized in Figure 12.6.

It is not that you, the facilitator, are continually in charismatic time, but you are modulating the voice into it on occasion, to say things of human depth and significance. Such intermittent use of charismatic time is appropriate for:

- Culture-setting statements such as proposing group values and ground-rules.
- Making contracts about basic objectives and methods.
- Making important permission-giving statements – for example, to the wounded child within the participants.
- Implanting suggestions into the group consciousness and process.
- Handling critical incidents in the group process.
- Expounding some basic idea.
- Introducing the deeper point of an exercise.
- Underlining a vital piece of feedback.
- Appreciating what has been said or done.
- All those interventions which affirm participants' basic humanity.

A key issue in such use is that your voice becomes anxiety-free. It is charged with the power of your presence. It is pregnant with who you really are. The tone, the rhythm, the slower speed reveal that some deeper, confident reality within you is in charge of your manner of delivery. You have empowered your behaviour from a wellspring within, which the up-hierarchy has liberated. It is this non-verbal manner to which, above all, people respond. It is the real language to which the soul of the listener responds. Once a listener feels empowered by this, then he or she is ready to do business positively with the content of what is being said. But if the non-verbal manner of voice and posture is precipitate and anxious, the listener is already predisposed to have difficulty with the content of speech. This is the simple and fundamental point which, in my experience, many facilitators have not, in practical action, grasped.

The crucial test of competence in the use of charismatic time is the ability to be fully present, without any anxiety, during the intentional silences within your delivery. When people practise charismatic speech, they can shift into appropriate speed, rhythm and tone of voice, but often baulk at the use of significant silence, since residual anxiety is confronted by this.

The thing to do in the silence is to feel your presence, to beam it out through posture, gesture, facial expression, the use of the gaze and relative position, and in and through this very process to be fully attuned to the presence of all your listeners. In this inner deed, in the depths of its silence, you come to know, to hear, and to draw forth, their fullness of being. Empowered within, you are empowering without. I have found it useful to encourage facilitators to feel the silence in terms of several of their own heart-beats.

So the purpose of such silence, which in fact lasts for no more than a few seconds, is to underline what has been said, to let its unstated implications unfurl, to let it generate imaginal and emotional resonance, to honour the reality of the listeners – giving them time to take in what you are saying, to respond to how you are being, to process all this within – and to affirm that the relationship of being together is more basic than speech.

Speaking in clock time also requires attention. People need to practise talking in clock time, without going on too long, and ridding it of the cooped-up smell of anxiety and tension. When facilitators are at ease with themselves in their presence, then their clock time speech is more laid back, briefer. If they are not in this way at ease with themselves, they often say too much. Yet it is *always* clear to the attentive listener when they have said just the right amount and should stop.

## Emotional Tone of Voice

At level 2 in the up-hierarchy I mentioned tone of voice alongside timing, and said that I mean mainly the emotional tone, but include also physical tone or timbre, volume and pitch. The emotional tone of the voice can convey many different qualities. It can be warm or cold, lively or dull, interested or bored, and so on. It is quite distinct from physical tone or timbre. A voice can sound physically like a foghorn or a French horn, yet each of these different timbres can carry a wide range of varied emotional tones.

For some people, the emotional tone of voice gets hijacked by early traumatic history. There gets incorporated in it a chronic inflection of pleading or defiance or whatever other defensive attitude the wounded child adopted in order to survive. This inflection is present whatever the person is saying in whatever circumstance. It is not clear why this defensive displacement occurs in some and not in others. But if a facilitator has it, then it makes sense to retrain the voice and become free of it, otherwise participants in groups will be thrown subliminally into parent-type transference by it. If at the same time because of other aspects of what the facilitator is doing they are cast into child-type transference, then they are going to be in a bit of a muddle.

Physical tone, or timbre, is to do with the structure of the voice-box and of the resonating cavities, and as I say is independent of emotional tone in the sense that the same basic timbre can carry many very different emotional tones. However, there is also an important connection between them. Timbre is a product of the proportion in which the fundamental physical tone is combined with the harmonics or overtones. There is not much I can do about the basic structures of my voice-box and related parts which produce the fundamental tone. But there is a great deal I can do about two closely related things: how I put the breath through the voice-box and how I set other spaces in the body resonating. In this way I can control not only pitch and volume, but I can also to a degree modify the timbre by altering the range of overtones, also their proportion in combination with the basic tone.

My view is that emotional tone is *carried* by a subtle modification of timbre due to small variations in the range and proportion of overtones, interacting with small variations of pitch and volume. All these variations are the effect of how the voice-box and other structures are being used by control of the breath and resonance. This use is managed in the experiential body, the inner felt body-image, and is directly influenced by our emotional and spiritual state.

On the one hand, this use can be cramped by continuous emotional inhibition. As I said earlier, personal power is the original soul taking charge of its earthly location. Our culture is repressive of this process. The voice has direct access to this original being, so if the basic timbre of the voice is under social restraint and its full resonance unused, the full emotional tone of the embodied soul is constantly subdued.

On the other hand, the original uninhibited signature of the voice can be recovered through various techniques of voice production, especially those involving singing. In charismatic training, the trainee is invited to let the emotional tone of the voice *emerge* out of integrated postural presence, to speak from the belly, from the fullness of being here now. Physically, the timbre acquires more resonance, more overtone richness, and emotionally the voice reveals warmth and original value, and becomes empowering for the soul of the listener.

## *Phonetic Command*

I must remind the reader, who may be feeling daunted by this analytic separation of all the many aspects of human expression, and thus wondering however to put it all together in conscious behaviour, that multi-modal functioning is entirely normal to human beings, who love it. It is no problem, but a natural joy, for people to integrate seeing, hearing, smelling, touching, moving, memory, fantasy, reflection, mood, pleasure and intention all in one short sequence of behaviour. In the same way, putting together all the elements of the up-hierarchy of expressive modes is exhilarating and agreeable, the more so because this way of being, suppressed in our culture, releases deep well-springs of personal empowerment.

Phonetic command is the third part of level 2, after timing and tone of voice. It is about the sounds you make in speaking, the pattern of noises you utter. Tune in to a radio programme in a language you do not understand, and listen to the sound of the language just as sound, a stream of patterned noise. Any such language is made up of a relatively small number of phonemes, a phoneme being the smallest segment of sound that can differentiate two words.

The so-called Received Pronunciation of British English has 44 phonemes according to one common analysis, 24 consonant sounds and 20 vowel sounds. Each phoneme may have several variations called allophones. Thus the phoneme 'p' sounds different in 'spot' and 'pot', since in the latter the 'p' is pronounced with a puff of breath, but not in the former. And each phoneme has one or more features to do with whether it involves the vocal cords, lips, tongue, nasal passages, and so on. English phonemes are quite distinct chunks of sound, but in some other languages there are phonemes which are distinguished by variations of tone on the same basic sound (Aitchison, 1987).

I mention all this simply to raise the reader's consciousness about an aspect of voice that normally disappears from awareness because we are so preoccupied with what we mean by the sounds we are uttering. But the sound *qua* sound has an impact all of its own. So my proposal is that facilitators let their felt presence in the whole experiential body manifest as the music of vocal sound. The sound they produce then has melodic qualities carried by the tone of voice and the rhythmic timing. Abram (1996) writes eloquently about the expressive qualities of voice as the foundation of language.

## Command of Language

In the up-hierarchy of personal empowerment, you let the tone and timing of voice, and music of sound at level 2, shape the command of language at level 3, that is, the choice of words and grammatical structures, the linguistic pattern you use. It is notorious how often facilitators can disempower their own facilitation by riddling their speech with verbal and grammatical detractors. They do this either by subtly undermining themselves, or by putting their listeners down in some implied way. Their choice of words, the forms of speech, show noticeable hints of pleading, apology, fear of rebuff, appeasement, diffidence, insecurity, uncertainty on the one hand; and rebuke, bossiness, condescension, disapproval, dislike, irritation, impatience and suchlike on the other. It is not that any of these things are grossly explicit in the language, but are implicit in the selection of terms and syntax. So the facilitator does not say 'I am too anxious to propose this' but 'I wonder whether perhaps you would mind trying this out'.

All this can be cleaned up from below, so to speak, in using the up-hierarchy. If facilitators are fully present, their experiential body integrating pelvis and lower limbs, belly, heart, larynx and head, and if timing and tone of voice and music of sound are marshalled out of this presence, then a lot of linguistic detractors will simply drop out of their speech. They start talking with their own true inner authority, honouring both themselves and their listeners. To the extent that this does not occur in training exercises, trainees need to be interrupted as soon as they slip into a verbal or grammatical detractor, and to be invited to run the statement again free of all negativity. Several re-runs may be necessary for some trainees to establish such freedom.

## Command of Content of Speech

The command of language, just considered, is the basis, also at level 3, for taking charge of the content of speech. So the selection and shape of your language, emerging out of all the prior levels of the up-hierarchy, influences *what* you say, the ideas and information, judgments and opinions you put forward. This is where the up-hierarchy and the down-hierarchy meet.

The down-hierarchy is conventional in the culture. It starts at level 4 and works downward by control to level 1. Thus we normally have some purpose in mind in relating to others, let this shape the meaning of what we are going to say, which in turn will select the words and linguistic structures, which will influence the tone, timing and sounds of voice; then posture, gesture, facial expression and relative position will adapt accordingly.

I think that facilitators in their early days rely heavily on the down-hierarchy, having carefully worked out their objectives and their programme – which shape what they say in front of the group. With more experience they disengage from it, keep their goals and plans more distant from their immediate behaviour, and let their presence before the group and their attunement to its energy field shape what they say. But they still have goals and plans in setting up the group, and these will quite properly also exert influence on what they say before the group.

The first meeting place of the two hierarchies is at level three in the content of speech, in what the facilitator is saying. The pre-existent objectives and programme of the facilitator in organizing the workshop – which proceed from the down-hierarchy – will have some general bearing on everything he or she says during it, and from the back of the mind will shape the broad sweep of his or her facilitation.

At the same time what in detail is said at this moment and in this given context in the workshop will be shaped by the up-hierarchy. Most times these immediate, existentially responsive statements will be in accord with the broad guiding plans of the down-hierarchy. But not always, for sometimes the realities encountered through the use of the up-hierarchy and its grounding attunement to the group life, will mean a discontinuity between what is said and pre-existent plans.

For the most part, through well-established habit, the down-hierarchy can be left to look after itself, so that the facilitator can empower him or herself with conscious use of the up-hierarchy. Thus the content of statements is simplified, gets down to basic ideas and principles, when it emerges from integral presence shaping vocal and verbal command. Innate intelligence shines through, uncluttered by unnecessary parentheses and qualifying clauses. Meanings are informed by the lucid beams of the heart.

As well as content of speech, there is the timing of that content – when it is said; and its direction – to whom it is said, whether to the group as a whole or one or more persons in it. These two vital aspects of speech behaviour go right back to level 2 of the up-hierarchy, and were mentioned as the first part of it.

## Command of Purpose

The final stage of the up-hierarchy is to allow the purposes and intentions you have in mind to be shaped by the whole of the preceding levels. These levels include your personal presence and rapport with the group, your sense of when to speak and to whom, your timing and tone and sounds of voice, your command of language and of content. As all these are working, emerging one out of the other, they shape and reshape the purposes which lie behind what you are saying. These purposes thus become existentially attuned: flexible, adapted and appropriate to what is happening.

As with the meaning of your speech, the purposes behind it will also be influenced by the down-hierarchy objectives and programme which you bring to the group and which have been expressed in the publicity for it. So level 4 is the second place where the two hierarchies quite properly interact.

This interaction at level 4 is usually tacit and unstated. Often the purposes which arise out of the up-hierarchy will be broadly consonant with your original objectives and programme. At other times, you may be silently modifying and adapting your original objectives and programme to suit the emerging realities of group process. Where there is radical dissonance between the two, renegotiation with the group about its agenda may be required.

## The Down-hierarchy of Facilitator Principles

The down-hierarchy starts at level 4, the level of purposes and intentions; and this level controls level 3, the meaning of what is said; and so on. I intend to look only at level 4. There are three main sorts of purposes and intentions involved here.

1. **Group objectives.** These are the published objectives and the provisional programme of the group. They define the group for prospective applicants to it, and are stated in the prospectus for it.
2. **Technical principles.** These are the technical facilitator principles which you intend to use in pursuing the published objectives and realizing the programme. This book is devoted to what I regard as some of the main ones, such as balancing the use of hierarchy, co-operation and autonomy in managing the dimensions of planning, meaning, confronting, feeling, structuring and valuing.
3. **Moral principles.** These are overarching ethical norms, of which I believe there are three primary ones, and I review these in the next section.

These three sets of intentions are the guiding lights of the down-hierarchy. Together they provide a kind of continuous sunlight which enables the manifold growths of behaviour within the up-hierarchy to flourish.

## Guiding Moral Principles of Facilitation

Every facilitator will have their own explicit or implicit set of such basic principles. I present below three of my own. I am not talking about intermediate moral principles such as telling the truth, keeping promises and contracts, which I shall take for granted in this discussion, but about the ultimate ones, those which support us in realizing our most cherished values, and on which the intermediate ones themselves rest.

1. **The principle of love.** I define this, for facilitators, as the commitment to provide conditions within which people can in liberty and co-operation, and with appropriate hierarchy, determine and fulfil their own true needs and interests. How to provide these conditions is dealt with by the group objectives and programme, and by the technical principles, both mentioned in the previous section.
2. **The principle of impartiality.** This means that facilitators are committed to giving everyone in the group equality of consideration. Time and attention are distributed among participants fairly. This does not mean that each participant gets the same time and attention from the facilitator as every other. It means that differences of treatment can be justified by relevant differences between the participants concerned. It is these relevant differences that get

equality of consideration: each person's special needs and interests are considered equally. As a result everyone is treated both differently and fairly.

3. **The principle of respect for persons.**   This could also be called the principle of respect for autonomy. It is clearly implicit in the statement of the principle of love, but merits special mention. It means that facilitators are committed to honour the right of every person to make autonomous choices about what they do or do not do in any group, and to be given adequate information about any proposed activity so as to be able to make an informed choice about it.

So here we have three transcendent principles to guide the whole facilitation enterprise. But without the immanent growth of living soul within the up-hierarchy, they become as nothing.

## Training Exercises for the Cultivation of Charisma, Dynamic Presence, Personal Power

As presented below, these exercises presuppose a training context, where people are working in pairs or small groups.

### Experiential presence
Stand up and arrange your experiential body so that you can be present throughout it all at once. Find your way into the exhilarating feeling of simultaneous extension in all directions. Your posture will assume a stance like those found in the *mudras* (sacred postures) of Tantric practice, or in the martial arts such as Tai Chi and Aikido: knees somewhat bent, legs well grounded, arms out from the side, elbows bent; spine, neck and head aligned with a subtle feeling of levity, the back elongated and widened. Now move slowly, maintaining this same experiential presence throughout your moving form, co-ordinating the integrated, extended awareness from the *hara*, the centre of gravity – and levity – within the lower abdomen. Form into pairs and share your findings with each other. End with experience-sharing in the whole group.

### In and out of presence
Work together in pairs and stand opposite each other. In silence, without any dialogue, one person practise shutting down, then opening up, full awareness in the experiential body, moving their mental attitude to and fro several times from being slouched half-

asleep in it to being fully present throughout it. When moving into presence in this exercise stay within the limits of 'normal' posture. Give a report on the felt difference between these two states of being, then hear feedback from your partner. Reverse roles. End with experience-sharing in the whole group.

### Belly-heart-head presence

People work in pairs. Each partner takes a turn doing all the following, first seated and then standing. Place your left hand on your lower abdomen and say 'I am present in my belly' and occupy awarely the whole of the lower experiential body. Then on your chest and say 'I am present in my heart', while entering thoracic space and integrating it with the lower body. Then on your larynx and say 'I am present in my voice', while entering the throat, integrating it with the thorax and the lower body. Then on your forehead and say 'I am present in my head' re-aligning the head, neck and spine with the larynx, the chest and the lower body. Finally, while feeling the total integrated posture from within, affirm the four statements one after the other, ending with the statement 'I am present'. Follow with report from self on the experience and feedback from partner. End with experience-sharing in the whole group.

### From stasis to presence

People work seated in pairs. Each partner takes a turn at role playing any short piece of facilitator talk, speaking it first of all crouched in a typical state of contracted postural stasis, and then again with integrated postural presence, ending with a report from self on the experience followed by feedback from partner. End with experience-sharing in the whole group.

### Parking with presence

This exercise is a piece of homework. Park your car in a limited space between two other parked cars. Practise doing this by becoming aware of the experiential form of the car, of the space it is to enter, and of the relative positions of the two. So you have a felt sense of the whole configuration of car and parking space known all at once from within. Indwell this configuration while manoeuvring the car, supported of course by visual perspectives in physical space. Note the greater ease with which you can park the car when doing so with presence, compared with trying to manoeuvre it exclusively from limited physical perspectives.

*Sharing experiential space*
People work in pairs. Partners move slowly and silently around each other. Become conscious within the shared experiential space that includes the total postures and relative positions of each of you. Practise sustaining this all-at-once grasp of shared experiential space while facing and looking at the other, while side by side and catching only a glimpse of the other in the corner of the visual field, and while being back to back and unable to see the other. The challenge is not to get sucked back into attending entirely to perceived perspectives in physical space. Experience-sharing in pairs and then in the whole group.

*Interacting within shared experiential space 1*
People work in pairs. Partners approach each other, shake hands and say 'Hello', all the while having a felt sense of the total spatial form of the two person interaction from within your shared experiential space. Often the handshake and the 'Hello' will throw you out of experiential space awareness into restricted physical space awareness. So keep practising until your consciousness is no longer distracted and contracted by the social convention. Experience-sharing in pairs and then in the whole group.

*Interacting within shared experiential space 2*
People work in groups of four and for several minutes have an informal conversation on what has been going on so far in the training programme. At the same time practise indwelling, in experiential space, the whole shared configuration of the group, feeling from within it everyone's total spatial gesture in relation with everyone else's. Ordinary social interaction has built into it hidden norms of contracted spatial awareness, of living in space as exclusively perceptual and physical. So during the conversation you need to remind yourself to resist these tacit norms, and stay in subtle expanded inner space. Experience-sharing in the small groups and then in the whole group.

*Pervasive empathy when listening*
People work in pairs. Partners take it in turns to talk for some minutes about your plans for their next main holiday. As listener, practise being aware within the whole of your own experiential body and expand this to include awareness of the relative positions of both of you, this spatial configuration being felt as a whole from within it. Then you indwell more particularly the experiential space of the speaker and get a felt sense of how he or she is being and

manifesting within that space, noticing how this correlates with all the perceived cues of breathing, posture, gesture, facial expression, voice and speech. After each turn, the listeners share their experience with their partners. End with experience-sharing in the whole group.

### Pervasive empathy when speaking

Work in the whole group if it is not too large, or in two sub-groups each in a room of its own. Everyone in turn comes and stands at the front of the group and talks for a minute or two in a role play making opening statements in some group they are about to run. When it is your turn, practise being fully present throughout your experiential body and extend this to include the whole shared experiential space of the room, the emotional energy and attitude of everybody in it. If your awareness contracts back into exclusive physical perception, just gently expand it again. A short report after each turn, then general discussion at the end.

### Moving in shared experiential space

People work in small groups of six. Everyone takes a turn as facilitator in a role play choosing some important piece of facilitation they normally do. In your turn establish yourself in your personal presence and in pervasive rapport with the group, and indwell this shared experiential space while doing your facilitation. Give yourself permission to move freely within this space throughout the facilitation without worrying at all about whether it is fitting or appropriate to go here or go there; just follow the currents. After your turn give yourself feedback, and hear feedback from the group. End with experience-sharing in the whole group.

### Moving between clock time and charismatic time

I invite people to work in pairs; and I have a small gong. Partners take turns over several minutes of describing the place where they live. I have instructed them to start the description in ordinary clock time mode, and that at the first stroke of the gong they are to shift over, continuing the description in charismatic time. At the next stroke of the gong they go back into clock time and so on. The listener just listens, but uses hand gestures to slow the speaker down if charismatic speech degenerates back into clock speech. After each turn, the speaker gives his or her report on the experience, followed by feedback from the listener. End with experience-sharing in the whole group.

### Applied charismatic time

People work in groups of four or five. Each person takes a turn as facilitator in a short role play practising the use of charismatic timing in one of the areas mentioned: culture-setting statements, making contracts, permission-giving statements, implanting suggestions, handling critical incidents, the exposition of some basic ideas, the deeper point of an exercise, underlining a vital piece of feedback, and so on. Each person chooses whichever of these is most pertinent. A paragraph of delivery is sufficient; then feedback to self, feedback from peers, and several re-runs to take account of feedback and deepen the practice. End with experience-sharing in the whole group.

### Applied clock time

People work in groups of four or five. Each person takes a turn as facilitator in a short role play practising the use of speaking in clock time to introduce some exercise (a) describing how to do it and (b) giving the rationale for doing it. Each listener puts up a hand when they feel the facilitator has said enough about (a), and likewise about (b). The facilitator stops both (a) and (b) whenever he or she feels it is appropriate to do so. Each turn is followed by feedback to self and feedback from the others. The feedback can consider not only the length of speech, but also any undertow of tension and anxiety. End with experience-sharing in the whole group.

### Conscious emotional tone

I have to hand various verses by Blake, Shelley, Wordsworth, Tennyson, Swinburne and other suitable poets. They are stanzas that are lyrical, sonorous, emotionally, imaginatively and spiritually evocative. In small groups people take turns to declaim one stanza with conscious command of timing and especially emotional tone of voice, generating this tone out of the fullness of their original presence. There is a report on the experience from self and then feedback from the others, and perhaps a second or third go to get deeper into the command of tone. End with experience-sharing in the whole group.

### Applied emotional tone and timing

People work in small groups of four or five. Each person takes a turn as facilitator in a short role play practising the use of charismatic emotional tone, as well as timing, in one of these areas: culture-setting statements, making contracts, permission-giving statements, implanting suggestions, handling critical incidents, the exposition of some basic ideas, the deeper point of an exercise, underlining a vital piece of feedback, and so on. Each person chooses whichever of these is most pertinent. A paragraph of delivery is sufficient, then feedback to self, feedback from peers, and several re-runs to take account of feedback and deepen the practice. End with experience-sharing in the whole group.

## Listening to speech as melody

This exercise is prepared for overnight. Members of the group who speak foreign languages and are familiar with their literature come to the session with well-known lyric poems written in those languages. These poems are read to small groups of those who do not understand the language being used. The listeners listen to the stream of phonemes as melody carried by the tone and rhythm of the speaker's voice, without in any way trying to understand or divine what the poem is about. They then share their experiences of this melody, describing its qualities. Later the speaker gives a brief precis of the poem in English, and this is followed by more discusssion. End with experience-sharing in the whole group.

## Glossolalia as melody

People work in groups of four. Each person takes it in turn to practise *glossolalia*, that is, speaking in tongues for a few minutes. This simply means you make up a language: a stream of sounds compounded into 'words' and 'sentences', using a wide range of phonemes which may be entirely imaginary, or which may come from any language you have ever heard. Out of your conscious presence, you voice phonemes as a melody carried by the tone and rhythm of your voice, without in any way bothering about what the sounds mean. You imagine you are doing this in relation to one of your own back-at-work groups. The listeners first of all give feedback on the qualities of the vocal 'music' produced, then later they discuss what they imagine it could have meant. End with experience-sharing in the whole group.

## Speaking with melody and meaning

People work in groups of four. Everyone takes it in turn to be a facilitator in role play speaking to a back-at-work group about any chosen significant topic. As facilitator, you become fully present, and speak one paragraph in English, attending fully to the phonemes – letting their melody as a pattern of sound be carried by the tone and rhythm of your voice. Give some feedback to yourself on this melody, and hear feedback from the group. Then have a rerun or two to become more at ease in producing agreeable sounds as such while using them to convey meaning. End with experience-sharing in the whole group.

### Empowering language for speaker and listener

People work in groups of four or five. Everyone takes a turn as facilitator in a short role play to practise doing a piece of facilitation they feel anxious about. They use the up-hierarchy model, being grounded in their presence and using charismatic and clock time as appropriate, and allowing all this to shape the language they use. The listeners only attend to the facilitator's language, and interrupt it as soon as any word, phrase or grammatical structure is either self-disempowering or an implied put-down to the recipients. The facilitator attends to being present and restates what was said until all agree it is empowering to both speaker and listener. End with experience-sharing in the whole group.

### Total up-hierarchy

People work in groups of five. Everyone takes a turn as facilitator in a role play introducing some important piece of theory, or rationale for practice, in your chosen field. Deliver this exposition out of the total up-hierarchy, grounded in your presence, out of which vocal timing (moving between clock and charismatic time), tone and sound, command of language and thus content emerge. After feedback from self and others, take one or two reruns to deepen the effect. Such reruns are an important part of any training exercise. End with experience-sharing in the whole group.

# 13 The Structuring Dimension

After a look at charismatic matters in the previous chapter, I return to continue a detailed account of the core model of the six dimensions and three modes of facilitation. In this chapter I discuss the fifth and structuring dimension. The question here for you, the facilitator, is: how can the group's learning experiences be structured? What form is the learning going to have, and who is going to give it that form? Your concern is with the learning environment, and with experiential methods, structured exercises and their genesis.

## Planning and Structuring an Exercise

The planning and structuring dimensions overlap in the area of structured exercises. Planning interrelates topics, time, resources, learning methods and assessment; and methods include exercises. When planning a course you may select certain forms of exercise and give them appropriate places in the programme. The form of an exercise includes its design and the decision-modes used in running it, that is, how it is to be supervised – whether you direct it as it is going on, you do this co-operatively with the participants, or they manage it on their own.

Planning, then, can include the selection of design and decision-mode for an exercise. It may specify both these aspects of every exercise in great detail, or it may give only a bare outline of the forms of exercises to be used at various points in the programme, or it may do no more than imply that exercises of some sort will be used.

The structuring dimension is to do with the immediate and active implementation of the plan. It is at the workface, managing the current learning of these participants at this point in their course. It may modify a detailed plan and adapt it to the evident needs of the learners, or change it radically, or abandon it entirely. It may give substantial body to an outline plan.

The structuring dimension deals with the existential and situational realities of learning – with what goes on when you are face to face with your learners. It is concerned with giving full working form to the methods of learning. Hence it is under the structuring dimension that I consider in detail the design of exercises and the way the decision-modes can be used in their supervision.

Of course, the planning dimension deals with the course programme as a whole, with the timetabling of topics, resources, assessment, and all the methods, not just with the structure of exercises. And the structuring dimension is also concerned with others' ways of giving form to learning as we shall see. However, the nature of the overlap – and of the distinction – between these two dimensions in the area of structured exercises is important to grasp. It is presented in Figure 13.1.

| | Planning dimension | | Structuring dimension |
|---|---|---|---|
| | *Place of exercise in course programme* | *Design of exercise* | *Supervision of exercise* |
| **Hierarchy:** *you alone* | | | |
| **Co-operation:** *you with group* | | | |
| **Autonomy:** *group alone* | | | |

**Figure 13.1**   *Planning and structuring an exercise*

This diagram shows that the timetabling for use of an exercise falls under the planning dimension, and the actual supervision of it under the structuring dimension (although the plan may indicate what sort of supervision is to be used). The design of it can fall under either: the plan may include a detailed design of an exercise; or it may indicate that the design is to be worked out at the time, in which case it falls under the structuring dimension. And even a design worked out at the planning stage may have to be modified in the actual learning situation.

The diagram also reminds us that decision-modes used in timetabling an exercise, those used in designing it, and those used in supervising it, can all be different. You may directively insert into the timetable an exercise the design of which is to be negotiated between you and the group at the time, and which when put into action is to be supervised entirely autonomously by the group.

To say that you have designed an exercise may literally mean that you have created it. For convenience, I also take it to mean that you may have chosen it from the existing repertoire of exercises in the literature.

## *The Experiential Learning Cycle*

The basic way to structure and interweave the four kinds of learning and understanding – conceptual, imaginal, practical and experiential, as defined in Chapters 1 and 6 – is to use an experiential learning cycle. There are various overlapping versions of this cycle, and I introduce a conveniently condensed one here. It combines both the trainer's and the trainee's roles. A more detailed discussion of the ins and outs of the cycle, and of its varieties, is presented in the next chapter.

Suppose the group is learning some interpersonal skill. The trainees start with some conceptual understanding, listening to the trainer make descriptive statements about what is involved in exercising this skill. They then move to imaginal understanding, as the trainer demonstrates the skill, or shows a video, so they can form an image of the sequence of behaviours that manifest the skill. This guides them in practising the skill, where they start to get practical understanding of how to do it. Practice brings the skill into relation with another person; and so they enter into an experiential understanding of the dynamic encounter with the other. Practising the skill interacts with the dynamic of the encounter: practical and experiential understanding continuously modify each other.

Then there is feedback on the practice, which starts the second cycle. Feedback returns the learners to conceptual understanding. It reflects on what went on in the practical and experiential phases of understanding, seeking to spotlight this through the use of words and concepts. It applies standards, picking out good and bad practice. This leads to a revised and enriched imaginal understanding, a better image of the form and sequence of behaviours; thence to better practice, and so on. Figure 13.2 maps out the cycles.

The upper level of the diagram represents the reflection phase, where thinking and imagination interact (shown by the two-way arrows); the lower level represents the action phase, where there is an interplay between one's behaviour and encounter with the other (shown by the two-way arrows). While the main thrust of the cycle is clear, the four kinds of learning are much more involved in each other at each stage than the diagram can show. Going round the cycle several times enhances learning, as each kind of understanding clarifies every other kind.

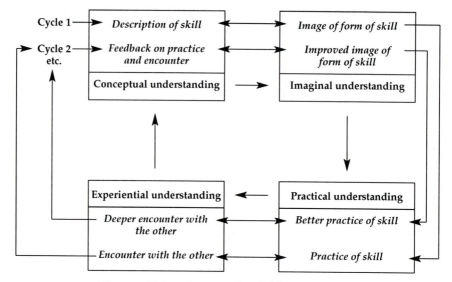

**Figure 13.2**   *An experiential learning cycle*

The experiential learning cycle, in this and other forms, is either used explicitly and formally in structured exercises; or in the broader sweep of the group's development as it moves between phases of active learning and times for review of what it is about. In advanced stages of learning, it can be developed into full-blown co-operative inquiry – see item 11, co-operative mode, meaning dimension, Chapter 6, and Chapter 7.

The version presented here, for interpersonal skills training, combines both trainer and trainee roles. You, the trainer, do the conceptual modelling of the skill, and some demonstration or illustration of it, at the start of the first cycle. The trainees discuss the conceptual model with you, and build up their imaginal understanding of the skill through attending to your demonstration. The trainees are on their own in the practical and experiential phases, and also when they return, at the start of cycle 2, to the conceptual level of feedback and reflection on practice, which takes place in the small practice sub-group. The feedback and reflection can be continued in the large group, with sharing between sub-groups, and involving you in the general review. What is learnt from this review is then taken back into practice to improve performance, and so on.

From the point of view of the decision-modes, first you are hierarchical in modelling, then the trainees are autonomous in practice, experience, feedback and reflection, then you co-operate with them in a general review, then they are autonomous again in practice, and so on. This sequence is examined in detail in the next section.

## *Supervision of an Exercise and the Experiential Learning Cycle*

The supervision of an exercise is about who takes responsibility for what, at different stages of the experiential learning cycle. An exercise which embodies this learning cycle includes several basic stages. Let us first go into more detail about the structure of the cycle given above for acquiring some interpersonal skill. Then the stages are:

1. **Modelling the skill conceptually and imaginally.** A verbal description is given of the skill, and of what it means to do it well. It is analysed conceptually; and presented imaginally by evocative accounts of instances and case studies. There may also be a live or video demonstration.
2. **Describing the exercise.** The exercise is designed and instructions are given in detail about its content and procedures: what it is about; the structure and sequence, who does what, the timing of each part. These first two stages are done when everyone is in the large group.
3. **Practice.** Participants now break into small groups, in which each member takes it in turns to practise the skill.
4. **Feedback.** In this part of the exercise each person who has taken a turn at practice gives feedback to self, and gets feedback from others, on her or his performance of the skill. Feedback immediately follows practice.
5. **Reruns.** The person who has just received feedback reruns the practice to take account of negative feedback, and so to get the practice in better shape. The rerun will again be followed by feedback to self and from the others. There may be two or three reruns, until the skill is on track.
6. **Reflection.** This is the part of the exercise in which, when practice and feedback and reruns for each person in the small group are finished, members reflect together on the issues that have arisen.
7. **Review.** The small groups reconvene in the large group, share some of the issues that arose in the small group reflection phase, review the skill model in the light of practising it, and perhaps also review the exercise design. After this, people may (or may not) repeat the sequence from 3 to 7.

Figure 13.3 shows these stages, with reflection and review shown on slightly different levels, since the former occurs in the small groups, and the latter in the whole group.

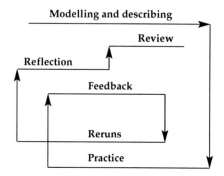

**Figure 13.3**    *Stages of an exercise*

Now the question is: who is responsible for different parts of this whole procedure? This takes us into the heart of the supervision of learning. I give here, in Figure 13.4, a diagram of the whole range of options for who can be responsible for what during the use of an exercise.

| Who supervises the stages of the exercise → ↓ | Hierarchy: *you alone* | Co-operation: *you with group* | Autonomy: *group alone* |
|---|---|---|---|
| *Modelling the skill* | | | |
| *Describing the exercise* | | | |
| *Practice* | | | |
| *Feedback* | | | |
| *Reruns* | | | |
| *Reflection* | | | |
| *Review* | | | |

**Figure 13.4**    *Options for supervising the stages of an exercise*

The bedrock of the exercise is, of course, practice, which is always and necessarily autonomous, in the hands of the learner. I shall return to this diagram under each of the three modes below.

## The Structuring Dimension: Hierarchical Mode

You take responsibility for structuring the learning process. You control its form. There are important ways of doing this before any active learning begins, as in the first two items below. Once the active learning starts, you supervise, directively, the use of the exercises you have devised. You do not actively involve the group in designing them, nor do you negotiate changes in the structures which you introduce.

1. **Pre-group structuring.** You have, of course, complete hierarchical control over the learning environment before the group meets. Here are some of the main issues you will need to consider when preparing to set up the group.
   - **Objectives, programme and learning methods.** What is the group for? How much of the programme will you pre-plan? What learning methods will you use?
   - **Facilitation and political profile.** Will you be alone or will you have a co-facilitator or an assistant facilitator? If so of what gender, and what will their role be? What mix of hierarchy, co-operation and autonomy will you use in facilitating the learning, and will this change as the group unfolds?
   - **Group composition.** Do you have any selection criteria to do with previous experience, education, age, sex, occupation, social class, nationality, psychological well-being, minimum and maximum numbers for the group? Do you need to interview and screen people for the group?
   - **Physical facilities.** How many rooms do you need, and of what sort? What sort of furnishings and fittings? Are you in chairs or on cushions? Is the group residential or not? Self-catering or not? In the town or in the country?
   - **Learning resources.** What kind of props and equipment do you need to facilitate learning: mattresses, clubs, masks, costumes, musical instruments, records, tapes, slides, CCTV, lights, books, diagrams, articles, photos, films, self-rating questionnaires, paper, paints, crayons, clay, incense, bells, etc?
   - **Fee.** How much will you charge? Are there bursaries, and for whom? Or is there a sliding scale? Does the payment that you are taking for yourself properly honour your status and competence? Or is it excessive?
   - **Advance publicity.** Does the brochure or the blurb make it unequivocally clear what the objectives, programme and methods of the group will be, a political profile of your facilitation, who is eligible to join it, who you are, and so on? The brochure presents the contractual basis for enrolment, and needs to say enough for applicants to make a fully informed choice to participate in the educational culture you are offering.

- **Voluntarism.** If the group is for some organization, have you checked out whether those attending are freely choosing to attend, or are being sent? Reject any pressure for people to be there.

2. **Culture-setting statements.** There are here a range of statements that help to establish a certain group culture that will enable learning to flourish. By propounding and recommending them, you are the hierarchical founder of that culture, creating the social structure of learning. They are announced at the outset of the group, with reminders and echoes from time to time after that. When you first announce them, always take time to seek the commitment and assent of group members. Seeking assent takes you into the co-operative mode; but the primary thrust of this intervention is hierarchical.

   - **Brochure reminder.** You run through the learning objectives, programme and methods, stated on your pre-course publicity, amplify and clarify them, and check out that everyone assents to them.

   - **Values.** You propose, for example, that the group becomes a place where there is safety and support, vulnerability and fallibility, honesty and risk-taking, emotional openness and appropriate self-disclosure, a spirit of inquiry, liberty and autonomy (voluntary participation), and confidentiality. You affirm the fundamental value of persons and personhood. You commend worthwhile ways of being which you feel will enable the group to fulfil its objectives of personal growth, skills building, or whatever.

   - **Discipline ground rules.** These are simple rules that assist learning by defining clear boundaries of behaviour. They include such things as arriving on time, returning from breaks on time, taking breaks only by group agreement, giving full attention when someone is working in the middle of the group, no smoking/eating/drinking during sessions, no physical violence to person and property, and so on.

   - **Decision-mode ground rules.** You make it clear what decision-mode, for choosing what the group does, you are going to use at the outset, and whether and how you may change the decision-mode at later stages of the group. In other words, this is a statement about what how you will make decisions on the planning dimension.

   - **Growth ground rules.** You commend a set of behaviours that will intensify personal learning and awareness, and appoint yourself their guardian – which means you point out when someone forgets a rule and invite them to restate what they have said in accordance with the rule. Here is one typical set, for a personal growth oriented group:

- Speak in the first person singular – 'I' instead of 'one' or 'we' or 'you' – in order to own fully what is being said.
- Address others in the second person – 'you' instead of 'her' or 'him' or 'they' – in order to encounter them fully and directly.
- Take risks in amplifying and disclosing what is going on inside you when it is going on, and be open to others doing the same, in order to learn more about yourself and others.
- Try to find the statement about your own experience that lies behind the question directed at someone else's experience. In this way you can become more aware of your own concerns.
- Try to spot and interrupt the defence of unawarely dumping and displacing your distress on others: in order to own your distress, work on it, and free yourself from it.

Culture-setting of this kind, with explicit assent from the group, sets a clear contractual basis for future learning in the group. It tends to disarm anxiety and tendencies to defensiveness from the start, and provides a contract which can be invoked to confront certain kinds of unaware defensive behaviour when they do occur. See item 7, hierarchical mode, confronting dimension, Chapter 10.

3. **The direction of exercises.** You design, supervise the introduction and use of a structured exercise as a means of experiential learning. Once active within the exercise, group members are, of course, autonomous, self-directed in their learning. But the form of the exercise, and overall supervision of it, are determined by you – in the hierarchical mode.

   The learner has the security of your hierarchical direction together with plenty of scope for autonomous practice within this structure. This is a powerful combination in early stages of skills-building and personal growth. The following sub-sections deal with various aspects of the direction of exercises.

   - **Experiential learning cycle.** With each exercise, you take people through this cycle, fundamental for learning. The seven steps of the procedure given earlier in this chapter can conveniently be reduced to three:
     - Step 1. A clear statement from you of the rationale of the exercise, the conceptual model behind it, followed by a clear

account of how to do the exercise, its time structure, the use of feedback, rerunning and reflection.

- Step 2. People do the exercise, usually in small groups, with some time for the action, some time for feedback (from self first and then from peers), some time for rerunning the action, if appropriate, and some time for reflection on the issues.

- Step 3. People come together with you in the whole group, for an exchange of reflection between the small groups, and for review with you of the conceptual model you presented at the outset.

You are the hierarch in designing the exercise and taking people through the first two stages. Thereafter, the decision-mode of supervision changes. Step 2 gives great scope for autonomous practice and feedback, and stage 3 is a co-operative review with you. See Figure 13.5.

| Who supervises the stages of the exercise | Hierarchy: *you alone* | Co-operation: *you with group* | Autonomy: *group alone* |
|---|:---:|:---:|:---:|
| *Modelling the skill* | X | | |
| *Describing the exercise* | X | | |
| *Practice* | | | X |
| *Feedback* | | | X |
| *Reruns* | | | X |
| *Reflection* | | | X |
| *Review* | | X | |

**Figure 13.5** *Hierarchical stages in the supervision of an exercise*

If you go round the small groups and make your contribution during feedback, reruns, practice and reflection, then the above table will also have Xs in the co-operation column on each of these four rows. Contributing to a rerun means that you propose it or give some feedback after it.

- **Procedural ground-rules.** These help to amplify and clarify step 2 above – autonomous practice and feedback. They maximize learning within the exercise. Two classic ones in skills-building exercises are:
  - Practice should always be followed by feedback. The best order of feedback in a role play is from protagonist to self,

from the other role players to protagonist, finally from observers to protagonist, followed by discussion.

- The protagonist should wherever possible rerun behaviours that are off track, until he or she gets them on track and knows what this feels like.

- **Uses of exercises.** Their overall use is as a method of experiential learning, which includes personal growth in all its aspects, and all kinds of personal and professional skills in handling oneself and others. They may be used as a set part of the overall programme, or in an impromptu way to relate to a live issue that emerges for one or more persons in the group. They can also be used to mark the stages of a group, and to influence its emotional dynamic:
  - To start a new group: to break the ice, get-to-know-you, loosen defences, reduce anxiety, clarify expectations, define needs.
  - To end a group: to review learning, plan transfer of learning to the outside world, deal with unfinished business, share appreciations, deal with separation anxiety, say farewell.
  - To open and close each day or session in an ongoing group: a ritual coming together for, and departure from, the shared learning.
  - To transform the emotional dynamic: see item 9, hierarchical mode, feeling dimension, Chapter 11.

It is also important to remember that the term 'exercise' as used here includes ritual and all kinds of charismatic and transpersonal structured experiences; and all kinds of expressive and celebratory structures.

- **The focus of exercises.** Exercises can be focused on the following: discussion within the group; decision-making within the group; encounter between people within the group; conflict resolution within the group; group process analysis; projects of all kinds; creativity and problem-solving; expressive skills; aesthetic skills; technical skills (e.g. clinical, mechanical, financial, etc.); management and organizational skills; interactive skills for personal and professional life; assertiveness skills; social change skills; personal and transpersonal growth.

  Personal and transpersonal growth may include: sensory awareness, breathing and body work, primal and general regression, monodrama, psychodrama, role play, re-evaluation and reintegration, guided fantasy and active imagination, sublimation and transmutation, attitude and belief-system restructuring, creative expression and celebration, goal-setting and life-planning, psychic awareness and subtle energy work, spiritual transformation through ritual, primary theatre, meditation and charismatic work. Many of these items overlap.

- **The content of exercises.** They can be about imaginary situations, either on the job or off the job. Whether on the job or off the job, the imaginary situations can be either typical, or bizarre and extreme. Alternatively, the exercises can deal with actual experience, here and now in the group, or with someone's past experience, or with someone's expected future experience. All of these, except here-and-now experience in the group, will involve the use of role play: one person in the central role practising some skill or exploring some experience, with other group members in supporting roles.

4. **Total, or partial, directive supervision.** All the structured exercises used may be designed and managed by you, or only some of them may be: others being designed and managed co-operatively with you or autonomously by the group. As you proceed through the history of a skills training group, you may include more and more co-operative, then autonomous, supervision.

5. **Autocratic, or consultative, directive supervision.** When introducing a structured exercise, modelling the skill and explaining the format, you may do this autocratically, without eliciting views from the group, and either with or without a supporting rationale. This is often best for beginners. Or you may introduce the exercise consultatively, in which case you elicit views from the group on the modelling and the format, but you may or may not take these into account when giving your final directions. When being consultative, you can be either facilitator-centred and present your own ideas before theirs, or group-centred and ask participants to share their ideas before yours; but in either case you make the concluding decision about the exercise. For more on all these distinctions, compare items 3 and 4, hierarchical mode, planning dimension, Chapter 5.

   As trainee skill increases, the more appropriate it is to move from autocratic to consultative forms of directive supervision, and then at later stages to co-operative and autonomous supervision.

6. **Directive choice of decision-modes for supervision.** You make a directive decision, autocratic or consultative, about what decision-modes to use in the supervision of learning exercises – whether they shall be hierarchical, co-operative or autonomous, in

what combinations and at what points in the procedure. This is a higher-level decision and comes before any of the previous entries on supervision. It, in turn, is preceded by 7, following.

7. **Decision-mode mastery for design and supervision of structures.**   As hierarchical facilitator, you need a clear grasp of all the different decision-modes and the various ways they can be applied to the process of learning by structured exercises. Figure 13.4 above shows the options.

8. **Directive choice of decision-procedures.**   You make a directive decision, autocratic or consultative, about what decision-procedures to use when facilitating co-operative decisions with the group about structuring the learning. For a reminder about the difference between decision-modes and decision-procedures, see Chapter 5.

9. **Unilateral review of structuring.**   On your own, you review the design of exercises, the sorts and uses of them, decision-modes and decision-procedures used in supervision. This may lead you to restructure some of these things.

## *The Structuring Dimension: Co-operative Mode*

You structure the learning methods with the group, co-operating with them in devising how the learning shall proceed. So group members participate with you in modelling the skill to be practised, in designing the content and procedure of structured exercises, and in supervising the running of them.

This co-operative approach between you and the group is appropriate for those who are in an advanced stage of learning, or who have a lot of professional experience in the field to which the learning applies.

It enables group members to relate directly the training exercises to their personal learning needs and goals, and to job-related situations and difficulties. At the same time, they can do this with guidance and assistance from you.

When no exercises are being used, your facilitation interacts with what people are saying and doing, so that the process is like an enabling dialogue. This relatively unstructured approach is appropriate for any stage of learning

The first intervention below sets the scene for all subsequent activities. Group members participate with you in defining the ethos of learning.

1. **Culture-setting contract.** Instead of making culture-setting statements and creating the culture unilaterally, as in the hierarchical mode, you work co-operatively with the group, eliciting from them their proposals for values and ground-rules, sharing your own views, and negotiating a final contract. You may need to prompt the group about possible values, about the different sorts of ground-rules – discipline, decision and growth – and of options within these; but the group is as active as you in defining and giving shape to the culture. For a reminder of the full range of culture-setting statements see item 2, under the hierarchical mode above.

2. **Co-operation on tailor-made exercises.** The group – or one or more members of it – participate with you in structuring the learning. Within this co-operative decision-mode it is probably best to use the decision-procedure of consensus.

   If the exercise is to practise some skill, the group participate with you in creating a model of what good practice is.

   You discuss the design of an exercise – the content of it and the procedures in running it – with those who are going to use it. They co-operate with you in modifying and shaping it until you all agree it may best meet their needs. In this way it can be tailor-made to fit their particular weaknesses and strengths, or the special circumstances of their work or life.

   The group co-operate with you in the final review stage, distilling learning out of the practice and reconsidering the original model of the skill in the light of all this. So Figure 13.4 now becomes Figure 13.6 below.

| Who supervises the stages of the exercise ──▶ | Hierarchy: *you alone* | Co-operation: *you with group* | Autonomy: *group alone* |
|---|---|---|---|
| *Modelling the skill* | | X | |
| *Describing the exercise* | | X | |
| *Practice* | | | X |
| *Feedback* | | | X |
| *Reruns* | | | X |
| *Reflection* | | | X |
| *Review* | | X | |

**Figure 13.6**   *Co-operative stages in the supervision of an exercise*

If you go round the small groups and make your contribution during feedback, reruns, practice and reflection, then the above table will also have Xs in the co-operation column on each of these four rows. If you are contributing to a rerun, this means that you propose it or give some of the feedback after it. Another modification is when you are hierarchical about modelling, and co-operative in designing and describing the exercise.

3. **Total, or partial, co-operative supervision.**   All structured exercises used may be designed and/or supervised co-operatively, or only some of them may be. Others being designed and supervised hierarchically by you or autonomously by the group. As a skills training group proceeds, you may include more and more co-operative, then autonomous, supervision.

4. **Negotiated, or co-ordinated, supervision.**   When co-operating with group members about designing and managing exercises, in item 2 above, you can either negotiate with them, or co-ordinate their thinking and decision-making. If you negotiate, you can be facilitator-centred and put your own ideas forward first, or you can be group-centred and invite participants to make their proposals before yours. And with any of these options, you will need to choose a decision-procedure: informal consensus will probably work best. All the basic distinctions made in 3, 4, 5 and 10, in relation to the co-operative mode, planning dimension, Chapter 5, apply here also. A brief visual reminder is shown below in Figure 13.7.

5. **Co-operative choice of decision-modes for supervision.**   Here you make a co-operative decision with the group, by negotiation or co-ordination, about what decision-modes to use in the

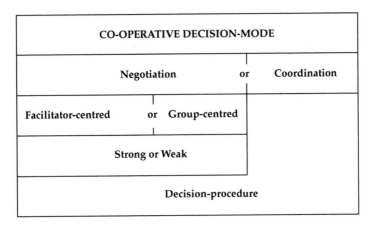

**Figure 13.7**   *Elements of the co-operative decision-mode*

supervision of learning exercises – whether they shall be hierarchical, co-operative or autonomous, in what combinations and at what points in the procedure.

6. **Co-operative choice of decision-procedures.**  You make a co-operative decision, by negotiation or co-ordination, about what decision-procedures to use within co-operative supervision. Often it is artificial and excessively formalistic to go to these lengths: informal consensus is the tacit choice.

7. **Co-operative review of structuring.**  You and the group take time out to review the structure of the learning that has gone on: the design of exercises, the sorts and uses of them, the use of decision-modes and decision-procedures. This may lead to various kinds of restructuring. The item overlaps with co-operative programme review, item 7, co-operative mode, planning dimension, Chapter 5.

8. **Ad hoc co-operative supervision.**  You are called in while a small group is busy with autonomous practice, to help out with some problem. Or you have already agreed with the group that you will go round visiting all the small practice groups in turn, contributing to feedback, reruns, practice and reflection.

9. **Process structuring.**  The ongoing process of an unstructured group is influenced, shaped and given special forms by your interventions – which support, elicit, interpret and confront. In this you co-operate, like a midwife, with the emerging behaviour of the group, creating a richer and deeper learning experience.

There are no given exercises here: the group is unstructured in that sense. But what people say and do becomes more authentic and open by virtue of your use of the facilitator's tool-kit.

## The Facilitator's Tool-kit

I reproduce here from my *Helping the Client* (Heron, 1990a), a bedrock range of facilitator interventions. They are all very simple and go together. Their purpose is to unfold group members' self-discovery with minimal input from you. They enable you, if you use them well, to be highly effective while maintaining a low profile.

### Be here now

This is the everyday mystical one. You are centred, present, with your awareness unencumbered, in the moment that is now. This has nothing to do with what you are saying or your social behaviour, it's all to do with how you are being. You are not distracted by the concerns of the past or future. You are fully aware of the present, but not caught up in or anxiously engaged with it. You are intensely in the moment, and yet not at all of it.

Some simple bodily adjustments can aid entry into this state: you can relax your breathing and deepen it a bit; you can let go of all unnecessary muscular tension in your posture and find one that feels both comfortable and attentive. But the state is not to do with your body, it is to do with inner alertness. To use a metaphor, you are awake to the moment, not distractedly dreaming it.

### Be there now

The previous state seems to me to be a pre-condition of all effective eliciting facilitation. One reason for this concerns the mystical principle of the identity of the centre of being with the circumference of being. So to be here now is very much also to be there now. When you are attuned to your own centre, you are already very open to the reality of others. Within the 'I' is found the 'Thou'. All this is another way of talking about participative feeling, a unified affective field, personal presence, the up-hierarchy of empowerment, and interpersonal empathy, as described in previous chapters.

### Giving free attention

This is the extension from being here now, to being there now with the other. When you are here now, you have abundant free attention, which is not enslaved by past, present or future content, and which can dwell with and energize your group. Through participative feeling, you as a distinct, aware and focused being, commune with others.

This is a subtle and intense activity of your consciousness mediated by gaze, posture, facial expression, sometimes touch. It has the qualities of being supportive of the essential being and worth of group members independent of anything they say or do; of being expectant, waiting for the potential fullness of human beings to emerge in ways that are meaningful to them and their fulfilment; and of being wider and deeper than the content of their speech, encompassing all their body cues, their whole individual way of being and doing, their total living reality. It's also relaxed, a little laid back and benign.

### Simple echoing

You echo back the last word, or the last few words, a person said before pausing. The words are echoed back just as stated, or perhaps slightly rephrased, and without any interrogative inflection (i.e. not as an indirect question), and without any inflection that carries judgment or value-loading. Simple echoing is a way of conveying to people attention, interest, and above all an invitation to develop the theme in any way that is meaningful to them. So they can go on talking on their own chosen path, whereas any question, however open, leads off in a certain direction.

### Selective echoing

You are listening very fully and with fine tuning to everything a person is saying. You then reflect or echo back something not at the end but from the middle of the speech, some word or phrase that carries an emotional charge or stands out as significant in its context. Again there is no interrogative inflection or any other kind of inflection on your echo. This gives space for people, if they wish (they may not), to explore more fully and in any chosen direction the hidden implications of the reflected word or phrase. Selective echoing is usually used to follow the speaker deeper into territory already entered. But it can be used to echo something that leads into new territory.

### Open questions and closed questions

Here is a simple but central polar pair of interventions. The open question does not have one right answer, but gives plenty of space for the group member to come up with several possible answers, e.g., 'What do you remember about your first school?' The closed question only has one answer, the right one, e.g., 'What was the name of your first school?' The distinction between open and closed is not an absolute one. Some questions are ambiguous, e.g., 'Do you believe in school?' may be heard as open or closed. And there are degrees of openness (or closure), e.g., 'What do you remember about your first school?' is more open than 'What do you remember about the head-mistress of your first school?'

In general, open questions tend to be more eliciting than closed questions simply because they give more scope for self-directed exploration and discovery. But there is no hard and fast rule: it depends on the context and the timing. In any case, the skilled facilitator can ask both open and closed questions as and when appropriate, and can control the degree of openness on open questions.

Highly anxious facilitators, compulsive helpers, often have difficulty with mastering open questions. Their anxiety contracts their questioning into the closed form. Hence they may have anxious participants worrying about whether they dare give an answer in case they get it wrong.

Questions, whether open or closed, need to be participant-centred and tuned in to the participant's reality, rather than facilitator-centred and deriving from your curiosity or determination to be proved right, etc.

There are three final points. Questions can be balanced between following and leading. They can be asked of one person, or of the whole group. They also give you the opportunity to be confronting and consciousness-raising, as well as purely eliciting.

### Empathic divining

When a group member says something that has an implicit feeling, thought or intention which is lurking between the lines and which is not fully expressed, you divine this unstated content and put it back to them. So if someone says, in a certain context, and with a certain kind of tone and inflection, 'I can't say any more', then you may say 'It seems as though you are quite frightened'. You are divining that part of the speaker's attitude of mind that is just below the surface of what is being said, and that is affecting how it is being said. It may be a feeling, a belief or an intention, or some mixture of these. You will pick it up mainly – within a given context – from the form of words and the tone of voice, aided perhaps by facial and other bodily cues. You express it always as a statement, never as a question, with an opening such as 'It sounds/seems as though you ...'. You can also use it when a person is not speaking, but full of facial and postural cues; then you say 'It looks/seems as though you ...'.

This intervention often needs a little practice before people get it right. It is a very precise test of empathy. The key to success is only to divine what is actually emerging between the lines. Sometimes you may put back something that goes way down below any lurking content, and this throws the speaker in too deep too soon. Sometimes you may 'divine' your own projected agenda.

Empathic divining overlaps with giving an attributive interpretation (see item 5, hierarchical mode, meaning dimension, Chapter 6). But the latter can go beyond empathic divining and penetrate to something that is hidden by the lines, not just showing through them.

Empathic divining can also be used with confronting intent and effect, to raise consciousness in people about some emerging attitude which they are defensively trying not to acknowledge. When applied to distress-charged statements and distress-charged facial and other bodily cues, it may also be used with cathartic effect, bringing the distress further up toward, or even into, discharge.

Empathic divining may also be applied to the group process as a whole, in which case it is based on the verbal and non-verbal cues of several group members over a recent time-period. It then states some as yet unidentified issue which is starting to emerge through the group dynamic. Your intent may simply be to elicit, or it may also be to confront.

### Checking for understanding

This intervention, a special case of empathic divination, is only used when someone, groping for words, says something confused or contradictory. You try to divine what they want to say, tidy up their statement to express this clearly, and put it back to them with the preface, 'Let me see, are you saying that …?' Then they can either agree; or disagree, clarify what they meant, and get back on a more coherent course.

The intervention can also be used for some dialogue or group discussion which lacks coherence. You pick out from the confused exchange what might be the primary issue and relevant points. You put this back to the group as a whole, and seek clarification from anyone in the group, not only those involved in the talk.

### Paraphrasing

You rephrase in your own words something important which a participant has expressed. This manifests solidarity, shows you are really listening and understanding. And it gives people a chance to check their formulation against yours, and so find out if they have said what they really wanted to say. This is on a smaller scale than logical marshalling, which is next.

### Logical marshalling

Whereas empathic divining deals with what is sensed between the lines, logical marshalling deals with what is on the lines of what group members have been saying. You organize the explicit content of a whole chapter of the discussion, summarize it, maybe interrelate parts of it, maybe indicate directions in which it seems to be leading, and put all this back succinctly to the group. This may prompt members to review and revise their train of thought and feeling; or it may provide a springboard for launching off in some new direction.

The above eleven entries can be set out in a simple diagram which represents the most basic items in the facilitator's tool-kit, as in Figure 13.8.

All the tools can be used for eliciting. Empathic divining overlaps with interpreting, and can be used for confronting and for moving toward catharsis. Questioning can also be used for confronting. Both questioning and divining can focus on facial and other bodily cues,

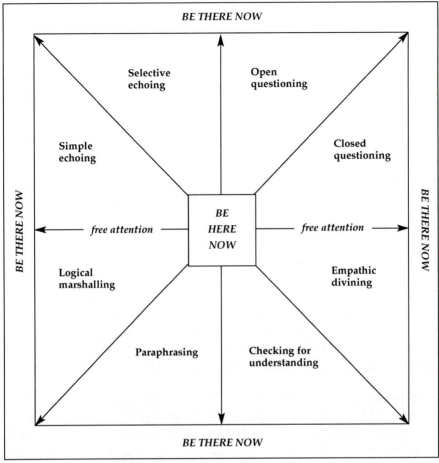

**Figure 13.8** *The facilitator's tool-kit*

when a person is not speaking, as well as on content and mode of speech.

The tool-kit is a box made up of four smaller boxes, each of which is divided diagonally into two compartments, for two related interventions of the same basic sort. It is useful, if you are a beginner, to have a copy of this diagram near you when working with a group, to remind yourself of the basic range of options available to you. Below are some more basic tools.

### Following, consulting, proposing or leading

When it comes to opening up new territory for the group, there are four options:

- Participants have already started to enter it and you follow.

- You consult group members and ask them where they want to go next, maybe referring back to items on an agenda agreed earlier. If there is a consensus about where to go, that's where you all go.
- You propose a change of area and seek participants' assent.
- You simply lead the group into new territory.

When proposing a shift or leading into it, you do so because:

- You divine it as seeking to emerge.
- You see it as appropriate to fulfil a balanced programme.
- There is a contract to cover it.
- Because it has been left unfinished from an earlier session.

The flexible practitioner will be able to use all these four as and when appropriate.

### Working with non-verbal cues

There are important cues evident in the facial expression and body language of group members who are not speaking. There are five basic kinds you can pick up on. Whatever else is going on, it is essential to scan the whole group with your eyes at regular intervals so that you can spot these cues and work with them as appropriate.

- **Picking up on pensive cues.**   You ask the open question 'What are you thinking?' of a group member who has that typical brief reflective facial expression, indicative of an inner reaction to what other people in the group are saying. The person may not verbalize the thoughts unless asked; but when expressed they often enrich the interaction. 'What are you thinking?' is an open question rather than a closed one. There is no single right answer. The pensive person's presenting thought is usually at the leading edge of a whole cluster of related thoughts.
- **Picking up on wanting-to-speak cues.**   You put an open question such as 'What is your view?' to someone whose facial and other movements show that they want to say something. Or eye contact, and bringing in the person with a hand gesture and saying their name, will be sufficient.
- **Picking up on emotional cues.**   These cues may combine with pensive cues, or wanting-to-speak cues, or may be evident on their own. They show shock, surprise, delight, loving care, irritation, impatience, anxiety, and so on. You can use empathic divining, 'It looks as though you …'; or open questioning, 'How are you feeling?' Again, the presenting emotion may well have other, sometimes quite different, facets.

- **Picking up on cathartic cues.** This is a special case of the previous entry. The eyes, facial expression, other bodily cues, show that distress emotion is coming up, moving toward discharge. The fists are clenched (anger); the lips and jaw are trembling (fear); the eyes are filling with tears (grief); laughter is about to break out (embarrassment). Empathic divining may bring the distress a little nearer identification, ownership, acceptance and release. So for filling eyes you may say 'It looks as though you're holding on to so much hurt and pain'. For sustained discharge, of course, you will move over into full-blown cathartic interventions.
- **Picking up on alienation cues.** The facial expression and perhaps the posture show that a group member is alienated, has mentally and emotionally cut out of the group, and is sunk in their own internal process. You can use empathic divining and say 'It looks as though you ...'. Or you can gently ask an open question: 'What is going on for you right now?'

*Bring in, draw out, shut out*
You scan the group regularly with your eyes to pick up on non-verbal cues among those who are not talking. From these, you can bring in one person by eye contact, hand gesture, questioning, divining. You can draw out someone who is already talking by eye contact, hand gesture, echoing, questioning, divining, checking for understanding, paraphrasing, marshalling. You can shut out someone who is talking, with a deft gesture from one hand, while simultaneously bringing in someone else with your other hand. You can do this without any words, like a traffic cop. Or you can also add words – and question, divine, check for understanding, paraphrase or marshal what the current speaker has just said, and put this to someone else for comment. Thus you keep a low profile while effectively managing contribution-rates, eliciting self-discovery and interpersonal learning in the group. Figure 13.9 below shows the options.

In the top box on the left of this diagram, there are those elements of your behaviour that underly your use of the ten further items. Being present means being here now, being there now and giving free attention, as I have described these above. Scanning means continuously looking round the group to pick up non-verbal cues of the five kinds given above. Timing means making your intervention deftly, surely and without inappropriate time-lag. Choice of words refers to the diction and also to the grammatical form of verbal interventions. Paralinguistics refer to your manner of speech and include: emotional tone of voice; volume and pitch of sound; rhythm and rate

| | BRING IN | DRAW OUT | SHUT OUT |
|---|---|---|---|
| **Being present**<br>**Scanning**<br>**Timing**<br>**Choice of words**<br>**Paralinguistics**<br>**Body language** | | | |
| **Eye contact** | | | |
| **Gesture: traffic cop** | | | |
| **Simple echoing** | | | |
| **Selective echoing** | | | |
| **Open questioning** | | | |
| **Closed questioning** | | | |
| **Empathic divining** | | | |
| **Checking for understanding** | | | |
| **Paraphrasing** | | | |
| **Logical marshalling** | | | |

**Figure 13.9**    *Managing contribution rates*

of speech; use of inflection and emphasis; use of pauses and silence. Body language covers your use of relative position, touch, posture, facial expression, gesture and eye contact. Relative position is a potent feature of facilitation: where you sit or stand in relation to the whole group or to one person with whom you are working; when and how you move from one position to another. See also the account of dynamic presence and the psychophysical modes of relating in Chapter 12.

In the list of ten interventions, the first two are non-verbal – eye contact and gesture. These are the two non-verbal behaviours most used in controlling contribution rates and managing interaction in a group. Traffic cop refers to simultaneous hand gestures. One hand is held up to shut out the current speaker, the other hand is beckoning to bring in someone else.

10. **Elicit–inform gradient.**   When you are eliciting contributions from the group in a reflection or review phase, in open discussion, you may also want to agree with, or disagree with and correct, what group members say; and to impart further information. This is also the group seminar or tutorial situation. You then need the elicit–inform gradient, shown in Figure 13.10.

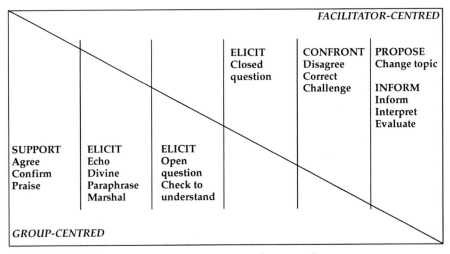

**Figure 13.10**  *Elicit–inform gradient*

It includes basic items from the facilitator's tool-kit, given in item 9 above, together with several other verbal interventions. The eight eliciting interventions of the tool-kit are included in the second, third and fourth columns in Figure 13.10. To these are added supportive interventions on the group-centred side, and confronting, proposing and informing ones on the facilitator-centred side. The items given under each of these further categories are self-explanatory. You could also add, alongside supportive interventions at the group-centred end, cathartic interventions, in the form of releasing tension through laughter. Be group-centred earlier on and facilitator-centred later on.

## The Structuring Dimension: Autonomous Mode

You give space for group members to devise their own forms of learning, and to manage the process by themselves. This is the heart-land of autonomous learning. Participants are not only being self-directed in practice, but they are also being self-directed in managing the process of learning. They are creating and supervising the structures and procedures that mediate their learning.

1.  **Autonomous design and supervision of structures.** Where there is skills-building or growth work in small groups, you delegate to each group the design and supervision of whatever structures it uses. Small group members confer about the design to meet their special learning needs and goals. There are different kinds and degrees of delegation here.

- **Contractual delegation.**  The contract you make with the group may cover time and general learning objectives only, and everything else is delegated. Members practise, for a given period, any skill they choose, in terms of any exercises and forms of peer supervision they devise. Or the contract may cover time and a specific learning objective – to practise a particular skill – and the choice of exercise and the way of supervising it are delegated. Or the contract may specify the time, the skill and the main method such as role play – and everything beyond that is delegated.
- **Functional delegation.**   You delegate different design and supervision functions to different people in the small group. Some people are to create the model of good practice, others are to design content (what the exercise is about), others are to design procedure (how the exercise is done), and yet others are to devise forms of peer supervision of the exercise. You also delegate a process whereby these three sub-groups can integrate their work. Functional delegation presupposes some form of contractual delegation about time, learning objectives, kind of exercise to be used.

For full-blown delegation, the supervisory table now appears as in Figure 13.11, the only co-operation with you being in the final review phase. This table shows very complete delegation. It could be much more piecemeal and limited, with Xs in some of the other rows and columns.

2.  **Total, or partial, delegation of design and supervision.**   All the structured exercises used may be designed and/or supervised autonomously, or only some of them may be, others being

| Who supervises the stages of the exercise | Hierarchy: *you alone* | Co-operation: *you with group* | Autonomy: *group alone* |
|---|---|---|---|
| *Modelling the skill* | | | X |
| *Describing the exercise* | | | X |
| *Practice* | | | X |
| *Feedback* | | | X |
| *Reruns* | | | X |
| *Reflection* | | | X |
| *Review* | | X | |

**Figure 13.11**    *Autonomous stages in the supervision of an exercise*

designed and supervised hierarchically by you or co-operatively by you and the group.

3. **Autonomous choice of decision-modes for supervision.** Group members decide on their own what decision-modes to use in the design and supervision of learning exercises – whether, among themselves, they shall be hierarchical, co-operative or autonomous, in what combinations and at what points in the procedure. This item could also refer to a group which chooses to bring you (or some other facilitator) back in to be hierarchical or co-operative.

4. **Autonomous choice of decision-procedures.** Group members decide on their own what decision-procedures to use when co-operating together within autonomous design and supervision of learning.

5. **Autonomous review of structuring.** Group members on their own take time out to review the structure of the learning that has gone on: the design of exercises, the sorts and uses of them, the use of decision-modes and decision-procedures. This may lead to various kinds of restructuring. It overlaps with autonomous progamme review, item 7, autonomous mode, planning dimension, Chapter 5.

6. **No facilitation of structures phase.** You announce a phase in which you will not offer structures or exercises, but leave group members to devise these among themselves. You may, of course, still be active on other dimensions.

7. **Autonomous monitoring of structuring.** In this extension of the initiative clause (see item 9, autonomous mode, planning dimension, Chapter 5) you have created a climate of shared leadership, in which group members spontaneously propose ways of structuring their learning – independent of and along-side your management of this dimension.

8. **Trainer–trainee delegation.** You delegate the role of devising and also facilitating structures to a group member for a period, in the whole group or in training sub-groups, followed by feed-back to that person. Both this and the previous strategy presup-pose that the group will have received some kind of training in presenting and working with structured exercises, or with process structuring.

9. **Autonomous projects.** You delegate to small groups the task of working on their own on a project of their own choice, consistent with the overall objectives of the course. This is a project other than skills building and so does not fall under the previous analysis of design and supervision of structures. It

goes with item 3, autonomous mode, planning dimension, Chapter 5.

10. **Self-directed client.** In personal growth work, participants choose what methods to use, whether psychodrama, body work, transpersonal work, and so on; and also direct themselves in the use of the method. This is the approach in co-counselling when the client opts for a free attention only contract. It can be used in any context to help internalize skill in method.

11. **Facilitator as self-directed client.** You take time in the group for your own development and learning, setting up a personal growth structure to meet your own needs for development and change. As an exemplary member of the group, you motivate risk-taking and initiative in others.

12. **Autonomy lab.** You set up a whole workshop, or a major part of a workshop, as an autonomous learning environment. You explain the model and invite group members to contract into it. Inside the lab, the group is leaderless. The learning resources of the lab are the group members themselves with their particular skills and experiences, physical resources such as books, articles, tapes, CCTV, etc., and yourself. You only do anything when asked by one or more participants to meet some specific learning need.

   Group members exercise total initiative and autonomy in deciding what their learning needs are, how to meet them, in what order and with whom. Everyone has the challenge of structuring their own learning experience, pacing and changing it, through negotiation with others. A useful instruction before the lab is to invite each person to prepare a list of what they want to get from or with others, and what they have to offer to others. The lab starts with all these lists posted up. Everybody studies these lists prior to negotiating meeting their needs and/or those of others. When not being called upon as a resource, you go around meeting your own learning needs. For a full account, with guidelines for setting up the lab, see item 13, autonomous mode, planning dimension, Chapter 5.

13. **Leaderless group.** The only way in which a group can be totally autonomous in forming its own learning environment, is if you encourage it to come into being as a leaderless peer group, from which of course you are absent. To the extent that you advise the group in advance about values, ground rules, experiential exercises, you give it a hierarchical impulse.

# *14* *Varieties of the Experiential Learning Cycle*

In the previous chapter on the structuring dimension, I presented a conveniently condensed and accessible version of the experiential learning cycle, including both trainer and trainee roles in the one cycle. In this chapter, I discuss the cycle in greater depth, exploring its inner structure, relating it to my distinction between the self and the person, to superlearning and to the roles of teacher and student.

## *Primary and Secondary Cycles*

In order to get deeper into the structure of the experiential learning cycle, it is important to note that there are two different and intimately associated versions of it, one being included as a phase within the other. Originally people defined the cycle as a movement from a phase of experience to a post-experience phase of reflection. Now it is acknowledged that within the phase of experience itself there is an ongoing learning cycle. 'In any experience there is a natural process taking place within the learner in which what is being taken in is processed, affects the learner and can provide the basis for action' (Boud and Walker, 1992: 167). These authors borrow from Schön (1983) the term reflection-in-action to name this process, and consider that it involves noticing and intervening. In other words, there is a simple feedback loop during experience. You notice what is happening, take account of this in your intervention, notice the outcomes of the intervention, and so on.

This is closely related to Torbert's more elaborate idea of action inquiry, which involves consciousness in the midst of action, a special kind of widened attention that embraces one's intuition or vision of ends, one's reasoned or felt strategy, one's present action, its outcomes and what is going on in the outside world. Such action inquiry not only notices all these, it also identifies and corrects, in the midst of action, incongruities among them (Torbert, 1991: 219–238).

Boud and Walker (1991, 1992) point out that this reflection-in-action cycle within experience is part of a wider learning cycle in which there is preparation for the experience before it begins and digestion of it and reflection on it after it is over. It is important to separate out these two cycles very clearly. The first I call the primary experiential learning cycle; the second and wider cycle, which includes the first as a stage within it, I refer to as the secondary experiential learning cycle. For convenience I will simply use the terms primary cycle and secondary cycle. The primary cycle can be entirely internal to and autonomously managed by the learner, once the experience begins. The secondary cycle is managed by the facilitator.

However there are cases where the teacher is generating the learners' experience in the earlier stages of the primary cycle, as in the original form of superlearning: Lozanov's suggestopedia applied to language teaching (Lozanov, 1978; Schuster and Gritton, 1986; Hooper-Hansen, 1992). I outline this kind of superlearning in terms of primary and secondary cycles in a later section of this chapter; and discuss the wider issue of teacher-managed or student-managed experience in the primary cycle of any kind of experiential learning.

In Chapter 3, I distinguish between the open self and the whole person, and I refer the reader back to that distinction. There can be primary and secondary cycles involving both the open self and the whole person, thus yielding a fourfold scheme, and this chapter also outlines each of the four. All these various options, and the issues involved in choosing between them, simply point to the fact that the field is still in early stages of development and awaits a lot more experiential inquiry. And it is in the spirit of inquiry that I put forward this range of models.

## *The Open Self Primary Cycle*

Experiential exercises used in learning subjects of any kind such as accountancy, chemistry, geography, astronomy can contain within them the open self primary cycle. This involves mainly emotion, imagery (perception, imagination and memory), discrimination and action. These are all intentionally brought forward and integrated in the learning process. In terms of the up-hierarchy model introduced in Chapter 3 and applied just to these four individuating functions, the ground of the cycle is positive emotional arousal. This empowers the learner to enjoy a variety of imaginative experiences, including seeing, hearing and moving. These in turn underwrite and sanction the conceptual discrimination, the propositional structures which are the cognitive rationale of the exercise. And these provide the basis for their intentional application in actions which the learner takes within the exercise.

These, then, are the four basic elements of the open self primary cycle: positive emotional arousal, varied imaginative experience, conceptual structuring, intentional action. This is the fundamental order of influence and potency: emotional arousal brings life to imaginative experiences, which provide the imaginal warrant for conceptual maps, which give the rationale for action. Once the exercise is under way, the primary ground of its internal learning cycle is emotional arousal. A previous discussion of this is given in Heron (1992: 227–238).

The cycle is illustrated in Figure 14.1. Suppose the exercise, fully described in advance by the teacher, is that the learners relate to each other within the space of the room to represent the interactive properties of different chemical substances. First, they are emotionally aroused by a brief active game, and in anticipation of the exercise. Second, they move and relate physically in different specified ways. Third, they consult handouts or wall charts which give a conceptual model of chemical interactions; and they identify which ones which they have just symbolized in their respective movements. Fourth, they use this model to vary their ways of physically relating, for example, by becoming different substances.

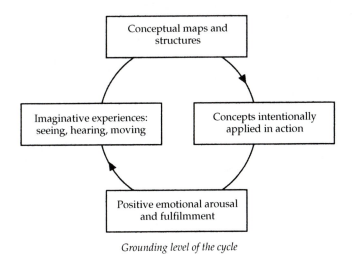

Conceptual maps and structures

Imaginative experiences: seeing, hearing, moving

Concepts intentionally applied in action

Positive emotional arousal and fulfilment

*Grounding level of the cycle*

**Figure 14.1** *The open self primary cycle*

This in turn gets them more emotionally involved and imaginatively engaged with the configuration of interactions going on between them, which sharpens their discrimination of the conceptual model, which further guides their interactions, and so on. The internal learning cycle here is the way in which imaginative experience, conceptual model and intentional action continuously inform and illuminate each other, through their grounding in emotional arousal.

The participate functions of feeling and intuition are tacitly involved. The learners will have a latent feeling of participating in a common field of experience, of being compresent with each other. They will subliminally and intuitively grasp the whole perceived pattern of their interactions and its consonance or otherwise with the conceptual structures.

So the self here is open. It is not compulsively activist. It is seeking to learn from aware interflow between emotion, perception and other imagery, conceptual structures and action. The discrimination of conceptual structures will deepen from time to time, depending on the subject, into more elaborate reflection. And the process of this primary cycle rests on the tacit evocation of feeling and intuition. Figure 14.2 shows another way of portraying the open self primary cycle.

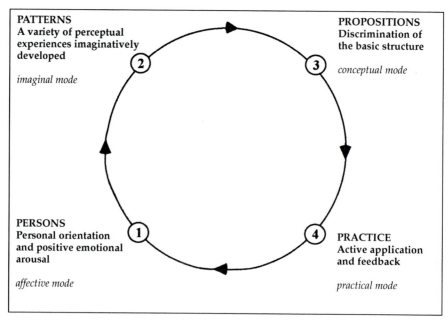

**Figure 14.2**   *The open self primary cycle*

# The Open Self Secondary Cycle

The secondary cycle is one which the facilitator prepares the learners for the primary cycle experience beforehand and enables them to process it afterwards. Whereas the primary cycle follows the basic up-hierarchy converted into a continuous sequence, the secondary one is what elsewhere I have called the reversal cycle (Heron, 1992: 29, 243). This reverses part of the basic cycle and uses the conceptual mode to redirect the imaginal from its habitual set.

The facilitator therefore adopts it when seeking to initiate students, who are used to the closed self cycle of traditional learning (see Chapter 3), into the open self primary cycle of experiential learning; and in general, since all egos tend to close again, to inaugurate an open self attitude in any group. The secondary cycle is emotion-discrimination-imagery-action, while the primary cycle is emotion-imagery-discrimination-action. So it seeks to re-vision the imaginal through prior conceptual structures.

Let us suppose you are discussing the notion of action in the philosophy of mind. One aspect of this topic is the distinction between action and intention, that is, between an action such as raising the hand and what the person concerned meant by that action, what it was intended to achieve. You decide to use an experiential exercise focused on this theme. You take the learners through the following secondary cycle which includes at stage 4 the exercise as a primary cycle.

## Stage 1

### Affective
Before launching into the topic of action and intention, you can ask the learners to work in pairs or small groups and take turns to identify positive and negative emotional responses to it simply as a bare topic, to affirm the positive responses and to work with the negative by owning them and letting go of them, or by cognitive reframing, emotional discharge or meditative transmutation. This honours the individual history which people bring to their learning and alerts them to their initial personal experiential stance within the topic. You may then give some direct or indirect suggestions which affirm the value of this stance and which build up a positive emotional climate for learning.

## Stage 2

### Conceptual

You now give a brief overview theoretical input about the distinction between action and intention. You discriminate between the two basic concepts and related ones and reflect on their theoretical implications. This leads into informal question and answer and discussion with the whole group.

## Stage 3

### Imaginal

You then present illustrations, instances, demonstrations, personal experiences, dramatic portrayals, stories, pictures – whatever shows the leading ideas of the theoretical input in living imagery. In the same illustrative and demonstrative way, you describe the experiential exercise you are going to invite everyone to do next.

## Stage 4

### Practical

You invite everyone now to do an exercise using the four stages of the primary cycle as described earlier – positive emotional arousal, imaginative experience, conceptual structuring, intentional action. So this primary cycle as a whole is within stage 4 of your secondary cycle. Working in pairs, each partner takes it in turn to do the following. Out of your positive arousal, you imaginatively improvise a series of significant gestures and postures and settle in one of them. Holding the posture and gesture, you then discriminate three different intentions it may have, and state them aloud. So if you settle on holding out a hand, you say 'I am testing for rain', 'I am waiting for change' and so on. Then you take each of these intentions in turn and devise a different posture and gesture for it.

## Stage 5

### Affective

The first three stages are a preparation for the exercise done in stage 4, and now we start the digestion of it. You ask the learners to go deeper into their personal experiential stance, opened up initially in stage 1. What positive and negative emotions were involved in doing the exercise and also in watching it being done by one's partner? This may mean reliving it through literal, phenomenological description in order to catch the emotional nuances. Invite learners to celebrate, affirm and develop the positive emotional responses; to work with the negative by owning them and letting go of them, or by cognitive reframing, emotional discharge or meditative transmutation. The importance of attending to emotional concomitants of experience was well underlined by Boud et al (1985) in their original paper on promoting reflection in learning.

Resolving negative emotion in these ways presupposes that they are impediments to learning. This may not always be the case. They may be anxieties and disquiets that point to some fundamental flaw in the structure of the exercise, or in the concepts on which it is founded. So it is important to differentiate between negative emotional responses that are blocks to learning and those that indicate ways in which it needs to be reorganized, either practically or conceptually or both together.

## Stage 6

### Conceptual

Learners are now invited to identify and discuss together all the conceptual issues that arise from the exercise, and to relate these to the topic and the theoretical input of stage 2. So the exercise and the topic are used to inform, illuminate and modify each other. This is the reflection phase of the secondary cycle, and one of its most important. Learners here are doing one or more of four things:

- They are cultivating a personal view of the topic, one that honours and manifests at the conceptual, reflective level their personal stance in the world.
- They are testing for a valid view, one that is consistent with experience.
- They are developing a coherent view, one that is internally consistent.
- They are unfolding a practical view of the topic, one that draws out its implications for personal action and/or social policy.

Reflection can be aided by means of a dialectical interplay with imaginal processes, using graphics, diagrams, spontaneous or directed imagery, movement, mime, sound, music, story, allegory, metaphor, analogy, role play, case-studies, instances, demonstrations, brainstorming, synectics, lateral thinking, and suchlike.

The reflective process of stage 6 can start in the exercise pairs, then develop in groups of four, then continue in the whole group with you the facilitator joining in. There is a sharing, review and discussion in

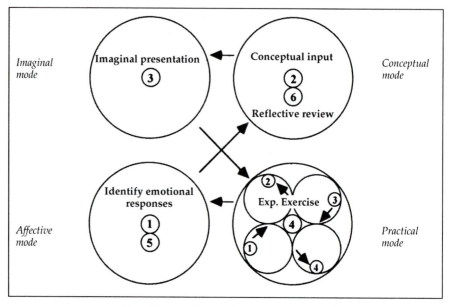

**Figure 14.3**    *The facilitator's open self secondary cycle*

the large group of all the issues that emerged in the pairs and fours. You relate all this where relevant to your original theoretical input, correcting it, amending it, adumbrating it in the light of what people are saying. The process may be developed further in written work. Figure 14.3 shows the facilitator's secondary cycle and, embedded in it at stage 4, the students' primary cycle, its internal stages represented by four rotating circles.

The secondary cycle could end here, or it could be carried on to include another primary cycle, as follows.

## Stage 7

### Imaginal

Learners break into small groups and participate in giving illustrations, instances, demonstrations, personal experiences, dramatic portrayals, stories, pictures – whatever brings out the issues of the conceptual review of stage 6 in living imagery.

## Stage 8

### Practical

Everyone now goes back into pairs to redesign the experiential exercise in the light of the last two stages, and to take it through the four stages of the primary cycle.

### Stage 9

*Affective*
Repeat and deepen stage 5.

### Stage 10

*Conceptual*
Repeat and deepen stage 6.

This, then, is the open self secondary cycle, which the facilitator uses to loosen up the closed self and empower it to maximize learning both within the primary cycle while it is going on, and from it in retrospect after it is over. It encourages students to integrate and enhance awarely in learning all the individuating functions: emotion, perceptual and other imagery, conceptual discrimination, action. In relation to the participatory functions (see Chapter 3), there is a strong focus in the secondary cycle on *reflection*, well grounded in personal experience and emotional awareness; *intention* is widened throughout the secondary cycle; there is a tacit evocation of *feeling* in the mutuality and compresence of peer learning, and of *intuition* in the grasp of perceptual patterns and imaginative experiences and their relations with conceptual structures.

The convenient version of the experiential learning cycle in Chapter 13 is basically that of a secondary cycle, and condenses the primary cycle into it without identifying the fact, and so does not show the detail of how they interact. Hence the version in this chapter, which also adds in a useful stage of identifying emotional responses.

## Primary and Secondary Cycles in Superlearning

Superlearning is an interesting species of open self, holistic learning. The essence of superlearning technique, originating in Lozanov's suggestopedia (Lozanov, 1978) and developed more widely as suggestive-accelerative learning (Schuster and Gritton, 1986), is assimilating varied presentations – visual, auditory, kinaesthetic – of the subject matter as a whole at the imaginal level, before analysing and conceptualizing it. This follows a basic precept of the up-hierarchy that full absorption of the imaginal patterning, as such, of material to be learnt facilitates its subsequent conceptual mastery. Indeed the method accords with the whole of the up-hierarchy model. I use below an example from learning a language, the classic application of the method (Hooper-Hansen, 1992).

I must emphasize that the up-hierarchy model, based on the four psychological modes, which I am using here to categorize the super-learning stages is not one which superlearning people use. Their own rationale derives from a mixture of brain science, suggestion therapy, memory research, conditioning theory, learning preferences, and so on. In my terms, however, their method is a form of open self learning, which involves both a primary and a secondary cycle. The primary cycle is as follows.

## Stage 1

### Affective

This stage coincides with the second and runs right through it. Students are relaxed while listening to the music described in stage 2: their feeling of attunement within themselves and within their situation is enhanced; and positive emotions are stimulated.

## Stage 2

### Imaginal

While classical music plays, the teacher reads the foreign language text out loud with dramatic variations of tone and volume related to the music. The students listen and follow the text with a translation and are invited to associate images with what they hear. Then while Baroque music plays, the same text is read in normal voice and the students relax and listen with eyes closed. The text is 1000–1500 words, which is long by conventional standards. At this stage the text is being taken in as a whole, as a presented imaginal pattern, mainly auditory, with visual and associative back-up.

## Stage 3

### Conceptual

The teacher now goes through the text as students read it aloud, and provides grammatical analysis and explanation of logical connections. This is done in short bursts interspersed with activities and games which apply the analysis, so there is overlap with stage 4.

## Stage 4

### Practical

This is a phase of much freer autonomous practice, in which students put the language to use in their own way using role plays, games and other activities.

Superlearning emphasizes multiple presentations at the imaginal stage, evoking varied internal imagery, appealing to sight, hearing and the kinaesthetic sense, and involving peripheral as well as central perception, eg through coloured informative posters on the wall. This multi-perceptual approach is carried through into the practical stage of active learning. Superlearning also stresses the grounding importance of the affective stage, emphasizing the value of the following: relaxation; a positive, confident, buoyant emotional climate; co-operation and mutual support among students; the facilitative presence, bearing, voice and behaviour of the teacher.

In taking students into the primary cycle, the teacher also uses a version of the secondary cycle, to encourage students – in my terms – to move from a closed self state to an open one. Remember this secondary cycle goes affective-conceptual-imaginal-practical, in this case as follows (Schuster and Gritton, 1986).

## Stage 1

*Affective*
The students are invited to go through a series of physical and mental relaxation exercises, to which are attached various suggestions to create a confident, positive emotional attitude to learning.

## Stage 2

*Conceptual*
The teacher gives a conceptual preview of the content of the lesson, an 'advance organizer' (Ausubel, 1960). It may be preceded with a brief outline review of the previous lesson.

## Stage 3

*Imaginal*
This conceptual preview is combined with some acting, demonstrations, stories, songs, playing with objects, by the teacher to illustrate or surround what is being said.

## Stage 4

*Practical*
The teacher now takes the students through all four stages of the primary superlearning cycle, as outlined above.

This whole approach honours all the individuating functions of emotion, perceptual and other imagery, conceptual discrimination, active practice. It makes a strong tacit use of feeling through the use of physical and mental relaxation in opening the secondary cycle, and through the use of music in the primary cycle. Likewise there is evocation of tacit intuition in the latent grasp of meaning that goes on unnoticed during the different presentations in stage 2 of the primary cycle.

## Teacher-managed and Student-managed Learning

The experiential learning cycle I described in the 'Open self primary cycle' section I will call BEL, for basic experiential learning. And the superlearning or suggestive-accelerative learning primary cycle, I will name SAL. In both BEL and SAL, the primary cycle is designed by the teacher, but in terms of its management, the student in SAL is more passive during the primary cycle. The teacher runs the first three stages of the SAL cycle for the receptive students, who only become active in the fourth stage. In the example I gave of a BEL cycle, the students were busy in different ways with self-managed activities in stages one, two and four.

Again in the secondary cycle, the SAL student is passive in stage 1, being relaxed by the teacher; while the BEL student is independently exploring emotional responses in stage 1. Also in a later stage of the BEL secondary cycle, the student is engaging in autonomous and considered reflection, in a way which does not occur in the SAL account.

What this brings out is that the use of the experiential learning cycle, primary or secondary, can involve more or less self-managed student activity within it, and correspondingly less or more teacher direction of the learning process within it. Clearly students need initiating into open self holistic learning by the teacher's overall *design* of primary and secondary cycles. What is not clear is when and how much it is desirable for the teacher to be actively directive and controlling *inside* one or other of the stages of each cycle.

The choice is between a form of experiential learning in which students are mentally and physically relaxed and the teacher generates an experience for them, and a form in which students generate experience for themselves. Which of these two approaches to use may in part be to do with the subject, the level at which it is being taught, the stage reached in the course, and the teacher's flexibility in moving between teacher-managed and student-managed methods.

The two approaches are not mutually exclusive: they can be brought bear upon each other and interfused in various ways. For example, the SAL method can be made more student-centred in the primary cycle. Take the learning a language example given above. After a teacher-centred phase and when basic pronunication is mastered, students could start to work in pairs or small groups, taking it in turns to read the foreign text aloud to each other to music in the active and passive concert manner.

The virtue of this more student-centred approach is that it combines the method of relaxed receptivity and indirect learning with a significant element of autonomy early on, putting the method in the hands of the students to explore and manage in their own way, and thereby understand more closely how it works for them. Finally, students can become not only involved in self-management *within* the experiential learning cycle, they can also become involved in the design *of* it, co-operatively with the teacher, or autonomously in peer learning groups.

## The Whole Person Primary Cycle

The primary experiential learning cycle involves action inquiry – being conscious of what you are doing and of its outcomes while you are doing it, and managing and modifying what you are doing out of this awareness. In open self learning, this consciousness is mainly involved with emotion, imagery (perception, memory, imagination), conceptual discrimination and action; the participatory modes of feeling and intuition are involved tacitly, and reflection is engaged with explicitly from time to time in the secondary cycle.

In whole person learning, this consciousness is expanded to involve, intentionally, both participatory and individuating functions: feeling and emotion, intuition and imagery, reflection and discrimination, intention and action. So we have here a much more comprehensive kind of action inquiry. A good example of this at work is in the domain of counsellor training, where the trainee (female) is practising counselling skills with another trainee (male) who is being a real client.

### Stage 1

*Affective*
The trainee practises feeling attuned to the total presence of her client, resonating empathically with his whole way of being. At the

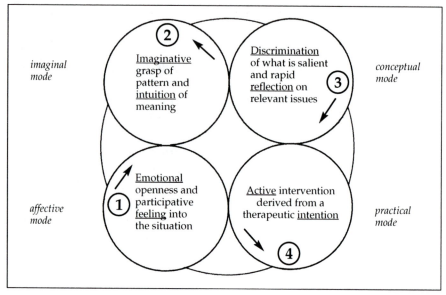

**Figure 14.4**   *The whole person primary cycle*

same time, the trainee is attending to her own emotions, dissociating from any restimulation or projection. She is managing awarely both feeling and emotion.

## Stage 2

### Imaginal

The trainee attends to a wide range of perceived images of the client, the whole presented pattern of his behaviour: not simply what he is saying, but how he is saying it in all the different paralinguistic aspects of voice, his body posture, gestures, facial expressions, use of eyes, breathing. At the same time she is taking all this in intuitively as a whole, divining its significance, what revelation of meaning it makes about the client. Here she is consciously engaged with both intuition and imagery at the preverbal level.

## Stage 3

### Conceptual

The trainee discriminates selectively among all this data, rapidly classifying it, and with quicksilver reflection evolves a working hypothesis about the client's process. This hypothesis will be in implicitly verbal form. The trainee is now involved with reflection and discrimination.

## Stage 4

### Practice

She converts her hypothesis into a practical intervention based on an underlying therapeutic purpose. She is using intention and action.

This is an inquiry and learning cycle since the client's response, noted in stages 1 and 2, to interventions made in stage 4, can modify hypotheses generated in stage 3, which alter interventions in stage 4, and so on. If this comprehensive kind of action inquiry is generalized to any kind of experiential exercise, then it can be stated as follows.

## Stage 1

### Affective: emotion and feeling

At the emotional pole of the affective mode, the student surfaces both positive and negative emotions involved in the experiential exercise, harnessing the learning power of positive emotional connections, and resolving negative emotions that obstruct learning. At the feeling pole, the student participates fully in the experience, resonating with and indwelling what is going on. This means a deepened awareness of the normal ground-state of empathic attunement. Felt acquaintance with the content of experience is no longer minimal, but raised into a full and enriched consciousness. The student opens to the distinct presences within the experience and feels their immaterial qualities, their unique signatures and gestures of being.

## Stage 2

### Imaginal: imagery and intuition

While participating in the experience, the student is open to the total configuration of its imagery in perception, memory and imagination; and intuits what the inherent pattern of the experience, its structure and process, is declaring about its domain of being. The student also intuits what connections there are between the pattern of this experience and the configurations of other related experiences. What is important here is that the student stays at the level of pure intuition of imagery, of its total pattern, its ontological declaration, its correspondences with other patterns of experience, without trying to conceptualize or analyse any of these things. The intuition of pattern here may be aided and realized by the use of drawing, painting, movement, mime, metaphor, analogy and related imaginal methods, during or after the experience.

## Stage 3

*Conceptual: discrimination and reflection*

The student disengages from the felt and intuited experience to discriminate and classify its content in conceptual terms; and to reflect on this content, converting intuitions into propositions including intellectual models and maps, tentative generalizations, possible theoretical implications and suchlike. The student is making connections between deeply felt and intuited personal experience and conceptual frameworks of a general kind.

## Stage 4

*Practical: intention and action*

The student now looks at the practical implications of the reflective phase in general terms, for example, with respect to social policy; considers personal intentions it may be appropriate to adopt for future experience and experimentation, and makes action-plans as appropriate. If the stages are run in cyclic fashion, then stage 4 re-designs the exercise for a second cycle and launches it off with the relevant actions.

The participate functions of feeling, intuition, reflection and intention subsume their correlative individuating modes. Feeling into the situation encompasses a variety of changing emotional states. Intuiting meaning is exercised in relation to the perceptual and other imagery involved. Reflection presupposes a number of classificatory discriminations having been made. And intention implies, or explicitly formulates, a plan for action.

The significance of the up-hierarchy – affective-imaginal-conceptual-practical – corresponding to the four stages is that the more deeply each stage is entered into, the more it enriches and empowers the subsequent one. Feeling attuned and processing emotions empower intuitive, imaginal grasp, which is full of latent conceptual content and so enriches the explicit reflective stage, which in turn empowers intention about practical ends.

This account of the whole person primary cycle in terms of the up-hierarchy of the modes is, I believe, rather more substantial than current accounts of experiential learning. In particular it brings to the forefront the grounding importance of conscious feeling as resonant participation in the situation. This feeling of acquaintance, empathy, attunement is *sui generis* and *in situ*. It is an original capacity of the psyche in its own right and is already in place. It is a precondition of all experience, but one which the prevailing world-view disregards in favour of over-hasty intellectual control. The point about stage 1 is not to rush past felt acquaintance in order to get concepts going, but to dwell in it and deepen it on its own account and in its own terms. This provides experiential learning with its immanent spiritual ground.

The corollary of this is the cultivation, in stage 2, of imaginal grasp: the ability to live in patterns of imagery – from perception, memory and imagination – interweaving them, combining and recombining them, until there is an intuition of relevant meaning inherent in the configuration. In pure imaginal meaning, conceptual content is inchoate, latent, in seed form. We are dealing here with meaning that is intrinsic to imagery, prior to all explicit conceptualization. Again our over-intellectualized culture wants to skirt hastily round all this, and make straight for the conceptual highway. This is paradoxical since the giants of this culture, such as Max Planck and Albert Einstein, were quite clear about the essential role of creative imagination as the ground of intellectual theory-making (Koestler, 1964; Hadamard, 1945).

This whole person primary cycle is therefore counter-cultural in its account of stages 1 and 2. It is even more counter-cultural in proposing that stage 1, the stage of participatory feeling, is already a spiritual stage. As the person opens up to embrace this grounding principle of all experience and give it space to expand within ordinary consciousness, however modestly, he or she is directly in touch with a potential for all-embracing unitive awareness. Whole person learning is already a spiritual activity. It does not have to incorporate some transcendental self that is outside the domain of everyday experience. It only needs to acknowledge, affirm and unfold the ever present ground of it. This effectively closes the gap which has hitherto existed between the transpersonal domain and the world of learning.

## The Whole Person Secondary Cycle

I return to the example of training counsellors used at the start of the preceding section. The trainer uses the secondary cycle to prepare trainees for the primary one and to digest it after it is over. The sequence is similar to the open self secondary cycle, and includes at stage 4 the primary cycle of counselling practice.

## Stage 1

*Affective*
You, the trainer, invite the trainees to work in pairs or small groups and take turns to work on positive and negative emotional responses to the impending exercise of counselling practice, to process any interpersonal agendas between those who are going to work together, and to affirm and celebrate their participation in the training process. You may give some direct or indirect suggestions which also builds up a positive emotional climate for training. The trainees then ground themselves in mutual attunement, being present with each in the mode of feeling, in some form of interactive meditation or ritual.

## Stage 2

*Conceptual*
You now give a brief theoretical account of the counselling process, identifying the stages of the counsellor primary cycle, the participatory and individuating functions involved in the action inquiry, and whatever else is pertinent at this stage of training. This leads into informal question and answer and discussion with the whole group.

## Stage 3

*Imaginal*
You then present illustrations, instances, demonstrations, personal experiences, dramatic portrayals, stories – whatever shows the leading ideas of the theoretical input in living imagery. In the same illustrative and demonstrative way, you describe the training exercise you are going to invite everyone to do next.

## Stage 4

*Practical*
You invite everyone now to do a practice counselling session using the four stages of the primary cycle, as described earlier in the first part of the previous section. So this primary cycle as a whole is within stage 4 of your secondary cycle. Working in pairs, each partner takes it in turn to be the counsellor for the other as real client.

The counsellor is alerted to participate fully in this experience through feeling and emotion, intuition and imagery, discrimination and reflection, intention and action; and to be aware of the mutual influence of these on each other. This is the internal learning, the action inquiry, of the primary cycle. After trainees end their turn as counsellor, they give themselves feedback on their handling of the four stages of the cycle and receive feedback from their partner who was the client.

## Stage 5

*Affective*
The first three stages were a preparation for the exercise done in stage 4, and now we continue the digestion of it, already launched with the feedback in stage 4. What positive and negative emotions were involved as counsellor and in response to the other as counsellor? These are processed as much as time allows. Positive responses are celebrated; negative ones are worked on either as projections and displacements, or as signs of uneasiness with the process and as cues to what went wrong with it.

## Stage 6

*Conceptual*
Trainees identify and discuss together all the issues that arise from the practice, and relate these to the theoretical model put forward in stage 2. So the practice and the model are used to illuminate each other. This reflective process can start in the training pairs, then develop in groups of four, then continue in the whole group with you the facilitator joining in.

Learners here are doing one or more of four things:

- They are cultivating a personal view of counselling practice, one that expresses their own stance in life.
- They are testing for a valid view, one that is consistent with their experience
- They are developing a coherent view, one that is internally consistent.
- They are unfolding a practical view, one that is effective in and for action.

Such reflection can be aided by means of a dialectical interplay with imaginal processes, using graphics, diagrams, spontaneous or directed imagery, movement, mime, sound, music, story, allegory, metaphor, analogy, role play, case-studies, instances, demonstrations, brainstorming, synectics, lateral thinking and suchlike.

## The Multi-stranded Alternative

The experiential learning cycles so far considered weld their use of different aspects of the person together into a coherent sequence that has, in my interpretation of them, an underlying theory about the structure and dynamics of the person and their relation to learning. But it seems to me that any programme of learning must benefit if these different aspects are brought to bear upon it, each in a single strand, without these strands being related to each other in some dynamic pattern. In other words they are invoked in a somewhat *ad hoc* way according to mood, intuition, energy level, convenience, logistical factors to do with available space at any given time, and so on.

Each strand is left to find its way across the gap of time or intervening strands to influence every other strand. In Chapter 3 I call this multi-stranded *learning*, if the strands are *inside* the learning process, that is, applied to the subject matter of learning. And I refer to multi-stranded *activities* if the strands are *alongside* the learning but not applied to its content: they minister to the whole person who takes time out to do them in order to enhance subsequent learning.

What is important is that there is a good balance among the strands, a fair representation of each of them, and that all the major ones are thus represented. It is also probably a good thing if there is some kind of balance between those that are inside the learning and those that are alongside it. Such a multi-stranded programme has the virtue of avoiding doctrinaire notions of personality and learning dynamics. In other words, it argues that there is some positive influence between the strands but does not insist it must flow this way or that. It only presupposes some view about what the main components of personhood are. This gives great freedom to the facilitator and to the participants to explore the use of holistic learning without being tied down by any strict format.

See Table 11.1 in Chapter 11, for a comprehensive range of options for multi-stranded learning and activities, arranged under affective, imaginal, conceptual and practical modes of learning.

# 15 The Valuing Dimension

This chapter concludes my presentation of the core model of the six dimensions and three modes of facilitation with an account of the final, sixth and valuing dimension. On this dimension, you are seeking to create a climate of respect for persons and personal autonomy, in which group members feel valued and honoured, so that they can become more authentic, disclosing their true needs and interests, finding their integrity, determining their own reality and humanity.

This is not the personal autonomy of the Cartesian ego, an isolated, self-reflexive consciousness independent of any context – what Charlene Spretnak calls the Lone Cowboy sense of autonomy. It is, rather, 'the ecological/cosmological sense of uniqueness coupled with intersubjectivity and interbeing ... One can accurately speak of the "autonomy" of an individual only by incorporating a sense of the dynamic web of relationships that are constitutive for that being at a given moment'. (Spretnak, 1995: 5)

## The Person

By a person, I mean the soul manifesting in alert, aware action: a being celebrating their self-determination in conscious deeds, within the dynamic web of their culture and the cosmos. A person emerges through their expressed intentions in relation with their context. 'I choose, and become a distinct person, in connectedness with a wider whole.' Through sensitively and intelligently electing to do something, in relation with the human and more-than-human world, the potential person becomes actual.

Hence the person is a self-creating being, in relationship of many kinds. The sum total of my past acts constitutes the person I have become today. Within the context of interbeing within which the everyday self is embedded, I am shaping my personality, making myself through my daily choices.

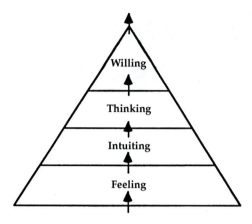

**Figure 15.1**    *The person*

The person is a seamless whole, an interacting system which in simplified form has four psychological modes of being: willing is the diamond apex whose facets are cut by the aware discrimination of thinking, which is made wise by the holistic receptivity of intuition, and grounded, through feeling, in participation in the wider reaches of culture and cosmos. This is shown as a pyramid in Figure 15.1, which is a lean version of Figure 3.4 in Chapter 3.

The pyramid, as arrowhead, is pointing towards deeds: the four psychological modes converge upon enterprise and endeavour. From our felt participation in the world, we open intuitively to grasp a total situation, then discriminate thoughtfully in order to act within it. This corresponds with the manifold, epistemological learning pyramid, Chapter 1, shown again in Figure 15.2.

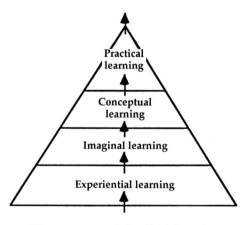

**Figure 15.2**    *Manifold learning*

A person, through the manifold of learning encounters the world (experiential learning), identifies patterns of form and process in it (imaginal learning), which is the basis for the development of language and knowledge (conceptual learning), and this is applied in a wide range of skills (practical learning). Some skills are acquired in infancy before the mastery of language, but the vast majority of human skills develop in the context of linguistic competence.

This basic thrust of human learning is also a cycle, moving from encounter with the world, through imaginal grasp and reflection, to action in the world, and thence to new encounter, and so on round the cycle. In Chapter 14, I call this the primary experiential learning cycle. It has superimposed upon it another dynamic, when persons make their learning more intentional and revisionary by using the secondary experiential learning cycle, also described in Chapter 14. The four stages of this cycle make another sequence, a continuous self-generated loop, through the basic learning pyramid, as in Figure 15.3.

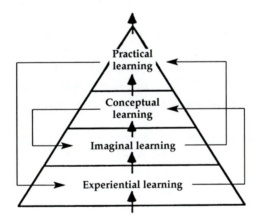

**Figure 15.3**  *The secondary learning cycle*

In Chapter 14, I presented this secondary cycle for use by a facilitator to aid learning in some group. But it is also for the autonomous person living as a self-creating and self-transfiguring being. For the secondary cycle deconstructs conservative rigidities acquired by limited use of the primary cycle. It uses conceptual ability to re-vision our imaging of reality, which in turn radically changes our actions, so that we encounter a new world.

## States of Personhood

Autonomy-in-connectedness and the creation of personhood, through living and learning, clearly admit of degrees. There are many different states of personhood from those in which it is largely potential to those in which it is actualized in many ways. The behaviour of a deranged and deluded person may be unawarely pushed around by all kinds of forces, yet it may still exhibit little areas where minimal self-determination is exercised. To refer to someone like this as a 'person' is both to affirm those areas and the individual's capacity for increasing the range of self-determined behaviour. Such a one is in reality more a potential person than an actual one. It follows that personhood, manifest in any full sense, is an achievement.

In truth, there are as many different mixes of potential and actual personhood as there are people, in this world and in other dimensions of being. But certain broad types of mix can usefully be identified, as follows. In the first three below, the autonomous person is more embryonic than actual, although less so as we go through them.

1. **The deranged person.** Behaviour is erratically and chaotically subject to psychic, psychosocial and physical influences, into which the person has little or no insight and over which they have little or no control. They do not see that their autonomy is being buried by the invasion. Voluntary choice is minimal and severely restricted.

2. **The compulsive person.** Behaviour is in certain ways rigid, maladaptive, repetitive and relatively unaware. The person can see that their autonomy is oppressed by these restricted ways of being, but has little insight into their origins or into how to get rid of them. Most of us are compulsive in some areas of our behaviour, slipping in and out of distress-driven victim, oppressor, rescuer and rebel roles. The problem lies in buried, out-of-date mechanisms of emotional survival, and the repressed early pain, discussed in Chapter 4. In non-compulsive areas there may be greater or lesser scope for voluntary choice, real autonomy, unless these are constrained by the next item.

3. **The conventional person.** Behaviour unreflectively conforms to the prevailing norms of the wider culture, and of the smaller social groups within it, to which the person belongs. The person may have some, little or no awareness that such conformity constrains really autonomous behaviour; but the more conscious they are of the hindrance, so much the less is their compliance unreflective.

Furthermore, the person may be conventional in some areas of behaviour while autonomous in others. And finally, a person may convert conventional behaviour into autonomous behaviour without changing its external form, because the person can see the point of it and can make it their own.

Here are some thoughts on the relations between the deranged, compulsive and conventional states of personhood:

- Deranged behaviour is the extreme of compulsive behaviour, but without the compulsive person's awareness that it limits autonomy, and without the compulsive persons ability to adapt, more or less, to conventional society. Deranged behaviour is too unaware to conform to convention; it is sub-conventional.

- Some compulsive behaviour is also conventional behaviour, since some conventions are compulsions writ large as social norms. Other compulsive behaviour is non-conventional but tolerated, such as drunkenness within limits. And yet other compulsive behaviour is unconventional, and may further be regarded as deviant or anti-social.

- Much conventional behaviour is non-compulsive, and this is what I include under 3 above. Either it is a matter of intelligent social coherence, even though people adhere to it through unreflective conformity; or it has symbolic significance as a form of the culture; or it is an arbitrary social practice, based perhaps on some mixture of ignorance and custom.

In the second group of different mixes of potential and actual personhood, autonomy is no longer embryonic – it is born. The person is more actual than potential: significant voluntary choice is now being exercised. But there are increasing degrees of freedom and self-determination, of the emergence of the person, involved in the following group.

4. **The creative person.** Behaviour is genuinely autonomous in some major areas of human endeavour: parenthood and the family; friendship, relationship and intimacy; education; social and political action; the professions; the arts; the sciences and the humanities; economics, commerce and industry; agriculture; and so on. The person has values, norms and beliefs to which they are internally committed, and to which they give systematic, creative expression in one or more of these domains of action. Their choices transcend unreflective conformity to the prevailing beliefs, norms and values of these domains. But the resultant sensitive, intelligent and reflective autonomy is still relative to the

cultural context and content on which the reflection is exercised. While conformity is unawarely and reactively relative to its social context, autonomy is awarely and proactively relative to its social context.

5. **The self-creating person.** Autonomous behaviour now becomes reflexive. The person becomes self-determining about the emergence of their self-determination. They consciously take in hand methods of personal and interpersonal development which enhance their capacity for voluntary choice, for becoming more intentional within all domains of experience and action. This means at least three things.

- **Unravelling.** They are at work on restrictions that come from their past, dealing awarely with the limiting effects of childhood trauma and social conditioning. The individual is committed to uncover and dismantle compulsive, and unreflectively conventional, behaviour in every area of living.

- **Receptivity.** They attend carefully to the deliverances of the receptive mind, the background field of everyday consciousness, the participatory reach of the imaginal and the affective dimensions of their nature. To become more aware about the exercise of choice and personal power, means also to open more fully to holistic intuition of, and felt participation in, the different realms of being. We need to resonate fully with the background in order to act with relevance in the foreground. External, outgoing action is balanced with attentive passivity. The person will listen as well as speak, be taught as well as teach, notice what is there as well as create what is different.

- **Relationship.** Various forms of association with other persons and the presences of nature become paramount, on the principle that personal autonomy entails connectedness. It only emerges fully in aware relationship with other autonomous persons and the more-than-human world around. It then becomes clear that autonomy is interdependent with two other basic values of social life, co-operation and hierarchy.

This whole process of self-creation, which starts in a largely humanistic mode, dealing with basic issues for the emerging person in this world and in the accessible aspects of the soul, leads over sooner or later into the next category.

6. **The self-transfiguring person.** Autonomy now reaches out to uncover latent powers within the soul, and to extend ordinary consciousness into realms that were seemingly above it or below it. The person freely chooses, as an extension of their self-

determination, to unfold their access to universal consciousness, and to unseen powers and presences; to become attuned through participative feeling to the rhythms and manifold forms of creation; and to plumb the depths of the psyche to open to indwelling, immanent spiritual life. Fired by faith, the person uses diverse keys to self-transfiguration, working in the heights, in the middle ground, and in the depths, of the soul (Heron, 1998a).

## *The Cross and Circle*

Experiential learning is about the emergence of personhood. To use a geometric metaphor and an ancient symbol, the horizontal bar of the compulsive and conventional states is at right angles to the vertical bar of the creative and the self-creative states of personhood. From the point of intersection, the circle of self-transfiguration can expand. See Figure 15.4.

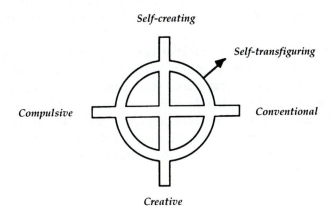

**Figure 15.4**   *The states of personhood*

To use a weaving metaphor, the warp of the compulsive and conventional, interlaces the woof of the creative and self-creating dimensions of personhood, forming the fabric of our being, which can be shaped into the garment of self-transfiguration.

To use an organic metaphor, the conventional dimension provides the social ground, the compulsive dimension the loam out of which the plant of the creative person can grow, bearing self-creating leaves and the bloom of self-transfiguration. In all these metaphors I include the deranged person as a limiting case of the compulsive.

## *The Valuing Dimension: Hierarchical Mode*

By your statements, your proposals, your acts and your presence, you manifest directly to group members your commitment to their fundamental worth as persons. You take strong initiatives in going forth to value people.

1. **Culture-setting statements.** This overlaps with the same entry, item 2, hierarchical mode, structuring dimension, Chapter 13. Please refer back to this passage. The whole of it, in different ways, is about respecting and honouring people, but in particular the following passage:
   - **Values.** You propose, for example, that the group becomes a place where there is safety and support, vulnerability and fallibility, honesty and risk-taking, emotional openness and appropriate self-disclosure, a spirit of inquiry, liberty and autonomy (voluntary participation), and confidentiality. You affirm the fundamental value of persons and personhood. You commend worthwhile ways of being which you feel will enable the group to fulfil its objectives of personal growth, skills building, or whatever.
2. **Reaching out.** You take initiatives in reaching out to those in the group who are in moments of crisis and affliction, offering your support and skills. You make your care and concern evident in facilitative word and deed.
3. **Validation.** You appreciate a group member, affirming their intrinsic nature, their qualities, their deeds, to enhance their confidence and self-worth. You affirm the group as a whole for its commitment and growth.
4. **Positive feeling.** Where appropriate, you directly express your love, affection, liking for a person and how they are being.
5. **Holding and touching.** Where appropriate, you go forth to hold or touch a person when working or needing support. Your physical presence is nurturing and valuing through contact.
6. **Authenticity.** You manifest, in direct action, three aspects of authenticity.
   - You are genuine, keeping in touch with your feelings and your own reality: you are there as a person, not alienated, cut off and mechanical within the role.
   - You keep in touch with the real issues in the group, those that engage the group with growth and change.
   - You are immediate, alert to the energy of the group, the spirit that moves through it in surprising and unexpected ways, and you take initiatives to respond to that energy.

7. **Active charisma.** You actively manifest your presence, your charismatic way of being, as and when appropriate, in and through your interventions. This is the inward spiritual power of the human person. I have also called this, when training facilitators, distress-free authority and charismatic authority. You manifest dynamic presence through the up-hierarchy of empowerment, and enter shared experiential space, as described in Chapter 12. Being charismatic and hierarchical in the early stages of training, to enable people to be more autonomous and co-operative later on, is a basic principle of facilitation.

## The Valuing Dimension: Co-operative Mode

Here you are inclusive, interactive, collaborating with persons in their emergence, in a manner that is founded on respect for their right to self-determination. You are creating a community of value and mutual respect, by eliciting and sharing in this community.

1. **Honouring co-operative choice.** When you invite someone to do some piece of personal development work in the group, you always respect their right to choose to do it or not. So you ask them whether they want to make that choice. If they give you double messages, you hang in with them until they make an unequivocal choice, and then you respect this, whatever it is. If they overtly choose to do the work, then you are truly doing the work with them, not on them or for them. If they choose not to do it, then your honour their right to grow when they want.

2. **Co-operation.** Working with the group on all the other dimensions, in the co-operative mode, is a basic way of valuing and respecting personhood, and its right to, and need for, both self-determination and connectedness. The art is to know when to move from the hierarchical mode – which provides security for the embryonic development of self-determination – to the co-operative mode. It can be unwise to rush into the co-operative mode.

3. **Mutual affirmation.** You collaborate with the group in introducing and setting up a culture in which mutual affirmation occurs. Your prompt and encourage the group to adopt the following:

    ● **Nurturing.** It becomes an accepted form within the group for members to greet, part, sustain and nourish each other through physical contact.

- **Validation.**   In ritual circles and spontaneously at other times, group members learn verbally to express positive feelings – to affirm, appreciate and celebrate each other.
- **Support.**   When anyone has personal work to do, members will give that person time, attention, care and support.

4. **Mutual authenticity.**   You collaborate with the group in introducing and sustaining a climate in which each person manifests, in direct action, three aspects of being authentic.

- Being genuine, keeping in touch with personal feelings and personal reality: being there as a person, not alienated, cut off and mechanical within the role.
- Keeping in touch with the real issues in the group, those that engage it, those at the leading edges of its task and its process.
- Being immediate, alert to the energy of the group, the spirit that moves through it in surprising and unexpected ways, and taking initiatives to respond to that energy.

5. **Facilitating participants' charisma.**   Everyone has the ability to cultivate their personal presence, to manifest their authentic spiritual power. You facilitate the expression of this through charismatic training, for which exercises are given at the end of Chapter 12.

## The Valuing Dimension: Autonomous Mode

You create space for the exercise of individual and group autonomy, the right of persons to be self-determining, their need to be self-creating – in the area of respect for persons, validation and celebration. And simply by being in your presence – as distinct from responding to your acts – people become more self-valuing.

1. **Delegation.**   You can delegate to one member, for an agreed time, in the whole group or in sub-groups, the role of facilitating the group with particular attention to the valuing dimension. This is followed by feedback to that person.

2. **Validation exercise.**   You set up small groups in which members learn in their own way to affirm and celebrate both themselves and each other.

3. **Giving space for autonomy.**   All the strategies on the other dimensions in the autonomous mode are ways of manifesting respect for persons and their need for self-determination independent of any co-operation and interaction with you. The

facilitator who cannot grant this kind of autonomy is acting out their own anxiety about lack of inner freedom and self-determination.

4. **Enabling presence.** You participate awarely in the experiential field of the group, filling it with abundant free attention: an intense, silent activity of consciousness that encompasses and enhances the autonomy of all those present. It means being fully present, in and through the psychophysical modes of relating (see Chapter 12), in the underlying affective field of the group. So your enabling presence is mediated by hearing, the gaze, facial expression, posture, gesture and position relative to others; and when you are active, by voice, speech and on occasion touch. It is supportive, alert, expectant and invisibly beckoning, waiting for each person in the group to emerge in ways that are meaningful for that person and their fulfilment. It is outside your own distress and anxiety. Its reach is wider and deeper than the manifest behaviour in the group. It is attuned to the potential in each person, to the underlying real issues, to the movements of transforming energy within the group.

5. **Going inward.** You are centring yourself, finding your own reality, visiting an internal watering place, tapping the inner universe, finding the well-spring, the deep indwelling source, of your own emerging person. This is the inner ground for enabling presence.

6. **Self-disclosure.** This overlaps with being a self-directed client, item 10, autonomous mode, structuring dimension, Chapter 13. You affirm your own autonomy and self-worth, and in this way inspire other members to do the same. You may disclose:
   - Your beliefs and attitudes about general issues outside the group.
   - Your thoughts and emotions about your life-experience outside the group.
   - Your thoughts and emotions about what is going on inside the group at this time, and about the persons concerned.
   - Your own personal anxieties, conflicts, tensions as these arise within the group process.
   - Your delights, celebrations, strengths as these arise within the group.
   - Your own personal growth work as self-directed client, supported by the attention and care of the group.

7. **A culture of autonomous authenticity.** This is not a strategy. It is a consequence of all the strategies on all the dimensions, especially the valuing dimension. Group members:

- Are genuine, keep in touch with personal emotions and personal reality. Each is present as a person, not alienated, cut off and mechanical within the role.
- Keep in touch with the real issues in the group, those that engage its deep commitment, those at the leading edges of its task and its process.
- Are immediate, alert to the energy of the group, the spirit that moves through it in surprising and unexpected ways, and take initiatives to respond to that energy.

So group members are self-determining in diverse authentic activities and ways of being. I repeat here the range from Chapter 4.

- **Task-oriented.**   The group is outgoing, busy with planning, working on a project, practising some particular skill, busy with a structured exercise, undergoing some experience, exploring some issue, engaged in theoretical study. Members co-operate in learning, in problem-solving and decision-making.
- **Process-oriented.**   The group is ingoing, examining its own psychosocial process, seeking to understand how it is functioning.
- **Expressive.**   The group is active with celebration and creative expression in word, art, music, song or movement.
- **Interactive.**   Group members are engaged in interpersonal work and feedback, giving and receiving impressions, sharing attractions and aversions, withdrawing and owning projections.
- **Confronting.**   Members are engaged in creative conflict resolution, in supportive confrontation.
- **Personal work oriented.**   Individual members are taking time for personal growth work. Each one has a turn, working in pairs or small groups, or with you in the presence of the whole group. This work covers a wide spectrum, from cognitive and analytic self-discovery, through emotional disclosure, regression and catharsis, to transmutation and transpersonal development.
- **Charismatic.**   The group is attuning to psychic and spiritual energies, entering altered states of consciousness and action, engaged in ritual, expressive spirituality, silent meditation.

# *16 Learning to be a Whole Person*

In Chapter 3, I distinguished between learning some subject matter or skill by holistic methods, and learning how to be a whole person. The former, I said, is to do with educational development, which may have personal development by-products; the latter is to do with personal development full-on. In this chapter, I look at this latter business of learning how to be a whole person. So we enter the world of personal growth, interpersonal skills, social change, ecological awareness, and transpersonal unfoldment.

## *The Self-creating Person*

The distinction between holistic learning of a subject or skill, and learning to be a whole person, is the difference between dipping down into the deeper reaches of yourself in order to master some external knowledge or specific behaviour, and dipping down into deeper reaches of yourself in order to integrate with them. In the former you open the self up only while learning, and only for the purposes of learning. In the latter you open the self up so that it will be open for living, and restrictive blocks and contractions may be permanently dissolved.

There are, of course, cases where the two things start to merge. Thus some forms of whole person learning within a domain, such as the counselling training used as an example in Chapter 14, will themselves involve basic elements of personal development applicable in life generally.

In terms of the up-hierarchy model of the person introduced in Chapter 3, learning to be a whole person means integrating the individuating functions of emotion, imagery, discrimination and action with the participatory ones of feeling, intuition, reflection and intention, within oneself, in face-to-face relation with others, and in concern for wider cultural and ecological issues. The person is embarked on the phase of self-creating of becoming intentional about liberation from the trauma of childhood and the constraints of social conditioning, and about releasing the deep potential of the affective and imaginal nature

He or she is dealing with old emotional fixations, developing integrated functions in interpersonal behaviour and in promoting cultural and ecological change, and acquiring a psychic, subtle and spiritual perspective – which begins the process of self-transfiguration (Chapter 15 above; Heron, 1992).

## *The Whole Person as a Web of Relations*

If holistic learning of a subject raises issues of what a whole person is, even more so does learning how to be a whole person. General systems theory, increasingly evoked as a post-positivist paradigm (Bateson, 1979; Capra, 1983; de Vries, 1981; Jantsch, 1980; Koestler, 1964, 1978; Laszlo, 1972), commends itself as a framework for thinking about personhood.

In systems thinking, a whole person is to be defined not simply in terms of the integration of all internal parts, but also in terms of the integration with wider wholes of which the person is her or himself part. In other words a whole person is to be defined in terms of both internal and external relationships. The inner nexus and the outer nexus are interdependent in a total web of relations. Here is my current model of this web.

1. **Intrapersonal.** At the core of the web is the internal structure and dynamics of the person: the four psychological modes – affective, imaginal, conceptual and practical – each with their polar participatory and individuating functions, related in terms of the up-hierarchy. And at the core of all this is immanent, indwelling spiritual life, the interior ground and source of the psyche.
2. **Interpersonal.** Intrapersonal, internal relations are set within the nexus of face-to-face interpersonal relations. What goes on within me is interdependent with past and current encounters with others.
3. **Cultural.** Interpersonal relations are embedded within the nexus of a sub-culture and a culture. By a culture I mean a language, and social structures with their established roles, practices and rituals, their pervasive values, norms and beliefs; and a sub-culture is one component part of all this.

4. **Ecological.** A culture is framed within the nexus of the ecological domain. 'Ecology' in its original usage in biology refers to the involvement of the organism with its environment. I use it here to mean the connections between a whole culture and its environment. First and foremost, I mean the engagement/dialogue/relationship (or alienation) between the people in a culture and the more-than-human world of nature and all its diverse entities and presences. Secondly, all those relations of a receptive kind, where the culture is embedded in what the planetary environment delivers, such as night and day, climate, the seasons of the year, its basic geography and endowments, the solar system and wider galactic environment, and so on. Thirdly, I mean the culture's economic relations in the use of natural resources in industry and agriculture, and the various sorts of interactions involved in town and country planning, communication and transport systems, wildlife conservation, climate control, waste disposal and so on.

5. **Transplanetary.** The ecological domain and all the previously listed parts of the web are set within the nexus of the transplanetary field. By this I mean two things, first the realm of the psychic and the subtle; and second the unitive field of universal consciousness. The term often used here, and I have used it myself elsewhere (Heron, 1992), is 'transpersonal'. But if we are defining the personal as necessarily included within the interpersonal, the cultural and the ecological, then the term 'transplanetary' seems more apposite.

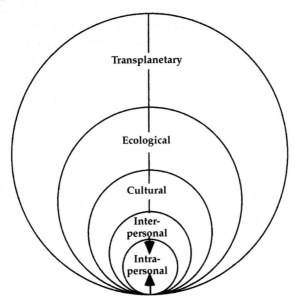

**Figure 16.1**   *The whole person as a web of relations*

The total web can be conceived as a set of circles sharing a common peripheral point, with the intrapersonal circle the smallest and the transplanetary the largest, as in Figure 16.1. Each circle is influenced by its relations with every other, the inner circles being more affected by everything else than the outer circles. To take just two adjacent circles, the total ecological environment has more effect on human culture than the other way round. Each circle has a relative autonomy: it has a degree of independence from the influence on it of all the other circles. The relative autonomy and self-regulation of the planet as a biological structure has been put forward as the Gaia hypothesis (Lovelock, 1987).

In Figure 16.1 the circles are all grounded in a common point. This is to symbolize that through the intrapersonal ground of feeling, as I have defined it in Chapter 3, with its source in immanent spiritual life, the person has the capacity to participate in all the circles and differentiate between them.

Given the logical structure of this model, you could argue that the latent capacity for autonomy is greater for each successive inner circle simply because it has a more dense web of relations with which to engage and on which it can exert its influence. So the individual person has the greatest *potential* for autonomous functioning with an interconnected whole. There is also the pragmatic reason that unless individual persons have the maximal capacity for independent action, they are going to be permanently overwhelmed by the sway of all the encircling forces.

What the model propounds, therefore, is that while individuals are most subject to all the combined effects of the web, they also have the greatest potential capacity to change it. There is a two-way influence: a down-hierarchy from the circumference to the centre, and an up-hierarchy from the centre to the circumference. While the down-hierarchy is always actual in the lives of persons, their role as the ground of the up-hierarchy can be in various states from the potential to the less or more actualized. This two-way process is represented by the arrows in Figure 16.1.

## *A Working Definition of a Whole Person*

What this model brings out for the definition of a whole person is that to be one involves the complete web. A whole person means someone who is in a set of whole interpersonal relations in a whole culture in a whole planetary environment integrated with its trans-planetary field. In each case here, whole means developing in orchestrated harmony. Since the web is not in this state, but is torn and damaged, such a definition is about the end-state of human development. As a definition for today, it is unrealistic and inapplicable. So we have to choose one that is more workable.

The next closest definition, it would seem, is that whole persons are those who have exercised their relative autonomy to integrate their intrapersonal life – so far as this is possible within a total web that is limited – and who are involved in a combined interpersonal, cultural (socio-structural), ecological and transplanetary change programme of activities and commitments. In other words since they cannot now be in a whole and healed web, they are seeking to bring one about. Whole persons are internally together change-agents of a rather comprehensive kind. They are defined in terms both of relative psychological integration and of holistic initiatives in the other four interdependent spheres. Whole personhood is faced with a paradox. Until all spheres are healed and hale it cannot be achieved, and it can only be achieved by making them so.

What is clear on a systems view is that the purely individualistic account of personhood is at an end. A person is a vast web of inner and outer relations, and all our respective webs overlap and interweave. And the outer relations beyond the intrapersonal are multidimensional. As well as culture, nature and cosmos, they include the psychic or subtle and the spiritual.

## The Agenda for Learning to be a Whole Person

The agenda for learning to be a whole person now extends from personal, intrapsychic growth, through interpersonal skills, to organizational and political change and development, thence to environmental development, and transplanetary (transpersonal) development. This agenda might involve developing the underdeveloped, or the undeveloped, aspects, or both. What is either underdeveloped or undeveloped furls out to cover all the other four spheres beyond the immediate intrapersonal one. We can now no longer present the personal growth agenda as one which is separated off from these wider issues; and vice versa.

Because of the breadth of the agenda, learning to be a whole person is necessarily a piecemeal enterprise. We cannot do it all in one workshop or one course, or in one phase of life-experience, but will bring the underdeveloped and the undeveloped things on bit by bit, here and there. Nor do I believe we can be dogmatic about which of the five spheres to start in, as long as it is acknowledged that whichever one we begin with all the others will sooner or later have a claim upon our attention; and as long as the presenter of any one of them is regularly pointing to its connections with the others. This is an age in which different people do indeed start in every one of the five spheres, and progressively add others to it on an idiosyncratic path of development. And this is no doubt as it should be in our multifarious universe.

My own preference is to give first place to the intrapersonal sphere on the grounds that working on hidden emotional distress will reduce its tendency unawarely and compulsively to distort behaviour in other spheres. More positively by unfolding our capacity for feeling, for resonant attunement with and participation in our world, we find the ground within for integrating all the spheres and for grasping their interdependence. Here are just some of the items within each sphere which may be on the total agenda.

1. **Intrapersonal.** Healing the wounded child within, and discharging its repressed distress; using the complementary method of transmuting distress; being able to exercise aware control of emotion of all kinds; unfolding the expressive power of positive emotion; cultivating the grounding capacity for feeling participation in the world and the wider universe as a distinct being within it; releasing the depths and power of the imaginal mind, including extrasensory competence; integrating thinking and action with the depths of the affective and imaginal being.
2. **Interpersonal.** Relating to others free of hidden projection and unaware displacement; managing harmoniously the boundaries between togetherness and separation, communality and privacy; moving flexibly between the relations of co-operating, following, leading, and being autonomous; balancing giving and receiving; balancing supportive care with supportive confrontation; having a wide range of informal intervention skills – prescriptive, informative, confronting, cathartic, catalytic and supportive; having a wide range of group process, group discussion and group decision-making skills.
3. **Cultural.** Being clear about the sources and processes of social oppression in its various forms; education as social transformation not cultural transmission; social empowerment through consciousness-raising and community action; re-visioning of their situation by oppressed minorities; mutual support networks of various special interest groups; transforming social structures from within by political initiatives, persuasion, organizational development methods, and techniques of soft revolution;

balancing hierarchy, co-operation and autonomy in organizations run as learning centres; challenging rigid social structures from without by direct nonviolent action; creating innovative social practices in different spheres of life; devising rituals to enhance the meaning of important occasions in life; decentralization and federalism; creating alternative institutions, social structures, nuclear societies and self-generating, self-transforming cultures.

4. **Ecological.** Cultivating dialogic and participatory relationships with mineral, plant and animal entities, the earth and its processes as a whole, the solar system, and the galaxy; green consumerism – biodegradable products, natural cosmetics, organic additive-free foods, lead-free petrol, recycled paper, artificial furs, vegetarian diet; recycling of paper, glass bottles, cans, rags, plastic, cars, and ultimately all natural resources; ethical investment in ecologically clean companies; ecologically sound control of pollution and waste; population control; reduction of animal husbandry; promotion of animal rights, reduction of animal vivisection; preservation of rare species, wildlife, wilderness areas, the countryside, forests, topsoil, irreplaceable resources; planting trees; self-regulating eco-economics, abandonment of undifferentiated economic growth; soft technology, solar energy and energy from other renewable resources; industrial democracy, work co-operatives, overlap of worker, owner, manager roles; work flexibility, ownwork, work portfolios; reduction of defence budgets; reduction of expropriation of profits by multinational companies from the third world.

5. **Transplanetary.** Development of subtle energies and faculties in human beings; use of subtle energies within nature; co-operation with creative forces, powers and presences in the subtle worlds; consciousness-raising about the influence of the deceased; development of unitive awareness in and with the world; resonance with universal consciousness; evocation of the immanent divine; invocation of the transcendent divine.

## Locations, Domains and Cycles

The diverse items given in the previous section mean that learning to be a whole person involves at least six different locations: within the psyche; everyday face-to-face social interactions; the classroom or group room; the work-place as change arena; community consciousness-raising, support or action groups of various kinds; the wider multi-dimensional universe. The first is in the intrapersonal domain, the second in the interpersonal, the third, fourth and fifth in the cultural/ecological domains; the sixth in the transplanetary domain.

The distinction between learning in the world and in the classroom made at the outset of Chapter 3 is no longer tenable in any rigid way: the two here stream in and out of each other. The primary experiential learning cycle, with its four stages, introduced in Chapter 14, in relation to holistic learning of a subject or a skill, is taken out into the world and applied in living, in each of the domains of the whole person nexus. This is shown in Figure 16.2. Learning to be a whole person goes out to the world and through the world, transfiguring it with spirit.

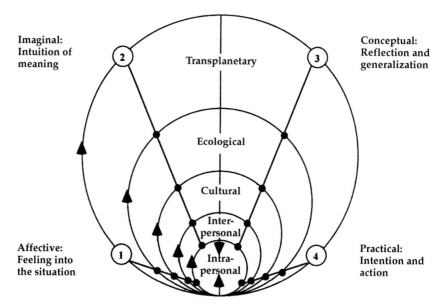

**Figure 16.2**   *The whole person web of relations and the primary experiential learning cycle*

## A Self-generating Culture

What this entails is individual and co-operative action inquiry within a learning culture. Each person, in the everyday process of his or her personal and professional life, is adopting a form of action inquiry, a primary experiential learning cycle. This consciousness-in-action involves, intentionally, both participatory and individuating functions: feeling and emotion, intuition and imagery, reflection and discrimination, intention and action. So you do four interdependent things:

- You feel into and participate fully in the immediate situation, notice and manage your emotional responses to it.
- You grasp intuitively the significance of the total perceived pattern of what is going on, and this includes a vision of how this pattern needs to develop.
- You discriminate conceptually the salient features of all this and reflect rapidly on the issues involved.
- You formulate a relevant strategic intention and act upon it. This takes you into a new relation with the situation, and the cycle starts again.

Again these several elements influence and revise each other in cyclic feedback fashion, resolving dissonance, deepening learning and worthwhile living.

Torbert's account of action inquiry (1991) overlaps with this. By extended consciousness-in-action, he means widening your attention to encompass your vision of goals, your strategies to achieve them, your current actions and their outcomes, and what is going on in the world around. It also means noticing and amending, either through action or internal revision or both, incongruities between these components of your lived inquiry.

In the whole person web of relations, such action inquiry will have its idiosyncratic private strands, its shared and face-to-face strands with people at home and at work, and its more collective strands within a learning organization and a wider learning culture, all of which take account of ecological and transplanetary concerns. It will involve primary cycles of living and learning; with time out in secondary cycles for review, reflection and goal setting. The totality of all this I call a self-generating culture, a society whose members are in a continuous process of learning and development, and whose forms are consciously adopted, periodically reviewed and altered in the light of experience and deeper vision (Heron, 1987, 1997).

Torbert presents a similar notion. For him, personal action inquiry 'aims at creating communities of inquiry within communities of social practice'. It exhibits 'transforming power' which 'operates through peer cultures, liberating structures, and timely actions. Cultures are truly peer-like, structures are liberating, and actions are timely, if they simultaneously promote widening inquiry about what is the appropriate mission, strategy, and practice for the given person or organization or nation, while accomplishing established objectives in an increasingly efficient, effective and self-legitimizing manner' (Torbert, 1991: 100).

A self-generating culture is thus one whose forms its members continually recreate through cycles of experiential learning and inquiry. It has several strands.

1. **Decision-making.**  Persons need to explore forms of decision-making, so that in their different sorts of association they can balance the claims of deciding by oneself, deciding co-operatively with others, and deciding for others. These forms need to be adopted intentionally, subject to periodic review, with an accepted procedure for changing them. I assume this same conscious learning process, without stating it, for all the points that follow.
2. **Association.**  Persons need to explore different forms of association in daily living and working, so that they can find ways of balancing the claims of being and doing things alone, together with others, or beside others.
3. **Economics.**  Persons need to explore forms of economic arrangement so that they can awarely choose different ways of distributing and combining the roles of owner, manager and worker; and choose different forms of income and wealth distribution.
4. **Ecology.**  Persons need to explore ways of caring for their planetary environment, sustaining and enhancing its dynamic eco-system.
5. **Education.**  Persons need to explore forms of providing for children and young people of all ages: how they are to be cared for, raised and educated, and by whom. They need to explore forms of education and training for the personal and professional development of adults, which include methods for dealing with individual and social overload of emotional distress, and methods for subtle and spiritual unfoldment
6. **Intimacy.**  Persons need to explore forms of intimacy, that is, ways of giving social form to their sexual and nurturance needs. The point about this form – whether it is open bonding, closed bonding, celibate bonding, serial bonding, or any other – is that it is chosen awarely in the presence of others, that there is a support network for it, and that there is an acknowledged social process for changing the form.
7. **Conflict.**  Persons need to explore forms of conflict resolution: different ways of dealing with hostility and tension, irrational outbursts, irreconcilable opinions, broken agreements, confusion of purpose, and so on. They need to devise such forms, have them in readiness, and learn to use them when they are relevant.
8. **Rituals.**  Persons need to explore and improvise rituals, special events, holidays and feast-days, to celebrate, mark, or mourn the

great recurring themes of their individual, social and planetary lives: birth, coming of age, relationships, graduations, visits, arrivals and departures, beginnings and endings, the seasons, solar and lunar cycles, death, and so on. They need to explore, receive and improvise rituals: to foster their inward, occult and spiritual development; to interact with the unseen worlds, their powers and presences; and in communion to attune to the presence within, beyond, and manifest as, creation.

## Whole Person Values

In the model of the five spheres and their learning agendas, there is implicit a set of values. This set is encoded in the notion of a harmonious system in which larger wholes include smaller wholes, or to state it in complementary language, smaller parts are subsumed in larger parts. Parts at the same level co-operate in relations of mutual interchange and reciprocal action. Wider wholes have influence over the parts they contain. Single parts have a relative autonomy of function both in relation to co-operative relations with their peers and in relation to influence from wider wholes. Single parts thus have influence on their peers and on their wider wholes. The total system exhibits autonomy, co-operation, down-hierarchy and up-hierarchy. These are its four forms of power, control, effect, guidance, direction or influence: self-influence, peer-influence, down-influence and up-influence. They are illustrated in Figure 16.3.

This model derives as I have said from a modified general systems theory. But it is also influenced by the notion of organic unity in aesthetic theory (Beardsley, 1958), by logical analysis of the concept of

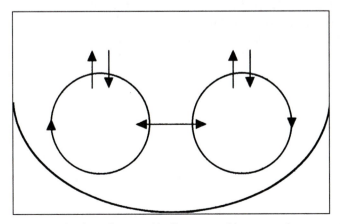

**Figure 16.3** *The four forms of influence: self-, peer-, down- and up-*

a whole (Nagel, 1963), and by theory of value (Perry, 1954). It seems to point to some archetypal, federal concept that crops up in many domains of inquiry. I have stated it in the form that makes most sense to me. But all stated versions contain some or all of the basic elements I have included.

Translated into a combined account of human values and human rights, it comes out something like the following. As stated, this version extends only through the intrapersonal, the interpersonal and the cultural spheres.

1. **Human integration is intrinsically worthwhile.**  Each person has a right to unfold and harmonize all different aspects of him or herself.
2. **Human self-determination is intrinsically worthwhile.**  Each person has a right to determine and fulfil in his or her own way his or her basic needs and interests.
3. **Human co-operation is intrinsically worthwhile.**  Persons have a right to meet together to determine and fulfil together their shared needs and interests.
4. **Human up-hierarchy is intrinsically worthwhile.**  Persons have a right to participate in decisions that serve their welfare, whether in the home, the community, the workplace, the larger society or the world.
5. **Human down-hierarchy is intrinsically worthwhile.**  Persons have a right to make decisions that serve the welfare of others, including the four previous items, whether in the home, the community, the workplace, the larger society or the world.
6. **Human conflict-resolution is intrinsically worthwhile.**  Persons have a right to co-operate in resolving (a) conflicts between personal needs and interests and shared needs and interests, and (b) up-hierarchy and down-hierarchy claims.
7. **Human diversity in unity is intrinsically worthwhile.**  Persons have a right to meet together to celebrate and affirm their different states, needs, interests and claims.

The values of self-determination and co-operation are importantly interdependent. There is no real co-operation going on unless it is between self-determining people; and self-determination is achieved and exercised in co-operative relations with others similarly engaged. Nevertheless they do not coincide. There is an element of relative independence in each: some valid self-determination is non-co-operative; and some co-operation compromises everyone's self-determination.

The values of up-hierarchy and down-hierarchy are likewise inter-dependent. There is no valid down-hierarchy, decision-making for others, unless up-hierarchy participation has authorized it; and up-hierarchy participation presupposes there is some valid down-hierarchy to participate in. But again there is relative independence: some valid up-hierarchy influence can be to oppose the down-hierarchy, or create an alternative to it; and some valid down-hierarchy decisions can properly be made – as in a sudden and unforeseen contingency – without any authorization to make them.

Many modern accounts of values and rights omit the down-hierarchy item. This seems to me to be a serious mistake. It is prob-ably omitted because it has been and is being so badly misused in terms of oppression and exploitation. But these abuses do not serve 'the welfare of others' and so fall outside my definition. A worthwhile down-hierarchy principle affirms the right of people to exercise responsibility, care and consideration for others, in a social context where the other principles are appropriately honoured.

The main thing that characterizes down-hierarchy decisions in the social sphere is social size. With a small face-to-face group, co-operative and consensus decision-making can be used. With a large federation of smaller social groups, federal decision-makers will be authorized by the groups to decide some things without consulta-tion, and to canvas and consult the groups on other issues. But even with these latter issues, crisis and rapid change may call for non-consultative decisions.

If societies move to more and more decentralization, so that strong up-hierarchy influence can be exercised by people in their local communities on many aspects of their living and working, then there will be a correlative need for federal bodies up to the global level, where the down-hierarchy influence will be strong. Global decision-makers, authorized through up-hierarchies to make certain sorts of decisions non-consultatively, will have awesome responsibility and power.

In everyday life, the down-hierarchy principle is inalienable. You may be in one of many positions in which you have a right and a duty to make decisions that serve others, and this without consulting them, because they are too traumatized, too young or too ill or too old or too ignorant and unaware, too far away, because there is no time to do so, and so on.

The principle also applies in the sphere of special expertise. This is an area where it has been much abused, in the sense that in many professions the experts could consult the laity a great deal more before making their decisions. Even so, there can come a point when lay persons defer because they are out of their depth and have to say 'You decide for me'.

The up-hierarchy principle is strongest in the intrapersonal sphere, within the psyche, where it can have unimpeded reign in ordering the relations between the psychological modes and functions. At the deepest level within the psyche, it is manifest as autonomous individual innovation, grounded in indwelling and immanent spiritual life (Heron, 1998a). The principle is strong in interpersonal, face-to-face groups where each person can have a lot of say in shaping any corporate decisions that are made. In the wider social groupings of the cultural sphere, the principle moves from strong to weak along a spectrum from the very local and decentralized to the very global and federal.

In the total ecological sphere, even in ecologically competent societies, up-hierarchy influence is much less than in the cultural sphere since so many environmental parameters are immune to its influence – night and day, planetary geography, and so on. In the transplanetary sphere of subtle worlds, hardly anyone knows what is going on in them in any reliable way in terms of decisions being taken by presences brooding over earthly affairs and so intentional up-hierarchy influence is virtually zero.

This may change in the future, when we may enter an era of two-world politics, in which people in this world seek representation on those decision-making councils in the other which preside over human societies. In the present climate of physical world chauvinism, this notion will appear fanciful and extravagant. For more on the subtle dimension of experience, see *Sacred Science* (Heron, 1998a).

Conversely, if the thesis of physical and subtle worlds is correct, then at present the non-consultative down-hierarchy principle is strongest at the transplanetary level: the Creatrix/Creator/and her/his hierarchies do not confer with human beings about the design of their psychological and physical endowments, their physical and psychic environment, or the social possibilities which these delimit. As I say, this one day may become different. The down-hierarchy principle is strong but accessible for human influence in the ecological sphere, and becomes progressively less dominant through the cultural and the interpersonal and is weakest in the intrapersonal.

Many moralistic and psychological systems for organizing the intrapersonal sphere have noted (a) that the down-hierarchy controlling principle is innately weak and (b) that chaotic and primitive sorts of up-hierarchy influences seem to be at work, such as desires and passions and selfish and irrational impulses. This has led them to try to install down-hierarchy forms of psychological control with high intellect (Plato) or rational conscience (Bishop Butler) or the reality-oriented ego (Freud) taking charge of the whole, with one or two subordinates helping out.

This has not worked very well, largely in my belief-system because the intrapersonal sphere is innately an up-hierarchy zone. Properly understood, chaotic up-hierarchies are the precursors to deeper, more enriching and more creative ones that can harmonize with those of other persons, and with the outer spheres on the great web of person-hood. I have already outlined my version of such a creative and worthwhile up-hierarchy within the person. And in *Sacred Science* I put forward the view that we can be co-creative with very ground of our personhood, immanent spiritual life (Heron, 1998a).

# 17 Approaches to Social Change

Continuing the theme of the previous chapter, this chapter looks at personal development as individual and collective action inquiry involved with structural change of the culture. It reviews three different theoretical approaches to social structures, distinguishes between liberation within and transfiguration of the human condition, and between opposing oppression and fulfilling rights. It concludes with the different group options available for working explicitly on the transformation of social structures, with the issues of concern to which the facilitator can alert any such group, and with some techniques of soft revolution.

## Personal Development and Structural Change

The peer supervision and peer unfoldment groups considered in Chapter 9 will tend to have as their outcome minor or major transformations of individual behaviour, in the sense of people developing existing values in their lives or realizing new values. These individual transformations can start to have some effect in changing the face-to-face quality of life in the surrounding culture. As I said at the outset of Chapter 9, a culture ceases to be oppressive, and starts to be enhancing when its members meet in small groups to revise its norms, values and social practices in their individual lives, personal and professional.

In terms of my model of the person as a web of relations – intrapersonal, interpersonal, cultural, ecological and transplanetary – the cultural impact of the groups I have discussed is mainly as a result of work done in the intrapersonal and interpersonal domains. What I want to look at in this chapter is personal development and action inquiry construed as cultural transformation that works directly at the cultural level, addressing cultural issues as such.

By my culture I mean my mother tongue, and the social structures

– the associations and organizations – within which my life is conducted, with their established roles, practices and rituals, their pervasive values, norms and beliefs. If I emigrate from the culture into which I was born, then I have two cultures, the one I bring with me as part of my history and the one I have moved into. To sharpen the discussion I shall use the terms 'social structure' or simply 'structure' and 'structural' to cover all that I mean by culture.

## Three Kinds of Structural Theory

To be committed to structural change presupposes some theory about what is wrong with current structures and about an alternative way of ordering society. On the diagnostic side, there are three sorts of theories that I believe are relevant and need each other, but are often found in total divorce from each other.

The first kind is to do with psychosocial dynamics, which depicts the interlocking of personal pathology and social pathology. The second is about political–economic macro-analysis, identifying corruptions of political and economic power in light of moral values and notions of a just social order. The third is to do with the transpersonal and is about social structures in relation to spiritual reality and the life divine.

An example of the first sort of theory about psychosocial dynamics is given by Jackins (1983) who holds that the repressed, wounded child within is stuck in a rigid pattern which includes a maladaptive victim response plus an internalization of the oppressive behaviour that caused it. The pattern has recorded in it the external oppressor's behaviour. He extends this theory of the distress pattern to generate a theory of social oppression. Persons who carry such a pattern will act out the internalized oppression against themselves as self-invalidation, and against people in their own oppressed group or in other oppressed groups within society. This effect of the oppressed oppressing the oppressed through the internalization of old external oppression, is its most damaging effect.

Certain oppressions play a key role in society in relation to other oppressions. Jackins singles out the oppression of young people by adults as the foundation for the installation of all other patterns of oppression. So far so good, but thereafter the theory rapidly degenerates into a millennial form of neo-Marxism, extremely vague on structural reform and totally devoid of any transpersonal awareness.

Theories about political–economic macro-analysis have a distinguished history from Plato's *Republic* through the views of More,

Rousseau, Fourier, Godwin, Owen, Blanc, Proudhon, Bakunin, Kropotkin, Marx and many others. A contemporary example of this tradition, refreshingly free of doctrinal bias, is provided by the Movement for a New Society which sprang out of a Quaker action group formed in the late 1960s in Philadelphia (Gowan et al, 1979).

They criticize the society of the USA as based on the private profit system whereby people can accumulate wealth through passive ownership thereby resulting in a massive concentration of economic, political and military power among a small elite – at the expense of real democracy, distributive justice, the planetary eco-system and the third world. However, their powerful analysis is not related in any way to psychological pathology in the individual, nor to the transpersonal dimension of human experience.

An example of an extreme transpersonal account of human culture is provided by the early Wilber (1983) who regards both individual persons and the cultures they generate as illusory substitutes for absolute spirit. They are projections of a hidden and denied longing for spirit, projections which displace this longing in a false and misbegotten direction. The end result of this kind of theory is that the only really valid moral imperative is for people to practise meditation so that they can lift themselves out of the illusions of personhood and cultural pursuits and enter 'non-dual awareness'. This theory reduces psychosocial dynamics and political–economic processes to nothing but spiritual pathology, and leaves everybody looking for the nearest guru to effect their transcendental release.

This kind of view is an extreme form of transcendental reductionism. It fails to honour the divine as One and Many, reducing the Many to illusion and acknowledging only the One. What is needed, by contrast, is a vision of personhood and culture as potential expressions of divine manifestation and differentiation within the realm of the Many. Self-transfiguring persons in self-transforming cultures become a creative enterprise with living divinity.

## *Liberation Within and Transfiguration of the Human Condition*

It seems to me that these three kinds of theory need each other, suitably adapted and amended to engage with each other. The idea that the oppressed need to work, psychologically, on the internalized oppressor and interrupt its tendency to oppress other oppressed people, replacing this with mutual aid, needs balancing with clear ideas about structural reform and how progressively to realize it. But this combination of the psychosocial approach and the political–economic structural approach is concerned, quite properly, with liberation within the human condition. To be effective I think it needs to be complemented by transfiguration of the human condition. As I have said, I do not mean by this a rejection of the human condition as illusory, but a transformation of it by knowing it as included within the subtle realms and the life divine. On this view the human person is an expression of divine multiplicity, unfolding through transfiguration into ever greater differentiation and manifestation.

## *Opposition Actions and Fulfilment Actions*

The words 'liberation' and 'struggle', often used about the realization of a more just social order, are problematic. If we do not struggle against oppressive power, seeking to liberate other people from its exploitation and abuse, we fail in humanity and fellow feeling. If we do struggle against it, we inevitably give it substance and affirm its being by our very effort. One solution to this dilemma is to notice that all rigid, oppressive systems are run by compulsive anxiety in the oppressors and are thereby constrained to operate in terms of a restricted grid of options. The oppressors seek to generate even more fear in the victims so that they will conform to severely limited parameters of behaviour and social structure.

The transcendental solution to this has always been to lead people into the spaces the oppressive system does not command. In the old days these were physical, geographical spaces. Nowadays they are psychosocial and structural spaces. Rather than oppose abuse, the social transformer creates alternatives in spaces of this kind, spaces which the oppressors' anxiety makes it difficult for them to accept as existing. The trouble with active opposition is that it may be in the grip of the fear induced by the oppressor, and so can act out that fear in confrontation, which affirms the power of the offensive system even while opposing it.

Once outside the hold of this fear, then the reformer has the open vision for innumerable options which the compulsive oppressor cannot see. Confronting reaction is replaced by creative proaction. There are critical occasions when direct realization of some human right in a given situation is the same thing as challenging rigid social structures from without by direct action. But the realization of the right is more important than the challenge to the oppression.

The basic distinction here is between taking action to oppose abuses of human and planetary rights, and doing things which directly seek to fulfil those selfsame rights. (By planetary rights I mean the rights of all parts of the total planetary eco-system to be in mutually supportive balance with all other parts.) So we have opposition actions and fulfilment actions. Fulfilment actions may at the same time be opposition actions, but that is not their primary motive. Opposition *per se* has the potential problem of being fed by the compulsive and fixated rebellion of childhood. At its worst this means choosing targets that are too big and that result in repetitive ineffectiveness – a symbolic re-enactment of the fruitless struggles of the rebellious child.

Opposition *per se* also has the problem that the identity of the opposer becomes parasitic on the existence of the evil empire, and therefore supports it by needing it. The compulsive rebel is still dependent on the abuse of power which he or she struggles against, and is addicted to struggling with the fear which such abuse provokes. If, on the other hand, the prime end and reason for action is the fulfilment of human rights, rather than simply opposition to their abuse, then the agents concerned draw their identity from newly realized good rather than from the established bad, and will have more power and effect as a result.

## Structural Change Options

Working on structural change at its own level has many forms, each of which is an arena for personal development and individual and collective action inquiry. In terms of the primary and secondary experiential learning cycles discussed in Chapter 14, the group members' endeavours in the world, their learning while doing, are the primary cycles; and these together with reflection and discussion on them at the group meetings are the secondary cycles.

The following groups may be created and sustained by a strong leader for a period, they may be facilitated on a rotating basis, or they may run as peer groups on an agreed format. They all have to be conscious in the exercise of decision-making, finding a good balance between autonomy, co-operation and hierarchy. They will wisely be holistic in method and use the multi-stranded approach, incorporating elements from the several strands given under item 9, hierarchical mode, feeling dimension, Chapter 11.

1. **Social change theory seminars.**   These are consciousness-raising study groups which research and reflect on the issues of change. Activism without this prior study can be blind, misplaced and ineffective. I have outlined three interrelated areas of theory – the psychosocial, the political–economic and the transpersonal. What seems critical is what these three approaches have to say to each other, and what active strategies such dialogue engenders. It makes sense for such seminars to use holistic methods which include:

   - Personal work on the emotional distress patterns that sustain addiction to oppressive systems both as victim and oppressor.
   - A moral–political intellectual critique of the existing social order, interdependent with visions of a new society with first-step strategies that move toward it now, with both these wings backed up where possible by relevant research data.
   - Transpersonal attunement through the use of ritual, group resonance and inner unfoldment.

2. **Community action groups.**   These are relatively small groups of people, variously affiliated by friendship, family, religion, social or occupational ties, who meet regularly to develop their ability to engage in some form of direct action for social change, in relation to any issue which is of concern to them. I repeat here the distinction made above between taking action to oppose abuses of human and planetary rights and doing things which seek to fulfil those selfsame rights and which, more generally, enable diverse forms of human flourishing. For the reasons stated, fulfilment actions seem preferable to opposition actions for their own sake, and while the former may have a powerful impact as opposition actions that is not the reason for their execution. A community action group can include:

   - **Community development.**   The group works directly, with or without the support of local government, to meet local needs and interests and deal with local issues, enlisting support and action from all those affected. This may involve social empowerment through consciousness-raising and appropriate action; revisioning and restructuring of their situation by oppressed minorities.
   - **Mutual aid.**   The group sets up a mutual aid network within which people do work for each other on a reciprocal basis, in relation to an agreed range of tasks and an agreed system of exchange of labour, as in current Local Exchange and Trading Systems in the UK.

- **Peer self-help.** The group organizes a mutual support association whose members share a common need for experience sharing, succour and social action to manifest their rights and advanced their welfare. This may be in relation to a physical disability (congenital defect, later trauma, degenerative disease); social deviance (drug dependency, alcoholism, disabling social and psychological distress); life-crisis (divorce, separation, single parenthood, rape, physical violence, bereavement, redundancy, retirement); minority values (homosexual and lesbian life-styles, euthanasia, gender emancipation); and so on.
- **New society education and action.** The group is busy with raising its own and society's consciousness, with identifying and promoting relevant action, about cultural and ecological issues: the human right to participate in decision-making in every type of social activity from industrial democracy to religious democracy, work co-operatives, green consumerism, consumer exploitation, recycling, pollution, abuse of the environment, animal rights, economic abuse of the third world, self-regulating eco-economics, soft technology and renewable energy, reduction of defence budgets.

3. **Occupational action groups.** These are groups that are affiliated exclusively by occupational ties. All the members of any group are from the same occupation, but not from the same organization or place of work (although some of them may be). Their commitment is to seek the extension and fulfilment of human and planetary rights within their own trade or profession and to create a climate for realizing more advanced views on psychological, social and political, ecological and transplanetary issues. They are likely to be active at professional conferences, meetings, committees, in-service training sessions, and so on. But initially they will be entirely *ad hoc* and not part of the formal structure of the profession.

4. **Organizational action groups.** These are groups of people who work together on the same organization. They may have the same occupational role, or they may be a mix of different occupations who work together. The commitment is to seek organizational change in the direction of increased self- and peer determination of the sorts indicated in the Appendix. The social structure is changed from within by political initiatives, persuasion, organizational development methods, and techniques of soft revolution. The aim is a better balance of hierarchy, co-operation and autonomy in the organization run as a learning system. This sort

of group will also initially be *ad hoc*, bringing its influence to bear informally through face-to-face dialogue, and also through formal organizational meetings of various kinds.

5. **New institutions.** All the previous activities converge on the creation of new institutions, the social structures of a new society. This seems a much wider arena for action than many people suppose, provided one is not in the grip of the fear which runs the prevailing system. Producers' and consumers' co-operatives, forms of community and village life which span the poles of privacy and communality, alternative schools, holistic medical clinics, these and many more require new skills in co-ownership, co-management and co-working: a challenge for any group of persons to live out a worthwhile way of life.

What need clarity are: awareness of group process issues and openness to the subtle and spiritual dimensions of experience.

## Facilitation for Structural Change

The facilitator as social change agent can take intitatives in setting up any one of the above groups, and can alert its members to the issues which they may need to be aware of and take charge of if the group is to succeed. Some of these are:

- **Emotion.** The group members may need to be able to separate out old hurts from present realities, and not to displace distress from the past on to other people and into current agendas; to have ways of working on distress that it stirred up within its members by its actions in the world and its internal deliberations.
- **Group process.** The group may need a good working awareness of group dynamic isses.
- **Feeling.** The group may need to open to its capacity for participative feeling and resonant attunement.
- **Power.** The group may need to take charge of its way of making decisions, to have a model of decision-making that is fully participative, consciously chosen and adhered to and systematically reviewed from time to time. It may need to rotate roles of facilitation, control and responsibility within the group on the basis of an honest assessment of competence and skill. It may need, in short, to get a working balance between autonomy, co-operation, and hierarchy.
- **Inclusion.** The groups may need to experiment with methods of discussion which ensure that everyone present has a voice and is

heard. These methods can be reviewed and modified in the light of experience of them.

- **Gender.** The group may need to be alert to the ways in which gender stereotypes can invade the behaviour and reactions of both men and women, and to have strategies for interrupting this and establishing enlightened gender relations.
- **Inquiry.** The group may need time to reflect on and learn from its actions in the world; and to study background material and reflect on that and its relevance to group goals and experience. Social structures become centres of learning and action inquiry, going through cycles of experience and reflection.
- **Co-operation.** The group may need to replace the conventional norm of competition with one of co-operation, mutual aid and skill sharing.
- **Conflict.** The group may need to have available strategies of conflict resolution and the awareness to use them when a conflict impasse is reached.
- **Confrontation.** The group may need to be open to challenge and confrontation about its activities and assumptions by any one or more of its members, so that its does not get trapped in radical conformity and consensus collusion. It may need a climate in which it is possible for its members to give each other person-to-person negative feedback in a fundamentally supportive and respectful way.
- **Affirmation.** The group may need to take time for its members to appreciate each other, their qualities and deeds and creations.
- **Celebration.** The group may need time for rejoicing and festivity and fun, for loving affirmation of people flourishing in their world, and for the celebration of differences among people.
- **Ritual.** The group may need to create new rituals that deepen the meaning of shared living and working, and celebrate its resonance with divine life and energy.

## Techniques of Soft Revolution

The following are simple strategies for introducing change in rigid institutions by those who are working members of them:

- Appeal to the stated values of your institution in order to launch radical practices within it.

- Appeal to the precedent set by another arm of the establishment in order to innovate in the arm of the establishment where you work.
- Always confront face-to-face the person in your institution who is the prime mover of malicious attempts, by slander or action, to undermine your initiatives for change.
- Launch innovations in the open spaces between the rigid grid-lines of the closed system of your institution.

Here are some more strategies. They are based on *managing* the limited mental and emotional state of those who block change. The strategies are all morally questionable, and any legitimacy they may have is situational.

- Shame those who block change with an impassioned appeal to basic human morality.
- Intimidate those who block change with copious relevant research references.
- Appeal to the vanity of those who block change by telling them how much they will be applauded in the wider community for promoting the innovation.
- Flatter the dominance of those who block change by telling them how much you need and are dependent on their support.
- Appeal to the greed of those who block change by demonstrating convincingly that the change you propose, when implemented, will show a profit.
- Play on the moral delusions of those who block change by telling them that you know they have the human compassion and ethical insight eagerly to want to promote the innovation you are proposing.
- Play on the determination to prove you wrong by telling those who block change that you believe there is no way they will feel able to support the change you have in mind.
- Appeal to the hidden angel in those who block change by being the most extreme devil's advocate in advancing reasons why the institution should not adopt the change you propose.

# 18 The Creation of a Facilitator Style

This concluding chapter considers some of the factors that may contribute to the creation of a facilitative style. Among other things, it includes details of facilitator training and criteria of facilitator competence; it looks at issues of research and social change; and it ends with a simple method of self-assessing your style.

## The Style is the Person

There are some imponderables about a person that constitute their given uniqueness and distinctness of being, and manifest unmistakably in the way they relate to others. This is original or archetypal style, like a person's signature in action. It is not acquired or created. It just becomes more fully revealed as behaviour becomes more and more authentic.

## Personal Values

Your facilitator style will reflect what you deeply value about human development, what you hold to be really worthwhile forms of human flourishing. For my part, I value autonomy, co-operation and hierarchy – and in that order. By autonomy I mean a state of being in which each person can in liberty determine and fulfil their own true needs and interests. By co-operation I mean mutual aid and support between autonomous persons. And by hierarchy I mean a state of being in which someone takes responsibility in doing things to or for other persons for the sake of the future autonomy and co-operation of those persons: this is part of parenthood, education and many professions. See also the end of Chapter 16.

## Personal Principles

I mean here guiding norms for action that follow from personal values. They are moral principles of high generality. An important one I use in group work is that of respect for persons: each person should be given a free and informed choice about any personal work or group activity, and should be enabled to be autonomous, and co-operative with other such persons. See also the end of Chapter 12.

## The Purpose and Composition of the Group

What the group is set up to achieve, its learning objectives, will of course have a strong influence on your facilitator style. So too will the level of skill and relevant experience in group members. Both these factors will affect the way you use the modes of hierarchy, co-operation and autonomy in running the group.

There are many different ways you can combine these modes. Figure 18.1 is a final reminder. At the top are the elements of a course: learning objectives, learning programme, assessment of students, evaluation of the course. Next are the four elements of the programme: the topics or subject matter, their allocation over time, the human and physical resources available for learning/teaching, and the learning and teaching methods. Then come the seven ways the modes can be combined, giving seven basic kinds of educational polity.

| Objectives | Programme | Assessment | Evaluation |
|---|---|---|---|
| Topics | Time | Resources | Methods |
| | Hierarchy | Co-operation | Autonomy |
| 1. | *You decide all* | | |
| 2. | *You decide some* | *You with group decide some* | |
| 3. | *You decide some* | *You with group decide some* | *Group decide some* |
| 4. | *You decide some* | | *Group decide some* |
| 5. | | *You with group decide some* | *Group decide some* |
| 6. | | *You with group decide all* | |
| 7. | | | *Group decide all* |

**Figure 18.1**   *Anatomy of educational decision-making*

## Personal Development

The more you, the facilitator, have done personal development work – both in healing the memories through deep regression and catharsis, and in opening up to transpersonal energies and domains – the more flexibility you have within yourself for facilitating these and other processes within your group. Also for moving around freely within the dimensions and modes of facilitation presented in this book.

Working on yourself enables you to keep clear of the pitfalls of the counter-transference, referred to in Chapter 4. If you unawarely project your own hidden distress on to the group, this either contaminates your interventions, making them degenerate rapidly, or it keeps you rigidly contained within a very limited range of interventions. If you are closed to the transpersonal, you miss opportunities for the group to participate in the wider reaches of awareness and reality.

## Training

Good training helps you create your facilitative style, above all by alerting you to a comprehensive range of issues and options, a large repertoire of policies and strategies. It gives you a broad canvas and a wide palette. The purpose of this book, as a basis for training, is to stretch your facilitative imagination, to appreciate the great reach and subtlety of the enterprise.

The basic elements of effective training are discrimination, modelling, practice and feedback (Cross, 1976).

### Discrimination
You need to be able to discriminate within a wide repertoire of policies and strategies, to know what's what within it, to be able to pick and choose appropriately from it. You need to be able to assess your own strengths and weaknesses in relation to this repertoire: which bits of it are you good at, and which not?

### Modelling
You need a model of good facilitation: verbal descriptions or videos or live demonstrations of what it is to make interventions well, in words, in manner and in timing. Modelling has a further aspect. Many facilitators at the start of their careers have modelled their style on that of some established group leader whom they admire and respect, because they resonate with his or her style. This kind of apprenticeship at a distance and by identification has much to

recommend it. It gives the beginner a secure platform on which they can eventually evolve and discover their own style.

### Practice

You need the opportunity to practise interventions, especially those you are not good at, in role plays or for real in small groups, and when it goes wrong, to rerun the practice until it goes right.

### Feedback

You need feedback on your practice from your peers and your trainer, so you can learn how you slip off the track and can get confirmation when you are on it. Feedback during training needs to be enlarged from time to time to include sessions of self- and peer assessment, and of collaborative assessment with your trainer, on your overall performance. This is followed, at the end of training, by a further process of self-, peer and trainer accreditation: what you, your peers and your trainer agree in authorizing you to do as a facilitator out there in the community.

Figure 18.2 presents an outline account of training methods under each of the four basic components of training.

| **Discrimination** *Learning a repertoire of skills* | The trainer presents a repertoire, a map of skills and degenerations. Trainees learn it with discrimination training. Trainees use it to assess their strengths, weaknesses and training needs. |
|---|---|
| **Modelling** *Seeing the repertoire modelled* | The trainer models the skills with metacomments:<br>• As on-the-job trainer now.<br>• In special demonstrations.<br>• In over the shoulder micro-skills modelling.<br>• Through case histories, video records.<br>The trainer presents criteria of competent facilitation for discussion. |
| **Practice** *Practising the repertoire* | Trainees practise skills in areas of need, with feedback and reruns, with:<br>• A real here and now group.<br>• Real past or future events: re-enactment or projected rehearsal.<br>• Imaginary scenarios: either typical, extreme or bizarre.<br>• Restriction exercises, stretch exercises.<br>Trainees do course design exercise, with presentations and discussion. |
| **Feedback** *Getting feedback on one's practice* | Trainees get feedback on their practice from self, peers, trainer. Self-, peer, trainer assessment of competence, using agreed criteria. Self-, peer and trainer accreditation about type of trainee's future work. |

**Figure 18.2**   *Basic methods for training facilitators*

## Professional Development

Professional development continues the learning process during your working career. One valuable form of it is to join a self- and peer supervision group with other facilitators. In such a group each person takes turns sharing critical or problematic incidents from their recent work, receiving comment and feedback from the other group members. See Chapters 8 and 9.

Other forms of professional development include: self-monitoring during your work; self-assessment after your work using memory, or audio-visual replay; peer assessment from colleagues who work in the same group with you; feedback from members of the group you have led, face to face at the end of a group, or via questionnaires sent in after the group. Assessment and feedback can be on two things: your interventions and style of facilitation; and on the programme and range of activities and methods used. A tool for self-assessment of your facilitator style, using the model of this book, is given at the end of the chapter.

## Criteria of Excellence

Another way of creating a style is to consider the criteria in the light of which you would judge a facilitator to be competent. There are many overlapping versions of such a set of criteria. Here is one account for the personal and interpersonal development facilitator, which you may like to reflect on – and modify. I state it in terms of you, the facilitator.

1. **Authority.**  You have distress-free authority, and do not displace your own hidden pathology through your interventions.
2. **Confrontation.**  You can confront supportively, and can work effectively on unaware projections and other defensive forms within the group.
3. **Orientation.**  You can provide clear conceptual orientation, as appropriate, in and among the experiential work.
4. **Care.**  You come over to group members as caring, empathic, warm and genuine.
5. **Range of methods.**  You can handle effectively both deep regression and catharsis, and transpersonal work; and you have a wide repertoire of techniques and exercises for personal and interpersonal development.

6. **Respect for persons.** You can in practice respect fully the autonomy of the person, and the right of participants to choose when to change and grow.
7. **Flexibility of intervention.**   You can move deftly and flexibly, as every situation needs, between interventions within one dimension, between the different dimensions and between the modes, so that the group dynamic can flourish with growth and learning.

## *Research*

There has been a lot of conventional, old paradigm research on experiential groups – with before and after studies, control groups or comparable groups – the researcher external to the group process. Much of this research has been about the effect of groups on participants, especially after the group is over. But the research method itself is alienated. It does research on groups, rather than with groups. To do research on people rather than with people is to treat them as less than people. While there have been positive findings using this approach, they are still vitiated by the assumptions of the method.

In the first and 1977 precursors to this book, I wrote at considerable length about this issue. Since then, I and others have written a great deal more about the negative case against the old method, and about new paradigm research, which, in the form of co-operative inquiry, does research with people. So rather than repeat or revise the earlier text, I refer the reader to some of the relevant literature since 1981 (Reason and Rowan, 1981; Heron 1996a, 1998a; Heron and Reason, 1997; Reason, 1988, 1994).

Co-operative inquiry breaks down the distinction between researcher and subject, and moves between the poles of reflection and action. The initiating researcher co-opts the group members as co-researchers who contribute to the thinking that generates, designs, manages and reviews the research; he or she also joins them as co-subjects, who undertake the actions and experiences that are being researched. See Chapter 7.

Experiential learning groups, when they use the experiential learning cycle, as depicted in Chapters 13 and 14, are already busy with an incipient form of co-operative inquiry. It lends itself readily to transformation into full-blown forms of person-centred research.

What does research contribute to the way in which you create a facilitator style? Conventional, old-style research on trainer effectiveness has, within its severe limits, affirmed the value of 2, 3 and 4 in the list in the previous section on criteria of facilitator excellence (Bolman, 1976).

More to the point, the new paradigm of co-operative inquiry can inspire a whole way of facilitating groups, by elevating learning to participative research, moving between the poles of reflection and experience. And the references cited a few paragraphs above include many accounts of co-operative inquiries in specific fields, from which specialist facilitators can cull findings to enhance their style and practice.

It is, however, important to remember that research with persons does not tell you, through its findings, what is really worthwhile or what you ought to do, for these things are a matter of moral vision, not of empirical inquiry. But collective reflection within the ambience of a co-operative inquiry may enhance insight into basic ethical values and principles. And the outcomes of the inquiry may show what is involved in the effective (and ineffective) realization of that insight.

## *Social Change*

How does a commitment to social and political change affect and shape your facilitator style? It can certainly determine what sort of workshops you run as defined in terms of their main objectives. The following list cuts – in slightly different way – through the same cake as the list in the section on structural change options, Chapter 17.

1. **Personal, cultural/planetary, and transplanetary issues.** You may want to run workshops that always deal with existential and archaic anxiety in the context of cultural/ planetary anxiety and of transcendental anxiety (see Chapter 4 for these four sorts of anxiety). Personal distress is seen as bound up with cultural oppression and lack of global awareness, also with spiritual disorientation. My belief is that personal and interpersonal development will increasingly be seen as interdependent with both planetary commitment, by which I mean a concern with fostering the well-being of all life forms and their habitat, locally, nationally and globally, and with transplanetary awareness (see Chapter 16).
2. **Transfer to life-style and life-planning.** You may want to include in your workshops time for members to commit themselves to revisions of their life-style and life-plan, or you may choose to let this process happen by spontaneous transfer, after the workshop.
3. **Professional, organizational and community development.** You may be committed to change the existing social system from

within, by working for new attitudes, skills and methods within existing professions, organizations and community associations.

4. **Soft revolution and non-violent training.** You may want to confront more directly the rigidities of the existing social system, by training people in creative subversion of oppressive institutions, or non-violent interruption of their activities. See here the caveats discussed in Chapter 17.

5. **Alternative network training.** You may want to train and set up peer self-help networks that constitute an alternative to existing institutional and professional services. There are self-help mutual aid groups for those in life-crisis, or with special physical or social disabilities, or oppressed by prejudice and discrimination, or with special revisionary and reforming interests; and of course for personal and social development and awareness – as in co-counselling networks.

6. **Alternative institutions.** You may want a workshop to prepare for the setting up of alternative kinds of institution: in industry, commerce, medicine, education, the family, community and so on.

## *Making a Self-assessment Profile of Your Facilitator Style*

Here is a simple and accessible self-assessment schedule. Take a copy of the form in Figure 18.3. Consider just one course or workshop which you have recently completed, or which is well under way. Assess your facilitation of it by entering, in each of the 18 boxes, one of the following: too much, about right, too little, not applicable.

Enter a figure from 1 and 5 beside 'too much' and beside 'too little'. So 'too much 1' means just a bit too much, and 'too much 5' means far too much. And 'too little 1' means just a bit too little, and 'too little 5' means far too little. With all the boxes filled in, you have, with respect to the workshop or course concerned, a profile of your facilitation, and you can see at a glance where you judge your strengths and weakness to lie. If you repeat the self-assessment for each of several workshops and courses, you can then compare and contrast the different self-assessments, and note the strengths and weaknesses they have in common, thus obtaining a more general profile of your facilitation.

| DECISION-MODES → and DIMENSIONS ↓ | HIERARCHY Direction Facilitator does it FOR people | CO-OPERATION Negotiation Facilitator does it WITH people | AUTONOMY Delegation Facilitator gives it TO people |
|---|---|---|---|
| PLANNING the programme of learning and development | | | |
| UNDERSTANDING and making sense of experiences, images and ideas | | | |
| CONFRONTING and raising consciousness about defences, distortions and avoidances | | | |
| FEELING the presence and managing the emotional dynamic of the group | | | |
| STRUCTURING the current learning activity of the group | | | |
| VALUING choice and creating a climate of celebration and respect for persons | | | |

**Figure 18.3**  *Form for self-assessment profile*

# Appendix: The Manager as Facilitator

This appendix takes the core model of the six dimensions and three modes of facilitation, as described in the main body of the book, and applies them, with suitable modification, to the role of the manager.

## Group Room and Workplace Learning

In Chapter 16, I proposed a model of the whole person in terms of a nexus of internal and external relations from the intrapersonal through the interpersonal, the cultural, to the ecological and transplanetary. I also suggested that learning to be a whole person, personal development, can no longer be confined to the intrapersonal and interpersonal spheres in the group room, but also streams out, through personal and collective action inquiry, into the cultural, the ecological and the transplanetary realms. In this chapter I wish to follow this stream and explore personal development as a process that goes on in the workplace. If the workplace becomes an arena for personal development in my extended sense, then the work leader or manager becomes a facilitator of such work-based development. How does such a facilitator-manager go about it?

In answering this question I shall adopt the same basic model used throughout this book. It was originally devised for facilitators of experiential learning groups. It was conceived as a manual – both conceptual and practical – for those whose job it is to direct and elicit whole person learning in personal growth groups, interactive skills groups, management training groups, staff development groups and the like. But the learning process which flows from the group room to the workplace falls within the same fundamental modes and dimensions. The principles remain the same, only the way they are defined, ordered, presented and used is noticeably modified by the new context; and one dimension is renamed.

So I shall apply the model to the business of managing a team that has a task in the world. The main focus is on occupational tasks, although the model can be applied to leadership of recreational or social tasks.

There is an important difference between personal development in the group room and personal development in the workplace. In the group room the primary goal is personal development, and any effect out there in the world is often left for each person to work out later. A task team's goal is to have an effect in the world, and personal development in the workplace is subsumed within that end. In the group room, change in the world is secondary and a later consequence of learning in the group; in the workplace, personal development within the team is an essential component of changing things in the world, and is thus more grounded and fulfilling.

Before applying the model, I shall take a look at the organizational revolution currently afoot that makes the idea of the manager as the facilitator of personal development in the workplace plausible and relevant.

## The Organizational Revolution

Doctrines of human rights are marching inexorably forward, advancing from the political to the economic arena: in particular what in the previous chapter I called the up-hierarchy principle – the doctrine that every human being has a right to participate in decisions that affect his or her needs, interests and activities. This right for workers to participate in managerial decision-making is reinforced by a right for increased self-determination at the site of work. And this in turn is enhanced by the spread of educational and psychological values of personal fulfilment and expression.

At the same time there is a pronounced tendency in the modern world toward large organizations. If these become monolithic, hierarchical bureaucracies, then three interrelated problems set in: unmanageable complexity, relative inefficiency and human alienation among staff. So the organizational revolution stems from the need for manageable complexity and for efficiency; as well as from needs for participation, self-determination and self-realization for persons at work. And it is made more feasible in format by rapid advances in automation, computers, artificial intelligence and the whole range of new information and communication technology.

Some features of this revolution (Handy, 1985; Garratt, 1987) are as follows:

1. **Democratic representation.** Employees have formal representation at board level, and so participate democratically in central
   decision-making.
2. **Autonomous work groups.** Employees are in small self-
   managing, peer supervision groups, organizing their own work
   and quality control.
3. **Co-ownership and co-management.** The traditional distinction between owner, manager and worker starts to break down.
   Workers and managers become co-owners with other shareholders. Management is diversified and its functions shared by
   all staff in different ways and at different levels. At one extreme
   of this tendency is the full-blown co-operative whose workers
   are the primary shareholders, and who hire their managers on
   contract.
4. **Consent cultures.** Organizations inform, confer with and
   consult their staff, rather than control them.
5. **Flexible management.** The manager is one who can move
   awarely and appropriately between the three modes of making
   decisions *for* people, making decisions *with* people, and delegating decision-making *to* people.
6. **Project teamwork.** Management shifts from classical unity of
   command at the upper reaches of a hierarchical pyramid, to
   project teams of specialists. These teams are co-operative and
   horizontally structured, with overlapping and variable functions, and last only as long as the task requires. Adhocracies.
7. **The learning organization.** Organizations see themselves as
   learning systems, in which human resource development is
   continuously applied within them to make them self-
   transforming.
8. **The shift from wages to fees.** This means paying people fees
   for work done independently to a certain standard, rather than
   paying wages for time spent under managerial control. Work
   becomes professionalized.
9. **Contracting and networking.** The large organization
   contracts-out work to a network of independent professionals –
   individuals and teams.
10. **Federalism and devolution.** Large organizations shift to the
    federal model, with a central secretariat serving and supporting
    a network of many small human-sized and semi-autonomous
    enterprises.

Item. 5, flexible management, is the special theme of this chapter,
which seeks to provide a comprehensive repertoire for the manager

who wants to facilitate personal development in the workplace in a way that enhances the team fulfilling its task. This means moving between the three modes of decision-making on each of the main dimensions of management.

Flexibility of management style is fundamental to the concept of the manager as personal development facilitator. Such a manager is one who can direct the team, can negotiate with the team, can delegate power to the team, and can switch between these three modes as appropriate. What is fundamentally involved is a reconciliation of four realities:

- The personal autonomy of the worker.
- The authority of the manager.
- The claims of the organization.
- Benefit to the world.

## The Manager, the Team and the Task

The manager may be formally appointed to the role by an organization, formally elected in some democratic way by team members or their representatives; self-appointed to recruit and lead a team; given the role by custom, convention and social practice; or informally selected.

By a team I mean more than just a loose association of people co-operating together. It has at least enough structure for someone in it to have a managerial role that is acknowledged by its members; and for it to have a clearly defined task in the world, also acknowledged by its members. So a team is partly defined in terms of management and task. I shall use the term 'teamwork' to mean 'a team with a leader engaged upon its task'. More formally and fully stated, a team can be defined in terms of four interacting features:

1. **Persons and tools.**   The team consists of suitably skilled people with the equipment they need to do the work.
2. **Goals and plan.**   The team has a task, consisting of work objectives and a programme of work.
3. **Roles and rules.**   The team has a defined social structure of roles and rules which specify members' working functions and inter-relations.
4. **Power and control.**   The team has a system of power and control, whereby decisions are made. I return to these features of a team later on.

The team may be an organization, or may be employed by one – working within it, or on contract for it. The team may be appointed or elected. It may be an independent group with a self-appointed task; it may be an informal impromptu task group. But it is by definition a group of people with an accepted manager who are working together on a project that engages them with the world.

The notion of a team is a relative one. It is system-oriented: it can be a whole including lesser wholes. An organization is a large team containing sub-teams, its various departments. Each department is a medium-size team containing further smaller sub-teams. There are selective teams, such as department heads; and so on. I leave to the reader to choose what part of a total system their use of the word 'team' refers to, and to adapt the meaning of my text accordingly.

By the task I mean an undertaking to act in a certain way in the social and physical world to fulfil a stated purpose. The term can be used for occupational, social, and recreational enterprises. It can be extended to the social fringe to include, for example, a team which conceives its task as the management of the ceremonial life of a religious community.

All this makes the phrase 'the manager of a team with a task' have a very wide potential application. It can refer to anyone who is seen by himself and a group to be guiding the group to do something in the world. But, as I have already said, I shall be writing here about the world of work, of occupational tasks. There are basically four kinds of occupational task (which I deal with later):

1. **Renewal tasks.**   They deal with servicing equipment, in-house education and training, relaxation, recreation.
2. **Development tasks.**   They create new forms and content for the three other kinds of task, and develop work in new directions.
3. **Production tasks.**   They are productive of goods or services.
4. **Crisis tasks.**   They deal with emergencies, unexpected contingencies or catastrophes.

## Dimensions and Modes of Management

I now give an overview of the dimensions and modes of management. By the *dimensions* of management I mean six different basic issues in relation to which the manager can influence the team in fulfilling its task. In my model, there are the six main parameters for managing any working group. By the *modes* of management I mean three different ways the leader can make decisions within each of these dimensions: by direction, by negotiation, or by delegation.

These dimensions, appropriately redefined, are basically the same as the six dimensions of facilitation discusssed in the main part of this book. I have renamed one of them: the operating dimension below is the revised name for the earlier structuring dimension. And I present them in a different order. This is not particularly important. It just brings out a perspective on the management dimensions that is portrayed in Figure A.1 below.

## The Six Dimensions of Management

1. **The operating dimension.** This is the operational aspect of management. It is to do with guiding implementation of the plan, with methods of supervising work in the field, with ways of structuring the activities in the workplace. The management issue is: How can the work-in-progress of the team be supervised and managed?

2. **The planning dimension.** This is the power aspect of management. It is to do with decision-making about the objectives, the work goals of the team, and an integrated programme to realize those goals. The management issue here is: How can decisions about the objectives and work-plan of the team be made?

3. **The confronting dimension.** The confronting aspect of management is to do with raising team members' consciousness about distorted behaviour that is disturbing job satisfaction, work effectiveness or both together. The management issue is: How shall the team's consciousness be raised about these matters?

4. **The meaning dimension.** The meaning aspect of management is to do with five interrelated aspects of the meaning of work:

   - The knowledge required to do the task.
   - The learning acquired in doing it.
   - Knowledge of the effects of doing it.
   - The meaning the work has by virtue of its nature and how it is put together as an intelligent whole.
   - The meaning the work has because of its wider moral and social significance in the world.

   The management issue here is: How shall all five kinds of meaning be given to and found in the task of the team?

5. **The valuing dimension.** This is the intuitive, moral aspect of management. It is to do with creating a work culture with core values, with an ethos of respect for persons and for their planet, one in which team members can be genuine, fulfilling their rights, duties and interests as human beings in their ecological context. The management issue is: How can a work culture with core values, and a climate of respect and integrity, be created?

6. **The feeling dimension.** This is the concern for the affective aspect of management, which includes:

   - Managing the fulfilment of human needs and interests in and through work – job satisfaction.
   - Dealing with emotions and interpersonal relationships within the team where these are involved in or influence the task.
   - Attending to empathy, attunement, participation, resonance, rapport of people in their total setting.

   The management issue is: How shall job satisfaction, emotions, relationships and resonance within teamwork be handled?

These six dimensions interweave and overlap, being mutually supportive of each other. Nevertheless, I hold that each one has an independent identity and cannot be reduced without remainder to any one or more of the other five. They are all needed, together, in conscious use, for effective management. The manager as facilitator of personal development at work is one who can move with flexible response among them.

From the point of view of a culture of personal development in the workplace, the grounding, underpinning dimension is that of participative feeling (see Chapter 3). Supported by it, at the next level are valuing and meaning and occasionally confronting. At the third level, based on the levels below and shaped by the requirements of the outside world, are planning and operating. This is depicted in Figure A.1, which also shows correlations between the six dimensions and the psychological modes of the up-hierarchy discussed in Chapter 3.

The How question stated under each dimension raises an issue in two parts. One part is about what method or strategy will be put forward in any decision made. The other part is about who will make that decision – the manager alone, the manager and the team together, or the team alone. This second part takes us into the three *modes* of management, given in the next section.

| THE WORLD | | |
|---|---|---|
| *Level 3* | Operating<br>Planning | *Practical mode* |
| *Level 2* | Confronting<br>Meaning<br>Valuing | *Conceptual mode*<br>*Imaginal mode* |
| *Level 1* | Feeling | *Affective Mode* |
| PERSONS | | |

**Figure A.1**    *The six dimensions between persons and the world*

## The Three Modes of Management

Each of the six dimensions of management can be handled by the manager in three different modes. Each mode provides a different answer to the question as to who should make decisions on strategies for each dimension. Hence I call the modes decision-modes.

1. **The hierarchical mode.**   Here you, the manager, direct the work of the team, and decide issues for the team. You lead from the front by thinking and choosing on behalf of the team. You supervise on-site work by direction, decide on the programme of work, confront resistances, give meaning to the work, manage satisfaction in the group, and choose values for and inspire them in the work force. As manager you exercise power over the team.
2. **The co-operative mode.**   Here you share your authority and decide issues with the team. You collaborate and consult with team members, prompting and enabling them to participate in the management process. You supervise on-site work with the team through negotiation; you negotiate the programme of work; you initiate conjoint consciousness-raising about resistances; you confer about the meaning of work; you consult about satisfaction and feelings; you confer about the values of the team and collaborate in creating a climate of mutual respect. You lead from within the team, generating, sustaining and guiding a working collective. As manager you share power with the team.
3. **The autonomous mode.**   Here you delegate authority to the team members; decisions on issues are made by the team. You

affirm the autonomy of its members, do not manage things for them, or with them, but give them freedom to manage things their own way, without any intervention. With your support, but without direction from or collaboration with you, they use peer supervision on-site, evolve their programme of work, find ways of confronting their resistances, give meaning to their work, manage their needs and feelings, elect their own values and create a climate of peer respect. The team is a self-directed peer group. As manager you affirm the power that is exercised autonomously by the team.

Working in the autonomous mode, delegating power, is a good measure of the manager as facilitator of personal development at work. It does not mean the abdication of responsibility, the dereliction of duty, which is involved in pushing on to others what one cannot be bothered to do oneself. It is not oppressive and exploitatory. Nor is it patronizing and parental. It is the subtle art of creating conditions within which people can exercise self-determination both to fulfil themselves and to meet the requirements of the task.

These three modes deal with the politics of the workplace, with the exercise of power in managing the six dimensions of teamwork. They are about who has control and influence. Who makes the decisions about what team members do, and when and how they do it: the manager alone, the manager and team together, the team alone? The three modes of direction, negotiation and delegation are in a higher order political dimension that runs through all the basic six, as shown in Figure A.2.

The effective manager – as facilitator of personal development in the workplace – is someone who can use all three modes on each of the six dimensions as and when appropriate; and is flexible in

|  | Operating | Planning | Confronting | Meaning | Valuing | Feeling |
|---|---|---|---|---|---|---|
| Hierarchy: direction |  |  |  |  |  |  |
| Co-operation: negotiation |  |  |  |  |  |  |
| Autonomy: delegation |  |  |  |  |  |  |

**Figure A.2** *Dimensions and modes of management*

moving from mode to mode and dimension to dimension – as and when appropriate. This is no doubt a counsel of perfection. But it broadens the imagination of the manager to keep the total 18-part grid of options in the back of the mind.

Too much hierarchical direction, and team members become dependent and unenterprising, or hostile and resistant, or overtly conformist and covertly deviant. They wane in self-direction – the core of all effective work. Too much negotiation may undermine clear direction by the manager, and self-determination by the team. Too much delegation by the manager and autonomy for the team may result in confusion of purpose.

Each team, depending on its personnel, its task and organizational context, will require a different balance of these three modes. And any given team may need this balance to change at different phases of its work. At the outset, perhaps, clear hierarchical management; in the middle phase, co-operative and shared management; and in the later phases, complete delegation and team autonomy. But there is no rule here: it all depends on the team, the task and the context.

The modes can include each other. A hierarchical manager who hires a team can subsume elements of co-operation and autonomy in his or her style, deciding unilaterally what job the team will do, deciding co-operatively with them how long it will take, and delegating to them all decisions about methods and ways of working.

Conversely, an independent team decides on its task, then hires a manager and contracts with him or her the different respects in which his or her leadership style will be hierarchical, co-operative and autonomous. The team's autonomy contains the other modes. So the modes can be interwoven in many different ways.

To illustrate this, we can apply the three modes to each of the following: the goals of the task, the programme of work to realize goals, and the methods of working, as in Figure A.3.

|  | Task Goals | Task Programme | Task Methods |
|---|---|---|---|
| Hierarchy | Manager alone | Manager alone | Manager alone |
| Co-operation | Manager with team | Manager with team | Manager with team |
| Autonomy | Team alone | Team alone | Team alone |

**Figure A.3**  *Configurations of power in the workplace*

This gives 21 ways of combining hierarchy, co-operation and autonomy in decision-making about the task: 21 configurations of power in the workplace. At one extreme, the manager alone decides on the goals, the programme, the methods. At the other extreme, the team alone decides all these things, so it has no manager.

In between are 19 ways of distributing power between manager and team with respect to the goals, the programme and the method of work – some more obviously relevant than others. Nor does this take into account possible combinations within each column, for different sub-goals, programme parts, etc.

## *Task and Process*

Three of the management dimensions deal primarily, but not exclusively, with the task of the team: the operating, planning and meaning dimensions. Operating is about ways of managing on-site work, planning is about the goals and programme of work, and meaning is about the knowledge needed for and generated by work.

The three other dimensions – confronting, valuing and feeling – deal primarily, but not exclusively, with the process in the team. By process I mean what is going on within people and between people as the task proceeds. While powerfully influenced by the task, process can always be described in relative independence of it.

The confronting dimension is about the resistances, blocks, avoidances, distorted behaviours within the team. The valuing dimension is about core values and norms, workers' rights – whether these are being respected, and whether the team can function with integrity. The feeling dimension is about the satisfactions and emotions arising out of the work and the working conditions, about the quality of interpersonal relationships, and the rapport of people with their total setting.

One important part of the meaning dimension, the inherent meaningfulness of work, is closely related to job satisfaction on the feeling dimension.

The three modes too are about a central aspect of process: the business of making the decisions. Decision-making also can be described – in terms of who and how – without any reference to what aspects of the task are being decided about. If we put all this on the grid, with the application of each of the modes being the application of a process (P) on either a task (T) or a process (P) dimension – as these have been just been defined – then we get the allocation as in Figure A.4.

|  | Operating | Planning | Confronting | Meaning | Valuing | Feeling |
|---|---|---|---|---|---|---|
| Hierarchy: | PT | PT | PP | PT | PP | PP |
| Co-operation: | PT | PT | PP | PT | PP | PP |
| Autonomy: | PT | PT | PP | PT | PP | PP |

**Figure A.4**   *Task and process related to dimensions and modes*

What this brings out is that, from the point of view of management style, the comprehensive leader needs three times as much process awareness and proficiency as task competence. Within the grid, the term P for process occurs 27 times, T for task 9 times.

## Eighteen Basic Management Options

I now present an overview of the dimensions and modes combined into 18 basic options for the team manager. For convenience I have numbered each option as in Figure A.5. Do not be misled below by the simplified statement of each option. The different modes within each dimension are not mutually exclusive. They can all be used on the same task, at different times, and for different aspects of the given dimension.

1.  **The operating dimension: hierarchical mode.**   You manage on-site work for the team. You are directive in supervising your team at the workface: you tell people what to do, and intervene in what they do.

|  | Operating | Planning | Confronting | Meaning | Valuing | Feeling |
|---|---|---|---|---|---|---|
| Hierarchy: | 1 | 4 | 7 | 10 | 13 | 16 |
| Co-operation: | 2 | 5 | 8 | 11 | 14 | 17 |
| Autonomy: | 3 | 6 | 9 | 12 | 15 | 18 |

**Figure A.5**   *Dimensions and modes of management (numbered)*

2. **The operating dimension: co-operative mode.** You supervise on-site work with the team. You negotiate with team members on how they do their work: supervision is collaborative, decisions at the workface involve you and them.

3. **The operating dimension: autonomous mode.** You delegate the supervision of on-site work to the team. The team becomes an autonomous work group, managing their own day-to-day tasks, practising self-directed peer supervision.

4. **The planning dimension: hierarchical mode.** You determine work goals for the team and do the planning to realize them, deciding unilaterally on the content and time-scale of the work programme.

5. **The planning dimension: co-operative mode.** You determine goals and plan the work programme with the team. You are committed to negotiate, to take into account and seek agreement with the views of team members in devising the content and the time-scale of the plan.

6. **The planning dimension: autonomous mode.** You delegate goal-setting and the planning of the work programme to the team. You are getting out of the way, leaving the team to work out its own schedule.

7. **The confronting dimension: hierarchical mode.** You interrupt distorted behaviour, raise consciousness about its effects and its source, and do this directly for team members – in such a way that those concerned may awarely alter their behaviour.

8. **The confronting dimension: co-operative mode.** You work with the team to raise consciousness about distorted behaviour. You prompt, invite, ask, compare and share views with them about the behaviour, its effects and its source. Consciousness-raising is collaborative.

9. **The confronting dimension: autonomous mode.** You hand over consciousness-raising about distorted behaviour to the team. You create a climate of support and trust within the workplace, so that the challenge to distorted behaviour occurs independently within the team, through self- and peer confrontation.

10. **The meaning dimension: hierarchical mode.** You make sense of what is going on for the team. You are the source of all relevant knowledge about the job, and of giving meaning to work events, making work meaningful.

11. **The meaning dimension: co-operative mode.** You invite team members to participate with you in generating understanding. You collaborate with them in generating all relevant knowledge about the job, and in giving meaning to work events, making

work meaningful. You give your view as one among their views and co-operate in making sense.

12. **The meaning dimension: autonomous mode.** You delegate knowledge and data gathering, interpretation, feedback, reflection and review to the team. Making sense of what is going on, giving work meaning, is autonomous, entirely generated by the team.

13. **The valuing dimension: hierarchical mode.** You create the core values for the culture for the team, the ethos of respect for persons and their planet. You take strong initiatives to care for team members.

14. **The valuing dimension: co-operative mode.** You collaborate with the team in developing the core values of its culture. You create a community of mutual respect, through dialogue about what the team stands for and about how it will manifest this.

15. **The valuing dimension: autonomous mode.** You delegate to the team the creation of its own core values and culture. You respect team members as self-governing persons who, in relation with each other, establish their own primary ethos and norms.

16. **The feeling dimension: hierarchical mode.** You take charge of the emotional being of the team for the team, decide what will maximize fulfilment and satisfaction at work, and implement it. You think for team members, judging what ways of managing emotions and interpersonal relations will suit them and their work best. You initiate basic rapport and resonance.

17. **The feeling dimension: co-operative mode.** You negotiate with the team ways of maximizing fulfilment and satisfaction at work. You manage the emotional life of the team collaboratively, discussing with members different ways of handling working relations, and of creating underlying attunement and resonance.

18. **The feeling dimension: autonomous mode.** You delegate to the team ways of maximizing fulfilment and satisfaction at work. You give the team space for the process of managing its own emotional and interpersonal life, and for generating participative attunement and resonance in its own way.

## *Personal Development in the Workplace*

The manager as facilitator of personal development in the workplace selects from among these 18 options to create a managerial style that progressively moves toward more delegation to team members. This means:

- Increased self- and peer determination at the site of work in managing quality and productivity.
- Increased participation in policy-making and planning.
- Increased self- and peer regulation and discipline in handling wayward behaviour.
- Increased self- and peer initiative in generating knowledge and understanding through work, and in giving meaning to work.
- Increased self- and peer commitment to generate and sustain core values.
- Increased self- and peer attention to job satisfaction, whole person satisfaction within the conditions of work, interpersonal relations, and rapport within the total setting.

The operative word here is 'increased'. It does not mean total or absolute, but just increased, delegation compared with the traditional norm of over-control from above. It will need balancing with negotiation and direction.

An important point is that the more these self- and peer processes increase, the greater the decentralization of work. And that also means, as I discussed earlier, that there will need to be a correlative increase in federal co-ordinating centres, and therefore an increase at these centres in certain kinds of down-hierarchy direction. This developmental polarity is the challenge of the future. What underlies it are the basic whole person values outlined at the end of Chapter 16: the values of integrated self-determination, co-operation with peers, up-hierarchy, and down-hierarchy exercise of responsibility. The more self- and peer determination at the decentralized end of the scale, the more down-hierarchy responsibility at the federal end of it. Personal development at the workplace means that everyone there has an experience of these polar values – bridged by the up-hierarchy of participative decision-making – interacting to enhance everyone's personal development and the work being done.

The increases in self- and peer processes are not brought about by immediate massive delegation, but by a graduated developmental sequence in which direction, negotiation and delegation are progressively mixed in varying proportions. Such a programme may typically start with a strong element of direction and move toward a significant amount of negotiation and delegation. But such generalization is misleading. It is impossible to give any detailed account of this sort of development, since it is entirely situational. It depends on the nature of the team: what its task is – whether renewal, development, production or crisis, the kind of organizational or professional culture in which it is embedded, what stage in its history has been reached, who its members are, their education and experience, their level of personal and professional development.

## *Transforming Power*

The manager who is using direction, negotiation and delegation (hierarchy, co-operation and autonomy) in varying proportions in order to empower personal development in the workplace – in the form of increased self- and peer determination – is exercising a higher-order kind of transforming power. It is equivalent to the redefinition of political authority in the learning environment which I discussed in Chapter 2. Through his or her own action inquiry in using the three decision-modes, the manager is seeking to create a team whose members are also engaged in self- and peer action inquiry, and who see their work as an arena for experiential learning.

I borrow the term 'transforming power' from Torbert for whom it means seeking to empower others through the creation of 'liberating structures' within organizations. Such structures are ones in which there is a sense of shared purpose among subordinates, an increasing self-direction among subordinates, and a commitment to generate quality work among subordinates. They are structures which simultaneously cultivate among members both quality improvement and other aspects of productivity on the one hand and action inquiry and personal development on the other. 'If liberating structures succeed organizational members will increasingly take executive responsibility, will increasingly treat one another as peers, and will increasingly create their own liberating structures' (Torbert, 1991: 100).

For Torbert, the leader exercising transforming power of this kind essentially invites mutuality and participation in power; but will also use what he calls unilateral, diplomatic and logistical power to further this end. There is therefore a strategic irony in the whole business. This is similar to my proposal that the manager use hierarchy, co-operation and autonomy in flexible and imaginative ways in order eventually to elicit more self- and peer determination among team members along the six dimensions of management. See also my idea of a self-generating practitioner community as part of a self-generating culture (Heron, 1997).

## *The Team Dynamic*

By the team dynamic I mean the combined configuration of mental, emotional and practical energies in the team at any given time; and the changes which this configuration undergoes at different phases in the team's existence, in response to several interacting factors. These influential factors include:

- The structure of the team.
- The tasks of the team.
- The motives of team members.
- Critical issues to do with the team's organizational context.
- Critical issues to do with the team's wider social context.
- The influence of ideology.
- The authority of the manager.
- The vision of the manager.

To have a consistent feel for and overview of the team dynamic is a central key for the manager as facilitator of personal development and liberating structures in the workplace. The rest of this chapter outlines my theory of such an overview, and covers each of the above items in turn, with a look at distorting forms of the team dynamic, after the item on motives. So the whole of what follows is an extended map of the field within which transforming power is exercised. It is offered as a cartography that may facilitate strategic thinking for the facilitator of team members' personal development in the workplace.

## The Structure of the Team

As I wrote earlier, any team, as the concept is used in this book, can be defined in terms of four interacting features. Each feature itself consists of two interdependent factors.

1. **Persons and tools.** The term 'persons' refers to the particular people through whom the team is made manifest, its present personnel, their skills and level of competence; and 'tools' to the equipment and technology which they use on the job. Without trained persons and their tools or technology there is no actual team. In general, the sort of persons recruited to join the team will influence its process, as will the kind of technology used by it. Technology can have a very strong influence indeed on how the team functions as a social structure. Thus the new information and communication technologies are capable of supporting radically new organizational forms – which allow much more autonomy at the workface. It is the very development of these technologies that

makes more and more possible the kind of flexible management style which I am advocating.

2. **Goals and a plan.**   The term 'goals' refers to the team's working objectives and 'plan' to the programme which enables these objectives to be realized. Together they define the task of the team: they state what it is about. The basic different kinds of task are analysed in the next section. The task of a team is a primary determinant of its dynamic – or should be.

3. **Roles and rules.**   The team has a more or less evident social structure which specifies members' working functions and inter-relations. The term 'roles' refers to the different positions in the social structure of the team, and 'rules' to their job-descriptions and responsibilities. This social structure is independent of whoever happens to be occupying the roles at any given time. And within one organization, the same person may have different roles in several teams.

4. **Power and control.**   The team has a system whereby management decisions are made. It has a *de facto* command procedure – which may not always correspond with how that procedure is defined on paper. The procedure may be different for longer-term policy and planning decisions as against day-to-day executive and operational decisions. But the team is always managed by one or more persons somehow. The term 'power' refers to who is doing the managerial decision-making, and 'control' to what procedures they use in doing it.

The first two of these are interdependent: workers and their tools must be suited to the task and vice versa. The second two are also interdependent: the social structure will define the allocation of power and control, and those in power can redefine the social structure of roles and rules. In a rational world, the last two should be grounded on the first two: the structure of roles and rules and allocation of power and control should be devised so that they are best suited to the people involved, their equipment and the nature of the task.

The four features are shown in Figure A.6. The duality within each arm of this figure can generate tension and requires internal accommodation. The four arms themselves are in dynamic tension with each other: a creative compromise between mutual support and mutual antagonism. They also provide a template for a set of manifold correlations, tendencies to alienation and distortion, that illuminate the dynamic of any team. I consider these affinities first of all from the standpoint of the different sorts of task.

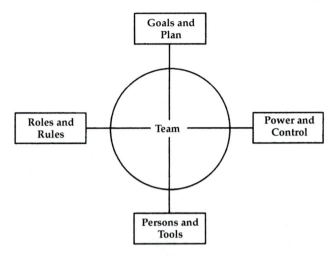

**Figure A.6**  *The four features of a team*

## *The Tasks of the Team*

Earlier, I outlined four very general yet very relevant ways of classifying the tasks of a team. Every team will be involved with each of these four kinds of task at different times in its history. At the same time each team will focus strongly on one kind of task. The four kinds are shown in Figure A.7.

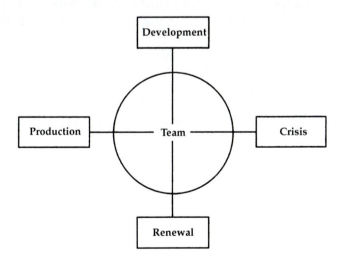

**Figure A.7**  *The four tasks of a team*

1. **Renewal tasks.** The work of the team is to service, replace or update equipment and introduce new technologies; to undertake education and training, professional and personal development; to relax, refresh and re-create people; to gestate for the next phase of activity. All sorts of technical service teams, staff development and training teams, welfare teams, recreational facility teams specialize in renewal tasks.

2. **Development tasks.** The team's work is to innovate, to develop work in new directions and by new methods, and to solve problems to make this possible. A secondary but important aspect of such work is to solve the problems that arise in closing down old directions and old methods – the innovation of closure. Research and development teams specialize here.

3. **Production tasks.** The work of the team is to sustain some form of production, in a steady state, or in phases of expansion or contraction. The vast majority of teams specialize in tasks of this sort – in two basic categories:
   - Tasks productive of goods, together with the diverse tasks that support the producers, such as producing and distributing raw materials, marketing and distributing the goods.
   - Tasks productive of services, together with the diverse tasks that support the servers and market their services.

4. **Crisis tasks.** The job of the team is to deal with sudden emergencies, disturbances, dangers, difficulties and critical events. Examples of specialist teams here are: fire-fighting teams, police teams, medical teams, military teams; and all kinds of trouble-shooting teams.

Renewal and development tasks have a bearing upon each other. Unless people are well educated and trained and in good physical and mental shape, they cannot develop their work in new directions; and through development work they deepen their learning and their motivation. Renewal and development are also best seen as the ground and support of production and crisis tasks, otherwise goods and services, and the solution of problems in delivering them, fall by the wayside of social and technological change. An organization that is a developing one is also a learning organization in which personal growth can take place.

There is some affinity between *renewal* tasks and the *persons and tools* feature of a team. Renewal is to do with meeting the training and recreational needs of the persons in the team, and with servicing, updating or replacing their tools.

There is some affinity between *development* tasks and the *goals and*

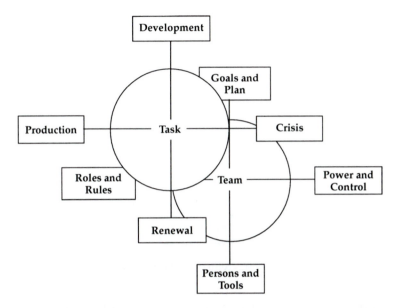

**Figure A.8**  *Affinities between team tasks and team features*

*plan* feature of a team. Development work means re-thinking what the team is seeking to achieve and how it is going about achieving it.

There is some affinity between *production* tasks and the *roles and rules* feature of a team. The continuous and sustained production of goods or services needs a well-defined organizational structure with clear functions and job-descriptions attached to a variety of different roles, and with clear allocation of responsibilities.

There is some affinity between *crisis* tasks and the *power and control* feature of a team. Dangers and emergencies require a clear and strong focus of command and command procedures in the team that copes with them.

Each kind of *task* can skew the team dynamic by giving undue emphasis to the corresponding *feature* of the team. To be preoccupied with one sort of task can result in the related feature being overdeveloped at the expense of other features. I return to this point later on. Figure A.8 lays out the affinities between different sorts of task, and different features of a team.

## Motives of Team Members

The dynamic of the team is also strongly affected by the sources of its members' actions. There appear to be four basic kinds of motive

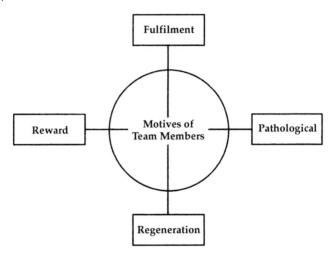

**Figure A.9**    *Motives of a team members*

which in various combinations can explain the behaviour of people who work in a team or an organization, and which influence the dynamic. They are shown in Figure A.9.

1. **Regeneration motives.**  Members of a team need to renew their skills and themselves: to take time to learn and develop on the job, for further education and training, including training in the use of new technology, for rest, relaxation, refreshment, recreation and inner recovery. At a deeper level, regeneration motives point to the need of people to be *self-creating*: to take charge of their own growth and unfoldment as persons. This means increasing their capacity for voluntary choice in relating to their own internal processes, and to the outer world of society and nature. At a still deeper level, they include the need for *self-transfiguration*: the transformation of the personality by openness to the transplanetary sphere as I described it in Chapter 16.
2. **Fulfilment motives.**  Here we have the needs of team members to be fulfilled by what is intrinsic to the work they do. The motive is to achieve job satisfaction *per se*. People need to be *creative*: to realize, express and fulfil their human capacities, talents, values and aspirations in what they do. They need their work to be within their autonomous control; to be mentally stimulating and challenging; to engage with their special interests and abilities; to have variety and scope; to engage co-operatively with others; to be worthwhile and in a good cause, realizing some wider end.

3. **Reward motives.** These are the needs of team members for things that are extrinsic to the actual nature of the work itself: needs for pay, for security, for career prospects, for status and recognition, to belong to a group. These extrinsic rewards of work are part of everyone's work motivation.
4. **Pathological motives.** These are relatively unaware compulsions, rooted in old, repressed emotional trauma and hurt, which produce distorted, distress-driven forms of behaviour. The four classic compulsions are to be an oppressor, a victim, a rebel and a rescuer. These four pathological roles can be acted out in various ways in teamwork. The whole team dynamic can be warped by them.

The first three – regeneration, fulfilment and reward motives – are the basic triad. They can be (a) satisfied and in balance; (b) frustrated, causing much work-related distress; (c) unbalanced and overdone in some direction, because of the nature of the task, or the wider social and economic situation, or because of pressure from pathological motives. Where the team, for whatever reason, is too preoccupied with one or other of these sorts of motive, then the team dynamic and its organizational structure will be distorted.

## Distorted Forms of the Team Dynamic

Alienation or fragmentation occurs within the team dynamic, when team members become bound to one of the four main features of the team, and become estranged from the other three. The one to which they are bound develops in a distorted way, at the expense of the others. There are tendencies for certain correlations to occur between the sort of team feature to which people become bound, the related task, and the related motive.

However, these correlations as presented below are only parts of a purely theoretical model of four types of limiting case. The dynamic of teams in the real world will be more complex and composite. The purpose of the model is to provide a template of affinities and tendencies, which may aid diagnosis within bewildering realities. It overlaps with that of Roger Harrison (Harrison, 1972; Handy, 1985), but differs extensively in the way it maps out four organizational *pathologies*, whereas he is concerned with organizational *ideologies*.

One basic principle, invoked in all the 4 points below, is that of *social inertia*: the tendency of any social form, once it has been set up in one context, to stay as it is, and to be transferred where possible without change or with minimal change to other contexts.

1. **Person-bound.**   Teams that focus strongly on renewal tasks – education and training, professional and personal development, recreation – tend to become person-bound, caught up in the satisfactions of self-renewal, and the consummation of regeneration motives. Purely personal needs and interests predominate. Decision-making power becomes subservient to the fulfilment of renewal needs: and this is at the expense of the team's social structure, and of meeting its goals and plan of work. Decision-making may tend toward the autonomous mode, each person doing their own thing. Absorption in renewal tasks can undermine all the other sorts of task.

   ● **Effect of renewal tasks on persons.**   When renewal tasks are sanctioned, people let their hair down, become absorbed in pursuing personal needs and interests, in reviving, refreshing and realizing themselves. Everything else tends to go by.

   ● **Effect of regeneration motives on persons.**   Renewal tasks, if at all imaginative and person-centred, open people up to the deeper possibilities of self-realization. Regeneration motives, once awakened and given a little scope, flower into full-blown self-actualizing motives – which can dramatically reinforce the absorbing nature of renewal tasks, and may lead a person completely to abandon their current work arena in search of something more self-realizing.

2. **Problem-bound.**   Teams that are preoccupied with development tasks, as in R & D and problem-solving work, tend to become problem-bound, too absorbed in goals and plan issues, too identified with fulfilment motives. This means that decision-making control becomes subservient to a preoccupation with problem-solving tasks and the pursuit of technical know-how, and this is at the expense of a coherent social structure, and of personnel welfare. Decision-making may be entirely in an *ad hoc* co-operative mode of informal mutual consultation. Development tasks are over-emphasized.

   ● **Effect of development tasks on goals and plan.** When a team is looking at new ways of doing things, its longer term objectives can get distorted by overfocus on the immediate problem. Decision-making is distracted by current work from the wider sweep of goal-setting and planning.

   ● **Effect of fulfilment motives on goals and plan.**   Development and problem-solving tasks can yield a lot of personal fulfilment: they satisfy needs for autonomy, creativity, intellectual interest and stimulation, challenge, and so on. So the immediate and absorbing intrinsic satisfactions of the work reinforce the distraction away from managing the team's longer-term goals and plans.

3. **Role-bound.** Teams committed to production tasks, to maintaining the production of goods and services, tend to become role-bound bureaucracies. They may become more concerned with the roles and rules of their social structure than the goods and services it is supposed to produce, and too strongly influenced by reward motives. This means that decision-making power becomes subservient to the roles and rules of organizational structure, and this is at the expense of production itself, of development tasks, and of personnel welfare. Decision-making is in the hierarchical mode, perhaps after some real or nominal consultation. In a chronic bureaucracy, all four sorts of task may suffer.

- **Effect of production tasks on roles and rules.** In order to maintain a steady flow of goods or services, the team needs a clear allocation of functions to different roles, with rules defining who does what with whom and when and how. This structure, once set up, may tend to become an end-in-itself, with those who run it rigidly preserving or enlarging its form for its own sake, regardless of changes in the product and demand in the wider world. In such bureaucratic fixation on an out-of-date form, decision-making ceases to command effective production, and is ill-adapted to crisis management, welfare tasks, and development tasks.

- **Effect of reward motives on roles and rules.** People at work need pay, security, some status and recognition, and to belong to an organized group. A well-defined system of roles and rules can meet all these needs, offering a significant range of extrinsic rewards to the workers. Reward motives may strongly reinforce the tendency for the system to become an end-in-itself, because the more it is sustained and elaborated with status and pay scales, the more it will also satisfy reward motives.

4. **Power-bound.** Teams that focus a lot on crisis tasks, as in police, military and medical work, incline to be power-bound. They may tend to exaggerate power and control issues, and may be influenced by pathological motives. This means decision-making is in the hierarchical mode, without any prior consultation, in which strong central command becomes oppressive and is carried too far – at the expense of organizational structure, of fulfilling team

goals, and of the needs of personnel. In task terms, crisis task attitudes distort non-critical service tasks, development tasks, and welfare and training tasks.

- **Effect of crisis tasks on power and control.**  When crises are afoot, dominant command is needed. But dominant command may also be unawarely and inappropriately transferred to non-critical service and other tasks – where its habits of mind and forms of social control are restrictive and counter-productive. The team or organization as a whole then inclines toward autocracy. It lacks the awareness and flexibility to adopt different forms of decision-making for different sorts of task.
- **Effect of pathological motives on power and control.**  When power and control are distorted into autocratic forms, under the influence of crisis tasks, they also become prey to the influence of pathological motives. The compulsion unawarely to act out repressed pain in oppressor and victim roles can readily further distort the exercise of dominant command. Those who command can become compulsively oppressive; those who obey may slip into old victim scripts. The autocracy starts to become irrational, and severely distorted.

| Distorted Form | Feature of Team | Type of Task | Sort of Motive |
|---|---|---|---|
| Person-bound | Persons and tools | Renewal | Regeneration |
| Problem-bound | Goals and plan | Development | Fulfilment |
| Role-bound | Roles and Rules | Production | Reward |
| Power-bound | Power and control | Crisis | Pathological |

**Figure A.10**  *Distorted forms of the team dynamic related to feature, task and motive*

Figure A.10 sets out the affinities so far proposed. I stress again that reality is much more complex than these simple correlations indicate. Different motives can run into each other: thus elements of pathology may be involved with each of the other three sorts of motive. Different tasks may overlap. The model provides only initial orientation within a problem.

## *Diagrams of the Distorted Forms*

The distorted forms of the team dynamic are shown in Figures A.11 to A.14. In each form, there are three degress of emphasis, represented by the size of the boxes and the size of the title in them: the most at the top and the least at the bottom, with medium emphasis in the middle. The smallest box represents the greatest casualty of the distortion.

In the person-bound distorted form, Figure A.11, autonomous immersion in the satisfaction of personal learning or recreational needs is at the cost of organizational structure and clear corporate decision-making. The team can lose its way without coherent objectives and plans. A classic example is the staff development course where the members have much scope for self-determination in curriculum design. The task of planning can disintegrate in person-bound chaos and anarchy.

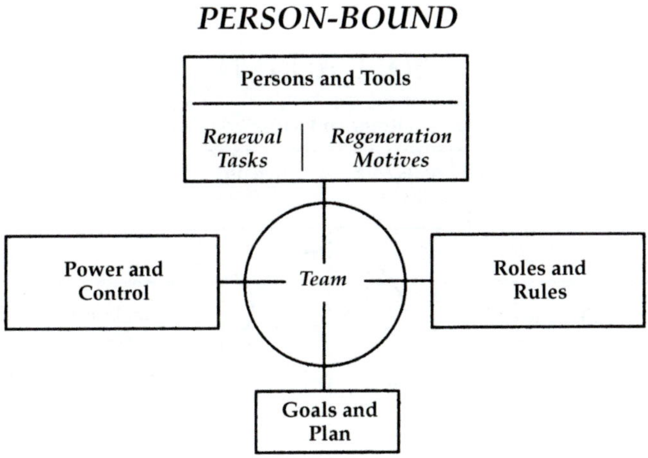

### PERSON-BOUND

**Figure A.11**  *The person-bound distorted form of the team dynamic*

In the problem-bound distorted form, Figure A.12, overemphasis on the task of innovation and problem-solving is at the expense of effective command and team structure. The challenge of a breakthrough into some new approach becomes obsessive. People become exhausted, overworked and ineffective.

In the role-bound, bureaucratic distorted form, Figure A.13, the preoccupation with organizational structure is at the expense of the effective use of people and a rational programme that fits the task. Relevant and resourceful decision-making disappear and become totally subservient to sustaining the bureaucratic status quo.

## PROBLEM-BOUND

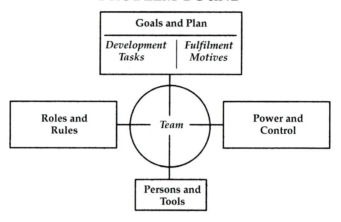

**Figure A.12**   *The problem-bound distorted form of the team dynamic*

## ROLE-BOUND

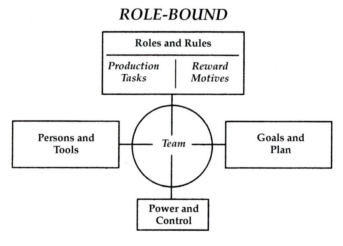

**Figure A.13**   *The role-bound distorted form of the team dynamic*

In the power-bound autocratic distorted form of the team dynamic, Figure A.14, excessive hierarchical command and control from the top is at the expense of coherent objectives and planning, and of the effective use of people. Teams and organizations that deal with critical situations, may allow the strong hierarchical command that is appropriate at actual times of crisis, to extend inappropriately into other non-critical areas of work. There is no coherent social structure that enables this distinction to be made in practice.

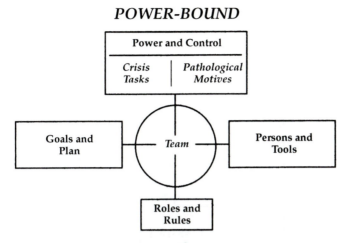

**POWER-BOUND**

**Figure A.14**  *The power-bound distorted form of the team dynamic*

Extreme forms of autocracy are caught in a vicious circle. Because of their persistent oppression, they are faced with the permanent crisis of resistance and rebellion, which reinforces the autocratic command structure.

I must stress again, that these are conceptual models only, abstract portraits of negative limiting cases. The diagnostic tool is not the patient, just as the map is not the territory. Reality is more mixed and varied. The actual team or organization may combine selective aspects from several of these models. Power-bound and role-bound forms may combine; problem-bound and person-bound forms may combine. A team at different times in its life and under the influence of different tasks may tend in each of the four directions.

There are two pairs of polar opposites. The power-bound is most at odds with the person-bound. Excessive central command has no tolerance of excessive personal autonomy; and vice versa. Likewise, the role-bound is most at odds with the problem-bound. A rigid system of roles and rules has no tolerance of the unpredictable flexibility of structure involved in obsessive problem-solving; and vice versa.

## The Organizational Context: Critical Issues

So far I have considered the influence on the team dynamic of the interaction between features of a team, the sort of task it has, and the motives of its members. If the team is part of a larger organization,

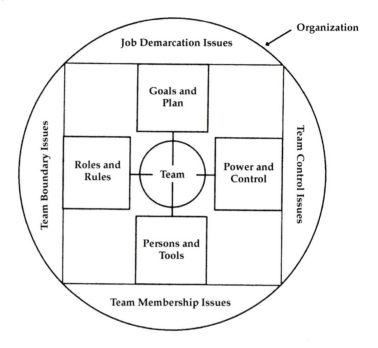

**Figure A.15**   *Critical issues between the team and the organization*

there are also certain critical, contextual issues that radically affect the dynamic. The issues arise between the team and the organization, and this in relation to each of the four main features of the team, as shown in Figure A.15.

1. **Team membership issues.**   Is the right person, in terms of skills and temperament, in the right team? Does one team within the organization have a stronger claim on existing personnel than another? Can different teams share access to needed equipment and appropriate technology? The issues are to do with the persons and tools.
2. **Job demarcation issues.**   What tasks belong to the team? Where is the line to be drawn between these tasks and those of other teams? The issues are to do with the tasks of the team, its goals and plan.
3. **Team boundary issues.**   What marks this team off from other teams within the organization? What roles are within the team? Which ones overlap with other teams? And with respect to these, are the respective responsibilities clear? The issues are to do with roles and rules.

4. **Team control issues.**   Does the organization control the team hierarchically, manage it consultatively, or confer upon it a high degree of autonomy? The issues are to do with power and control.

## The Social Context: Critical Issues

The team within its organization, or the independent team, is set in the context of the wider society. At this interface a further range of critical issues emerge to influence the team dynamic. Figure A.16 shows these in a second ring around the issues to do with the organizational context.

1. **Human and physical resources in society.**   The range of skills, and the level of skills development, needed in team members raise issues about what human and physical resources there are in the

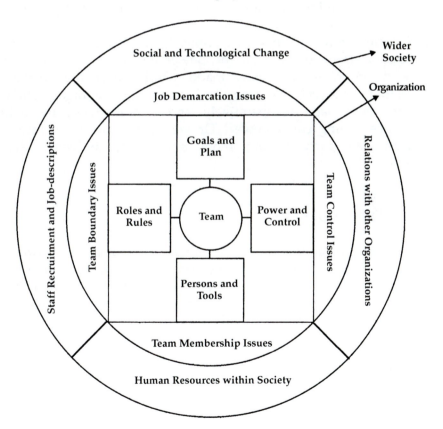

**Figure A.16**   *Critical issues between the team, the organization and the wider society*

wider society; about the scope and standards of education and training in the community; about the number of people with relevant skills; about the availability of equipment, goods and services, raw materials. Such issues relate to the persons and tools feature, and to renewal tasks.

2. **The rate of social and technological change.**  Social structures and technology in the wider culture are changing at a rapid rate. Every team needs to adapt its tasks to these developments; its work goals and work-plan will have to be evolved into new forms. The issues here relate to the goals and plan aspect of a team, and to development tasks.

3. **Staff turnover, recruitment and job-description.**  People change jobs, get dismissed, retire. The team has an identity and structure that is independent of any particular persons. It has to keep reaching out into the wider society to recruit people to fill its roles. The issues of staff turnover and recruitment influence job description and definition, organizational structure and career prospects – the roles and rules feature of a team.

4. **Relations with other organizations.**  The issues involved here have a strong bearing on the power and control aspect of a team. How are decisions made which affect the working relations between the team and some external organization? Are they made co-operatively and consultatively, by both parties having equal power? Or are they made hierarchically, with one party having more power and influence than another?

## The Influence of Ideology

By ideology I mean the core values of the team that define its priorities. They state what, ultimately, the team or organization is doing its task for. They define what intrinsically worthwhile state of affairs it is seeking to realize through its work. There seem to be four different sorts of value that can influence the team dynamic.

1. **The ideology of human and planetary flourishing.**  The integrated value-system here is that of personal development in co-operative relations of action inquiry with others, creating self-transforming learning organizations, combining decentralization and federalism, and nurturing the eco-system of the planet. Personal development expands through the entire whole person web from the intrapersonal through the interpersonal, to the

cultural (socio-structural), ecological and transplanetary spheres; and is committed to balancing self-determination, co-operation, up-hierarchy influence and down-hierarchy responsibility. See the later sections of Chapter 16.

2. **The ideology of social welfare.** The primary value of the team, the overriding principle of all its work, is the creation of greater welfare in the social system it serves.

3. **The ideology of profit.** The primary value of the team is the maximization of profit, as a result of the task, which is usually the production of goods or services of some kind. This value over-flows into the value of pleasure-seeking.

4. **The ideology of power.** The team is dominated by those who command it, and their ideology is to value the exercise of power for its own sake, as an end-in-itself. They are interested in the satisfactions of power, and more power, as such.

These four values are not mutually exclusive. Two or more of them can co-exist in mixed proportions within the ideology of a given team or organization. They also correlate somewhat, as shown in Figure A.17, with the affinities set out earlier in Figure A.10.

| Distorted Form | Feature of Team | Type of Task | Sort of Motive | Ideology |
|---|---|---|---|---|
| Person-bound | Persons | Renewal | Regeneration | Human-planet flourishing |
| Problem-bound | Goals | Development | Fulfilment | Social welfare |
| Role-bound | Roles | Production | Reward | Profit |
| Power-bound | Power | Crisis | Pathological | Power |

**Figure A.17** *Ideology correlated with distorted form, feature, task and motive*

I shall return to consider the role of these ideologies in the vision of holocracy, after the next section on the manager.

## *The Authority of the Manager*

I have so far considered six factors that influence the team dynamic: the structure of the team, its different sorts of task, the motives of its members, its organizational context, its social context, and its ideology. The seventh factor is the authority of the manager, which has two main aspects. Firstly, who appoints the manager; whence does his or her authority derive? And secondly, how does he or she exercise authority and control; what sort of decision-making model does he or she use? These two dimensions together create a portrait of the power of management.

Managers may be self-appointed, as with the founder of any business or other kind of organization. Or they may be appointed by those whom they then lead: I will refer to this as being peer-appointed. Or they may be appointed by some established source of authority which is over and above their own role and the team they lead: I call this being hierarchically appointed.

How managers exercise their authority in relation to the team takes us back to the modes of management discussed earlier in the chapter. They may be hierarchical and autocratic, making all decisions for the team and over it. They may be co-operative and consultative, negotiating and deciding things with the team. They may lead by delegation, giving maximum scope for autonomous decision-making within the team.

Putting these two dimensions together, we get a nine-part grid giving the basic forms of a manager's power, as shown in Figure A.18.

| Manages by →  Manager is ↓ | Direction: hierarchical decisions | Negotiation: co-operative decisions | Delegation: autonomous decisions |
|---|---|---|---|
| Self-appointed | | | |
| Peer-appointed | | | |
| Hierarchically appointed | | | |

**Figure A.18**   *The basic forms of a manager's power*

In a single team, the question is whether the terms of appointment specify how a manager shall exercise his or her authority. Self-appointed managers can set their own terms, and exercise power, flexibly and appropriately, by any or all the modes of direction, negotiation and delegation. Democratically or hierarchically appointed managers need to make sure that this kind of flexibility is not constrained by the terms of their appointment. The place or places of the manager on one or other of the three rows of the nine-part grid will have a strong influence on the team dynamic.

## The Vision of the Manager: Holocracy

I now come the final and eighth factor that influences the team dynamic. This is the vision of the manager. The limits of prevailing belief-systems about social and physical reality are a challenge to the realization of vision. And many strands now converging at the leading edge of cultural change suggest for any manager the vision of holocracy.

By this I mean that the manager – as a facilitator of personal development at the workplace – guides the team dynamic in the light of certain core values, a set of priorities organized as an up-hierarchy, in which the items listed below progressively inform, shape, support and empower those that follow later, as illustrated in Figure A.19. The holocratic leader seeks to be a mediator, a channel, for this up-hierarchy of influence.

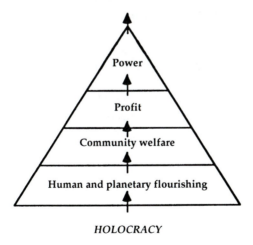

HOLOCRACY

**Figure A.19** *The holocratic up-hierarchy of ideologies*

### *Persons and tools, and the ideology of human and planetary flourishing, are first*

This means several things – at different levels.

- Working hours, conditions, and facilities are such that people can maintain high standards of refreshment, renewal and recreation.
- Personnel are fully educated and trained for their work. They have chosen it, are suited to it, and are fulfilled by it. They are equipped with appropriate technology, for the human relations and task side of their work, and for the eco-system of the planet. Learning in the job, for it and alongside it, extends into personal development (Mulligan, 1988).
- The culture of the organization is such that it is a self-renewing learning environment, adapting and changing its form and its technology as its members, through their personal development and action inquiry on the job, learn more about how to realize the holocratic vision. Thus it fulfils people's regeneration motives – deep needs to be self-creating and self-transforming. It upholds as paramount the ideology of personal development in co-operative relations with others, creating self-transforming organizations, combining decentralization and federalism, and nurturing the eco-system of the planet. It develops technologies that serve these ends.

This ideology sustains, nourishes and grounds the holocratic up-hierarchy. Thus personal development expands through the entire whole person web from the intrapersonal through the interpersonal, to the cultural (socio-structural), ecological and transplanetary spheres; and is committed to balancing self-determination, co-operation, up-hierarchy influence and down-hierarchy responsibility.

### *Goals and plan, and the ideology of social welfare, are second*

The task aspect of the team, and its commitment to the welfare of the society in which it is embedded and which it serves, are subordinate to the basic ideology of 1 above – human and planetary flourishing as defined.

- The work of the team makes some significant contribution to its local community – to its current welfare and to the development of this welfare into the future.
- It is organized to yield job satisfaction, to gratify fulfilment motives in team members – their need to be creative, to realize

their human capacities, to exercise autonomous control, to work co-operatively in a good cause, to have significant up-hierarchy influence.

- The goals of the team, its work-plan and methods are under regular review, involved in and keeping pace with social and technological change in ways that contribute to community welfare; and that integrate this concern for immediate social benefit with the wider sweep of cultural, ecological and transplanetary development.

### Roles and rules, and the ideology of profit-seeking, are third

The social structure of the team, its formal positions and job-descriptions, its allocations of function and responsibility, and the pursuit of profit, are guided first by the ideology of human–planetary flourishing and second by the ideology of local community welfare.

- Roles and rules are kept flexible and adaptable, responding to the requirements of the task, the needs of persons, and the use of appropriate technology, not restricting any of these through unnecessary rigidity. The roles of owner, manager and worker become co-extensive through the increased use of worker co-operatives.
- The team is structured to satisfy the external reward motives of its members – their needs for money, status, security, recognition, social belonging – in a way that is supportive of and not to the detriment of their intrinsic job satisfaction.
- The pursuit of profit from the production of goods or services is enjoyed within the wider ideologies of community and planetary welfare; as, for example, with so-called ethically sound firms. Profit is not maximized through the pursuit of undifferentiated growth but set within the context of a steady-state eco-economy. There is no entitlement to profit exclusively through ownership, except through the investment of pension funds and other funds that support those who are legitimately outside the total work force.

### Power and control, and the ideology of power, are fourth

The management of the team – how decisions are made, and the pursuit of power, are contained within and emerge from all the prior levels of the up-hierarchy.

- Pathological motives are kept out of managerial action.

- Charismatic authority and transforming power are used to enhance the spread of self-determination and peer supervision in the workplace.
- Managers are guides who can exercise their authority in the hierarchical, co-operative and autonomous modes with equal skill, flexibly moving between them as and when appropriate in order to express this up-hierarchy of values. Crisis situations are handled with an autocracy that does not then get transferred to other non-critical areas of teamwork.

Figure A.19 shows the holocratic up-hierarchy of ideologies as an arrow-head or pyramid. The ideology of human and planetary flourishing is the ground of the ideology of community welfare, of a social order that takes care of people; and these two ground, limit and transform the ideologies of profit and power. In terms of related correspondences, pathological and reward motives are grounded in fulfilment and regeneration motives. Renewal and development tasks provide the creative guidance and support for a self-developing culture of work on production and crisis tasks.

This, of course, is all part of a vision. The manager is seeking to mediate this vision; to engage with the tendencies within the team dynamic toward the distorted forms – power-bound, role-bound, problem-bound, person-bound – and to balance these tendencies into the holocratic form, thus facilitating personal development in the workplace.

# References

Abram, D (1996) *The Spell of the Sensuous*, Vintage Books, New York

Aitchison, J (1987) *Linguistics*, Hodder and Stoughton, London

Alexander, C (1979) *The Timeless Way of Building*, Oxford University Press, New York

Alexander, F M (1969) *The Resurrection of the Body*, Dell, New York

Allport, G (1958) The historical background of modern social psychology, in *Handbook of Social Psychology*, ed G Lindzey, Addison-Wesley, Cambridge, Mass

Assagioli, R (1965) *Psychosynthesis*, Penguin Books, Baltimore

Ausubel, D P (1960) The use of advance organizers in the learning of meaningful verbal material, *Journal of Educational Psychology*, **51**, pp 227–67

Barlow, W (1973) *The Alexander Principle*, Gollancz, London

Bateson, G (1979) *Mind and Nature: A Necessary Unity*, Dutton, New York

Beardsley, M C (1958) *Aesthetics*, Harcourt, Brace and World, New York

Bohm, D (1980) *Wholeness and the Inplicate Order*, Routledge and Kegan Paul, London

Bolman, L (1976) Group leader effectiveness, in *Developing Social Skills in Managers*, ed C Cooper, Macmillan, London

Boud, D (ed) (1988) *Developing Student Autonomy in Learning*, Kogan Page, London

Boud, D and Miller, N (eds) (1996) *Working with Experience*, Routledge, London

Boud, D and Walker, D (1991) *Experience and Learning: Reflection at Work*, Deakin University Press, Geelong

Boud, D and Walker, D (1992) In the midst of experience: developing a model to aid learners and facilitators, in *Empowerment through Experiential Learning*, ed J Mulligan and C Cooper, Kogan Page, London

Boud, D, Keogh, R and Walker, D (1985) Promoting reflection in learning: a model, in *Reflection: Turning Experience into Learning*, ed D Boud, R Keogh and D Walker, Kogan Page, London

Brennan, R (1991) *The Alexander Technique*, Element, Shaftesbury

Capra, F (1983) *The Turning Point*, Fontana, London

Cortazzi, D and Roote, S (1975) *Illuminative Incident Analysis*, McGraw-Hill, London

Cross, K P (1976) *Accent on Learning*, Jossey Bass, London

de Vries, M J (1981) *The Redemption of the Intangible in Medicine*, Institute of Psychosynthesis, London

Egan, G (1990) *The Skilled Helper*, Brooks/Cole Pacific Grove, Calif

Flavell, J (1963) *The Developmental Psychology of Jean Piaget*, Van Nostrand Reinhold, New York

Garratt, R (1987) *The Learning Organization*, Fontana, London

Gerth, H H and Mills, C W (eds) (1984) *From Max Weber: Essays in Sociology*, Allen and Unwin, London

Gowan, S, Lakey, G, Moyer, W and Taylor, R (1979) *Moving Toward a New Society*, New Society Press, Philadelphia

Hadamard, J (1945) *The Psychology of Invention in the Mathematical Field*, Dover Publications, New York

Handy, C (1985) *Gods of Management*, Pan Books, London

Harrison, R (1972) Understanding your organization's character, *Harvard Business Review*, May-June, pp 119–128

Harrison, R (1973) Developing autonomy, initiative and risk-taking through a laboratory design, *European Training*, **2**: pp 100–117

Hawkins, P and Shohet, R (1989) *Supervision in the Helping Professions*, Open University Press, Milton Keynes

Henry, J (1989) Meaning and practice in experiential learning, in *Making Sense of Experiential Learning*, ed S W Weil and I McGill, SRHE/Open University Press, Buckingham

Heron, J (1977) *Dimensions of Facilitator Style*, University of Surrey, Guildford

Heron, J (1982) Self and peer assessment, in *Handbook of Management Self-Development*, ed T Boydell and M Pedlar, Gower, London

Heron, J (1987) *Confessions of a Janus-Brain*, Endymion Press, London

Heron, J (1988) Assessment revisited, in *Developing Student Autonomy in Learning*, ed D Boud, Kogan Page, London

Heron, J (1989) *The Facilitators' Handbook*, Kogan Page, London

Heron, J (1990a) *Helping the Client: A Creative, Practical Guide*, Sage, London

Heron, J (1990b) *A Handbook for Leaders*, University of Surrey, Guildford

Heron, J (1992) *Feeling and Personhood: Psychology in Another Key*, Sage, London

Heron, J (1993) *Group Facilitation: Theories and Models for Practice*, Kogan Page, London

Heron, J (1996a) *Co-operative Inquiry: Research into the Human Condition*, Sage, London

Heron, J (1996b) Helping whole people learn, in *Working with Experience*, ed D Boud and N Miller, Routledge, London

Heron, J (1997) A self-generating practitioner community, in *Implausible Professions: Arguments for Pluralism and Autonomy in Psychotherapy and Counselling*, ed R House and N Totton, PCCS Books, Ross-on-Wye

Heron, J (1998a) *Sacred Science: Person-centred Inquiry into the Spiritual and the Subtle*, PCCS Books, Ross-on-Wye

Heron, J (1998b) *Co-counselling Manual*, www.dpets.demon.co.uk/cciuk/resources/manuals.html

Heron, J and Reason P (1997) A participatory inquiry paradigm, *Qualitative Inquiry*, 3(3), pp 274–294

Hillman, J (1975) *Revisioning Psychology*, Harper Row, New York

Hooper-Hansen, G (1992) Suggestopedia: a way of learning for the 21st century, in *Empowerment through Experiential Learning*, ed J Mulligan and C Griffin, Kogan Page, London

Huczynski, A (1983) *Encyclopedia of Management Development Methods*, Gower, Aldershot

Huxley, A (1963) *The Doors of Perception*, Harper and Row, New York

Hyde, L (1955) *An Introduction to Organic Philosophy*, Omega Press, Reigate

Jackins, H (1983) *The Reclaiming of Power*, Rational Island Press, Seattle

James, W (1890) *The Principles of Psychology*, Vols 1 and 2, Holt, Rinehart and Winston, New York

Jantsch, E (1980) *The Self-Organizing Universe*, Pergamon, Oxford

Jung, C G (1964) *Man and his Symbols*, W. H. Allen, London

Jung, C G (1977) *Psychological Types, Collected Works, Vol. 6*, Princeton University Press, Princeton

Kilty, J (1978) *Self and Peer Assessment*, University of Surrey, Guildford

Kilty, J (1980) *Self and Peer Assessment and Peer Audit*, University of Surrey, Guildford

Knowles, M S (1980) *The Modern Practice of Adult Education: From Pedagogy to Andragogy*, Follett, Chicago

Koestler, A (1964) *The Act of Creation*, Hutchinson, London

Koestler, A (1978) *Janus*, Hutchinson, London

Kolb, D A (1984) *Experiential Learning*, NJ Prentice Hall, Englewood Cliffs

Laszlo, E (1972) *Introduction to Systems Philosophy*, Gordon and Breach, London

Lipps, T (1903–6) *Ästhetik*, 2 vols

Lovelock, J (1987) Gaia: a model for planetary and cellular dynamics, in *Gaia: A Way of Knowing*, W I Thompson, Lindisfarne Press, Great Barrington, Mass

Lozanov, G (1978) *Suggestology and Outlines of Suggestopedy*, Gordon and Breach, New York

Margulies, A (1984) Toward empathy: the uses of wonder, *American Journal of Psychiatry*, **141**, pp 1025–1033.

Merleau-Ponty, M (1962) *Phenomenology of Perception*, Routledge and Kegan Paul, London

Miller, A (1987) *For Your Own Good: The roots of violence in child-raising*, Virago Press, London

Mulligan, J (ed) (1988) *The Personal Management Handbook*, Sphere, London

Mulligan, J and Griffin, C (eds) (1992) *Empowerment through Experiential Learning*, Kogan Page, London

Nagel, E (1963) Wholes, sums and organic unities, in *Parts and Wholes*, D Lerner, Free Press of Glencoe, New York

Perry, R B (1954) *Realms of Value*, Harvard University Press, Cambridge, Mass

Peters, R S (1966) *Ethics and Education*, Allen and Unwin, London

Postle, D (1991) *Emotional Competence*, Wentworth Institute, London

Reason, P (ed) (1988) *Human Inquiry in Action*, Sage, London

Reason, P (ed) (1994) *Participation in Human Inquiry*, Sage, London

Reason, P and Rowan, J (eds) (1981) *Human Inquiry: A Sourcebook of New Paradigm Research*, Wiley, Chichester

Reason, P and Torbert, W R (1999) Towards a transformational social science: a further look at the scientific merits of action research, forthcoming

Reid, T (1764) *Inquiry into the Human Mind on the Principles of Common Sense*

Scheler, M (1954) *The Nature of Sympathy*, Routledge and Kegan Paul, London

Schön, D (1983) *The Reflective Practitioner*, Basic Books, New York

Schuster, D H and Gritton, C E (1986) *Suggestive Accelerative Learning Techniques*, Gordon and Breach, New York

Skolimowski, H (1994) *The Participatory Mind*, Arkana, London

Spretnak, C (1991) *States of Grace: The Recovery of Meaning in the Postmodern Age*, Harper-Collins, San Francisco

Spretnak, C (1995) Embodied, embedded philosophy, *Open Eye: California Institute for Integral Studies*, **12**(1), pp 4–5

Swami Rama, Balletine, R and Swami Ajaya (1976) *Yoga and Psychotherapy*, Himalayan Institute, Honesdale, Pa

Thame, S (1978) A means of understanding human learning; the Alexander Technique, *Management Education and Development*, **9**(3), pp 202–205

Titchener, E B (1910) *A Textbook of Psychology*

Torbert, W (1991) *The Power of Balance: Transforming Self, Society and Scientific Inquiry*, Calif Sage, Newbury Park

Varela, F J, Thompson, E and Rosch, E (1991) *The Embodied Mind: Cognitive Science and Human Experience*, MIT Press, Cambridge, MA

von Bertalanffy, L (1972) *General Systems Theory*, Allen Lane, London

von Eckartsberg, R (1981) Maps of the mind: the cartography of consciousness, in *The Metaphors of Consciousness*, ed R S Valle and R von Eckartsberg

Weil, S W and McGill, I (eds) (1989) *Making Sense of Experiential Learning*, SRHE/Open University Press, Buckingham

Wilber, K (1983) *Up from Eden*, Routledge and Kegan Paul, London

# *Index*

The sharpest minds
need the finest advice.
**Kogan Page** creates
success.

**www.koganpage.com**

Lightning Source UK Ltd.
Milton Keynes UK
UKOW031803070312

188536UK00006B/8/P